THE CROWN OF LIFE

By the same Author

ON SHAKESPEARE
The Wheel of Fire (Tragedies)
The Imperial Theme (Tragedies and Roman Plays)
The Shakespearian Tempest (Symbolism)
The Sovereign Flower (Royalism; General Index)
The Mutual Flame (Sonnets and *The Phoenix and the Turtle*)
Shakespeare and Religion
Shakespearian Production
Shakespeare's Dramatic Challenge
Vergil and Shakespeare (Jackson Knight Memorial Lecture)

ON OTHER WRITERS
Poets of Action (Spenser, Milton, Swift, Byron)
The Starlit Dome (Wordsworth, Coleridge, Shelley, Keats)
Laureate of Peace; reissued as *The Poetry of Pope*
Lord Byron: Christian Virtues
Lord Byron's Marriage
Byron and Shakespeare
The Golden Labryrinth (on British Drama)
Ibsen
The Saturnian Quest (John Cowper Powys)
Neglected Powers (Powys; also Masefield, Brooke, Eliot, T. E. Lawrence)
Powys to Knight, Letters, ed. Robert Blackmore; contributions by G.W.K.
Symbol of Man (stage poses)

ON LITERATURE AND RELIGION
The Christian Renaissance (the New Testament, Dante, Goethe)
Christ and Nietzsche (Christian Dogma, Germanic Philosophy and *Thus Spake Zarathustra*)
Hiroshima (Literature and the Atomic Age)

GENERAL
Atlantic Crossing
The Dynasty of Stowe

DRAMA
The Last of the Incas

BIOGRAPHY
Jackson Knight: a Biography

POETRY
Gold-Dust

TAPE RECORDINGS
Shakespeare's Rhetoric
Shakespeare and the English Language } (Jeffrey Norton Publishers, USA)
Byron's Rhetoric
Shakespeare's Dramatic Challenge (sound, BBC; video-tape, Yeovil College; or from Keith Keating, Nassau Community College, Garden City, New York, from whom colour tapes can also be obtained)

The Crown of Life

ESSAYS IN INTERPRETATION OF SHAKESPEARE'S FINAL PLAYS

By

G. WILSON KNIGHT

Emeritus Professor of English Literature in the University of Leeds
Formerly Chancellors' Professor of English at
Trinity College, Toronto

Look down, you gods,
And on this couple drop a blessed crown;
For it is you that have chalk'd forth the way
Which brought us hither.
The Tempest, v. i. 201

METHUEN

LONDON and NEW YORK

Originally published by the Oxford University Press 1947
First published by Methuen & Co. Ltd 1948
Reprinted three times
Reprinted with minor corrections 1965
Reprinted 1969

First published as a University Paperback 1965
Reprinted four times
Reprinted 1982

Published in the USA by
Methuen & Co.
in association with Methuen, Inc.
733 Third Avenue, New York, NY 10017

ISBN 0 416 68770 9

Printed and bound in Great Britain by
J. W. Arrowsmith Ltd, Bristol

CONTENTS

PREFACE

THIS book is the culmination of twenty years' work on Shakespeare. It therefore seems fitting to reprint, as its introduction, my first published statement—apart from articles —*Myth and Miracle* (E. J. Burrow & Co., 1929). This essay was originally composed as a brief outline of a thesis which I regarded as my main contribution to Shakespearian studies, and for which I had for some time been trying to gain recognition in expanded form ; though, having published it, I have remained, hitherto, content to let it stand alone. The decision has probably been justified, since the considered analyses here offered have the advantage of incorporating discoveries from interim studies ; especially *The Shakespearian Tempest*, *The Olive and the Sword* and *The Starlit Dome*. Those two binding principles of Shakespearian unity, the tempest-music opposition and Elizabethan nationalism, are vital to any full appreciation of Shakespeare's last, and perhaps supreme, phase ; so, too, is the study of the romantic poets.

These essays were roughed out in the summer of 1944and revised during the following winter. After completing them, I looked through much of the work done on Shakespeare during recent years in this country, most of which I had read as it appeared, in case any important points of contact should seem to demand explicit reference ; though few seemed, on consideration, to do so. Rumours of recent advances in the United States of America on lines similar to those of my own studies I have tried, without success, to follow up by inspection of the books concerned : when conditions become again normal, it is to be hoped that they will find their way to British libraries. But, though my references to other workers are few, I am gratefully aware that my investigations have not been solitary, nor neglected. We have watched a change come over Shakespearian studies during the last two decades, to which my attempts from *Myth and Miracle* onwards may, I like to think, have contributed, perhaps originated, something ; though it will probably be wiser to consider such supposed origins as themselves symptoms rather than causes of a given movement. I would nevertheless express my gratitude to those writers on both sides of the Atlantic, who have, from time to time, made kindly acknowledgment to my findings, while also recognising that, the most potent influences being often unconsciously received, I have sometimes reason for gratitude where no such acknowledgment is made. Whatever the 'causes', beneficent influences have been active. It is no longer customary to rule out as unauthentic those scenes in Shakespeare that appear difficult or queer to-day : the reputation of the Folio editors has gone up. Obstacles, however, still remain. The Vision in *Cymbeline* and large parts of *Henry VIII* are still as suspect as were *Troilus and Cressida* and *Timon of Athens* in the days when I was writing the essays incorporated into *The Wheel of Fire*. The same battle has to be re-fought, and with the same weapons. Destructive criticism must be met, as it can only be met, in this and other spheres, by the constructive imagination.

Apart from *Myth and Miracle*, two of my present essays are expansions of already published work. An abbreviated version of my defence of the Vision in *Cymbeline* appeared in *The Times Literary Supplement*, and my arguments for the authenticity of *Henry VIII* were outlined in an article contributed to *The Criterion*, both in 1936. Line references are given throughout to the Oxford Shakespeare.

G. W. K.

Leeds, 1946

IN this reprint I have corrected the errors regarding the stage directions of *Pericles* on pages 47 and 63 to which I drew attention in the 'Prefatory Note' to the 1951 reissue of *The Imperial Theme*.

It is a pleasure to observe that the term 'Final Plays' is beginning to replace its misleading predecessor 'the Romances'; and to record that the reading of these plays advanced in the following pages appears already to have had an effect on stage production, both at Stratford and in London. Jupiter has at last been given his chance; the concluding scene of *The Winter's Tale* has received an interpretation in depth; and the pattern of *Henry VIII* is respected.

Leeds, 1952

G. W. K.

SINCE 1952 a few more traces of error regarding stage directions have been put right.

My 1929 text of *Myth and Miracle* is correctly followed below except for the addition of some reference numerals, some changes in punctuation and typography, the removal of a misleading stage direction and the correction of a grammatical error. The original end-notes are omitted, but I wish to record that they referred the phrase 'die into love' on p. 12 and the definition of God on p. 28 to Middleton Murry. I also owed to Murry, who was fond of using it, my quotation from Tchehov on p. 27. A general debt to Murry's influence was acknowledged in my original preface, though my reading of Shakespeare's last plays was never his, nor favourably accepted by him. My account of our relations appears in the volume *Of Books and Humankind*, Essays Presented to Bonamy Dobrée, ed. John Butt, 1964.

Colin Still's *Shakespeare's Mystery Play* (p. 226 below) was brought to my conscious notice by Still himself on the publication of *Myth and Miracle*. Later I found forgotten notes of an early review of it among my papers, and so its argument may have been an unconscious influence. I should perhaps recall that Dr. Hugh Brown, who was writing articles on Shakespeare in *The Hibbert Journal* at that time, after reading *Myth and Miracle* wisely urged me not to ignore in future the national, or royalistic, element in *Cymbeline*. Before my composition of *The Crown of Life* the late E. M. W. Tillyard had noted the temperamental differences of Guiderius and Arviragus; whether he was the first, I do not know. Shakespeare himself has, of course, given us the hint (pp. 158–9).

My first study of Shakespeare's last plays was a book entitled *Thaisa*, completed about 1928 but never accepted for publication. The typescript is lodged in the Shakespeare Memorial Library in the Birmingham Reference Library. The thesis was next summarised in an article 'The Poet and Immortality' in *The Shakespeare Review*, Stratford and London, for October 1928. After that I published *Myth and Miracle*.

G. W. K.

Exeter, 1965

I

MYTH AND MIRACLE (1929)[1]

I

IN this essay I shall consider the Final Plays, whose significance has not yet been recognized, as the culmination of a
series which starts about the middle of Shakespeare's writing
career and exposes to a careful analysis a remarkable coherence
and significance; and, by throwing them into direct relation
with their predecessors, show that those improbabilities of plot
texture and curiosities of the supernatural descending on the
purely human interest—as in *Pericles* and *Cymbeline*—are not
the freaks of a wearied imagination, as has been usually supposed; nor the work of that convenient 'incompetent coadjutor'
who is too often at hand when necessary to solve the difficulties
of Shakespeare interpretation; but rather the inevitable development of the questioning, the pain, the profundity and
grandeur of the plays they succeed. My method is to regard
the plays as they stand in the order to which modern scholarship
has assigned them; to refuse to regard 'sources' as exerting
any limit to the significance of the completed work of art; to
avoid the side-issues of Elizabethan and Jacobean manners,
politics, patronage, audiences, revolutions and explorations; to
fix attention solely on the poetic quality and human interest of
the plays concerned. Secondary considerations necessarily
condition the materials of a poet's work: but it is in the nature
of his accomplishment within and transcending those limits
that we must always search for the lasting significance of either
poet or prophet. For this reason, though I refer to the author
of the plays as Shakespeare, I leave any discussion of the questions of consciousness and unconsciousness, intention and
inspiration, as unnecessary to a purely philosophic analysis of
the text. To the critic of the poetry the word 'Shakespeare'
stands alone for the dynamic life that persists in the plays, and
any other 'Shakespeare' is a pure abstraction. We should avoid
irrelevancies. That spiritual quality which alone causes great
work to endure through the centuries should be the primary
object of our attention; and that quality is implicit in the

[1] The original text is here followed, but I have added a few notes.

printed page. My method is empirically justified: where other commentators have found incoherence and the inevitable 'incompetent coadjutor', it will show, wherever the Shakespearian rhythm or metaphor rings true, order, reason, and necessity.

II

It has often been observed that *Hamlet* reflects a mind in pain and perplexity; so, in different ways, do *Troilus and Cressida* and *Measure for Measure*. In *Hamlet* we are confronted by that mode of the spirit which sees the world of men and nature as an 'unweeded garden' (I. ii. 135); bereft of vision, tortured by too much thinking, obsessed with love's impurity and death's hideousness. In *Troilus and Cressida* the same idea recurs with reference to the frailty of romantic love. Both in the matter of love and death the thinking in these plays is essentially a time-thinking. Immortality of the spirit in time and decay of the body in time are both fearful to Hamlet; the inability of love to stand the test of time is a torture to Hamlet and Troilus. It is as though in these two plays all higher values were enslaved, and 'injurious Time' (IV. iv. 42) enthroned supreme, their antagonist and victor. In *Measure for Measure* the pain is less; the light of a pure Christian ethic shines through the play, and there is forecast of the stoic philosophy of the tragedies to follow. But the sex-satire is again powerful. Lucio, the foul-minded and careless wit, continues the hate-theme which makes Hamlet cry out against the universe as unclean, and which in the figure of Thersites receives one of its clearest and most exaggerated manifestations:

> Lechery, lechery ! Still, wars and lechery ; nothing else
> holds fashion : a burning devil take them ! (V. ii. 192)

This hate-theme, closely connected with time-thinking, and inimical to romance and religion and value, as such, eats into the thought of these plays, blighting, decaying. It is evident in the pain of Hamlet, the railings of Thersites, and the disgusting wit of Lucio. It cannot smell the rose for knowledge of the dung in which it was nurtured. *Othello*, which followed these plays, demands a different kind of analysis from its predecessors and successors in Shakespeare's progress, in view of its extreme classicism, its concentration on form, its purely aesthetic impact.[1] But it may be observed in passing that its plot perfectly crystallizes the thought of the preceding plays : the devil of cynicism, Iago—in whom is combined much of Hamlet, Thersites, and Lucio—causes the hero to distrust the thing of purity and innocence. Desdemona is betrayed, and Othello has slain the thing he loved.

Othello thus completes the first group, the group of problem plays : plays which reflect what William James calls 'the sick soul'. But if *Othello* completes this group, it as surely heralds the next. The next group, by viewing life in terms of passion and tragedy, gives a solution, as satisfactory as the solution of tragedy may be, to the baffled questions which preceded. It is a mistake to regard such plays as *Macbeth* and *Lear* as in essence pessimistic. Where humanity is shown as intrinsically grand, and his stage is the battleground of a mighty conflict, there is purpose and a noble destiny : where these things are in evidence there is no room for 'the sick soul'; and, conversely, 'the sick soul' has no knowledge of these things. *Macbeth* and *Lear* are characterized by the thunder of tragedy, and the mystery of eternity broods over a tragic close. The pessimistic and painful impact of *Troilus and Cressida* is largely due to the fact that the hero and heroine are left remorselessly alive : death would lend pathos and open vistas of eternity where pathos and eternity were not wanted. High tragedy and cynicism are incompatible. In *Macbeth* and *Lear* the Shakespearian symbol of tragic conflict—the storm or tempest—which had lent splendour to *Julius Caesar*, but had been avoided in the problem plays and only curiously and half-heartedly wedged into the plot of *Othello*,[2] now recurs in full force. Storm in the elements accompanies the thunder and lightning of the passionate heart of man. In *Lear* the suffering of mankind is sublimated into a noble, stoic destiny : Lear, Gloucester, Cordelia, Kent, Edgar, the Fool, endure their lot, and are aureoled with the halo of suffering. The play is a play of 'creative suffering'. All, it is to be noted, are brought by

[1] This statement now appears to me quite meaningless ; though I remember that I found it far from easy to break through the crust of conventional appreciation that had gathered round the content of what had for long been my favourite Shakespearian play.

[2] There is nothing 'half-hearted' about *Othello*, II. i. ; and I here disclaim any private knowledge as to the warmth of Shakespeare's interest in his own composition.

their own pain to a noble and exquisite apprehension of the pain of others : Hamlet thought only of himself. *Lear*, too, goes far to answer the questions of *Hamlet* on the matter of death. In *Lear* death is the end. There is no time-thinking of immortality. 'Break heart, I prithee break,' says Kent over Lear (v. iii. 314). Death is the sweet ender of suffering, and we are at peace with it, as we were never at peace with it in *Hamlet*. In the same way the hate-theme of the earlier plays is given sub-limity and tremendous meaning in *Timon*. Timon is the grand and universal hater—but only because he is by nature the grand and universal lover. The hate-theme is thus seen to be born of the aspiring spirit of man, un-at-home in its frail sepulchre of flesh, reaching out to infinity, crying for death because the world is unworthy :

> My long sickness
> Of health and living now begins to mend,
> And nothing brings me all things.   (v. i. 191)

In *Timon of Athens*—a great and neglected play—we are at peace with the sordidness and foulness of mankind. Again, the tempestuous passion of the hero is its own justification, and the close gives to the action the tragic framework of eternity. All these plays are to the reader what they must have been to the author, revelations of profundity and grandeur : the mystery of human fate—though still a mystery to the intellect—is intuitively apprehended as we endure to the end of great tragedy. In essence, our understanding is a mystic under-standing, and our sense of victory a mystic joy. Tragedy and our religion are inter-significant. The Christian cross is only the symbol of the greatest of tragedies.

Now it is important that we should observe the tremendous advance in optimism and the mystic apprehension of the tragic sacrifice which is marked by the next tragedy, *Antony and Cleopatra*. Death is here sublimated as the supreme good, and directly related to the theme of love. The protagonists, Antony and Cleopatra, it has been well said, 'die into love'. The love-problems and death-problems are resolved by being harmonized in the unity of death-in-love. It is difficult to speak adequately of the last two acts of this perhaps the greatest but one of Shakespeare's plays. In the cold forms of conceptual thought one can say that by synchronizing a fine moment of love-consciousness with the time-vanquishing act of death the timeless nature of that love-consciousness is made apparent; or that the death and love union represents a vision of immortality in terms of quality rather than quantity, of value rather than time. But the language of conceptual thought fails before the transcendent reality of this death-revelation. It must suffice to emphasize the mystic nature of that vision, and its tragic purification of the diseased love-satire of the problem plays. And one more fact must be noticed. The tempest and storm symbolism of the earlier great tragedies does not recur in *Antony and Cleopatra*, but gives place to a new mystic symbolism in the music that preludes the final sacrifice of love:

4 *Soldier.*	Peace ! what noise ?	
1 *Soldier.*		List, list !
2 *Soldier.*	Hark !	
1 *Soldier.*	Music i' the air.	
3 *Soldier.*		Under the earth.
4 *Soldier.*	It signs well, does it not ?	
3 *Soldier.*		No.
1 *Soldier.*		Peace, I say !
	What should this mean ?	
2 *Soldier.*	'Tis the god Hercules, whom Antony lov'd,	
	Now leaves him.	(IV. iii. 12)

The emergence of this music-symbolism at this moment of the tragedy is all-important for our understanding of the third group of plays. The furthest limit of direct representation is here reached: tragedy is merging into mysticism, and what is left to say must be said in terms not of tragedy, but of miracle and myth. The inner truth of the tragic fact will thus be explicated in the narratives of the last plays from *Pericles* to *The Tempest*, and their plots will reflect the poet's intuition of immortality and conquest within apparent death and failure. I will now notice the themes of miracle and music in those plays.

III

The stories of *Pericles*[1] and *The Winter's Tale* are remarkably alike. In both the hero loses his wife and daughter just after the birth of his child; in both the idea of a child's helplessness is synchronized with a sea-storm of the usual Shakespearian kind; in both the wife and child are miraculously restored after a long passage of time; and the revival of Thaisa, and the restoration of Marina and Hermione are accompanied by music. These plays are throughout impregnated by an atmosphere of mysticism. The theology is pseudo-Hellenistic. The Delphic oracle and a prophetic dream occur in *The Winter's Tale*; Hermione is restored to Leontes in a 'chapel' to the sound of music, Thaisa to Pericles in the temple of Diana, with the full circumstance of religious ceremonial.[2] The goddess Diana appears to Pericles. A reader sensitive to poetic atmosphere must necessarily feel the awakening light of some religious or metaphysical truth symbolized in the plot and attendant machinery of these two plays.

Cerimon, who raises Thaisa from the dead, is a recluse and visionary:

> I hold it ever,
> Virtue and cunning were endowments greater
> Than nobleness and riches : careless heirs
> May the two latter darken and expend,
> But immortality attends the former,
> Making a man a god.   (III. ii. 26)

The body of Thaisa, supposed dead, is cast ashore by the tempest in a coffin. Cerimon, by his magic, and with the aid of fire and music, revives her:

> Well said, well said ; the fire and cloths.
> The rough and woeful music that we have,
> Cause it to sound, beseech you.
> The viol once more : how thou stirr'st, thou block !
> The music there !—I pray you, give her air.
> Gentlemen,
> This queen will live ; nature awakes ; a warmth

[1] In a note to my original text I showed that I was not necessarily regarding *Pericles* as Shakespeare's work throughout.   [2] Indicated at V, i. 241–4.

Breathes out of her ; she hath not been entranc'd
Above five hours. See how she 'gins to blow
Into life's flower again !   (III. ii. 87)

This incident, with the exquisite conception of the character of
Cerimon, and the reviving of Thaisa, is one of the pinnacles of
Shakespeare's art: this scene and those of the restoration to
Pericles of his long-lost daughter and consort which follow,
are alone sufficient to establish my thesis that the author is
moved by vision, not fancy; is creating not merely entertainment, but myth in the Platonic sense. Now the theme of music
again occurs in the meeting of Pericles with Marina:

Pericles.   Now, blessing on thee ! rise ; thou art my child.
               Give me fresh garments. Mine own, Helicanus ;
               She is not dead at Tarsus, as she should have been,
               By savage Cleon : she shall tell thee all ;
               When thou shalt kneel, and justify in knowledge
               She is thy very princess. Who is this ?
Helicanus.   Sir, 'tis the governor of Mytilene,
               Who, hearing of your melancholy state,
               Did come to see you.
Pericles.   I embrace you.
               Give me my robes. I am wild in my beholding.
               O heavens, bless my girl ! But, hark ! what
                    music ?
               Tell Helicanus, my Marina, tell him
               O'er, point by point, for yet he seems to doubt,
               How sure you are my daughter. But, what
                    music ?
Helicanus.   My lord, I hear none.
Pericles.   None !
               The music of the spheres ! List, my Marina.
Lysimachus. It is not good to cross him ; give him way.
Pericles.   Rarest sounds ! Do ye not hear ?
Lysimachus. My lord, I hear.
Pericles.   Most heavenly music !
               It nips me unto listening, and thick slumber
               Hangs upon mine eyes ; let me rest. (*Sleeps*)
                                             (v. i. 215)

The blindness of past Shakespearian criticism is at no point
more completely in evidence than in the comments on this
play. To the discerning mind it will be evident that we are

here confronted with the furthest reach of Shakespeare's poetic and visionary power: if we except *The Tempest*, the latter half of *Pericles* has no equivalent in transcendental apprehension in all Shakespeare but the latter half of *Antony and Cleopatra* which on the plane of myth and symbolism it may be considered to interpret.

Almost of an equal beauty is the restoration of Thaisa in the Temple of Diana.

> *Cerimon* . . . Look ! Thaisa is
> Recovered.
> *Thaisa.* O, let me look !
> If he be none of mine, my sanctity
> Will to my sense bend no licentious ear,
> But curb it, spite of seeing. O ! my lord,
> Are you not Pericles ? Like him you speak,
> Like him you are. Did you not name a tempest,
> A birth, and death ?
> *Pericles.* The voice of dead Thaisa !
> *Thaisa.* That Thaisa am I, supposed dead
> And drown'd.
> *Pericles.* Immortal Dian !
> *Thaisa.* Now I know you better.
> When we with tears parted Pentapolis,
> The king, my father, gave you such a ring.
> *(Shows a ring)*
> *Pericles.* This, this : no more, you gods ! your present
> kindness
> Makes my past miseries sport. . . .
> (v. iii. 27)

That last thought of Pericles is to be echoed again, with clear religious and universal significance, in the Vision of Jupiter in *Cymbeline*. Now if, as is probable, the greater part of *Pericles* is the work of Shakespeare grafted on to an earlier play of different authorship, of which signs are apparent in some of the early scenes, it is not surprising that, after his composition of these supreme latter acts, he found another plot of the same kind for his next play; nor is it surprising that that next play, *The Winter's Tale*, though more perfect as a whole, lacks something of the paradisal radiance of *Pericles*. The great artist does not well to repeat himself: in *Pericles*, as the writer handles an old theme, some mystic apprehension of a life that conquers death has sprung to vivid form, as it were, spontaneously: a shaft of light penetrating into the very heart of death. The studied repetition that follows is less vital.[1] It will be sufficient here to point the recurrence of the themes of birth, restoration, tempest, and music, and to speak shortly of their significance in both plays.

In *The Winter's Tale*, the plot turns on Leontes' distrust of Hermione's conjugal loyalty. Now too much stress cannot be laid on the importance attached to infidelity in Shakespeare. The horror at the passing of love's faith is twin to the horror of death: the difficulty is quite as much a metaphysical as a moral one—Troilus cannot understand the patent fact of its existence. In *Hamlet* and *Troilus* these death and love problems are given dramatic form, and leave us distressed; in *Othello* the faithlessness-theme is crystallized into a perfected classic mould and makes a great play, but, since Desdemona dies untrusted, leaves us still pained. In *Antony and Cleopatra*, though the love of the protagonists is shown to us as untrusting and untrustworthy, a spiritual and passionate thing tossed tempestuously on the waters of temporal existence, yet, by the synchronizing of faith with death, we are left with a vision of a timeless instantaneous ascension in death to love, which is life. This tragic apprehension is explicated in narrative form in the parables of *Pericles* and *The Winter's Tale*. Leontes is guilty of Othello's distrust, and thinks Hermione dead. He suffers years of remorse, but at last she is restored to him, in a temple, with ceremony, and to the sounds of music. In Shakespeare the failing of love's faith is essentially a metaphysical difficulty, and one with the difficulty of loss in death: conversely, 'perfect love casteth out fear'. The infidelity-theme of *The Winter's Tale* is thus not essentially different from the loss of Thaisa at sea. In both we see the tempests of temporal conditions seemingly at war with the otherness of a purely spiritual experience.

In both these plays we have the theme of a child bereft of its mother and threatened by storm and thunder. The em-

---

[1] One's past 'critical' (as opposed to interpretative) pronouncements are apt to make poor reading fifteen years later. I cannot remember ever having seriously held the opinion here expressed. *The Winter's Tale*, which I had known well for years, was, I think, shadowed for the moment by my recent discovery of *Pericles*.

phasis on tempests is insistent, and the suggestion is clearly
that of the pitifulness and helplessness of humanity born into a
world of tragic conflict. That the tempest is percurrent in
Shakespeare as a symbol of tragedy need not be demonstrated
here at length. Its symbolic significance is patent from the
earliest to the latest of the plays—in metaphor, in simile, in
long or short descriptions, in stage directions. The individual
soul is the 'bark' putting out to sea in a 'tempest': the image
occurs again and again. For instance, we have in *Macbeth*,

> Though his bark cannot be lost,
> Yet it shall be tempest-toss'd (i. iii. 24),

and in *Timon of Athens* (v. i. 205), we hear of

> . . . other incident throes
> That nature's fragile vessel doth sustain
> In life's uncertain voyage. . . .

and in *Pericles*, which contains perhaps the finest of Shakespeare's profuse storm-poetry in iii. i., Marina says (iv. i. 17):

> Ay me ! poor maid,
> Born in a tempest, when my mother died,
> This world to me is like a lasting storm,
> Whirring me from my friends.

Numerous other references could be given. The theme of
helpless childhood synchronized with storm in *Pericles* and *The
Winter's Tale* (iii. i.; iii. iii.) is significant, just as the tempests
in *Julius Caesar*, *Macbeth* and *Lear* are significant: poetic symbols of the storm and stress of human life, the turbulence of
temporal events reflecting and causing tempestuous passion in
the heart of man. Lastly, in these two plays we have the music
which accompanies resurrection and reunion. This music may
seem to perform a dual function: first, to suggest, as a symbol
of pure aesthetic delight, the mystic nature of the act being
performed; second, to anaesthetize the critical faculty, as does
the overture in a theatre, and prepare the mind for some extraordinary event. But these are in reality twin aspects of the
same function: for music, like erotic sight, raises the consciousness until it is in tune with a reality beyond the reach of
wisdom. 'Music, moody food of us that trade in love,' says

Cleopatra (ii. v. 1). Music in Shakespeare is ever the solace and companion of love, and love in Shakespeare the language of mysticism. For this reason the mystic happenings in these plays are accompanied by the theme of music. I will now pass to the third of the mythical plays, *Cymbeline*.

Many of the former elements recur in *Cymbeline*. We have the faithlessness-theme in which Posthumus distrusts Imogen, and Iago is resuscitated in the deceiver Iachimo. Posthumus' very name suggests the birth-theme of the two former plays : like Marina and Perdita he is cast unprotected into a hostile world. Cymbeline's long-lost sons, Guiderius and Arviragus, remind us of the lost children of Pericles and Leontes. We have again the idea of the apparently dead found to be alive. Guiderius and Arviragus think Imogen is dead, and even prepare to bury her. Solemn music sounds at her supposed death. Posthumus, too, is led to think Imogen dead independently. The same themes are evidently running in the poet's mind, but it is as though the artist tries hard to control them, to control the more directly religious apprehension that is beginning to make the writing of a normal play an impossibility. And this repressed instinct—if repressed it was—certainly has its revenge. In the Vision of Jupiter we have Shakespeare's clearest statement in terms of anthropomorphic theology of the significance of the themes I have been analysing in the final plays. Without analysis of the sequence of tragedies and myths the scene will appear dramatically unnecessary and crude: with knowledge of Shakespeare's state of mind in the writing of this play, when his imagination must have been burningly conscious not alone of human life, but of the mystic significance of it, which he had already touched in *Antony and Cleopatra* and *Pericles*, we shall find it quite reasonable that he should attempt a universal statement in direct language concerning the implications of his plot. The scene becomes, in fact, a priceless possession to the interpreter of Shakespeare. It has been often allotted in the past to the 'incompetent coadjutor'. I will shortly notice this, the central and, for the purpose of this paper, by far the most important, scene in the play.

Posthumus, in the depth of his misery and remorse, sleeps in prison. He has prayed to heaven to take his life, and finally

called on his love, whom he has mistrusted, whom he believes
dead through his fault:

> O Imogen !
> I'll speak to thee in silence.   (v. iv. 28)

There is next a lengthy stage direction, with a three times
iterated mention of music. Posthumus' father, mother, and
two brothers appear. And these figures chant, to a haunting
dirge-like tune of words, a piteous complaint to Jupiter. It is
important to observe the universal significance of their words,
and its direct bearing on the troubles and trials of Posthumus,
who has endured the same kind of suffering as Shakespeare's
other heroes. Jupiter is the 'thunder-master' who shows his
'spite on mortal flies'. The helplessness of Posthumus' birth
is remembered:

> *Mother.* Lucina lent not me her aid,
> But took me in my throes ;
> That from me was Posthumus ript,
> Came crying 'mongst his foes,
> A thing of pity ! (v. iv. 43)

If we consider that Iachimo is of the same kin as Iago and that
both are embodiments of the spirit of cynicism and devitalised
intellectual energy which blights the faith of Hamlet and
Troilus in human kind and the purposes of eternity, we can
find a poignant and universal note that is generally missed in
Sicilius' stanza:

> *Sicilius.* Why did you suffer Iachimo,
> Slight thing of Italy,
> To taint his nobler heart and brain
> With needless jealousy ;
> And to become the geck and scorn
> O' the other's villainy ?   (v. iv. 63)

I am not suggesting that Shakespeare intentionally allegorizes
here: but that Iago and Iachimo are products of the same
potentiality in his mind or soul, and that it is exactly that
potentiality that rings in the pain, the cynicism, and the loathing of the problem plays. The family of Posthumus end their
chant with fervent cries that justice be done. It is man's com-

plaint to God on behalf of those he loves. Jupiter appears and
answers their complaints as follows:

> *Jupiter.*   No more, you petty spirits of region low,
>   Offend our hearing ; hush ! How dare you ghosts
>   Accuse the thunderer, whose bolt, you know,
>   Sky-planted, batters all rebelling coasts ?
>   Poor shadows of Elysium, hence ! and rest
>   Upon your never-withering banks of flowers.
>   Be not with mortal accidents opprest;
>   No care of yours it is ; you know 'tis ours.
>   Whom best I love I cross ; to make my gift
>   The more delay'd, delighted. Be content ;
>   Your low-laid son our godhead will uplift :
>   His comforts thrive, his trials well are spent..
>   Our Jovial star reign'd at his birth, and in
>   Our temple was he married. Rise, and fade !
>   He shall be lord of lady Imogen,
>   And happier much by his affliction made.
>   This tablet lay upon his breast, wherein
>   Our pleasure his full fortune doth confine :
>   And so, away : no further with your din
>   Express impatience lest you stir up mine.
>   Mount, eagle, to my palace crystalline.
>   (*Ascends*)   (v. iv. 93)

As Jupiter vanishes, Sicilius makes majestic comment:

> *Sicilius.*   He came in thunder ; his celestial breath
>   Was sulphurous to smell ; the holy eagle
>   Stoop'd, as to foot us ; his ascension is
>   More sweet than our blest fields ; his royal bird
>   Prunes the immortal wing and cloys his beak,
>   As when his god is pleas'd.   (v. iv. 114)

Now, whatever we may think about the imaginative impact
of this scene as we read—we must remember that we miss the
heightened consciousness of the music that is indicated, and
the visual accompaniment of grouping and dance—two things
are certain: first, that there is nothing whatever in the style to
justify a critic who knows his Shakespeare in enlisting the services of the incompetent coadjutor; second, that, coming as it
does before the usual reunions at the end of the play, it clearly
points the necessity of my thesis in dealing with the similar

plots of *Pericles* and *The Winter's Tale*, that these miraculous
and joyful conquests of life's tragedy are the expression, through
the medium of drama, of a state of mind or soul in the writer
directly in knowledge—or supposed knowledge—of a mystic
and transcendent fact as to the true nature and purpose of the
sufferings of humanity. My primary intention here is not to
insist on the truth of the immortality shadowed forth in these
plays; but simply to indicate that they are of this mystic kind,
so that we may allot them their proper place in our assessment
of Shakespeare's achievement.

To-day we hear from theologians that immortality is a matter
of quality and value rather than something which can be
measured by time. Canon Streeter asserts that its truth can
only be expressed by myth or metaphor. Now the supreme
value to man is always love. What more perfect form, then,
could such a myth take than that of the restoration to Pericles
of his Thaisa and Marina, so long and so mistakenly supposed
lost ? It is, indeed, noticeable that these plays do not aim at
revealing a temporal survival of death: rather at the thought
that death is a delusion. What was thought dead is in reality
alive. In them we watch the fine flowers of a mystic state of
soul bodied into the forms of drama. The parables of Jesus,
which, through the medium of narrative, leave with the reader
what is pre-eminently a sense of quality rather than a memory
of events, are of the same kind. *Pericles* and *The Winter's Tale*
show us the quality of immortality in terms of victorious love
welling up in the beautiful plot of loss and reunion; and in
Cymbeline an anthropomorphic theology is introduced to
attempt an explanation and a valuation of the mystic fact.

IV

The artist expresses a direct vision of the significance of life,
and for his materials he uses, for purposes of imitation, the
shapes, the colours, the people and events of the world in
which he finds himself. But in course of the spiritual progress
to which he is dedicated it may happen that the implements of
outward manifestation in the physical universe become inade-
quate to the intuition which he is to express. Art is an extraverted expression of the creative imagination which, when

introverted, becomes religion. But the mind of man cannot altogether dispense with the machinery of objectivity, and the inwardness of religion must create, or discern, its own objective reality and name it God. Conversely, the artist, in process of growth, may be forced beyond the phenomena of actuality into a world of the spirit which scarcely lends itself to a purely artistic, and therefore objective, imitation. In *Cymbeline* Shakespeare is forced by the increasing inwardness of his intuition to a somewhat crude anthropomorphism in the Vision of Jupiter: and this anthropomorphic theology is inimical to artistic expression. *Cymbeline* contains a personal god called in to right the balance of a drama whose plot, like that of *Pericles* and *The Winter's Tale*, is incompatible with the ordinary forms of life; but this god, true enough to the religious intuition of the author, yet comes near to exploding the work of art in which he occurs. The form of dramatic art is necessarily extraverted and imitative; and Shakespeare has passed beyond interest in imitation. If a last work of pure art is to be created there is only one theme that can be its fit material. A prophetic criticism could, if *The Tempest* had been lost, have nevertheless indicated what must be its essential nature, and might have hazarded its name: for in this work Shakespeare looks inward and, projecting perfectly his own spiritual experience into symbols of objectivity, traces in a compact play the past progress of his own soul. He is now the object of his own search,[1] and no other theme but that of his visionary self is now of power to call forth the riches of his imagination.

Let me recall the outline of the Shakespearian progress. In the problem plays there is mental division: on the one side an exquisite apprehension of the spiritual—beauty, romance, poetry; on the other, the hate-theme—loathing of the impure, aversion from the animal kinship of man, disgust at the decaying body of death. This dualism is resolved in the tragedies: the hate-theme itself is finely sublimated in *Timon* by means of the purification of great passion, human grandeur, and all the panoply of high tragedy. The recurrent poetic symbol of tragedy in Shakespeare is 'storm' or 'tempest'. The third group outsoars the intuition of tragedy and gives us plays

---

[1] I was thinking of 'Thou art THYSELF the object of thy search', quoted from H. P. Blavatsky by William James in *The Varieties of Religious Experience*.

whose plots explicate the quality of immortality: the pre-dominating symbols are loss in tempest and revival to the sounds of music. It is about twelve years from the inception of this lonely progress of the soul to the composition of *The Tempest*.

Now on the island of *The Tempest* Prospero is master of his lonely magic. He has been there for twelve years. Two creatures serve him: Ariel, the 'airy nothing' of poetry; and the snarling Caliban, half-beast, half-man; the embodiment of the hate-theme. These two creatures are yoked in the employ of Prospero, like Plato's two steeds of the soul, the noble and the hideous, twin potentialities of the human spirit. Caliban has been mastered by Prospero and Ariel. Though he revolts against his master still, the issue is not in doubt, and the tunes of Ariel draw out his very soul in longing and desire, just as the power of poetry shows forth the majesty of Timon, whose passion makes of universal hate a noble and aspiring thing. These three are the most vital and outstanding figures in the play: for Shakespeare had only to look inward to find them. But there are other elements that complete the pattern of this self-revelation.

Prospero's enemies are drawn to the magic island of great poetry by means of a tempest raised by Prospero with the help of Ariel. In Alonso, despairing and self-accusing, bereft of his child, we can see traces of the terrible end of *Lear*; in Antonio and Sebastian, the tempter and the tempted, plotting murder for a crown, we can see more than traces of *Macbeth*. But, driven by the tempest-raising power of tragic and passion-ate poetry within the magic circle of Prospero and Ariel, these hostile and evil things are powerless: they can only stand spell-stopped. They are enveloped in the wondrous laws of enchant-ment on the island of song and music. Caliban, who has been mastered by it, knows best the language to describe the mystic tunes of Ariel:

> Be not afeard : the isle is full of noises,
> Sounds and sweet airs, that give delight, and hurt not.
> Sometimes a thousand twangling instruments
> Will hum about mine ears; and sometime voices,
> That, if I then had wak'd after long sleep,
> Will make me sleep again : and then, in dreaming,

> The clouds methought would open and show riches
> Ready to drop upon me ; that, when I wak'd,
> I cried to dream again.   (III. ii. 147)

The protagonists of murder and bereavement are exquisitely entrapped in the magic and music of Prospero and his servant Ariel. So, too, were the evil things of life mastered by the poetry of the great tragedies, and transmuted into the vision of the myths. The spirit of the Final Plays also finds its perfected home in this the last of the series. Here the child-theme is repeated in Miranda, cast adrift with her father on the tempestuous seas; here the lost son of Alonso is recovered, alive and well, and the very ship that was wrecked is found to be miraculously 'tight and yare and bravely rigg'd' as when it 'first put out to sea.' (V. i. 224). Prospero, like Cerimon over Thaisa, revives, with music, the numbed consciousness of Alonso and his companions; and, as they wake, it is as though mortality were waking into eternity. And this thought makes necessary a statement and a distinction as to the dual possible approaches to the significance of *The Tempest*.

First, we can regard it as the poet's expression of a view of human life. With the knowledge of Shakespeare's poetic symbolism in memory, we will think of the wreck as suggesting the tragic destiny of man, and the marvellous survival of the travellers and crew as another and more perfectly poetic and artistic embodiment of the thought expressed through the medium of anthropomorphic theology in *Cymbeline* that there exists a joy and a revival that makes past misery, in Pericles' phraseology, 'sport'. According to this reading Prospero becomes in a sense the 'God' of the *Tempest*-universe, and we shall find compelling suggestion as to the immortality of man in such lines as Ariel's when Prospero asks him if the victims of the wreck are safe:

> Not a hair perish'd ;
> On their sustaining garments not a blemish,
> But fresher than before.   (I. ii. 217)

So, too, thinking of sea-storms and wreckages as Shakespeare's symbols of human tragedy, we shall find new significance in Ariel's lines:

> Nothing of him that doth fade,
> But doth suffer a sea-change
> Into something rich and strange. (I. ii. 397)

Especially, if we remember that the soul's desire of love in Shakespeare is consistently imaged as a rich something set far across tempestuous seas, we shall receive especial delight in the song:

> Come unto these yellow sands,
>   And then take hands :
> Curtsied when you have, and kiss'd
>   The wild waves whist. (I. ii. 375)

Commentators divide into two camps and argue long as to the syntax and sense of those last two lines: is 'whist', or is it not, they say, a nominative absolute? And if not, how can waves be kiss'd? A knowledge of Shakespeare's imagery, however, is needed to see the triumphant mysticism of the dream of love's perfected fruition in eternity stilling the tumultuous waves of time. This is one instance of many where the imaginative interpretation of a poet, and a knowledge of his particular symbolism, short-circuits the travails and tribulations of the grammarian or the commentator who in search for facts neglects the primary facts of all poetry—its suggestion, its colour, its richness of mental association, its appeal, not to the intellect, but the imagination.

The second approach is this, which I have already indicated. *The Tempest* is a record, crystallized with consummate art into a short play, of all the themes I have discussed in this paper, of the spiritual progress from 1599 or 1600 to the year 1611, or whenever, exactly, *The Tempest* was written. According to this reading Prospero is not God, but Shakespeare—or rather the controlling judgement of Shakespeare, since Ariel and Caliban are also representations of dual minor potentialities of his soul. From this approach three incidents in the play reveal unique interest. First, the dialogue between Prospero and Ariel in I. ii. where Ariel is tired and cries for the promised freedom, and is told that there is one last work to be done— which is in exact agreement with my reading of the faltering art of *Cymbeline*:[1] second, Prospero's well-known farewell to

---

[1] A strange error : whatever our personal likes and dislikes, there is nothing 'faltering' in *Cymbeline*.

his art, where commentators have seldom failed to admit what Professor Saintsbury calls a 'designed personal allegory', and where I would notice that Prospero clearly regards his art as pre-eminently a tempest-raising magic, and next refers to the opening of graves at his command, thereby illustrating again the sequence from tragedy to myth which I have described; and third, Prospero's other dialogue with Ariel in v. i. where Ariel pities the enemies of his master and draws from Prospero the words:

> Hast thou, which art but air, a touch, a feeling
> Of their afflictions, and shall not myself,
> One of their kind, that relish all as sharply
> Passion as they, be kindlier moved than thou art ?
>
> (v. i. 21)

In poetic creation 'all is forgiven, and it would be strange not to forgive'; but the partial and fleeting flame of the poet's intuition may light at last the total consciousness with the brilliance of a cosmic apprehension. This speech suggests the transit from the intermittent love of poetic composition to the perduring love of the mystic.

Now these two methods of approach considered separately and in sequence are not so significant as they become when we realize that they are simultaneously possible and, indeed, necessary. Together they are complementary to *The Tempest*'s unique reality. For it will next be seen that these two aspects when considered together give us a peculiar knowledge of this act of the poet's soul in the round: so that the usual flat view of it which reads it as an impersonal fairy story—corresponding to my reading of it as an objective vision of life—becomes a three-dimensional understanding when we remember the implicit personal allegory. Only by submitting our faculties to both methods can we properly understand the play to the full. *The Tempest* is at the same time a record of Shakespeare's spiritual progress and a statement of the vision to which that progress has brought him. It is apparent as a dynamic and living act of the soul, containing within itself the record of its birth: it is continually re-writing itself before our eyes. Shakespeare has in this play so become master of the whole of his own mystic universe that that universe, at last perfectly projected in one short play into the forms and shapes of objective human existence, shows us, in the wreck of *The Tempest*, a complete view of that existence, no longer as it normally appears to man, but as it takes reflected pattern in the still depths of the timeless soul of poetry. And, since it reveals its vision not as a statement of absolute truth independently of the author, but related inwardly to the succession of experiences that condition and nurture its own reality, it becomes, in a unique sense beyond other works of art, an absolute. There is thus now no barrier between the inward and the outward, expression and imitation. God, it has been said, is the mode in which the subject-object distinction is transcended. Art aspires to the perfected fusion of expression with imitation. *The Tempest* is thus at the same time the most perfect work of art and the most crystal act of mystic vision in our literature.

V

An unduly personal criticism, it will be said. But that is not true. The critic who picks on this or that speech and then asserts, without due reference to other speeches or plays, that it has the final authority of Shakespeare's considered wisdom, is giving an unduly personal criticism: so, too, are those who take on themselves to decide arbitrarily that Shakespeare's intention is to show that one character more than another is justified, or that some scene or passage would not have been written save in deference to the public taste of his time; or those whose immediate understanding of the poetry has been over-much deflected from its true direction by the desire to search the world's literature and the records of contemporary events for 'sources'. All those are guilty of an unjust criticism, for they ever credit Shakespeare with their own tastes and aversions, and whenever they find some literary or historic tangent to the fiery circle of poetry, they think, by following its direction into the cold night of the actual, to expose the content of that burning star. But the critic who refuses the name of Shakespeare to any hypothetical figure of history but the creative impulse dynamic in the text of the plays; who yet views each play ever in its place among the completed works; above all, who gives attention to imaginative rather than literal similarities, and refuses to be led astray by any considerations but the hot pulse of passion and poetic significance that beats within the living work of art, and alone endues it with immortality—he, by consistently aiming at a sincere and personal poetic criticism can alone hope to succeed in gaining the true objectivity of interpretation. For the poetic reality alone is the subject of his work. Therefore the conclusions of this essay, based on a close and detailed attention to poetic and imaginative fact throughout the plays, are set beyond the hostile comment of the expert on contemporary history, the tracer of 'sources', and the critic who must ever think in terms of Shakespeare's 'intentions'. I have little to say of his intentions. Whenever I hazard a suggestion as to his awareness in uncreative consciousness of the sequence I have been tracing, I am content always to leave it a suggestion and no more. If we use the word Shakespeare in the interpretation of this sequence of plays it should be used as we use the word 'God': to signify that principle of unity and coherence within apparent multiplicity and disorder. But the necessity of recognizing the significance of this sequence, and especially of these Final Plays, is, indeed, imperative.

The progress from spiritual pain and despairing thought through stoic acceptance to a serene and mystic joy is a universal rhythm of the spirit of man. William James, in *The Varieties of Religious Experience*, quotes, among other instances, the doubts and inner torments that preluded the prophetic zeal of Tolstoy's later years. His description of the state of the 'sick soul' reads like a commentary on *Hamlet*, and it should be clear that the progress of other of his subjects from the state of sin to conversion and the conviction of salvation is but another expression of that rhythm which is to be found, too, in the progress from the hate-theme in Shakespeare's problem plays to the mysticism of *Pericles* and *The Winter's Tale*. A curious inversion has come about. The self-abasement of the Middle Ages has developed into the satire of Renaissance Europe, and Goethe's Mephistopheles is depicted as pre-eminently the scoffer and spirit of denial. Sin has become cynicism. But the same inward movement of the spirit can be traced in its different manifestations. The work of Dostoievsky reflects it; and Keats. It need not be a progress stretched across a span of years: in Shakespeare I have traced an exact miniature of the

succession of great plays to follow in the thought-sequence of
one speech of *Richard II*; and the same sequence is separately
apparent in some of Tennyson's early poems. As for my con-
tention that the Final Plays of Shakespeare must be read as
myths of immortality, that is only to bring his work into line
with other great works of literature. Tragedy is never the last
word: theophanies and reunions characterize the drama of the
Greeks: they, too, tell us that 'with God all things are possible'.
Again, in *The Book of Job*, which turns on the same question as
that which fires the greater plays of Shakespeare—the problem
of suffering and a tragic destiny—we get again the same
answer: after endurance to the end the hero has a mystic vision
of God, and then, in spite of reason and experience, we are told
that his original wealth and happiness are restored to him ten-
fold. Neither *The Book of Job* nor the Final Plays of Shakespeare are to be read as pleasant fancies: rather as parables of a
profound and glorious truth. The one attempts a statement of
the moral purpose of God to man, in face of an apparent uncon-
cern, offering striking parallels to the anthropomorphic theology
of *Cymbeline*; the Final Plays of Shakespeare, concerned on the
whole less with a purely moral issue, and except in *Cymbeline*
steering clear of definite theology, display plots whose texture
is soaked in the quality of romantic immortality. For in
Shakespeare, as at the conclusion of Goethe's *Faust*, we are
insistently aware of the quality of romantic love as in some way
intrinsically connected with the immortality of the human
spirit: so, too, Beatrice, not Vergil, guides Dante through the
spheres of Heaven.

I have left unsaid the two most significant of all comparisons.[1]
For what is the sequence of the *Divina Commedia*, *L'Inferno*,
Il Purgatorio, *Il Paradiso*, but another manifestation, in the
spatialized forms of medieval eschatology, of the essential
qualities of the three groups of the greater plays of Shakespeare, the Problems, Tragedies and Myths? And what are
both but reflections in the work of the two greatest minds of
modern Europe—children respectively of the Middle Ages and

---

[1] The Shakespearian sequence itself concludes with a play saturated in Christian feeling and
symbolism: *Henry VIII*. This I had not read for many years, assuming that the prevailing view
of it as mainly non-Shakespearian was correct. On the publication of *Myth and Miracle* my
attention was recalled to it by the late Edgar I. Fripp, when its importance was at once clear.

the Renaissance—of that mystic truth from which are born the dogmas of the Catholic Church—the incarnation in actuality of the Divine Logos of Poetry: the temptation in the desert, the tragic ministry and death, and the resurrection of the Christ? We should centre our attention always not on the poetic forms alone, which are things of time and history, but on the spirit which burns through them and is eternal in its rhythm of pain, endurance, and joy.

ADDITIONAL NOTE (1965)

Note that my conclusion asserted not 'dogmas' but the 'mystic truth' *behind* them; not 'forms' but 'spirit'. In view of certain current misconceptions, I here state that all my comparisons of Shakespeare and Christianity assume a preliminary recognition of their difference. Shakespearian drama lies within the tradition running from Aeschylus to Ibsen and Nietzsche as described in *The Golden Labyrinth*. Though it has obvious Christian contacts, it obeys no external dictates.

The grand discovery of *Myth and Miracle* was this—that Shakespeare's autonomous poetry corroborates the death-conquest announced by Christianity. Probably few readers have deeply understood it since Mr. T. S. Eliot, as he recorded when introducing *The Wheel of Fire*, found it—or he may have been referring to its unpublished predecessor, *Thaisa* (p. viii above; *The Sovereign Flower*, p. 9)—helpful, and subsequently sent me the inscribed copy of *Marina* now lodged in the Shakespeare Memorial Library at Birmingham. *Marina* was followed by *Triumphal March*, indirectly related to Beethoven's *Coriolan* and also—as there is reason to suppose—to Shakespeare's *Coriolanus*, though its central insight touches more nearly Section 35 (or II. 13) of Nietzsche's *Thus Spake Zarathustra*. New views on Shakespeare were at this brief period of Mr. Eliot's progress being incorporated into a visionary humanism to be distinguished from the religious orthodoxy of *Ash Wednesday* and *Murder in the Cathedral*, and of an assurance more direct and single than the *Four Quartets*.

I refer those in danger of confusing my Shakespearian interpretations with a doctrinal and dogmatic orthodoxy to pages 35, 79, 96–7, 128, 227, 251, 253, 277, 297, 314, 317 below; to my prefaces to the post-war editions of *The Imperial Theme* (p. xii) and *The Shakespearian Tempest* (pp. vii–viii); to the chapter 'Some Notable Fallacies' in *The Sovereign Flower*; and to my letters in *The Times Literary Supplement* of 7 January and 4 February 1965.

Even the impregnating Christianity of *Henry VIII* is countered, as my extended interpretation demonstrates, by strong sexual and royalistic emphases. The drama celebrates a state-church balance, at a moment of British history, that may be profitably compared with Ibsen's *Emperor and Galilean* (discussed in my *Ibsen*, 1962; pp. 31–46).

My interpretation of *All's Well that Ends Well*, which may be grouped with the essays of this volume (see pp. 127–8, note, below), has now appeared in *The Sovereign Flower*.

II

THE WRITING OF PERICLES

Submit—in this, or any other sphere,
Secure to be as blest as thou can'st bear :
Safe in the hand of one disposing Power,
Or in the natal, or the mortal hour.
All Nature is but Art, unknown to thee ;
All Chance, Direction, which thou can'st not see ;
All Discord, Harmony not understood ;
All partial Evil, universal Good . . .

Pope's *Essay on Man*, 1. 285.

I

THE problems raised by *Pericles* are unique. In no other Shakespearian play do we find so stark a contrast of (i) scenes of supreme power and beauty with (ii) scenes which no one can accept as Shakespeare's without disquietude. Two more facts must be faced: the first, that the play seems to have been extremely popular; the second, that it alone of the accepted canon was omitted from the First Folio.

The most questionable scenes, which occur early, are strange both in matter and in manner. The first, showing Pericles' suit for the hand of Antiochus' daughter and his reading of the riddle, is peculiar enough; what dramatic interest is raised sags soon after and it is hard to follow his later fears and successive flights with the requisite interest. The verse, too, is troublesome. The thought is clear and pointed, but the language seems weak; at the best, it lacks colloquial grip and condensed power and at the worst sounds like apprentice work; there are few striking metaphors, and rhyme bulks large. One begins by suspecting another hand, or wondering if Shakespeare is revising a script of his own dating back to the time of *The Two Gentlemen of Verona*, a manner suggested by Pericles' first lines :

> I have, Antiochus, and, with a soul
> Embolden'd with the glory of her praise,
> Think death no hazard in this enterprise. (1. i. 3)

Often one suspects the text which may be faulty. And yet, as against these suspicions, we are forced to recognize that everything is organic in story-value; more, that each scene, indeed the early scenes as a single unit, are imaginatively coherent, and the peculiar manner, on the whole, sustained. Moreover, little occurs that is indisputably unauthentic, and the thoughts at least, and even the action, recall other Shakespearian plays. Occasionally we meet lines that sound like late writing of the normal kind. Later, we have long sequences of apparently mature Shakespeare between work of the doubtful sort. The court scenes at Tarsus and Pentapolis are full of strange, often rhymed, rather formal, verse, but Pericles' arrival on the shore of Pentapolis in Act II., with its accompanying storm-poetry and fisherman's talk, has the Shakespearian stamp. Even the queer scenes seem to grow in power, perhaps because one gets acclimatized; after Act I. one is less inclined to doubt, and from Act III. onwards there is little but superlative, even for Shakespeare, strength. Finally, after a number of re-readings one begins to suspect some especial purpose in the passages of stilted verse, lending themselves, as they do, to semi-didactic comment and generalized statement. The style is often gnomic.

It is often supposed that Shakespeare was re-writing someone else's play. This is possible, though it may be wiser to suppose an earlier text of his own. Anyway, the allotment of unauthentic, early Shakespearian and late-Shakespearian passages, if such allotment is attempted, must be left to the reader's private judgement, since no certainty is possible. The general result is that, though the Folio editors rejected the play, we are in no position to do so. It was published under Shakespeare's name, fits, as we shall see, into the general progress of his later work, and is, even where the style appears doubtful, heavily loaded with Shakespearian reminiscence. It fairly obviously stands now as a whole for which Shakespeare must be considered responsible. As Lascelles Abercrombie argued in his *Plea for the Liberty of Interpreting*, non-authentic material can assume authenticity through incorporation, deriving sustenance from the new organism into which it has been incorporated, as when flesh is grafted on to a living body. It is the less easy to feel this in *Pericles* in that the queer scenes bulk so largely and seem to stand so firmly on their own feet; the problem is far different from the incorporation of Plutarchan passages in *Antony and Cleopatra*. But the strong Shakespearian continuation in Acts III, IV and V, apart from earlier fine scenes and the possibly misunderstood purpose of those considered dubious, certainly does something to render the whole, as a whole, impressive. We must accordingly be prepared to make a preliminary acceptance and see what comes of it.

Pericles is usually dated early in the group of Final Plays; that is, as a direct successor to the tragic sequence culminating in *Coriolanus* and *Antony and Cleopatra*. Now if we can imagine ourselves in Shakespeare's position at this turn in his writing career, we can penetrate a little more deeply.

The tragic spirit dominating the sombre plays from *Hamlet* and reaching its maximum intensity in *Timon of Athens* finally transmutes itself, as is the nature of such intensity, to a positive; the reversal being expressed crisply in Timon's 'nothing brings me all things' (v. i. 193). The full statement of this new positive is *Antony and Cleopatra*, less a tragedy than a triumphal song, wherein death is no longer gloomy but golden. The truth revealed is, of course, no logical proposition, but simply a dramatic coherence exploited by poetry (especially the poetry of Cleopatra's dream in Act V), and relying mainly on a sharp synchronization of death with love to create a new intensity that may be called, for want of a better phrase, essential life. If we can feel the transcendent power of this conclusion it is likely that Shakespeare did so too; which put him, as a dramatic artist, in a strange way.

There is meaning in Shakespeare's art; but that is not to say that Shakespeare has a meaning in his head and proceeds to express it in his art. His art is more than expression; it is creation, born from a fusion of his own thoughts, dreams and intuitions with a chosen narrative, the choice of which exists in the order of action, not in the order of thinking. The poet responds, perhaps without knowing why, to a certain tale; and the precise reason for his decision to follow up response with action must be as elusive and unanalysable, to himself and to others, as life itself. Therefore the truth that finally emerges, especially if it be so transcendent yet elusive a truth as that dramatized in *Antony and Cleopatra*, may well be one he cannot himself think, but to which, once created, he will look up as to a religious dogma of recognized validity.

A strong positive faith tends to render tragedy impossible. During the ages of faith great tragedy was, necessarily, not composed, since the one towering tragedy of the Mass left no room for lesser ritual; the account had been settled and man's destiny fixed. But with the Renaissance great drama, silent since Aeschylus, Sophocles and Euripides and their Roman followers, returns. The step from Aeschylus to Shakespeare is easy: in spite of Shakespeare's obvious Christian sympathies the two dramatists often seem more contemporaneous than either with Dante. They breathe the same air of questioning adventure, sharing the same brooding sense of blood and death as vast antagonists to the soul of man. Shakespeare was, no doubt, an outwardly conforming Christian; more, his plays witness continually a fervent Christianity on the plane of verbal poetry and human delineation; but in that which is equally, perhaps more, important, the infusing of poetic belief into his fable, his dramatic machinery of ghosts and revenge-themes, the driving of action to a climax of slaughter, the sense of death as death; in this Shakespeare is with Aeschylus; at the most, with Vergil, not with Dante. Though the thought-forms of Renaissance writers are often medieval, their creative art is not. And yet, having created his own positive in *Antony and Cleopatra*, Shakespeare the dramatist is in the position of a Christian writer; not, it must be re-emphasized, of an accepting Christian merely, since it would seem that he (i.e. Shakespeare the dramatist—I say nothing of Shakespeare the man) was always that, but of a wholly dedicated dramatic force; not just a believer, but an apostle; and with, as his new dramatic centre, not the Mass but the old and new testaments of his own life-work culminating in a victory over death. To put it bluntly: it would have been extremely difficult and most unlikely for a man who had written *Antony and Cleopatra* to start composing more *King Lear*s. He is, of course, able whenever necessary to put words at the disposal of tragic feeling, but he will plan no new whole of tragic intention; theoretically, he could, no doubt, do this, but, what is more decisive, he cannot *want* to do it. Though not guided by conscious belief, art cannot run too far counter to its own creative discoveries. There is a certain compulsion dictating the artist's choice.

So we have Shakespeare, a working dramatist, with a firm

sense of new plays to be written, but no clear knowledge of their nature. The problem has been created by his own past work and to that he probably looked for guidance; to the comedies, the histories, the tragedies; plays Roman and Greek, Nordic and Italian. But the inner or suffusing moods of *Twelfth Night*, of *Henry V*, of *King Lear*, are alike alien to his present, more religious, temper. He may well have looked to the moralities for a precedent. In this mood he handles whatever script lay behind the composition of *Pericles*, and elects to use it.

His choice was, very clearly, in direct line with the central poetic impulse that had carried him so far. In poetry of metaphor and simile, description, atmospheric suggestion, symbol and plot, his imaginative emphasis has, from *The Comedy of Errors* onwards, concentrated primarily on tempests and especially sea-tempests, with fortunate or, more often, illstarred ship-voyages: in the plots of the comedies, as running imagery throughout the histories, in the grander symbolism of the tragedies (e.g. *Troilus and Cressida*, I. iii. 31–54; *Othello*, II. i. 1–215; *Macbeth*, I. iii. 4–29), the emphasis persists. In choosing the story of *Pericles* Shakespeare is therefore basing his new structure on his own most instinctive symbol. To put it shortly: being at a loss, he chooses a story that gives full rein to his poetic passion for voyages, tempests and wrecks. With these he is thoroughly at home. More, the problem posed by his own poetry is solved by giving that poetry its head. He aims to compose a morality play around his own poetic symbolism as dogma. For the rest, we may expect him to rely here, and in succeeding plays, on his own past accomplishments in comedy, history and tragedy, redistributing and re-knitting their elements into yet more complex designs.

In past plays narrative has reached an extraordinary intensity, as in the regular stamping of unity on action by imagery and other atmospheric suggestion, and the synchronization of love and death in *Antony and Cleopatra*. Such unity-impact is itself close to the essential magic of Shakespeare's plays, and through it their artistic value and truth have matured. But now, making a fresh start, and relying on poetry as such, or rather on poetic magic (a new term is needed since 'poetry' covers the whole creation); that is, on the interpenetrating or underlying feeling which renders earlier stories beautiful or sublime; relying more deeply than ever before on this magic itself and alone rather than on a realistic coherence, the poet enjoys a new and indeed extreme relaxation, the very opposite of plot-compactness. For poetry is now expected to make, rather than to bind and harmonize, his story. The quality which formerly interpenetrated the story now *is* the story. Now the new tale supplies exactly the required looseness, being merely a succession of happenings linked by sea-journeys. We have poetry, as it were, writing itself and are to see what new thing unfolds. The resulting work will be nearer faëry-lore than realistic drama, though, in so far as it becomes interpenetrated with meaning, it will resemble parable; for parable is, precisely, a stringing out into narrative sequence of some single quality not readily definable; here, the essential magic of Shakespeare's world. We are not surprised to find the meaning grow in depth and stature as the narrative progresses.[1]

II

To pass to a direct interpretation. The events are linked by Gower who directs us with a series of choric speeches, the story of *Pericles* having been contained in Gower's *Confessio Amantis*.[2] How far the attempts at archaic phraseology are successful may be questioned; and so may the poetic value of these speeches in general; but, since their quaintness is clearly deliberate, and since they are crammed with typical Shakespearian imagery of tempests and wreck in association with 'fortune', they may be allowed to pass.

We start with Pericles' suit for Antiochus' daughter, who enters 'apparell'd like the spring' and appears a dazzling creature of intelligence, virtue and honour (i. i. 12–14). Pericles' praise is extravagant. But there is in it something a trifle feverish; it is the result more of fascination, almost lust, than love, resembling Orsino's passion for Olivia:

---

[1] As analogies to *Pericles* and *The Winter's Tale* compare the Inca drama *Apu-Ollantay*, the Hindu *Sakuntala*, and the Eleusinian *Mysteries*.

[2] The events of *Pericles* follow closely those in Gower's story of Apollonius of Tyre, while the use of Gower as chorus further points the relation. The deeper, or higher, implications of our play are absent from the older narrative.

> You gods, that made me man, and sway in love,
> That hath inflam'd desire in my breast
> To taste the fruit of yon celestial tree
> Or die in the adventure, be my helps,
> As I am son and servant to your will,
> To compass such a boundless happiness !   (I. i. 19)

The weak conclusion is certainly reminiscent of Shakespeare's early writing, but the speech is subtle enough. Notice the speaker's self-defence, not unusual in lust, attributing it, with some justice, to instinct divinely implanted. The image in the third line recalls certain passages in Dante, so fine an expert in the subtleties of the good and evil in human desire. The thing aimed at is specifically dangerous. Antiochus warns Pericles that the lady is a 'fair Hesperides' with 'golden fruit', guarded by 'death-like dragons' (I. i. 27–9). He continues with reminders of former suitors whose 'dead cheeks'—like those in Keats' *Belle Dame Sans Merci*—advise him to 'desist' from this mad engagement with death (I. i. 34–40). Pericles' suit is to depend on his solving of a riddle and failure means death; so, as it turns out, does success too, since the riddle concerns the lady's incestuous relationship with her father, a powerful and wicked king who will not tolerate his secret's discovery.

Our hero's adventure is a plunge into sin and death closely associated with ravishing desire. He has not actively sinned, except in giving way to a lustful and cheating fantasy, but the result is immersion into an experience of evil with accompanying disgust and danger. It is a fall in the theological sense. His eyes are now opened to 'this glorious casket stor'd with ill'; he has found 'sin' within the thing of beauty:

> You're a fair viol, and your sense the strings,
> Who, finger'd to make men his lawful music,
> Would draw heaven down and all the gods to hearken ;
> But being play'd upon before your time,
> Hell only danceth at so harsh a chime.   (I. i. 76–85)

The phraseology is intensely impregnated with moral and theological concepts ('lawful', 'heaven', 'gods', 'hell'). The evil exposed is a denial of a 'lawful music'; of the harmony of human marriage and procreation defined in Sonnet VIII, where father, mother, and child are described as making a single music. The creative order has been mutilated and hence the oblique confusions of the riddle itself:

> I am no viper, yet I feed
> On mother's flesh which did me breed ;
> I sought a husband, in which labour
> I found that kindness in a father.
> He's father, son, and husband mild,
> I mother, wife, and yet his child.
> How they may be and yet in two,
> As you will live, resolve it you. (i. i. 64)

Shakespeare's final work is aptly heralded by this inversion of that creative mystery which is to be from now on its emphatic and repeated theme. The poetry denounces this obscenity with thoughts of 'foul incest' (i. i. 126) and 'serpents' who breed poison from sweet flowers (i. i. 132–3). The black evil suggests *Lucrece* and *Macbeth*:

> Murder's as near to lust as flame to smoke
> Poison and treason are the hands of sin . . . (i. i. 138)

So Pericles flees from Antioch to escape the King's vengeance.

The short scene is clearly important. Though the verse may at moments recall Shakespeare's early manner, the philosophical impact lies clearly in advance of it. Moreover, the rhymed or otherwise stilted sequences suit the intention of the miniature 'morality'. The meaning is generalized: the King is less man than ogre, the lady less a lady than a ravishing *thing*: she is not even given a name, and her entry to music is correspondingly formal. The whole scene is a moral on the dangers attending visual lust, and recalls the moral undertones of the casket-scene in *The Merchant of Venice*, with its song on 'fancy' bred 'in the eyes' (*The Merchant of Venice*, iii. ii. 63; cp. 'eye' in our *Pericles* scene at i. i. 32), the lesson there of the golden casket containing a skull corresponding here to 'this glorious casket stor'd with ill' (i. i. 77). In both plays failure to read the riddles concerned is to be punished, the penalty in *Pericles* being death. The scene is impregnated with a grimness of intention surpassing anything in the earlier play, the antinomy of good and evil transcended in *Antony and Cleopatra* being now again powerfully distinct: the unity has fallen apart, as is, in the new style of myth-making, necessary, since that fine immediacy and coalescence is to be henceforth strung out again into narrative sequence. A further, semi-social, criticism of Antiochus as tyrant gives us a line or two of Shakespeare's mature best:

> The blind mole casts
> Copp'd hills towards heaven, to tell the earth is throng'd
> By man's oppression ; and the poor worm doth die for't.
>
> (I. i. 100)

The speech continues with gnomic rhymes: we have no choice but to accept the poetic amalgam as it stands.

After escaping to Tyre, Pericles is struck down with melancholia. He has had a blasting experience, not unlike Hamlet's, both suffering through knowledge of incest in one they love and falling into a mysterious gloom:

> Why should this change of thoughts
> The sad companion, dull-ey'd melancholy,
> Be my so us'd a guest, as not an hour
> In the day's glorious walk or peaceful night—
> The tomb where grief should sleep—can breed me quiet ?
>
> (I. ii. 1)

Pleasures 'court' his eye, but, like Hamlet ('I have of late, but wherefore I know not . . .'—*Hamlet*, II. ii. 313), he cannot enjoy them. His fear of Antiochus is, he half knows, irrational; and yet he realizes that his silence will be, like Hamlet's, an ever-living threat: Antiochus 'will think me speaking though I swear to silence' (I. ii. 19). His vague foreboding (like the Queen's at *Richard II*, II. ii. 1–72), burdened by fear and horror, expresses itself in such phrases as 'black as incest' (I. ii. 76) and 'his bed of blackness' (I. ii. 89). He seems to feel guilt, yet is uncertain how far the 'offence' is his own (I. ii. 92). The experience transmitted is both subtle and powerful, though the verse often remains, comparatively, weak:

> And what may make him blush in being known,
> He'll stop the course by which it might be known . . .
>
> (I. ii. 22)

That does not sound like late Shakespeare. There is a dialogue between Pericles and Helicanus containing typical Shakespearian thoughts on flattery, but couched in a poetry at its best recalling the early histories:

> If there be such a dart in princes' frowns
> How durst thy tongue move anger to our face?
>
> (I. ii. 53)

However, the sequence of emotions and events moves with steady assurance.

So Pericles sets out on his journeys. His first action is to be one of charity: he seems to make deliberately for Tarsus (I. iv. 88), which is suffering from a severe famine, with ships laden with provisions. Before his arrival we meet Cleon and Dionyza, the king and queen, moralizing on their misfortunes:

> *Cleon.*   This Tarsus, o'er which I have the government,
> A city on whom plenty held full hand,
> For riches strew'd herself even in the streets;
> Whose towers bore heads so high they kiss'd the
>   clouds,
> And strangers ne'er beheld but wonder'd at;
> Whose men and dames so jetted and adorn'd,
> Like one another's glass to trim them by:
> Their tables were stor'd full to glad the sight,
> And not so much to feed on as delight;
> All poverty was scorn'd, and pride so great,
> The name of help grew odious to repeat.
> *Dionyza.*   O! 'tis too true.
> *Cleon.*   But see what heaven can do! . . .   (I. iv. 21)

He continues with an extraordinary account of past luxuries and present necessity, saying how parents are ready to eat their erstwhile pampered babies, the passage driving home a contrast of superficial luxury and basic need. Such is heaven's judgement on man's wickedness:

> O! let those cities that of plenty's cup
> And her prosperities so largely taste,
> With their superfluous riots hear these tears:
> The misery of Tarsus may be theirs.   (I. iv. 52)

'Superfluous' directly reminds us of Lear's

> Take physic, pomp;
> Expose thyself to feel what wretches feel,
> That thou may'st shake the superflux to them,
> And show the heavens more just. (*King Lear*, III. iv. 33)

or Gloucester's:

> Heavens, deal so still !
> Let the superfluous and lust-dieted man,
> That slaves your ordinance, that will not see
> Because he does not feel, feel your power quickly.
>
> (*King Lear*, IV. i. 67)

The similarity in thought is as striking as the divergence in style: we are aware of profundity crudely expressed. Here the semi-gnomic stiffness suggests the kind of weakness critics have complained of in the verse Shakespeare allows to his gods and goddesses (e.g. Hymen, Hecate, Diana, Jupiter); which raises yet further possibilities.

On Pericles' appearance, they fear that his ships signify some hostile invasion taking advantage of their own weakness, but instead find an act of pure charity, Pericles disclaiming all protestations of 'reverence' and asking only for 'love' (I. iv. 99). Gratitude is poured on him and a statue set up in his honour (II. chor. 14). His own misfortunes have been used to relieve the sufferings of others (cp. *Romeo and Juliet*, v. i. 84 and v. iii. 42; *King Lear*, IV. i. 65–72). The scene, moralistic from the start, has turned into a little morality drama on the theme of good works and indeed recalls the parable of the ungrateful man in the New Testament; for, after being let off by Providence functioning through Pericles' charity, Cleon and Dionyza are to prove criminally ungrateful.

News of Antiochus' continued persecution makes a longer stay unsafe and Pericles leaves Tarsus. We have already in typical Shakespearian manner been introduced to tempests. A tyrant's revenge was a 'tempest' at I. ii. 98. Sea-voyages are here considered all but suicidal. Pericles when setting out from Tyre was spoken of as putting himself

> unto the shipman's toil
> With whom each minute threatens life or death.
>
> (I. iii. 24)

Thaliard, commissioned to murder him, takes it for granted that he has 'scap'd the land to perish at the sea' (I. iii. 29). Now, when Pericles again dares the waters, Fortune, in spite of his recent good works, is cruel. Gower describes how he puts forth into the dangers of ocean and is stricken by a thunderous tempest and roaring seas; how his ship is 'wrack'd and split' and the 'good prince' driven from shore to shore till the spite of 'Fortune' is satiated (II. chor. 27–38). Through the attempt at archaic language a typically Shakespearian range of thought and imagery is apparent. Pericles is cast up at Pentapolis.

The opening of Act II brings us closer than ever before to the Shakespearian tempest: we have, as it were, a close-up of this persistent terror that has for so long burdened the poet's imagination. Pericles enters 'wet' and speaks in the usual tradition:

> Yet cease your ire, you angry stars of heaven !
> Wind, rain, and thunder, remember, earthly man
> Is but a substance that must yield to you ;
> And I, as fits my nature, do obey you.
> Alas ! the sea hath cast me on the rocks,
> Wash'd me from shore to shore, and left me breath
> Nothing to think on but ensuing death :
> Let it suffice the greatness of your powers
> To have bereft a prince of all his fortunes ;
> And having thrown him from your watery grave,
> Here to have death in peace is all he'll crave. (II. i. 1)

The accent is clearly Shakespearian, though even here the virile tempest-verse tails off into rhyme. Notice that the elements are directly humanized as divine powers. We are made to feel that the hero has endured a series of trials and buffetings; in him mortality is getting a rough passage. The implications are again general. The speech says crisply in Shakespearian terms, 'Tragedy': that is its function.

The following Fishermen's dialogue preserves, in a different vein, the high standard of the opening. The men's names (II. i. 12, 14) 'Pilch' and 'Patch-breech' (referring to the nets) recall Hugh Oatcake and George Seacoal in *Much Ado About Nothing* (III. iii. 11) and Potpan in *Romeo and Juliet* (I. v. 1), while their description of the wreck points on to the Clown's and Miranda's similar descriptions in *The Winter's Tale* and *The Tempest*:

> *Third Fisherman.* Faith, master, I am thinking of the poor men
> that were cast away before us even now.

First Fisherman.   Alas ! poor souls ; it grieved my heart to hear
                    what pitiful cries they made to us to help them,
                    when, well-a-day, we could scarce help our-
                    selves.   (ii. i. 18)

The simple men are philosophical as well as sympathetic, and
their humour shows a moralizing depth unknown to Shakespeare's earlier prose rustics. One of them, marvelling 'how
the fishes live in the sea', is answered:

> Why, as men do a-land ; the great ones eat up the little ones ; I
> can compare our rich misers to nothing so fitly as to a whale ; a'
> plays and tumbles, driving the poor fry before him, and at last
> devours them all at a mouthful. Such whales have I heard on o'
> the land, who never leave gaping till they've swallowed the whole
> parish, church, steeple, bells and all.   (ii. i. 31)

'A pretty moral', says Pericles, aside (ii. i. 39), and continues
with a comment that would, with the necessary adaptation,
have well suited the gardener's comparison in *Richard II*
(iii. iv.) of state-affairs to his own humble profession, perhaps
our nearest equivalent to this scene, though there given verse,
partly to suit the wholly serious intention. This is Pericles'
remark:

> How from the finny subject of the sea
> These fishers tell the infirmities of men ;
> And from their watery empire recollect
> All that men may approve or men detect !
>   (ii. i. 53)

Notice again the stiff, gnomic, rhyme, here clearly fused with a
Shakespearian comment in a purely Shakespearian scene.
    Pericles introduces himself in terms of the clearest tragic
generality as

> A man whom both the waters and the wind,
> In that vast tennis-court, have made the ball
> For them to play upon, entreats you pity him ;
> He asks of you that never us'd to beg. (ii. i. 64)

The metaphor (to which the nearest Shakespearian equivalent
occurs at *King Lear*, iv. i, 36–7) is that of *The Duchess of Malfi*:

> We are merely the stars' tennis-balls, struck and bandied
> Which way please them.   (iv. iv. 63)

There follows more satire from the Fishermen on those (like Autolycus in *The Winter's Tale*) who make a better living out of begging than any workers, with comic play on the words 'beg' and 'crave'. Pericles speaks lines of strongest sinew:

> A man throng'd up with cold, my veins are chill,
> And have no more of life than may suffice
> To give my tongue that heat to ask your help . . .
>
> (ii. i. 78)

which again, however, tail off into a limp couplet. The warm-hearted men invite him to share their simple life and its homely comforts, the general warmth and kindliness overtopping both humour and satire. Sometimes Shakespearian comedy is dull, the play on words tedious, the satiric arrows too particular for a later age; here the humour is obvious and the thrusts general. Pericles words for us a natural response: 'How well this honest mirth becomes their labour!' (ii. i. 102). The scene is more than comic relief; its social philosophy is organic to the play's moralistic thinking. The king here is 'the good Simonides' (ii. i. 107):

Pericles.	The good King Simonides do you call him ?
First Fisherman.	Ay, sir ; and he deserves to be so called for his peaceable reign and good government.
Pericles.	He is a happy king, since he gains from his subjects the name of good by his government.

> (ii. i. 108)

The statement serves to crystallize the sense already transmitted of simple honesty and wisdom: we are in a good community. The society is not levelled, but the men are as happy and rich-hearted in their station as the King in his. This one always feels about Shakespeare's rustics, but never before was the expression so purposeful.

Pericles hears of the tournament to be held for the hand of the King's daughter, and there follows the chance discovery in the Fishermen's net of Pericles' armour:

> Help, master, help ! here's a fish hangs in the net, like a poor man's right in the law ; 'twil hardly come out. Ha ! bots on't, 'tis come at last, and 'tis turned to a rusty armour. (ii. i. 126)

It is poetically important that these simple fisher-folk are the

means of Pericles' retrieving of his fortune and that the sea
itself should so mysteriously redeem its cruelty by this sudden
shift of favour. The equation sea = fortune, hinted throughout
Shakespeare, is in *Pericles* emphatic and obvious. The rhythm
of events, nearly all concerned with 'fortune' and the sea, is a
pretty clear reading of the shifts of chance in human existence:

> Thanks, Fortune, yet, that after all my crosses
> Thou giv'st me somewhat to repair myself . . .
>
> (II. i. 131)

Again:

> It kept where I kept, I so dearly lov'd it ;
> Till the rough seas, that spare not any man,
> Took it in rage, though calm'd they have given 't again.
> I thank thee for't ; my shipwrack now's no ill
> Since I have here my father's gift in's will.
>
> (II. i. 140)

The accent is Shakespearian (cp. 'though calm'd . . . again'
with *The Tempest*, II. i. 259) though the end rhyme, as before,
falls limp. Pericles decides to try his luck at court. There is a
last happy touch in the Fisherman's hint:

> Ay, but hark you, my friend ; 'twas we that made up this garment
> through the rough seams of the water ; there are certain condole-
> ments, certain vails [=gratuities]. I hope, sir, if you thrive, you'll
> remember from whence you had it.   (II. i. 160)

Pericles' concluding words, though picturesque, are rather
trivial:

> Unto thy value will I mount myself
> Upon a courser whose *delightful* steps
> Shall make the gazer joy to see him tread.   (II. i. 169)

The weak adjectival emphasis—noticeable elsewhere in these
early scenes—might be Greene's, or even Marlowe's, or from
a young Shakespeare, younger than any of which we have
record, in imitation; or again, they may conceivably be mature
Shakespeare, looking, in this tentative play, for new things,
setting himself in a new-old manner for some specific purpose.

   The court of the good Simonides scarcely offers anything of
equivalent interest to the Fishermen's conversation, but its
atmosphere is well realized, and the events important. The
verse, and much else, is formal and the rhymes often awkward.

The stage-formality itself seems here more important than the verse; as when the various knights pass across with their devices and mottoes. The importance of such ceremonial grows throughout Shakespeare's final period, its nature being here satisfactorily captured by Malone's direction:

> A Public Way. Platform leading to the Lists. A Pavilion near it, for the reception of the King, Princess, Ladies, Lords, etc.
> (ii. ii)

The jousting is done off-stage, as in *Richard II*, and we move to feasting, music and dance after the manner of *Romeo and Juliet* and *Timon of Athens*.

We are continually pointed to Pericles' appearance of lowness and poverty. The other knights' blazonings are spectacular: a 'black Ethiop' against a 'sun', a knight pictured as overthrown by a lady, a 'wreath of chivalry', 'a burning torch', a hand surrounded by clouds and holding gold. Pericles' 'present' (probably the actual thing, not merely a device) is 'a wither'd branch, that's only green on top' (ii. ii. 16–44). The courtiers remark on his rusty armour and rude appearance, suggesting that he seems more at home with the 'whipstock' than the lance (ii. ii. 51). He is at the best 'a country gentleman' (ii. iii. 33), regarded rather as is Posthumus in *Cymbeline*, though he meets a worthier acceptance, for the good Simonides is, unlike Cymbeline, not to be deceived by appearances:

> Opinion's but a fool, that makes us scan
> The outward habit by the inward man. (ii. ii. 56)

Where the thought is clear enough, whatever may be wrong with the seemingly transposed phraseology. Others take their example from the King:

> Contend not, sir ; for we are gentlemen
> That neither in our hearts nor outward eyes
> Envy the great nor do the low despise. (ii. iii. 24)

King Simonides is always moralizing, often in gnomic rhyme, warning his daughter Thaisa of the duties incumbent on princes if they are to hold their subjects' respect (ii. ii. 10–13), and asserting the importance of honour, that is, the interchange of courtesies, after the fashion of Timon:

Knights.   We are honour'd much by good Simonides.
Simonides. Your presence glads our days ; honour we love ;
              For who hates honour, hates the gods above.

(II. iii. 20)

Simonides' sentiments, in both substance and manner of expression, are directly in line with those of the King's speech on
true and false honour in *All's Well that Ends Well* (II. iii.
124–51), a play whose early scenes abound in gnomic sequences
very like those in *Pericles*. A near equivalent to Simonides'
court will also be found in the early scenes of *Timon of Athens*,
where there are more analogies to the strangely stilted language
of *Pericles*, both in Timon's moralizing and Apemantus'
proverb-like commentary. In both plays we have a firm sense
of (i) true worth as independent of social rank and (ii) the
duties incumbent on high position: our court scenes follow
organically on the fishermen's talk. The thought, too, recalls
the two contrasted uses of gold in the early and late acts of
Timon, and its two directions (the casket and wealthy heiress)
in *The Merchant of Venice*. Simonides' remark on the folly of
reading worth by outward appearances is directly in line with
Bassanio's:

So may the outward shows be least themselves ;
The world is still deceiv'd by ornament.
              (*The Merchant of Venice*, III. ii. 73)

This truth, which is a central truth throughout Shakespeare,
is here dramatically lived before us, since Pericles, poor as he
appears, is really a king.

The most insistent impressionistic recurrence throughout
Pericles, except for the sea-voyages, concerns the balancing of
true and false values. We started with Pericles' infatuation for
a deceptive beauty compared to the golden apples of the Hesperides (I. i. 27) and turning out to be, like Morocco's choice,
a 'glorious casket stor'd with ill' (I. i. 77). We moved next to
the paradox of Tarsus once so wealthy with people over-
dressed and bejewelled and their food arranged more to please
the eye—cp. again 'eyes' in the Fancy-song of the *Merchant
of Venice* (III. ii. 63)—than the taste (I. iv. 21–9), but now
brought low by savage hunger; brought, that is, to realize its
ultimate dependence; brought up against basic fact; such fact

as is the natural air breathed by the admirable fishermen of Pentapolis.

Always in Shakespeare riches (gold, jewels, rich clothes, etc.) have two possible meanings: they may be shown as in themselves deceptive or they may, by metaphor, be used to reflect an essential good. So the rusty armour that had so often defended Pericles' father is compared to a 'jewel' (II. i. 168) and princes are like 'jewels' which need keeping bright to deserve respect (II. ii. 12). And now—since we have brought our list up to date—when Thaisa begins to fall in love with Pericles she says: 'To me he seems like diamond to glass' (II. iii. 36). The comparison of a loved person to a rich stone is, of course, among the most frequent of Shakespeare's habitual correspondences (e.g. *Romeo and Juliet*, I. v. 50; *Troilus and Cressida*, I. i. 105; *Othello*, v. ii. 346). Later—to push ahead in our narrative—courtiers round a sovereign are as 'diamonds' about a 'crown' (II. iv. 53). There is, too, a peculiarly interesting example of the reverse, ironic, use, when the 'high gods', sick of Antiochus' wickedness, let loose their 'vengeance':

> Even in the height and pride of all his glory,
> When he was seated in a chariot
> Of an inestimable value, and his daughter with him,
> A fire from heaven came and shrivell'd up
> Their bodies, even to loathing ; for they so stunk,
> That all those eyes ador'd them ere their fall
> Scorn now their hand should give them burial.   (II. iv. 6)

The passage renders actual the contrast of glorious appearance with inward pollution which first started Pericles on his wanderings. Of all our moralizings this passage, so strongly reminiscent of Greek tragedy, is the crown.

To return to Pericles' fortunes at the court of Simonides. Having proved victorious in the tournament, he is crowned with 'a wreath of victory' (II. iii. 10) by Thaisa who functions as 'queen o' the feast' (II. iii. 17), like Perdita in *The Winter's Tale*, with Simonides playing the kindly over-lord, and reminding her, as her father reminds Perdita, of her duties. Pericles remains very quiet—he is now extraordinarily humble—and meditative, comparing the King to his own father, once just such a 'sun' surrounded by star-princes, though he himself has fallen to the glimmerings of a 'glow-worm', and drawing there-from the moral:

> Whereby I see that Time's the king of men ;
> He's both their parent, and he is their grave,
> And gives them what he will, not what they crave.
>
> (ii. iii. 37–45)

Twice (ii. iii. 54, 91) Pericles' especial melancholy is noted. Simonides, a jovial host after the manner of Old Capulet and Wolsey, is worried, and urges on Thaisa her responsibilities:

> Princes in this should live like gods above,
> Who freely give to every one that comes
> To honour them . . .   (ii. iii. 59)

Prompted by her father she questions Pericles, with whom she has fallen in love: her bashfulness in approach is delicately managed. The scene works up to a dance. The whole situation is dominated by Simonides: kingly, courteous, moralistic, and jovial.

Simonides next dismisses all the suitors but Pericles, telling them that Thaisa has sworn 'by the eye of Cynthia' (ii. v. 11) that she will wear 'Diana's livery' (ii. v. 10) for a whole year: our first mention of the goddess, who is to assume such importance later. Simonides enjoys not only his ruse but also his daughter's self-willed determination, expressed in a letter, to marry Pericles or no one, the long story of Shakespeare's tyrannic fathers from Capulet to Lear being most delightfully reversed. Simonides admires the stranger-knight who is clearly a man trained 'in arts and arms' (ii. iii. 82), winning the tournament and showing himself both a skilful dancer (ii. iii. 102–9) and a skilled musician:

> I am beholding to you
> For your sweet music this last night ; I do
> Protest my ears were never better fed
> With such delightful pleasing harmony.   (ii. v. 25)

True, the adjectival verse sounds most unlike late Shakespeare, but it is followed at once by:

Pericles. It is your Grace's pleasure to commend,
        Not my desert.
Simonides.   Sir, you are music's master.
Pericles. The worst of all her scholars, my good lord.

> (ii. v. 29)

Which no one will question. Pericles is conceived as the perfect courtier (as defined by Castiglione) and even his tourneying praised as art:

> In framing an artist art hath thus decreed,
> To make some good, but others to exceed,
> And you're her labour'd scholar. (ii. iii. 15)

Music is regularly in Shakespeare the antagonist to tempests; and Simonides' peaceful court thinks automatically in artistic terms. There are throughout *Pericles* many noticeable artistic emphases, some of a new sort to be observed later; and all blend with the moralistic tone of thought, the ceremonious directions, and even the stilted, and often questionable, formality of the verse. Art, as such, seems to be getting a more self-conscious attention than is usual; which is scarcely surprising in a play where the myth-making fantasy seems, as in the recurring voyages, to be functioning with a new freedom.

Pericles remains humble, and when confronted with Thaisa's letter by the supposedly irate father asserts that he never dreamed of aiming so high. Like Prospero, Simonides keeps up the pretence of harshness, accusing him, as Ferdinand is accused, of treachery. So the scene is driven to its delightful conclusion:

> Therefore, hear you, mistress ; either frame
> Your will to mine ; and you, sir, hear you—
> Either be rul'd by me or I will make you—
> Man and wife. (ii. v. 81)

Simonides is a grand person and the scenes at his court, though blemished seriously by old play incorporations, bits of immature or hurried writing, faulty texts or evidences of genius at a loss—exact decision is impossible—remain of the highest Shakespearian standard in stage-organization, human delineation (Simonides and Thaisa), and the depicting of a chivalrous society (after the pattern of Theseus in *A Midsummer Night's Dream* and Timon in *Timon of Athens*). The neat, semi-humorous overturning of a tragic situation to reveal kindliness and joy is a clear precurser of other more important reversals in *Pericles* and later plays: while the rewarding of Pericles' humility forecasts the fortunes of Cranmer in *Henry VIII*.

Pericles' story has clearly been forming itself into a significant design. His first adventure was one of semi-adolescent fantasy bringing him up sharply against disillusion and a realization of evil; he next won merit by charitable deeds; was again rebuffed by fortune, only to find himself on the shores of a hospitable community rich in social wisdom and artistic feeling; and so to a love affair characterized not by daring and aspiration (as was the other) but by a profound humility and crowned with unexpected success. We are watching something like a parable of human fortune, with strong moral import at every turn.

Act III is introduced by a striking chorus, describing the still house after the marriage-banquet, the silence broken only by heavy snores and crickets at the 'oven's mouth':

> The cat, with eyne of burning coal,
> Now couches fore the mouse's hole . . .
>
> (III. chor. 5–8)

The association of marriage-feast, midnight and the sleeping house recalls the final scene of *A Midsummer Night's Dream*, though nothing there quite touches the warm realism of our short passage, which has a fine Shakespearian ring. The bride is 'brought to bed' by 'Hymen' (III. chor. 9). There follows a dumb-show depicting Thaïsa 'with child'. After revealing his royal identity Pericles sets sail, with his queen, for home; but the voyage is ill-starred:

> And so to sea. Their vessel shakes
> On Neptune's billow ; half the flood
> Hath their keel cut ; but Fortune's mood
> Varies again ; the grisled north
> Disgorges such a tempest forth,
> That, as a duck for life that dives,
> So up and down the poor ship drives.
>
> (III. chor. 44)

The action next opens with Pericles on ship-board addressing the storm. Sea-tempest, so long a favourite image, and brought so near to us in Act II, has become at last the focus of dramatic action, and never before was it given such poetic thunder as in Pericles' opening lines:

Thou God of this great vast, rebuke these surges,
Which wash both heaven and hell ; and thou, that hast
Upor the winds command, bind them in brass,
Having call'd them from the deep. O ! still
Thy deafening, dreadful thunders ; gently quench
Thy nimble, sulphurous flashes. O ! how Lychorida,
How does my queen ? Thou stormest venomously ;
Wilt thou spit all thyself ? The seaman's whistle
Is as a whisper in the ears of death,
Unheard. Lychorida ! Lucina, O!
Divinest patroness, and midwife gentle
To those that cry by night, convey thy deity
Aboard our dancing boat ; make swift the pangs
Of my queen's travails !   (III. i. 1)

The nurse brings the child with news of its mother's death:

O you gods !
Why do you make us love your goodly gifts,
And snatch them straight away ?   (III. i. 22)

Continually we are pointed to these seemingly meaningless shifts of fortune which characterize the action. Pericles now speaks to the child born, as it were, amid a living death, commenting on its rude welcome to the stage of life:

Thou hast as chiding a nativity
As fire, air, water, earth, and heaven can make,
To herald thee from the womb ; even at the first
Thy loss is more than can thy portage quit
With all thou can'st find here.   (III. i. 32)

Observe the exact mention of the elements, natural and divine. The storm is generalized; the child's birth shown as an entry into the turmoils of nature, widely understood, an entry into storm-tossed mortality recalling the crying child of old Lear's lunatic sermon (*King Lear*, IV. vi. 187); and when the child is called 'this fresh new sea-farer' (III. i. 41) only a response most insensitive to Shakespeare's storm-poetry in general, and his use of it in *Pericles* in particular, will limit the meaning to the immediate occasion. As again in *The Winter's Tale*, the association of child and tempest holds a general, if unemphasized, implication.

The superstitious sea-men insist that Thaisa be immediately

buried at sea and Pericles, with another passage of supreme
poetry, gives way:

> A terrible child-bed hast thou had, my dear ;
> No light, no fire : the unfriendly elements
> Forgot thee utterly ; nor have I time
> To give thee hallow'd to thy grave, but straight
> Must cast thee, scarcely coffin'd, in the ooze ;
> Where, for a monument upon thy bones,
> And aye-remaining lamps, the belching whale
> And humming water must o'erwhelm thy corpse,
> Lying with simple shells !   (iii. i. 57)

Nowhere else does Shakespeare's sea-poetry move with quite so
superb an ease, the one word 'humming' doing more than long
passages of earlier description; as though, in this extraordinary
story, with all the normal restrictions gone, except always for
the necessity of prime concentration on this favourite theme,
his deepest genius were enjoying a liberty hitherto unknown.
Perhaps only whilst desultorily working over an old plot in
which he scarce half-believed could such unsought-for excellence have matured. Notice that the text, when Shakespeare's
hand is indisputably at work, seems remarkably pure.

Pericles asks for spices, his 'casket' and 'jewels' (iii. i. 66),
and includes them, with some writing, in the coffin, which is
cast overboard. The ship makes for Tarsus.

We move to Ephesus, where we meet Cerimon, a descendant
of Friar Laurence in *Romeo and Juliet*, deeply versed in the
understanding of mineral and vegetable properties, and quite
at home with the inmost 'disturbances that nature works and of
her cures' (iii. ii. 37). He is a magician, of 'secret art' (iii. ii.
32), like Prospero in *The Tempest*. He is, too, noble, a man of
Timon-like lustre, renowned for his generosity, who has, like
Timon, 'poured forth' his charity, till 'hundreds' are indebted
to his skill, personal labours, and 'purse' (iii. ii. 43–8). He
defines his own life-wisdom for us:

> I hold it ever,
> Virtue and cunning were endowments greater
> Than nobleness and riches ; careless heirs
> May the two latter darken and expend,
> But immortality attends the former,
> Making a man a god.   (iii. ii. 26)

His art holds a deeper content

> Than to be thirsty after tottering honour
> Or tie my treasure up in silken bags
> To please the fool and death.   (III. ii. 40)

The contrast already suggested between the substantial and the ephemeral, the real and the deceptive, is here more sharply defined and given a personal centre. Cerimon is an almost superhuman figure living out a truth expressed throughout the New Testament, as in the parable of the rich man summoned by death, and such phrases as 'the body is more than clothes', 'consider the lilies of the field'.

We meet him at night-time, called from his rest to help shipwrecked mariners, while people comment on the storm in the usual Shakespearian manner, saying how it exceeds all previous experience. When servants bring in Thaisa's coffin, Cerimon's wryly humorous comment recalls the sea's throwing up of Pericles' armour at Pentapolis:

> If the sea's stomach be o'ercharg'd with gold,
> 'Tis a good constraint of fortune it belches upon us...
>   (III. ii· 54)

Gold is present, in spite of Cerimon's former repudiation, as a preliminary to the sudden disclosure of wondrous riches enclosing the sparkling richness of the supreme jewel, Thaisa. The chest has a marvellous scent: it smells 'most sweetly', with a 'delicate odour' (III.ii.60–1), phrases pointing on to *The Winter's Tale*, III. i. 1; and *The Tempest*, II. i. 44, 49. The body itself is

> Shrouded in cloth of state ; balm'd and entreasur'd
> With full bags of spices.   (III. ii. 65)

Pericles' written message asks that 'this queen worth all our mundane cost' be buried in return for the 'treasure' enclosed, and for charity's sake (III. ii. 70–5). Notice how Thaisa is surrounded by clustering impressions of wealth: they are to continue.

Cerimon sets to recover her with the help of 'fire' and 'music'. He gives his orders busily, in language aptly broken by colloquial pauses:

> Death may usurp on nature many hours,
> And yet the fire of life kindle again
> The overpress'd spirits. I heard

> Of an Egyptian, that had nine hours lien dead,
> Who was by good appliances recover'd. (III. ii. 82)

The reference to an Egyptian is peculiarly apt in a scene so
strongly reminiscent of the magic for which ancient Egypt was
renowned.[1] The miracle is now worked before our eyes:

> Well said, well said ; the fire and cloths.
> The rough and woeful music that we have,
> Cause it to sound, beseech you.
> The viol once more ;—how thou stirr'st, thou block !
> The music there ! I pray you, give her air.
> Gentlemen,
> This queen will live ; nature awakes, a warmth
> Breathes out of her ; she hath not been entranc'd
> Above five hours. See ! how she 'gins to blow
> Into life's flower again. (III. ii. 87)

Music, for so long Shakespeare's normal dramatic antithesis to
tempestuous death, becomes directly implemental ; and will be so
again, in *The Winter's Tale*, as the agent of Hermione's release.
Cerimon's skill goes beyond science, in the modern sense,
resembling rather the raising of the dead in the New Testament, a reading borne out by the reaction of those who attend:

> The heavens
> Through you increase our wonder and set up
> Your fame for ever. (III. ii. 96

Cerimon's next words mark the culmination of the imagery of
jewels and riches so persistent throughout *Pericles*:

> She is alive ! behold,
> Her eyelids, cases to those heavenly jewels
> Which Pericles hath lost,
> Begin to pa:t their fringes of bright gold :
> The diamonds of a most praised water
> Do appear to make the world twice rich. Live,
> And make us weep to hear your fate, fair creature,
> Rare as you seem to be ! (III. ii. 98)

'Rare' : the word is to characterize everything most wondrous
in this and later plays. The original direction—pointing on,

[1] The nearest equivalent in our poetry occurs, it would seem, in Shelley's use of Egyptian
lore in *The Witch of Atlas* ; see *The Starlit Dome*, pp. 232–3. An interesting analogy to the
restoration of Thaisa may be read of in Mr. P. Brunton's *A Search in Secret Egypt* (Rider & Co.),
pp. 169–70.

as did 'warmth' earlier, to *The Winter's Tale*—is 'she moves'.
The poetic excitement is breathlessly intense: we are watching
the key-incident that unlocks the whole range of Shakespeare's
later work. His imagery, his poetry, dictates the action. From
his earliest plays he has been deeply engaged with sea-tempests
and death; with true and false appearance; with riches, real and
unreal, in relation to love; and with wealth strewn on the sea's
floor (as in Clarence's dream), the treasures it has gorged; and
more than once with a jewel thrown into the sea, as a symbol
of love, for ever lost; and, continually, with music as an almost
mystical accompaniment of love, reunion, and joy. All are
together here, as the supreme jewel, Thaisa, is given back.

Her first words are, 'O dear Diana!' (III. ii. 105). She
wonders, like Lear waking after madness, where she is: 'What
world is this?' (III. ii. 106). The watchers marvel at the
strangeness of the act, this miracle 'most rare' (III. iii. 107).
But Cerimon hushes their exclamations of wonder and removes
Thaisa to a chamber of rest. Later he gives her the jewels from
the chest and she, despairing of seeing her lord again, decides
to take on a 'vestal livery' (III. iv. 10), and is accordingly
introduced by Cerimon to Diana's temple.

We have moved very far beyond gnomic rhymes and moral
precepts; beyond psychological lessons and social comment;
have advanced beyond ethic altogether to a dramatic disclosure
metaphysical rather than moral, indeed visionary rather than
metaphysical, as we watch life blossom and glow from the very
jaws of death, warmed into renewed existence by Cerimon's
fire and music. This is the new thing that has come, spontaneously, from Shakespeare's novel attempt in free narrative;
something quite unlike any previous incident; which yet could
not, perhaps, have been born before *Antony and Cleopatra*; but
which, once touched, insists on re-expression till the end.

Pericles leaves his child, called Marina because she was
born at sea (III. iii. 13), with Cleon and his queen Dionyza.
Cleon grieves for the 'shafts of fortune' that have so mortally
attacked their former benefactor, and Pericles answers:

> We cannot but obey
> The powers above us. Could I rage and roar
> As doth the sea she lies in, yet the end
> Must be as 'tis.   (III. iii. 9)

Thaisa's death is no peculiar misfortune, but rather the general
fate and fact of mortality. Pericles, worn with disaster, vows
'by bright Diana', who has by now become the play's presiding
deity, to leave his hair 'unscissor'd' until his daughter's marriage (III. iii. 27–9); and departs, after being recommended by
Cleon to 'the mask'd Neptune and the gentlest winds of
heaven' (III. iii. 36). The verse continues to maintain a high
Shakespearian standard.

Marina's education at Tarsus is described in the chorus to
Act IV. She is trained in both music and letters, and becomes so
generally admired that she rouses the Queen's jealousy on behalf
of her own daughter, Philoten. The two girls work in rivalry:

> Be't when she weav'd the sleided silk
> With fingers long, small, white as milk,
> Or when she would with sharp neeld wound
> The cambric, which she made more sound
> By hurting it ; when to the lute
> She sung, and made the night-bird mute,
> That still records with moan ; or when
> She would with rich and constant pen
> Vail to her mistress Dian, still
> This Philoten contends in skill
> With absolute Marina . . .   (IV. chor. 21)

The lines recall earlier remarks on Pericles' musical skill and
dancing. Music and poetry are normal Shakespearian interests, but the emphasis on needlework is both new and, as we
shall see, important. Now, jealous of Marina's excellences, the
wicked mother (a forecast of the Queen in *Cymbeline*, Philoten
corresponding to Cloten) engages Leonine to murder her.

Marina enters, grieving for the death of her nurse Lychorida.
She bears 'a basket of flowers' and speaks lines pointing on to
Perdita in *The Winter's Tale* and the burial of Fidele in
Cymbeline:

> No, I will rob Tellus of her weed,
> To strew thy green with flowers ; the yellows, blues,
> The purple violets, and marigolds,
> Shall as a carpet hang upon thy grave,
> While summer days do last. Ay me ! poor maid,
> Born in a tempest, when my mother died,
> This world to me is like a lasting storm,
> Whirring me from my friends.   (IV. i. 13)

'Carpet' may be tentatively referred to the new interest in arts of design that gives us Marina's needlework. The generalizing of a usual thought in the concluding lines is plain—no finer example occurs in Shakespeare—with death envisaged as the supreme separator, and therefore as tempest, tempests being continually felt elsewhere as the separators and antagonists of love. As the moment of Marina's own death seems to be approaching (she is talking with Leonine by the sea-shore) she wistfully recalls her birth:

> *Marina.* Is this wind westerly that blows ?
> *Leonine.* South-west.
> *Marina.* When I was born the wind was north.
> *Leonine.* Was't so ?
> (IV. i. 50)

She describes the storm; how Pericles galled his kingly hands at the ropes, the loss of life, the cries, the confusion. Asked again when this happened, she answers, 'When I was born' (IV. i. 58). The association of birth and tempest continues to exert strong poetic radiations.

Leonine reveals his murderous intentions, offering her, as Othello offers Desdemona, a space for prayer. The short following dialogue is rich with a peculiarly Shakespearian poignancy of emotional realism as Marina asserts her innocence and pleads for life, appalled at Leonine's impossibly wicked intention:

> I saw you lately
> When you caught hurt in parting two that fought . . .
> (IV. i. 86)

It reminds us of Arthur and Hubert in *King John*. The situation is saved by the Pirates, whom the dramatist uses as cavalierly as he uses the bear in *The Winter's Tale*. Leonine reports to the Queen that the murder has been performed.

Dionyza is a fine study, showing the same hard-headed, unsentimental approach to crime as Lady Macbeth and Goneril. Cleon is distracted at the supposed murder, remembering Marina's virtues:

> a princess
> To equal any single crown o' the earth
> I' the justice of compare. (IV. iii. 7)

What, he asks, will his wife tell Pericles? Her reply is terse
and uncompromising:

Dionyza.   That she is dead. Nurses are not the fates
            To foster it, nor ever to preserve.
            She died at night ; I'll say so. Who can cross it ?
            Unless you play the pious innocent,
            And for an honest attribute cry out
            'She died by foul play'.
Cleon.   O ! go to. Well, well,
            Of all the faults beneath the heavens, the gods
            Do like this worst.
Dionyza.   Be one of those that think
            The pretty wrens of Tarsus will fly hence,
            And open this to Pericles. I do shame
            To think of what a noble strain you are,
            And of how coward a spirit.   (iv. iii. 14)

Cleon answers exactly as does Macbeth when similarly taxed.
The dialogue recalls, too, Goneril's scene with Albany (*King
Lear*, iv. ii.), though it even exceeds earlier plays in its condensed clarity and psychological pith. How subtly, for
example, Cleon's weakness of will shows through his conscience-stricken protestations ('Well, well'.) Every phrase
tells, psychologically and dramatically, till the close:

Cleon.   Thou art like the harpy,
            Which, to betray, dost with thine angel's face,
            Seize with thine eagle's talons.
Dionyza   You are like one that superstitiously
            Doth swear to the gods that winter kills the flies ;
            But yet I know you'll do as I advise.
                                          (iv. iii. 46)

A formal ending, perhaps; but with what a deadly formality!
    In dumb-show we see Pericles coming to Tarsus, where he
hears of Marina's supposed death, and reads Dionyza's hypo-
critical inscription, on the carefully devised monument, in the
'glittering golden characters' (iv. iii. 44) with which she disguises her 'black villainy' (iv. iv. 44): as before, we have a
golden falsity and Pericles is again deceived. He suspects
nothing; receives this as but another stroke of fate; vows never
now to cut his hair, 'puts on sackcloth', and sets out to sea
(iv. iv. 28–9). His endurance reaches its limit:

> He bears
> A tempest, which his mortal vessel tears,
> And yet he rides it out.   (IV. iv. 29)

Utterly broken, he now leaves his course to 'Lady Fortune' (IV. iv. 48).

There is less necessity to speak at length of the brothel scenes at Mitylene, since their merits have been generally recognized. They recall *Measure for Measure*, with the stark contrast of purity and vice rendered sharper by bringing Marina, who corresponds (with many differences) to Isabella, actually inside the brothel and threatening her integrity. The harsh, yet often richly amusing, satire is of the finest and the persons of the Pandar, the Bawd and Boult generously realized. To this sink of iniquity Marina is sold by the pirates. The play's presiding deity, Diana, is aptly invoked:

> *Marina.* If fires be hot, knives sharp, or waters deep,
>   Untied I still my virgin knot will keep.
>   Diana, aid my purpose !
> *Bawd.*   What have we to do with Diana ? (IV. ii. 162)

The incongruity dramatized by Marina's hideous situation is painful, but even so a fine humour matures from it. Rather like Timon with the Bandits, she converts her would-be customers, who retreat shame-faced:

> *First Gentleman.* But to have divinity preached there ! Did you
>   ever dream of such a thing ?
> *Second Gentleman* No, no. Come, I am for no more bawdy-houses.
>   Shall's go hear the vestals sing ?   (IV. v. 4)

She speedily ruins trade, to her employer's exasperation.

Lysimachus' visit is given a detailed presentation. He is governor of Mitylene and enters with an unpleasant bearing, but there seems no evidence that he is (as has been suggested) playing a spy-part like the Duke in *Measure for Measure*, to nose out the city's vice: rather he is a loose young man, like Bertram in *All's Well that Ends Well*, of enough wealth and power to gratify his desires at will. Marina's talk, however, soon enough converts him to a shame-faced, though untrue, asseveration:

> I did not think
> Thou couldst have spoke so well ; ne'er dream'd
>   thou could'st.
>   Had I brought hither a corrupted mind,
>   Thy speech had alter'd it.   (IV. vi. 112)

He asserts that he 'came with no ill intent' and that to him now
'the very doors and windows savour vilely' (IV. vi. 120).
Notice the emphasis on Marina's 'speech': good-breeding in a
prostitute is considered unthinkable. The incident's handling
clearly assumes a conventional ethic which makes sharp distinction between masculine laxity and feminine impurity:

> *Boult.* The nobleman would have dealt with her like a
>   nobleman, and she sent him away as cold as a
>   snow-ball ; saying his prayers too.   (IV. vi. 152)

Even Boult, left alone with Marina and charged to break down
her defences, succumbs to her withering scorn. Finally she
urges (in a speech whose nervous broken rhythms serve a clear
purpose) her real value:

>   O ! that the gods
> Would safely deliver me from this place.
> Here, here's gold for thee.
> If that thy master would gain by me,
> Proclaim that I can sing, weave, sew, and dance,
> With other virtues which I'll keep from boast . . .
>   (IV. vi. 195)

Her offer to teach succeeds triumphantly: though recalling
Viola's in *Twelfth Night* (I. ii. 55–7), her profession of skill is
here far more important, since Marina is, as it were, art incarnate, an emphasis already strong and now driven home by the
following chorus:

> She sings like one immortal, and she dances
> As goddess-like to her admired lays ;
> Deep clerks she dumbs ; and with her neeld composes
> Nature's own shape, of bud, bird, branch, or berry,
> That even her art sisters the natural roses ;
> Her inkle, silk, twin with the rubied cherry . . .
>   (V. chor. 3)

Arts both of melody and of design[1] are included.

---

[1] Shakespeare's work is not normally rich in suggestion of the visual arts : see Professor
Fairchild' interesting monograph, *Shakespeare and the Arts of Design* (University of Missouri
Press). We shall, however, find such arts increasingly emphatic in the Final Plays.

The play's last movement starts on 'God Neptune's annual feast' (v. chor. 17); an occasion, that is, of propitiation to the controlling powers. Pericles arrives on a ship with 'banners sable, trimm'd with rich expense' (v. chor. 19), recalling former imagery of riches and textile art. Malone provides an exquisitely appropriate direction:

> On board Pericles' ship off Mitylene. A pavilion on deck, with a curtain before it ; Pericles within it, reclined on a couch. A barge lying beside the Tyrian vessel. (v. 1)

The contrast of peace with our earlier storm-scenes is strong. Pericles, who has not spoken for months, is in sack-cloth, with hair unshaven, fasting; a figure of grief, perhaps, in some undefined fashion, of remorse, for the fact of mortality in a universe that has robbed him of wife and child. Lysimachus sends for Marina, now famed in Mitylene for her arts and charm, to see if she can restore him.

The following action is another pinnacle of Shakespeare's art. Marina is brought to cure Pericles, as Helena cures the King in *All's Well that Ends Well*. Though she is no intentional magician, we are pointed, as with Cerimon, to a blend of divinity and art: she is to pit both her 'sacred physic' and 'utmost skill' (v. i. 74–6) against Pericles' stonelike, frozen immobility, his living death. She sings.

When Pericles awakes from his trance, she touches on her own sufferings, saying how she herself has 'endur'd a grief' that might well equal his (v. i. 88); how she is descended from a kingly stock, though brought low by 'wayward Fortune' (v. i. 90–2). Pericles, half-awake, stammeringly repeats her strange phrases. He looks in her eyes; something he half recognizes, but breaks off. We watch a re-enactment of Lear's waking to music into the presence of Cordelia. Questioned, Marina asserts that no 'shores' (i.e. land) can claim her birth, though she was 'mortally brought forth' (v. i. 104); an assurance dramatically serving to emphasize her momentary function of enacting, like Cordelia, a super-mortal presence (cp. 'Thou art a soul in bliss . . .' *King Lear*, iv. vii. 46) invading mortal grief. Pericles' interest is roused:

> I am great with woe, and shall deliver weeping.
> My dearest wife was like this maid, and such a one

> My daughter might have been : my queen's square brows ;
> Her stature to an inch ; as wand-like straight ;
> As silver-voic'd ; her eyes as jewel-like,
> And cased as richly ; in pace another Juno ;
> Who starves the ears she feeds, and makes them hungry,
> The more she gives them speech.   (v. i. 106)

Such riches-imagery ('silver' and 'jewel') we have already discussed: the last lines descend from *Antony and Cleopatra*
(ii. ii. 245).

Marina incorporates both the poetic worth of Thaisa and
the sacred magic of Cerimon; she is, as we have seen, all but
art personified. She is that to which all art aspires, which it
seeks to express:

> Prithee, speak ;
> Falseness cannot come from thee, for thou look'st
> Modest as justice, and thou seem'st a palace
> For the crown'd truth to dwell in.   (v. i. 121)

How finely is limned for us this spiritualized royalty, one with
that delicate power, or beauty, lying behind all Shakespeare's
royalistic tonings and reaching its subtlest flowering in his last
works. Marina incorporates an eternal essence of personified
Truth and Justice, able to awake belief in things elsewise
'impossible'; for she is herself, as Pericles observes, an image
of one formerly 'lov'd', supposed dead, but now miraculously,
it would seem, alive (v. i. 124–7).

Our lines have already suggested a painting, or, more
probably, a statue, a work of still, yet pulsing, intellectual, life;
Yeats' 'monuments of unaging intellect' in *Sailing to Byzantium*. Monumental art is Shakespeare's normal approach to eternity,[1] though his earlier use of it has been sparing and tentative.
We have already had two statues here; one to honour Pericles
(ii. chor. 14) and another with an inscription of 'glittering
golden characters' in memory of Marina (iv. iii. 44; iv. 34),
both at Tarsus. Yet more potent was the heart-seizing transference of 'monument' and 'aye-remaining lamps' to the glim-
mering ocean depths of Thaisa's burial (iii. i. 62–3). And now
comes the supreme and final expression:

---

[1] As in the Sonnets often and the conception of the last scene in *Romeo and Juliet*; where,
though 'eternity' is not explicit, the expressions of enduring time and vast death may be allowed
to constitute an 'approach', as in Gray's *Elegy written in a Country Churchyard*.

> Tell thy story ;
> If thine consider'd prove the thousandth part
> Of my endurance, thou art a man, and I
> Have suffer'd like a girl ; yet thou dost look
> Like Patience gazing on kings' graves, and smiling
> Extremity out of act.   (v. i. 136)

We remember Viola's 'Patience on a monument smiling at grief' (*Twelfth Night*, II. iv. 116); but these lines hold a deeper penetration. The whole world of great tragedy ('kings' graves') is subdued to an over-watching figure, like Cordelia's love by the bedside of Lear's sleep.[1] 'Extremity', that is disaster in all its finality (with perhaps a further suggestion of endless time), is therefore negated, put out of action, by a serene assurance corresponding to St. Paul's certainty in 'O death, where is thy sting?' Patience is here an all-enduring calm seeing *through* tragedy to the end; smiling through endless death to ever-living eternity.

And yet there is nothing inflexible, inhuman, about Marina: she remains at every instant a natural girl. Learning her name, Pericles, again like Lear, thinks he is being mocked, fears lest some 'incensed god' aims to make the world 'laugh' at him (v. i. 145). The paradox grows more intense. This amazing presence is yet human, a living girl:

> But are you flesh and blood ?
> Have you a working pulse ? and are no fairy ?
> Motion !—Well ; speak on. Where were you born ?
> And wherefore call'd Marina ?   (v. i. 154)

Life, as in Hermione in *The Winter's Tale*, breathes from the statued calm. There is more talk of her birth at sea (v. i. 158). Pericles thinks it all a deceitful dream (like that described so poignantly by Caliban in *The Tempest*):

> O ! Stop there a little.
> This is the rarest dream that e'er dull sleep
> Did mock sad fools withal ; this cannot be.
> My daughter's buried . . .   (v. i. 162)

He controls himself; asks her to continue; tries, with an effort, to talk reasonably. She recounts the attempt to murder her and

---

[1] A near equivalent outside Shakespeare is Byron's association of 'eternity' with 'love watching madness with unalterable mien' (*Childe Harold*, IV, lxxi–lxxii.). See, too, Cordelia's 'patience' and 'sorrow' at *King Lear*, IV. iii. 18.

her subsequent adventures. Her survival is, of course, given
a perfectly water-tight realism. On the plane of logical statement nothing unique has occurred, but such logic has at best a
secondary importance in drama. It is what we momentarily
live, not what we remember, that counts. Here the experience
dramatized is one of a gradual unfurling; an awakening to discovery of life where death seemed certain. The plot has been
manipulated specifically to generate this peculiar experience,
which next quite bursts its boundaries, and, expanding beyond,
automatically clothes itself in semi-transcendental phraseology.
The story is, anyway, a fiction; its threaded events, even less
than in most stories, count for little; all depends on what the
poet makes of them. The most realistic tension in the whole
play comes at these moments of amazing tragic reversal, at the
restoration of Thaisa by Cerimon and the amazing impact of
Marina's survival. In both we attend the unveiling of death
from off the features of life: this it is which generates the unique
excitement. The discovery is elaborately delayed, expanded,
played upon, allowed to grow more and more certain till no
doubt remains:

> O Helicanus ! strike me, honour'd sir;
> Give me a gash, put me to present pain,
> Lest this great sea of joys rushing upon me
> O'erbear the shores of my mortality,
> And drown me with their sweetness. O ! come hither,
> Thou that begett'st him that did thee beget ;
> Thou that wast born at sea, buried at Tarsus,
> And found at sea again. O Helicanus !
> Down on thy knees, thank the holy gods as loud
> As thunder threatens us ; this is Marina.   (v. i. 192)

The sea is now a 'sea of joys'; and notice the triple reference of
birth, death, and restoration 'at sea'; while we may recall that
our action is set on a ship, in calm water, on the occasion of
Neptune's feast. The new joy is proportional to the tragedy
('as loud . . . threatens us') being reversed.

Marina's self-discovery has clearly something divine about
it. In all her words she has 'been god-like perfect'; she has
brought Pericles 'another life' (v. i. 208). Pericles calls for his
garments; notices Lysimachus for the first time; and, after
somewhat perfunctorily greeting him, returns to his joy:

Pericles.	Give me my robes. I am wild in my beholding.
	O heavens, bless my girl ! But, hark ! what music ?
	Tell Helicanus, my Marina, tell him
	O'er, point by point, for yet he seems to doubt,
	How sure you are my daughter. But, what music ?
Helicanus.	My lord, I hear none.
Pericles.	None !
	The music of the spheres ! List, my Marina.
Lysimachus.	It is not good to cross him ; give him way.
Pericles.	Rarest sounds ! Do ye not hear ?
Lysimachus.	My lord, I hear.
Pericles.	Most heavenly music !
	It nips me unto listening, and thick slumber
	Hangs upon mine eyes ; let me rest. (*Sleeps*)

(v .i. 224).

The scene closes, as it started, in sleep, or trance: there is a double awakening, from sleeping to waking and from waking to some yet higher apprehension; we attend a dramatized awakening which culminates, beyond discovery and recognition, in the hearing of those heavenly harmonies which were contrasted, in *The Merchant of Venice*, with the 'muddy vesture of decay' (v. i. 64) preventing their reception. The scene enacts the breaking of those boundaries, an adventure into that music, or the irruption of that music into human life.

Pericles' sleep leads on to a direct theophany, or divine appearance, the first (except for Hymen and Hecate) in Shakespeare. Diana appears to Pericles as in a vision (v. i. 240) and directs him to Ephesus, where he is to sacrifice with her 'maiden priests' (v. i. 243) before all the people and recount his wife's death 'at sea' (v. i. 245)—the emphasis persists— and all his and his daughter's sufferings:

> Perform my bidding, or thou liv'st in woe ;
> Do it, and happy ; by my silver bow !
> Awake, and tell thy dream !   (v. i. 248)

Pericles starts up, crying:

> Celestial Dian, goddess argentine,
> I will obey thee !   (v. i. 251)

He immediately gives directions for the next, and final, voyage.

There follows first much 'pageantry' and 'minstrelsy' at
Mitylene (v. ii. 6, 7), and then they all sail for Ephesus:

> In feather'd briefness sails are fill'd,
> And wishes fall out as they're will'd.   (v. ii. 15)

The couplet neatly drives home the old metaphoric equivalence,
almost identity, of sea and soul.

Malone's final stage-direction is :

> The Temple of Diana at Ephesus ; Thaisa, standing near the
> altar, as high priestess ; a number of Virgins on each side. (v. iii.)

Cerimon is present. Pericles formally presents his account to
Diana, with the usual emphasis on death and birth 'at sea'
(v. iii. 5). Marina, he says, 'wears yet thy silver livery' (v. iii.
7), a phrase recalling Diana's 'silver bow' (v. i. 249), and
blending with earlier imagery of rich metals.

Hearing his account, Thaisa, now called a 'nun' (v. iii. 15)
by strange Christian transference (cp. *A Midsummer Night's
Dream*, i. i. 70–8, 89–90), faints, and Cerimon explains her
identity to Pericles, recounting how he himself opened her
coffin filled with 'jewels' (v. iii. 24). Thaisa recovers:

> O ! my lord,
> Are you not Pericles ? Like him you speak,
> Like him you are. Did you not name a tempest,
> A birth, and death ?   (v. iii. 31)

How precise and yet with what generalized, universal reverberations is this ringing of the changes on birth and death in
tempest. Our second reunion works up more swiftly than the
first to its climax. Pericles recognizes the hand of divinity,
crying 'Immortal Dian!' (v. iii. 37) and even half-wishing, as
did Othello before him, to dissolve at this high moment:

> This, this : no more, you gods ! your present kindness
> Makes my past miseries sport : you shall do well,
> That on the touching of her lips I may
> Melt and no more be seen. O ! come, be buried
> A second time within these arms.   (v. iii. 40)

All old questions of fortune and the gods are caught up into
this miraculous reversal which, glancing back, makes tragedy
in its short illusion a game, melted in the sun of union.

Marina, her 'burden at the sea' (v. iii. 47), is introduced to her mother: 'Bless'd, and mine own' (v. iii. 48) says Thaisa. The phraseology throughout these reunions is saturated in religious suggestion: this, our final scene, is aptly staged outside a temple, with Thaisa as high priestess. Cerimon, too, is regarded as a divine instrument, functioning very precisely as Christ Himself in the Christian scheme:

> *Pericles.* Now do I long to hear how you were found,
> How possibly preserv'd, and whom to thank,
> Besides the gods, for this great miracle.
> *Thaisa.* Lord Cerimon, my lord ; this man,
> Through whom the gods have shown their power ;
> that can
> From first to last resolve you.
> *Pericles.* Reverend sir,
> The gods can have no mortal officer
> More like a god than you. Will you deliver
> How this dead queen re-lives ?
> *Cerimon.* I will, my lord.
>
> (v. iii. 56)

'The gods', 'great miracle', 'power', a 'god': the impressions are piled on. We are directed to feel that a dead person 're-lives', and though Cerimon promises, as does Paulina in *The Winter's Tale*, an explanation, we do not hear it, in either play. We are left with a sense of wonder.

III

One should not, however, regard *Pericles* as a completely new departure. We rather feel as present fact those miracles already hinted by Kent's 'nothing almost sees miracles but misery' and by Lear's dying 'Look there ! look there!' (*King Lear*, ii. ii. 172; v. iii. 313). The dim shadowings of *King Lear* are turned to the light. The new play follows naturally on Timon's 'nothing brings me all things' (*Timon of Athens*, v. i. 193); on Romeo's dream of reunion beyond death (*Romeo and Juliet*, v. i. 1–11) and Cleopatra's of the universal Antony (*Antony and Cleopatra*, v. ii. 76–100). Nor is the use of a happy ending to a serious purpose wholly new: the earlier comedies, more serious works than is usually supposed, dramatized stories

of error dispelled, mistaken identity set right, reunion after
separation, generally in direct relation to tempests, as in *The
Comedy of Errors* and *Twelfth Night*. The two farces, *The Taming of the Shrew* and *The Merry Wives of Windsor*, show strong
morality endings. *The Merchant of Venice* is a parable on life
and money. *As You Like It* has a ceremonial conclusion, with
Rosalind for miracle-worker and Hymen for theophany, and in
Much Ado About Nothing the supposedly dead girl, Hero, is
found alive after all, her supposed death and return being
organized by a Friar functioning as a weak forecast of Cerimon
in *Pericles* and Paulina in *The Winter's Tale*. Cerimon's miraculous powers are clearly also akin to those of Helena in *All's
Well that Ends Well* (a late play that has never been satisfactorily dated and which may even have followed *Pericles*). The
conclusion of *The Comedy of Errors* is acted before a monastery,
with Aemilia discovered as an abbess by her husband precisely
as Pericles discovers in the high priestess of Diana's temple his
long-lost Thaisa. The structural elements in *Pericles* are not
all new; but the treatment gives them fresh, and explicitly
transcendental, meaning. Instead of a happy-ending romance,
or ritual, in the tradition of Lyly, with whatever validity such
fictions may be considered to hold—and it is probable that
they hold more than we normally suppose—we are here confronted by some extra dimension of validity. The depth and
realism of tragedy are present within the structure of romance.
The two extremes, happy and sad, of Shakespearian art coalesce
to house a new, and seemingly impossible, truth; as though the
experiences behind or within the composition of *King Lear* and
Timon of Athens were found not necessarily antithetical to the
happy ending but rather reached therein their perfect fulfil-
ment. Hence the sense of breath-taking surprise, of wonder
and reverence, in the reunions, and the cogent presentation of
the miracle-worker, Cerimon.

Pericles might be called a Shakespearian morality play. The
epilogue asserts as much, though it does no justice to the more
important scenes, which so tower above the rest and which it
would be a great error to relate too sharply to any known type
of drama. These, whatever we think of them, are spontaneous,
new creations. And yet, in spite of their superiority, they
cannot be isolated: *Pericles* is too thoroughly organic a play for

that, with all its running coherences of idea, image, and event. These demand a short retrospective comment.

There are the continual references to 'fortune' personified at IV. iv. 48 as 'Lady Fortune' (cp. *Timon of Athens*, I. i. 64), variously entwined with the sequence of sad and happy adventures and used rather as in *Antony and Cleopatra* with strong suggestion of 'chance'. The gods are referred to as in *King Lear*, though with a greater sense of their reality, beneficence, and intervention; as in 'you most potent gods' (III. ii. 63); the 'powers that give heaven countless eyes to view men's acts' (I. i. 72); 'we cannot but obey the powers above us' (III.iii. 9). The 'most high gods' quickly punish, with 'heaven's shaft', the wicked (II. iv. 3, 15), but are otherwise conceived as kindly (II. iii. 59). Such deities counter the chance-like concept of 'fortune'. Somewhat sterner are the Destinies, conventionally supposed as cutting the thread of life (I. ii. 108), and also the typically Shakespearian conception:

> Time's the king of men,
> He's both their parent and he is their grave. (II. iii. 45)

Religious reverence crystallizes into the personal deities of Neptune and Diana; the first to be related to our voyages and tempests, the latter of high importance at the end.

To pass to the more human essences. There are a number of variations concerning true and false value played on riches (gold, silver and jewels) following, as we have noted, the use of riches in *The Merchant of Venice* and *Timon of Athens*. Now in *Timon of Athens* the gold of the later action may be related to the aristocratic essence, the spiritual fineness of Timon himself; and something similar happens in *Pericles*. For our glitter of jewels and other riches blends naturally into the play's royalism, where again we have a divergence of directions, with distinctions drawn between the wicked and good princes (Antiochus, Cleon and Dionyza against Pericles and Simonides); the former tyrannous (I. ii. 103) and regarding conscience as unworthy of noble blood (IV. iii. 23–5); the others, chivalrous and relating princely honour to charity (I. iv. 85–96; II. iii. 24–6; 59–61).

Here we may approach a new subtlety creeping into Shakspeare's royalism: his emphasis on the discovery (by the owner or someone else) of a child's royal birth (in Marina,[1] Perdita, Guiderius, Arviragus, Miranda). Royal blood is felt mystically, spiritually, with Marina as a palace 'for the crowned Truth to dwell in' (v. i. 124). We are reminded of Wordsworth's child forgetting 'the glories he hath known and that imperial palace whence he came' (in the *Ode on Intimations of Immortality*); and of Coleridge's remarkable play *Zapolya*, specifically written on the pattern of Shakespeare's last plays, where the spiritual connotations of the discovery of royal blood are vividly felt. Where the later poets witness a 'spiritual' reality, Shakespeare works from a firmer basis of Tudor royalism: but he invariably develops that, as in his manipulation of Timon's innate aristocracy, into something more spiritual, chivalric, or Christian, with stress on generosity and humility (as with Theseus in *A Midsummer Night's Dream*). This development reaches its finest results in his semi-mystic approach to the royal children from *Pericles* to *Henry VIII*; and may delicately be referred to some yet more universal intimation concerning the royal birth and destinies of the individual human soul, widely understood; for the royal protagonist of drama is always primarily an objectification of the spectator's individual self; his 'I'; and certainly in *Pericles* the greatest moments are weighted by a sense of man's universal destiny. So, whatever our political principles, we find the royalistic image radiating its lines of force: and it is precisely this princeliness that renders the rich, kindly and even humorous (iii. ii. 54–5) Lord Cerimon, on whom sits the aristocratic lustre of Timon, more attractive than his great descendant Prospero, who, though of ducal status, is more coldly conceived. Both *Pericles* and *The Winter's Tale* hold a certain freshness that the later, more coherent, play lacks. Something is lost as miracle becomes assured.

These imaginative strands are all Shakespearian favourites; but their use is new. They are newly actualized: what was formerly imagery becomes dramatic fact. The old image of storm gives us 'enter Pericles, wet'; that of bark-in-storm becomes a stage-setting, with Pericles 'on shipboard ; the old association love = jewel is built into a personal sense of Thaisa's

---

[1] Professor D. G. James, in *Scepticism & Poetry*, has written interestingly on the discovery of Marina's royal birth.

and Marina's jewel-like worth; the love-image of jewel-thrown-into-the-sea (see *The Shakespearian Tempest*, pp. 64–9; 222–3) becomes Thaisa in her jewel-stored coffin (like Portia's picture in the casket) thrown overboard. Shakespeare's continual reference to pagan deities works up to the 'feast of Neptune' and actual appearance of Diana. Finally, music, for so long a dramatic accompaniment to scenes of love and reunion, becomes an active force in Cerimon's magic and explicitly mystical in Pericles' 'music of the spheres' (v. i. 231). A similar process develops the Friars of *Romeo and Juliet* and *Much Ado about Nothing*, both plot-manipulators within their dramas with a tendency to arrange false appearances of death, into the miracle-working Cerimon taking on the plot-manipulation of life itself and restoring the dead. Pericles is the result of no sudden vision: it is Shakespeare's total poetry on the brink of self-knowledge.

It is accordingly not strange that art, as such, should be given greater emphasis than hitherto; in stage-conception, ceremonious procession (as of the tourneying knights) and ritual quality; in dumb-show; in monumental inscriptions, and metaphors; in musical accomplishment (Pericles' and Marina's); in Marina's dancing and decorative needlework. The arts least emphasized in Shakespeare, the static arts of design, assume a new prominence, giving us the exquisite descriptions of Marina in monumental terms. Shakespeare's drama is aspiring towards the eternal harmony and the eternal pattern.

The new excellences are bought at a cost. Pericles himself is a passive figure, quite unlike Shakespeare's usual dynamic protagonists. He himself does nothing crucial; his fall is purely an awareness of evil, like Hamlet's, his good acts are perfunctorily set down, his repentance in sack-cloth and unshaven hair a repentance for no guilt of his own but rather for the fact of mortality in a harsh universe. He is here for things to happen to and forges little or nothing for himself; his most original actions are a series of escapes or departures; he is too humble to press his suit for Thaisa. He is really less a realized person than man, almost 'every man', in the morality sense, as the epilogue suggests. We can, however, improve on the epilogue by seeing the whole as a panorama of life from adolescent fantasy and a consequent fall, through good works to a sensible

and fruitful marriage, and thence into tragedy, with a re-
emergence beyond mortal appearances into some higher recog
nition and rehabilitation. The medium is myth or parable
supposedly, of course, realistic: we must not expect death to
be totally negated; Thaisa's father dies (v. iii. 78); Cerimon
cannot restore everyone (iii. ii. 7). But, as in parable always,
it is the central person, or persons, that count; and here the
deaths of Thaisa and Marina are shown, in the fiction, as false,
though with an intensity surpassing fiction.

Having worked through the play like this, we may well
question whether it is not as authentic as any of Shakespeare's
works. The bad lines may be due to a bad text, or lack of
revision (as one suspects at *Timon of Athens*, iii. v. 24–59 where
the mixture of broken metre and gnomic rhyme provides a
closely similar problem). The weaker rhymed passages, so
closely resembling those in *All's Well that Ends Well*, may be
a record of Shakespeare writing a tentative play and falling
back on rhyme for stability and inspiration, while also searching for a new formality to suit his growing itch for static design,[1]
until his normal manner starts to take control with staggering
results. It is, indeed, possible that he would always have
regarded his blank-verse colloquialisms, in both vocabulary and
rhythm, his virile growth of spontaneous, hurtling speech, as a
rough dramatic expedient, with a far greater approval than we
should grant accorded to his own rhymed couplets and formal,
gnomic, sequences, which, though we tend to ignore them, are
sprinkled fairly thickly throughout the plays. In *Pericles* a stiff
formality clearly serves a purpose in Marina's epitaph at iv. iv.
34; as does, too, the obviously intended quaintness of Gower,
whose speeches are often rich enough in content however queer
the form. If we accept, as we must, such passages, it is hard
to know where to stop; for the worst things one can always
blame a copyist or compositor—especially that most dangerous
workman who remedies some obscurity or hiatus by drawing
on his own poetic resources. The main problem is not confined
to *Pericles*: Prospero's epilogue in *The Tempest* has something

---

[1] The formal sequences of *All's Well that Ends Well* (to be, with those in *Pericles*, distinguished from Shakespeare's earlier formal and gnomic verse, as at *Romeo and Juliet*, ii. iii.
1–30 and *Othello* i. iii. 199–219) are, in their way, assured and powerful, as those in *Pericles*
are not ; which suggests that *All's Well that Ends Well* might be dated later than *Pericles*. See
my note on p. 128.

of the accent of Gower at v. ii., and Shakespeare's divine beings regularly speak a semi-formal but clearly authentic verse over which it is nevertheless hard to enthuse; as though there were some artistic intention to which our ears are not tuned. Against the argument for complete, or almost complete, authenticity we can observe: (i) the extreme badness of certain passages in the earlier scenes; (ii) that the bad text, if bad text it is, tends to improve whenever Shakespeare's voice is unquestionably being heard, though faulty lines occur in the final scene; and (iii) the almost unanswerable fact that the Folio editors, who alone were in a position to know the truth, rejected the play.

The obvious conclusion is that some much earlier play, either of Shakespearian or other authorship, shows through, mainly in the first half, but that it has been so modified by incorporation that we need not, from an interpretative view, be seriously disquieted. *Pericles* was published under Shakespeare's name during his life. The high standard of authenticity demanded by the Folio editors is witnessed alike by their own preface and the massive and detailed coherence of the material they published: such things do not happen by chance. But neither can the internal coherence of *Pericles*, far more precise than that of many a more famous Shakespearian work, be dismissed. Nothing is here forgotten: Antiochus' wickedness, Pericles' relief of the famine, the crime of Dionyza and Cleon, all are exactly remembered long after their purpose in the narrative sequence has been fulfilled; from first to last the Gower speeches have the whole action in mind; the various imagistic correspondences, cutting across divergences of style, knit the narrative into a unity. Every line, good or bad, serves a purpose: there are probably less extravagant irrelevancies than, say, in *Hamlet* or *King Lear* (e.g. the weak elaboration of *Hamlet*, I. ii. 79–81, and what might be called the delaying bombast of *King Lear*, I. iv. 299–311). The play appears to be carefully and critically composed: witness Gower's laboured apologies for the disrespect shown to the unities and even for the employment of a single language for different places (IV. iv. 7). Whatever we think of certain parts, the whole, as we have it, is unquestionably dominated by a single mind; that mind is very clearly Shakespeare's; and Shakespeare's, too, in process of an advance unique in literature.

III

'GREAT CREATING NATURE': AN ESSAY ON *THE WINTER'S TALE*

> But some man will say, How are the dead raised up ? and with what body do they come ? Thou fool, that which thou sowest is not quickened, except it die ; and that which thou sowest, thou sowest not that body that shall be, but bare grain, it may chance of wheat, or of some other grain : but God giveth it a body as it hath pleased him, and to every seed his own body.
>
> All flesh is not the same flesh ; but there is one kind of flesh of men, another flesh of beasts, another of fishes and another of birds. There are also celestial bodies and bodies terrestrial : but the glory of the celestial is one, and the glory of the terrestrial is another. There is one glory of the sun, and another glory of the moon, and another glory of the stars ; for one star differeth from another star in glory. So also is the resurrection of the dead.   1 *Corinthians*, xv. 35.

I

IN *The Winter's Tale* Shakespeare handles a similar narrative to that of *Pericles* with the infusion of a closer and more realistic human concern and a tightening of dramatic conflict. Pericles experiences a sense of evil followed by unmerited suffering; Leontes sins and endures a purgatory of guilt. Here the sackcloth and ashes of Pericles' martyrdom are given a profounder relevance.

The Winter's Tale has had a poor showing in commentary, having seldom been regarded as more than an inconsequential romance with fine bits of poetry; while even those who, during recent years, have regarded it as a serious reading of human affairs, have avoided, or slurred over, as though un-at-home with its nature, the crucial and revealing event to which the whole action moves: the resurrection of Hermione.

The play is in three main sections. The first is tragic; the second pastoral; the third must for the present be left un-defined. There is a strong suggestion throughout of season-myth, with a balance of summer against winter. Evil passions, storm, and shipwreck are contrasted with young love and humour. Maturity and death are set against birth and resurrection.

The action opens with a short prose dialogue between Camillo and Archidamus in which the simplicities of Bohemia are contrasted with the luxuries of Sicilia. The contrast is not later developed, and more important are the following remarks on maturity and youth. Leontes and Polixenes 'were trained together in their childhoods', though since separated by 'mature' responsibilities (I.i. 24–35). The picture is completed by thought of the boy Mamilius:

> *Camillo.*   It is a gallant child ; one that indeed physics the subject, makes old hearts fresh ; they that went on crutches ere he was born desire yet their life to see him a man.
>
> *Archidamus.*   Would they else be content to die ?   (I. i. 42)

Youth is conceived as a power; as a renewer of life and antagonist to death. Thus early is the central theme of *The Winter's Tale* set before us.

Polixenes also has a son whom he 'longs to see' (I. ii. 34), but Hermione presses his stay, asking about his and her own lord's youth together and of their 'tricks' as 'pretty lordings'. He answers:

> *Polixenes.*   We were, fair queen,
> Two lads that thought there was no more behind
> But such a day to-morrow as to-day,
> And to be boy eternal.
>
> *Hermione.*   Was not my lord the verier wag o' the two ?
>
> *Polixenes.*   We were as twinn'd lambs that did frisk i' the sun,
> And bleat the one at the other ; what we chang'd
> Was innocence for innocence ; we knew not
> The doctrine of ill-doing, no nor dream'd
> That any did. Had we pursued that life,
> And our weak spirits ne'er been higher rear'd
> With stronger blood, we should have answer'd
>   heaven
> Boldly, 'not guilty' ; the imposition clear'd
> Hereditary ours.   (I. ii. 62)

The 'eternal' consciousness of childhood is distinguished from the sin-born time-consciousness of man.[1] Polixenes' second

---

[1] One must, however, read no special meaning into Shakespeare's use here of 'behind' to denote the future. A similar use occurs at *Hamlet*, III. iv. 179, perhaps with a stage-sense of events awaiting their entrance. For a reverse, more normal, thought of a backward past see *The Tempest*, I. ii. 50.

speech defines a golden-age existence free from that 'hereditary' taint of fallen humanity which appears with the 'stronger blood', or passions, of maturity. Leontes, called from his reverie, excuses himself in similar terms; for he has been half-meditating and half-talking to Mamilius, calling him a 'calf' and saying how he needs 'a rough pash and the shoots that I have' to be like his father (I. ii. 128–9):

> *Leontes.*   . . . Looking on the lines
> Of my boy's face, methoughts I did recoil
> Twenty-three years, and saw myself unbreech'd,
> In my green velvet coat, my dagger muzzled,
> Lest it should bite its master, and so prove,
> As ornaments oft do, too dangerous :
> How like, methought, I then was to this kernel,
> This squash, this gentleman. Mine honest friend,
> Will you take eggs for money ?
> *Mamilius.*   No, my lord, I'll fight.
>   (I. ii. 154)

'Calf', 'kernel', 'squash', 'eggs' (also 'eggs' earlier at I. ii. 131): impressions of young life—remember the frisking lambs of Polixenes' speech—on various natural planes cluster. Polixenes, questioned as to his own 'young prince' (I. ii. 164), answers:

> *Polixenes.*   If at home, sir,
> He's all my exercise, my mirth, my matter,
> Now my sworn friend and then mine enemy ;
> My parasite, my soldier, statesman, all :
> He makes a July day short as December,
> And with his varying childness cures in me
> Thoughts that would thick my blood.
> *Leontes.*   So stands this squire
> Offic'd with me.   (I. ii. 165)

All humanity is compacted in the loved person, after the manner of Helena's 'Not my virginity yet . . .' in *All's Well that Ends Well* (I. i. 181). Childhood is shown as a redeeming force, subduing horrors. Mamilius is, at the play's start, dramatically central. Defined mainly by what is said to, or about, him, and especially by Leontes' by-play ('What, hast smutch'd thy nose?' at I. ii. 122), 'my young rover' (I. ii. 176) focalizes the poetry of boyhood and fills the stage.

This poetry is, however, countered by Leontes' rising jealousy conceived as evil in contrast to the golden-age of childhood. Leontes lives in the world of mature passion with attendant knowledge of evil, and consequent suspicion. More, his suspicion is an ugly thing, itself an evil; it is, practically, sin. The central emphasis in Shakespeare on conjugal trust and fidelity is patent: the deepest issues of good and evil are through it expressed. From Provençal lyric, through Petrarch, to Dante, romantic love is haloed with semi-divine meaning. At the Renaissance there is a further development: the romantic idea descends from fancy to actuality; it becomes practical, and therefore moral, in the ethic of marriage.[1] Now the dramatic implications of this change have received insufficient notice. Spenser's doctrine of marriage-love is less important than Lyly's dramatization of it: in Lyly the happy-ending love-drama, or love-ritual, not only releases drama from ecclesiastical domination but sets it firmly on a new course, which it follows still, thereby witnessing the unexhausted meaning, social and religious, of this persistent theme. In Shakespeare love-integrity is all but the supreme good, in both comedy and tragedy, the pattern being especially clear in *Othello*, with Desdemona as divinity and Iago as devil. Whatever may be our own social tenets, we must, in reading *The Winter's Tale*, be prepared to accept the Shakespearian emphasis as a preliminary to understanding. Great poetry seldom leaps direct at universal ideas for their own sake; its ideas are housed in flesh and blood; and there is a logic of incarnated thought, a blood-contact and descent from body to body, that does not necessarily correspond point by point to any conceptual chain. So, though Shakespeare writes here as a poet of the Renaissance as it specifically shaped itself in England with a plot-interest confined to suspicion of conjugal infidelity, the radiations set going concern the very essence of evil; sexual jealousy is shown as a concentration of possessiveness and inferiority developing into malice with Leontes' suspicion aptly enough called 'sin' (I. ii. 283) and the whole argument considered a matter of 'good and evil' (I. ii. 303). But opposite the hero stands his own child, whose very being is a wisdom and an assurance:

[1] To use C. S. Lewis' crisp phraseology in *The Allegory of Love* (VII, p. 340), 'The romance of marriage' succeeds 'the romance of adultery'.

Mamilius.   I am like you, they say.
Leontes.   Why, that's some comfort.
                                        (I. ii. 207)

The boy has broken into one of his father's interjectory paroxysms. The remark, and Leontes' reaction, are simple enough; but the dramatic context is already so loaded with meaning that the simplicity reverberates beyond itself. *The Winter's Tale* is more than a 'morality' play; and yet, with no loss of sharp human particularization, Mamilius stands before Leontes as Truth confronting Error.

Leontes is shown as a man inwardly tormented. His misery expresses itself in short, stabbing sentences of great force:

> Too hot, too hot !
> To mingle friendship far is mingling bloods.
> I have *tremor cordis* on me : my heart dances :
> But not for joy ; not joy . . .   (I. ii. 109)

His words jet from a similar nervous disorganization to that less vividly expressed in Macbeth's

> Why do I yield to that suggestion
> Whose horrid image does unfix my hair,
> And makes my seated heart knock at my ribs
> Against the use of nature ?
>   (*Macbeth*, I. iii. 134)

Leontes' early soliloquies contrast with his, and others', conversation when a more reasonable intercourse is demanded; he can mask his feelings. But, left to himself, his anguish comes out in hisses, jets of poison, carried over by sibilants and thoughts of stagnant water:

> Gone already !
> Inch-thick, knee-deep, o'er head and ears a fork'd one !
> Go play, boy, play ; thy mother plays, and I
> Play too, but so disgrac'd a part, whose issue
> Will hiss me to my grave : contempt and clamour
> Will be my knell. Go play, boy, play. There have been
> Or I am much deceiv'd, cuckolds ere now ;
> And many a man there is even at this present,
> Now, while I speak this, holds his wife by the arm,
> That little thinks she has been sluic'd in's absence,
> And his pond fish'd by his next neighbour, by
> Sir Smile, his neighbour . . .   (I. ii. 185)

The word 'hiss' occurs as a threat, drawing close. Hermione is 'slippery' (I. ii. 273). How poignantly the slime of this reptilian horror coiling round Leontes is countered by the little boy's presence, leading to the ugly dexterity of the wit on 'play'.

The spasmodic jerks of his language reflect Leontes' unease: he is, as it were, being sick; ejecting a poison, which yet grows stronger; something he has failed to digest, assimilate. Images of nausea pour out. His marriage is 'spotted', like a toad (cp. 'most toad-spotted traitor' at *King Lear*, v. iii. 140; and Othello's 'I had rather be a toad . . .' and 'cistern for foul toads to knot and gender in' at *Othello*, III. iii. 270 and IV. ii. 60); and this defilement is to him 'goads, thorns, nettles, tails of wasps' (I. ii. 328–9). Our most virulent speech of disgust involves the much-loathed spider:

> There may be in the cup
> A spider steep'd, and one may drink, depart,
> And yet partake no venom, for his knowledge
> Is not infected ; but if one present
> The abhorr'd ingredient to his eye, make known
> How he hath drunk, he cracks his gorge, his sides,
> With violent hefts. I have drunk, and seen the spider.
>
> (II. i. 38)

The studied build-up of the preceding lines injects a maximum of force into that final, icy, reserve. Indeed, Leontes' most vitriolic spasms get themselves out with a certain under-emphasis, not unlike Swift's general expression of nausea through *meiosis*; as though the extreme of satiric bitterness were always loath to risk suicide in the *katharsis* of luxuriant expression. Leontes' paroxysms never enjoy Othello's even swell and surge of fully developed emotion:

> Come, sir page,
> Look on me with your welkin eye : sweet villain !
> Most dear'st ! my collop ! Can thy dam ?—may't be ?—
> Affection ! thy intention stabs the centre :
> Thou dost make possible things not so held,
> Communicat'st with dreams ;—how can this be ?—
> With what's unreal thou coactive art,
> And fellow'st nothing : then, 'tis very credent

Thou may'st co-join with something ; and thou dost,
And that beyond commission, and I find it,
And that to the infection of my brains
And hardening of my brows.   (I. ii. 136)

From the boy and his 'welkin eye'—a phrase enlisting all
great nature's serenity and light—Leontes is being swiftly projected into instability; the universal 'centre' is gone, stabbed
by this supposed 'affection' (i.e. growing love) of Hermione
and Polixenes. The result is nightmare. The impossible has
happened: worse, it is even now happening ; the known
creation has had dallyings with the 'unreal', the 'nothing', and
thence given birth (as in *Macbeth*) to an only-too-real action of
hideous obscenity in the visible order. We are close to Macbeth's 'horrible imaginings' of his own as yet 'fantastical'
crime, with 'function smother'd in surmise' until 'nothing is
but what is not' (*Macbeth* I. iii. 137–42). In both plays we
have evil impinging as essential 'nothing', unreality, a delirium,
which yet most violently acts on the real. Leontes' whirling
sequence rises to the powerful and revealing 'infection of my
brains'—thereby half-admitting his own now poisoned thinking—and then drops into an understress, almost euphemism,
in 'hardening of my brows'. And yet that last reserve again
reflects a state the very opposite of repose: that of a man
tense, nerving himself to believe, to endure—more, to *be*—the
hideous, horned, thing. We are nearer *Macbeth* than *Othello*.

This spasmodic, interjectory, explosive style, however,
whirls itself once into a single rhythmic movement of towering
excellence, developing the 'nothing' of our last quotation into
a truly shattering reality.[1] 'Is whispering nothing?' asks
Leontes of Camillo, and continues with a list of love's advances,
jerked out in rapid fire, and concluding:

[1] Shakespeare's use of 'nothing' is variously important. Repetitions of the word carry a
weight of dramatic meaning at *Hamlet*, III. iv. 130–2 and IV. v. 173 ; *All's Well that Ends
Well*, III. ii. 77–105 ; and *King Lear*, I. i. 89–92 and I. iv. 142–50. Compare also *King Lear*
I. ii. 32 with *Othello*, III. iii. 36. In *Macbeth* it helps to characterize a nightmare state at I. iii. 141
and a general nihilism at v. v. 28 ; and in *Richard II* is used seven times to define a nameless
fear at II. ii. 1–40 and twice for a peaceful Nirvana-like dissolution at v. v. 38–41, the last
example pointing on to 'nothing brings me all things' at *Timon of Athens*, v. i. 191–3 (Bergson's
equation of 'the nought' with 'the all' in *L'Evolution Créatrice* is analogous). It tends to occur
at moments of crisis, or whenever what Nietzsche called the Dionysian element in tragedy is
breaking into the rational and Apollonian : for the accompanying poetic implications see *A
Midsummer Night's Dream*, v. i. 16. A good apocalyptic use occurs later in *The Winter's Tale*
at III. i. 11.

> . . . Is this nothing ?
> Why, then the world and all that's in't is nothing ;
> The covering sky is nothing ; Bohemia nothing ;
> My wife is nothing ; nor nothing have these nothings,
> If this be nothing. (i. ii. 292)

Nature's 'centre' and 'welkin' (sky) in the boy's eye (cp. 'the eye of Heaven' for the sun in Sonnet XVIII) were first (in our former speech) contrasted with 'nothing'; here the nihilistic horror itself assumes validity equal to that of the 'world' and 'covering sky': this contrast or identity (as Leontes claims) is, as we shall see, basic. Great nature is here our final term of reference, to which even evil must appeal, somewhat as Hamlet, from the depths of his melancholia, admits the firmamental splendour.

The victory of evil in Leontes' soul, its rise in philosophical status, is thus here matched, though only for an instant, by a corresponding mastery of rhythm, rather as in Macbeth's later speeches. One must beware of regarding tormented rhythms as a poetical goal. Possibly we over-rate Shakespeare's rough-handling of language to correspond to the twists and jerks of psychic experience, not unlike the helter-skelter impressionism brought to a self-conscious art by the justly praised and influential Hopkins. One can often approve a poet's disrespect to the tyrannies of rhythm and syntax; but there are dangers. Though Shakespeare indeed uses such a crammed, often cramped, manner elsewhere, the style is certainly most effective when expressing nightmare or disintegration: disrupted rhythms suit Brutus' and Macbeth's soliloquies before their half-intended murders (*Julius Caesar*, ii. i. 10–34; *Macbeth*, i. vii. 1–12). Shakespeare later allows himself more and more freedom in a manner which is perilously near to mannerism; and where no especial disorder, psychic or—as in a messenger-speech (as at *Cymbeline*, v. iii. 14–51)—physical is concerned, the result can irritate. With Leontes, however, the purpose has been patent; the disrupted style not merely fits, it explores and exposes, the anguish depicted.

That anguish is hell. Leontes half knows, too, that it is sin. He goes to Camillo, if not for absolution, at least for confirmation and collaboration:

> I have trusted thee, Camillo,
> With all the nearest things to my heart, as well
> My chamber-councils, wherein, priest-like, thou
> Hast cleans'd my bosom : I from thee departed
> Thy penitent reform'd. But we have been
> Deceiv'd in thy integrity, deceiv'd
> In that which seems so.   (I. ii. 235)

He wants Camillo to corroborate his own discovery. He is
nervous, tentative; something intimate is, as the confessional
phraseology hints, involved. But he is not asking advice ; the
least hint of disagreement rouses his fury. He now positively
wants his suspicions, which have become the dearest part of
him, confirmed:

> *Camillo.*   Good my lord, be cur'd
> Of this diseas'd opinion, and betimes ;
> For 'tis most dangerous.
> *Leontes.*   Say it be, 'tis true.
> *Camillo.* No, no, my lord.
> *Leontes.*   It is ; you lie, you lie ;
> I say thou liest, Camillo, and I hate thee ;
> Pronounce thee a gross lout, a mindless slave . . .
>   (I. ii. 296)

The phrase 'diseas'd opinion' is exact: Leontes seems to admit
disease, whilst insisting on his suspicion's truth. Opposition raises
a devil of self-defensive fury, rising to bombast and that type of
vulgar abuse so often symptomatic of a semi-conscious guilt.

His evil is self-born and unmotivated. Commentators have
searched in vain for 'motives' to explain the soul-states and
actions of Hamlet, Iago and Macbeth, without realizing that
the poet is concerned not with trivialities, but with evil itself,
whose cause remains as dark as theology: given a 'sufficient'
motive, the thing to be studied vanishes. In Leontes we have
a study of evil yet more coherent, realistic and compact; a
study of almost demonic possession. He reacts violently to
criticism: when Antigonus and others presume to argue, he
shouts 'Hold your peaces!' (II. i. 138); and when he hears that
Paulina is outside, Paulina who is to function throughout as
his accuser, almost as his conscience, he starts 'like a guilty
thing upon a fearful summons' (*Hamlet*, I. i. 148), as though
recognizing his natural enemy:

> How !
> Away with that audacious lady ! Antigonus,
> I charg'd thee that she should not come about me .
> I knew she would.   (II. iii. 41)

The last words have the very accent of neurosis, blackening
with defensive scorn the good onto which it projects its own
evil.

Leontes dimly recognizes that he is behaving as a tyrant,
using position and power to bolster up and enforce on others
a disease in himself. He is accordingly at pains to show himself as relying on his lords' advice on condition that they do not
oppose him:

> Why, what need we
> Commune with you of this, but rather follow
> Our forceful instigation ? Our prerogative
> Calls not your counsels, but our natural goodness
> Imparts this . . .   (II. i. 160)

He is insecure enough to want support, would convince himself of 'natural goodness'; but, failing support, will go his own
way. However, he has sent to the Oracle of Apollo for
'greater confirmation', realizing the danger of rashness and
wishing to 'give rest to the minds of others' (II. i. 179–92).
Tyrant though he be, he can still think constitutionally. Though
absolutely certain, he is yet not quite certain that his certainty
can maintain itself: paradoxes abound. He is on a rack of
indecision:

> Nor night, nor day, no rest ; it is but weakness
> To bear the matter thus ; mere weakness. If
> The cause were not in being,—part o' the cause,
> She the adultress ; for the harlot king
> Is quite beyond mine arm, plot-proof ; but she
> I can hook to me : say, that she were gone,
> Given to the fire, a moiety of my rest
> Might come to me again.   (II. iii. 1)

In the full flood of anger, when his lords kneel, imploring him
to spare the new-born child, he is indecisive and gives ground,
muttering: 'I am a feather for each wind that blows' (II. iii. 153).
We cannot admire him, as we admire Richard III, the later
Macbeth, and Milton's Satan, for a whole-hearted Satanism.
Nor can we sympathize, as with Othello. The emotion aroused

is rather a stern pity. He himself knows that to be mistaken
in such a matter were 'piteous' (ii. i. 181; cp. also iii. ii.
235). More, it is almost comic: Antigonus suggests that the
public scandal will raise everyone 'to laughter' (ii. i. 197).
Of all Shakespeare's jealous husbands Leontes is nearest to
Ford, existing in almost comic objectivity, though without
one atom's loss of tragic intensity. We have in him a sharp
personification of the blend so obvious in the wider design.

Tyranny and superstition are mutually related. Tyranny is
the forceful domination of a person in the semi-evil, semi-
neurotic, state of contemporary humanity. Were the tyrant
purely integrated, his absolute control might be a good; hence
the will in all royalist states to see the king as a superman of
goodness and wisdom, and the theological equation of Christ
= King. A tyrant normally makes power serve personal error,
opening the way for a number of illegitimate powers; at the
extreme, superstitious belief regarding the manipulation of
natural forces, and finally for beings of an infra-natural kind.
In Shakespeare's two full-length studies of tyranny in *Richard
III* and *Macbeth* the emphasis on ill-omened creatures, witchcraft,[1] and ghosts is thoroughly integral.

Now Leontes has, without knowing it, entered this domain;
and, by a transition well known to psychologists, tends to deny
vehemently the name of tyrant, whilst seeing in his opposite,
Paulina, the exact evil really lodged in himself. She brings
from the prison, where his wife lies, Leontes' new-born child-
daughter, challenging him with utter fearlessness, reiterating
the (to him—since he half fears its truth) maddening phrase
'good queen' (ii. iii. 58) and finally stinging him to madness
by actual presentation of the child. The opposition of childhood and evil, already made vivid by Mamilius, here reaches
its maximum dramatic intensity and rouses in Leontes a devil
that speaks directly in terms of black magic. Leontes now sees
Paulina as a witch and as she presents the baby shouts: 'Out!
A mankind witch!' (ii. iii. 67). He is, as Paulina coolly
observes, 'mad' (ii. iii. 71). His storming gets more violent
and excessively ugly:

---

[1] For witchcraft see *Richard III*, iii. iv. 66–71. Richard is, of course, continually compared
to ill-omened creatures, and is visited by eleven ghosts before Bosworth. The presence of all
these effects in *Macbeth* is obvious. See also 2 *Henry VI*, i. iv.

Traitors !
Will you not push her out ? Give her the bastard.
Thou dotard ! thou art woman-tir'd, unroosted
By thy dame Partlet here. Take up the bastard ;
Take't up, I say ; give't to thy crone. (II. iii. 72)

Notice the unchivalrous, ugly, scorn, the horror almost of
woman as woman, in 'Partlet' and 'crone', the latter suggesting
witchcraft; and also the continuation of our political emphasis
in 'traitors', to be repeated again by 'a *nest* of traitors' (II. iii.
81), subtly suggesting, as does 'Partlet' too, a growing identity, in Leontes' diseased mind, of creative nature with treachery. Against his words is Paulina's more religious threat to
Antigonus that his hands will be for ever 'unvenerable' (II. iii.
77) if he obeys; and her insistence that 'the root' of Leontes'
'opinion' is 'as rotten as ever oak or stone was sound' (II. iii.
89), driving home once more the all-important contrast of
Leontes' crime with the stabilities of nature. After her exquisite
description of nature's handiwork in the child's likeness to its
father, Leontes' reply is: 'A gross hag!' (II. iii. 107). The
more perfect the good presented, the more black it rises before
him; like Milton's Satan, only without knowing it (as Macbeth
knows it at the end and by so doing all but redeems himself),
Leontes has said, 'Evil, be thou my good'. His values are all
transposed and Paulina deserves a witch's death:

Leontes.   I'll ha' thee burn'd.
Paulina.   I care not ;
        It is a heretic that makes the fire,
        Not she which burns in't. I'll not call you tyrant ;
        But this most cruel usage of your queen—
        Not able to produce more accusation
        Than your own weak-hing'd fancy—something
                                                savours
        Of tyranny, and will ignoble make you,
        Yea, scandalous to the world.
Leontes.   On your allegiance,
        Out of the chamber with her ! Were I a tyrant,
        Where were her life ? she durst not call me so
        If she did know me one. Away with her !
                                        (II. iii. 113)

Paulina's phraseology ('heretic') is again orthodox and Christian. Leontes' 'on your allegiance' echoes Lear's scene with Kent

(*King Lear*, I. i. 122–82), where the psychology of tyranny was, though less subtly developed, very similar. Notice Paulina's reiterated emphasis on tyranny, and Leontes' violent reaction. He fears the thought, half-recognizes its truth; though, with some justice, defending himself *to himself*, adducing rational evidence; trying to crush the summoning conscience whose outward projection is, throughout the play, Paulina. He has, however, sunk deep into paganism, witnessed by his intention to have the child 'consum'd with fire' (II. iii. 133). His emphatic desire to *burn* suggests a complex of tyranny and paganism, not to be finally distinguished from that semi-pagan fear of paganism which led to the tyrannic burning of supposed heretics and witches. There is in both a submission to fear and a desire to leave no trace of the dreaded thing: hence Leontes' earlier thought that if Hermione were 'given to the fire' his peace of mind might return (II. iii. 8); and his recent threat to Paulina. Paulina, in opposition, represents the pure Christian conscience, together with common sense. Aligned with her are (i) the new-born baby and (ii) all those natural and human sanctities it symbolizes.

Nature rules our play. Despite the court-setting, nature-suggestion has been, from the start, vivid, introduced by Polixenes' opening lines:

> Nine changes of the watery star have been
> The shepherd's note since we have left our throne . . .
>
> (I. ii. 1)

The following dialogue is sprinkled with natural imagery in close association with youth—in the description of the two kings as 'twinn'd lambs that did frisk i' the sun' (I. ii. 67), the 'unfledg'd days' of boyhood (I. ii. 78), Leontes' use of steer, heifer, kernel and squash. A general pastoralism rings in the 'mort o' the deer' at I. ii. 119. Leontes sees his wife's supposed love-making as a bird's holding up of her 'bill' (I. ii. 183); and there are his more obvious animal-images of nausea already noted. Seasons, to be so important in the general design, are suggested by 'sneaping winds' at I. ii. 13 and twice actually mentioned: Polixenes' son 'makes a July's day short as December' (I. ii. 169), and we have Mamilius' contribution to the play's wintry opening in his unfinished story. 'A sad tale', he says, is 'best for winter' and continues:

Mamilius. There was a man—
Hermione.   Nay, come, sit down ; then on.
Mamilius. Dwelt by a churchyard. I will tell it softly ;
            Yond crickets shall not hear it.   (II. i. 24–30)

The 'sad tale' reflects the oncoming disaster; the boy's words characterize his father, dwelling close (as is hinted by a revealing image at II. i. 150) to death; the broken story is itself a little tragedy. But here all tragedies are firmly held within Nature's vastness. Hermione's thought of how Polixenes may 'unsphere the stars with oaths' (I. ii. 48) repeats the manner of *Antony and Cleopatra*: compare, too, Camillo's 'among the infinite doings of the world' (I. ii. 253) with the Soothsayer's 'in nature's infinite book of secrecy a little I can read' at *Antony and Cleopatra*, I. ii. 11. Nature here, however, whilst remaining vast, is normally less philosophically, more concretely, present. Three times already (I. ii. 137–9; I. ii. 293–4; II. iii. 90) we have found creation's firmamental and earthly steadfastness contrasted with the hideous instabilities of evil; and throughout Leontes' fall that solid 'world' and its 'covering sky' (I. ii 293–4; cp. also his 'You'll be found, be you beneath the sky' at I. ii. 179) are our touchstones of reality.

The close association of nature and human childhood has Christian affinities, and Christian tonings occur naturally among our positives. We have seen that Paulina employs them. When Polixenes calls Hermione 'my most sacred lady' (I. ii. 76), whilst admitting his own lapse, since childhood, into 'temptations', the adjective goes (as later at II. iii. 84 and v. i. 172) beyond formal courtesy. More direct is:

> O, then my best blood turn
> To an infected jelly, and my name
> Be yok'd with his that did betray the Best !
>   (I. ii. 417)

—though the immediate comparison (as at *Richard II*, IV. i. 170, 240; and *Timon of Athens*, I. ii. 48–51) still serves a human purpose. But here is something quite new and characteristic, indeed, the most characteristic possible, of *The Winter's Tale*. When the Gaoler doubts whether he should release the new-born baby from the prison without a warrant, Paulina answers:

> You need not fear it, sir :
> The child was prisoner to the womb, and is
> By law and process of great nature thence
> Freed and enfranchis'd . . .   (II. ii. 58)

'Freed': how the word contrasts with the stifling atmosphere
of Leontes' own enslavement to evil and imprisoning of Hermione. It is precisely this freedom of 'great nature', un-
possessive, ever-new, creative, against which Leontes' tyranny
has offended; and his offence is therefore also one against the
natural order whose very laws are those of creation and freedom; and therefore, too, of miracle.

'Great nature' is our over-ruling deity—hence the broad
phraseology of 'your mother rounds apace' (II. i. 16)– responsible for the miraculous perpetuation and re-creation of worn
and sinful man. Mamilius' likeness to Leontes is, as we have
seen, emphatic; as when, looking on his son, the father remembers his own boyhood (I. ii. 154–61), or sees the boy's smutched
nose as 'a copy out of mine' (I. ii. 123); while Mamilius himself remarks: 'I am like you, they say' (I. ii. 208). The emphasis reaches a climax in Paulina's presentation to the horrified Leontes of his new-born baby. We have had something
similar in Mamilius' play with the ladies and his talk of eyebrows (II. i. 7–15), but here is a greater passage:

> Behold, my lords,
> Although the print be little, the whole matter
> And copy of the father ; eye, nose, lip,
> The trick of's frown, his forehead, nay, the valley,
> The pretty dimples of his chin and cheek, his smiles,
> The very mould and frame of hand, nail, finger :
> And thou, good goddess Nature, which hast made it
> So like to him that got it, if thou hast
> The ordering of the mind too, 'mongst all colours
> No yellow in't ; lest she suspect, as he does,
> Her children not her husband's.   (II. iii. 97)

Notice the pretty irony of 'the trick of his frown': Leontes'
ugly wrath at this instant is reflected in the baby's puckered
brow. Notice, too, the slight but important reservation as to
whether Nature also orders the mind, less an assertion of
difference than symptom of the will to drive natural supremity

to the limit, in spite of traditional distinctions which are nevertheless remembered. Observe the exact and objective description of human lineaments, with a maximum of love's intimacy, yet so purified of any clouding, or glamorous, passion or sentimentality that we are nearer to Blake's 'minute particulars' than to the physical descriptions in *Venus and Adonis*; and yet the physical is even more intensely, though quietly, preserved; the speech is, of course, maternal rather than erotic. The identification, through love, is so complete that objectivity supervenes with a purity and realism the precise antithesis to the other objectivity of Leontes' hideous command to carry hence 'this female bastard' (II. iii. 174), where the one adjective 'female' houses a whole philosophy of cynical materialism. Paulina's speech lives the play's doctrine on the sanctity of human creation and the miraculous doings of 'nature': it is thus deeply Christian. Such is the antagonist to Leontes' sin and the tragedy it draws swiftly down; a thing already of such power that Hermione's final resurrection shall be no madness. It is easy to see why Leontes' possessing devil is so violently roused: it recognizes its antagonist in the baby. The dark powers in *Macbeth* are similarly opposed by a crowned and tree-bearing child. So our dramatic conflict of delirious evil against the stabilities of nature works through conversations about boyhood and the stage-presence of the attractive Mamilius, to this final opposition, with Paulina as directing agent. Mamilius' presence was always the more eloquent for his few speeches; and the apparently helpless new-born baby (in Wordsworthian phrase 'deaf and silent', yet reading 'the eternal deep' and 'haunted for ever by the eternal mind', in the *Immortality Ode*) is necessarily even more potent.

Though often Christian in impact, the natural majesty explored is also in part Hellenic, relating directly to our controlling god 'great Apollo' (II. iii. 199), the sun-god, and his oracle at Delphos.[1] Leontes sends 'to sacred Delphos, to Apollo's temple' to solicit, in Christian phrase, the god's 'spiritual counsel' (II. i. 182, 185). Cleomenes and Dion return awestruck, deeply impressed by the island's (it is so considered) 'delicate' climate, the 'sweet' air and general *fertility* (III. i. 1–3;

[1] The word appears to be an amalgam of Delphi and the island Delos : it is considered an island. For 'Delphos' as the home of the oracle compare *Paradise Regained*, I. 458.

cp. *The Tempest*, ii. i. 43–9, 55); and even more by the temple, the 'celestial habits' and 'reverence' of the 'grave' priests and the 'sacrifice' so 'ceremonious, solemn and unearthly'; while the actual voice or 'burst' of the oracle was as a terrifying judgement, 'kin to Jove's thunder' (iii. i. 3–11: cp. the thunderous appearances of Jupiter in *Cymbeline*, v. iv. 93, and of Ariel in *The Tempest*, iii. iii. 53). They pray that 'great Apollo' and the package sealed by 'Apollo's great divine' may quickly turn all 'to the best' and disclose something 'rare' (iii. i. 14–21); the word 'rare', used already at iii. i. 13, being frequent on such occasions throughout this and other of the Final Plays (as in 'rarest sounds' at *Pericles*, v. i. 233). Apollo is both a nature-deity and transcendent; though a god of sun-fire (as is clear later), his revelatory voice makes the hearer 'nothing' (iii. i. 11), the word already used to define Leontes' ghastly experience. Apollo is as mysterious and as awful as Wordsworth's gigantic mountain-presences; he is both the Greek Apollo and the Hebraic Jehovah. In him the play's poetry is personified.

Hermione is brought to trial. Leontes opens the proceedings with a disclaimer:

> Let us be clear'd
> Of being tyrannous, since we so openly
> Proceed in justice . . .   (iii. ii. 4)

His fear, as before, marks a recognition; the tyranny in his soul he would film over by a show of judicial procedure. Hermione's defence is characterized by lucidity and reason; her 'integrity' (iii. ii. 27) is in every syllable; she is expostulating as with a nervous invalid. She wields a martyr-like strength:

> But thus : if powers divine
> Behold our human actions, as they do,
> I doubt not then but innocence shall make
> False accusation blush, and tyranny
> Tremble at patience.   (iii. ii. 29)

She aims to increase his already obvious discomfort; that is, to appeal to his 'conscience' (iii. ii. 47). She is being condemned by his 'dreams' (iii. ii. 82); we should say 'fantasies'. Her language grows more and more coldly convincing:

> Sir, spare your threats :
> The bug which you would fright me with I seek.

To me can life be no commodity :
The crown and comfort of my life, your favour,
I do give lost ; for I do feel it gone,
But know not how it went. My second joy,
And first-fruits of my body, from his presence
I am barr'd, like one infectious. My third comfort,
Starr'd most unluckily, is from my breast,
The innocent milk in its most innocent mouth,
Hail'd out to murder . . .   (III. ii. 92)

Notice the vivid physical perception and nature-feeling in 'first-fruits' and 'milk'; we shall find such phrases elsewhere. The calm yet condemnatory scorn of Hermione's manner shows a close equivalence to that of Queen Katharine on trial in *Henry VIII* (II. iv.). Both are daughters of a foreign king suffering in a strange home. Hermione is 'a great king's daughter' (III. ii. 40), daughter of 'the emperor of Russia' (III ii. 120–4): compare *Henry VIII*, II. iv. 13, 46; III. i. 81–2, 142–50. Both appeal, with a similarly climactic effect, to the highest known authority, Queen Katharine to the Pope and Hermione to the Oracle:

                    . . . but for mine honour
Which I would free, if I shall be condemn'd
Upon surmises, all proofs sleeping else
But what your jealousies awake, I tell you
'Tis rigour and not law. Your honours all,
I do refer me to the oracle :
Apollo be my judge !   (III. ii. 111)

The request is granted by one of the lords : in the ritual of both trials the King is half felt as a subject before the majesty of law.

So Cleomenes and Dion swear on a ' sword of justice' (III. ii. 125) that the 'holy seal' (III. ii. 130) is intact; and the package is opened. Hermione and Polixenes are cleared and Leontes revealed as 'a jealous tyrant', who must live 'without an heir if that which is lost be not found' (III. ii. 133–7). Truth is thus vindicated by the voice of supreme judgement accusing Leontes of lawless tyranny; but the devil in him is not easily exorcized. At first he will not submit; asserts blasphemously that 'there is no truth at all in the oracle' (III. ii. 141); probably seizes the paper and tears it to shreds, insisting that the trial

continue, thereby revealing his utter subjection of justice to the
egotistic will. But now, following sharply on his impious dis-
regard, comes news of Mamilius' death. No dramatic incident
in Shakespeare falls with so shattering an impact; no reversal
is more poignant than when, after a moment's dazedness,
Leontes' whole soul-direction changes:

> Apollo's angry ; and the heavens themselves
> Do strike at my injustice.   (III. ii. 147)

Great nature, the giver of children, can as easily recall them:
that nature is, here, the transcendent Apollo, who both guides
and judges. Leontes' crime, be it noted, is one of 'injustice'.
Hermione faints and is taken away by Paulina.

Leontes next speaks two revealing phrases: 'I have', he
mutters, 'too much believed mine own suspicion'; he admits
'being transported by my jealousies' (III. ii. 152, 159). He has
allowed himself to be temporarily possessed, dominated, by
something in himself which, given power, has 'transported'
him, that is, changed his nature as by magic (cp. 'translated' at
A Midsummer Night's Dream, III. i. 125). By this inward
usurpation the essence of tryanny and injustice has lodged in
him, only to be exorcized by the violent impact of his crime's
actual result: Mamilius' illness was first brought on by Hermione's disgrace (II. iii. 13–17). Now Leontes, having awakened from his delirious dream, speaks with a new simplicity:

> Apollo, pardon
> My great profaneness 'gainst thine oracle !
> I'll reconcile me to Polixenes,
> New woo my queen, recall the good Camillo . . .
>   (III. ii. 154)

But his punishment is not over. Paulina returns, and with a
long speech of considered vehemence says exactly what wants
saying, because now only can its import register:

> What studied torments, tyrant, hast for me ?
> What wheels ? racks ? fires ? What flaying ? or what
>   boiling
> In leads, or oils ? what old or newer torture
> Must I receive, whose every word deserves
> To taste of thy most worst ?   (III. ii. 176)

Suggestion of tyranny here reaches its climax; though Paulina refers to 'thy tyranny together working with thy jealousies' (III. ii. 180), they are two aspects of one reality, one complex, from which Leontes' actions have flowed. Paulina, comparing him to a devil (III. ii. 193), lists his crimes, with bitter irony suggesting (what is a half-truth) that they are none of them his fault; and concluding with news of Hermione's death and a demand for vengeance from Heaven. Throughout, she is playing on his conscience; more—she is his conscience.

Hermione, she says, is dead, and the man who could resurrect her must needs be worshipped as a god (III. ii. 208):

> But, O thou tyrant !
> Do not repent these things, for they are heavier
> Than all thy woes can stir ; therefore betake thee
> To nothing but despair. A thousand knees
> Ten thousand years together, naked, fasting
> Upon a barren mountain, and still winter
> In storm perpetual, could not move the gods
> To look that way thou wert. (III. ii. 208)

The association of winter and penitence, though not itself new (see *Love's Labour Lost*, v. ii. 798–815), assumes here a new precision. Paulina's voice, so hated before, now matches Leontes' own thoughts and is accordingly desired:

> Go on, go on ;
> Thou can'st not speak too much : I have deserv'd
> All tongues to talk their bitterest. (III. ii. 215)

Rebuked for her forwardness, she answers:

> I am sorry for't :
> All faults I make, when I shall come to know them
> I do repent. (III. ii. 219)

She is, indeed, repentance incarnate: that is her dramatic office. Now she recognizes that Leontes is 'touch'd to the noble heart' (III. ii. 222), nobility, in the chivalric tradition, involving Christian virtues; but, in apologizing for reminding him of what he 'should forget', she only further defines her office; and the more she emphasizes and lists the sorrows she will not refer to, the loss of Leontes' queen and children, as well as her own lord, the more she drives home on him his grief (III. ii.

223–33). He, however, prefers 'truth' to 'pity'; would live into, perhaps through, the purgation of remorse; and ends speaking of the 'chapel' where his queen and son are to be buried, and where he will attend in sorrow so long as 'nature' gives him strength (III. ii. 233–43). His last words hold a subdued dignity; his speech is calm and lucid; he is now, as never before, kingly.

No full-length Shakespearian tragedy reaches the intensity of these three acts: they move with a whirling, sickening, speed. Leontes is more complex than Othello as a study of jealousy and more realistically convincing than Macbeth as a study of evil possession. In him are blended the Renaissance, man-born, evil projected through Iago and the medieval supernaturalism of the Weird Sisters. He and his story also include both the personal, family, interest of *Othello* and the communal, tyrannic, theme of *Macbeth*, whilst defining their relation; that is, the relation of emotional and sexual unhealth to tyranny; hence the repeated emphasis here on 'tyrant' and the opposing concepts of justice and constitutional law. Macbeth's crime is an act of lustful possessiveness to be contrasted (as I have shown at length in *The Imperial Theme* and *The Shakespearian Tempest*) with the creative kingship of Banquo in association with child-images and nature; while conjugal jealousy is a concentrated exaggeration of domestic ownership and domination, sexually impelled. Each dramatic theme is enriched by mingling with the other, and we accordingly find Leontes marking an advance in Shakespeare's human delineation: the poetic and philosophic overtones of Hamlet, Lear and Timon are compressed into a study as sharply defined as the Nurse in *Romeo and Juliet* and as objectively diagnosed as Ford, Malvolio and Parolles. Hence the violent detonation.[1]

The play's morality interest, though less surface-patent than that of *Pericles*, will be clear. But a warning is necessary. Though Shakespeare writes, broadly speaking, from a Christian standpoint, and though christianized phraseology recurs, yet the poet is rather to be supposed as using Christian con-

---

[1] My own stage experience suggests that Leontes demands more nervous energy of the actor than Macbeth, Othello, Lear or Timon. This new realism depends partly on a new restriction in imagery. In the Histories persons use figurative language often glaringly 'out of character'; in the Tragedies there remain serious discrepancies. The Final Plays show, normally, a satisfying coalescence. See also W. H. Clemen's *The Development of Shakespeare's Imagery*.

cepts than as dominated by them. They are implemental to his purpose; but so too are 'great Apollo' and 'great nature', sometimes themselves approaching Biblical feeling (with Apollo as Jehovah), yet diverging also, especially later, into a pantheism of such majesty that orthodox apologists may well be tempted to call it Christian too; but it is scarcely orthodox. *The Winter's Tale* remains a creation of the Renaissance, that is, of the questing imagination, firmly planted, no doubt, in medieval tradition, but not directed by it. There is a distinction here of importance.

And now, as an echo to our court-tragedy, our action enters, as it were, the elemental background of all tragedy; the wild and rugged Bohemian coast, with threatening storm. We are behind the scenes, where the organizing powers fabricate our human plot. The skies are ominous, as though Heaven were angry at the work in hand (iii. iii. 3–5), for Antigonus, exactly obeying Leontes' command, has brought the child to this 'remote and desert place', where 'chance may nurse or end it' (ii. iii. 175, 182). It is to be thrown on the mercies of nature:

> Come on, poor babe :
> Some powerful spirit instruct the kites and ravens
> To be thy nurses ! Wolves and bears, they say,
> Casting their savageness aside have done
> Like offices of pity.   (ii. iii. 184)

The ruling powers have, however, themselves taken charge, directing Antigonus to this fierce and rugged spot. 'Their sacred wills be done' (iii. iii. 7), he says. He recounts how Hermione has appeared to him in a dream, 'in pure white robes, like very sanctity'—again a forecast of Queen Katharine —so that he regarded her as a 'spirit' come from the 'dead'; and tells how she directed him to leave the child in Bohemia. The dream was so convincing that it seemed more real than 'slumber'; and he therefore deduces that Hermione 'hath suffer'd death' and that, the child being in truth Polixenes', it is Apollo's will it be left in his kingdom (iii. iii. 15–45). He is wrong about the child, but right about Hermione; or again wrong as to both. His ghostly account, with its suggestion of present deity, is the more powerful for the inhuman grandeur of its setting. So, either 'for life or death', he leaves the baby upon the 'earth' of this inhospitable place; buries it, as a seed, to live or die, praying, 'Blossom, speed thee well'; entrusting it to forces beyond man's control, while hoping that the treasure he leaves may help to 'breed' it (III. iii. 40–8). The child is enduring, as it were, a second birth, with the attendant risks, the synchronization of storm and birth recalling *Pericles*. The spot is, as we have been told, famous for its beasts of prey. The storm starts and Antigonus is chased off by a bear.

The incident is as crude as the sudden entry of pirates in *Pericles*. But, as so often there, Shakespeare is moulding events from his own past imagery. His recurrent association of tempests with rough beasts, especially bears (as at *King Lear*, III. iv. 9–11), is here actualized: the storm starts, the bear appears, and we have a description of shipwreck. We must take the bear seriously, as suggesting man's insecurity in face of untamed nature; indeed, mortality in general.

This scene is a hinge not only for the story but also for the life-views it expresses. We are plunged first into the abysmal smithies below or behind creation, in touch with ghostly presences and superhuman powers; but next, as one dream dissolves into another, we pass from horror to simple, rustic, comedy. We met a precisely similar transition in *Pericles*, where the fishermen fulfilled an office closely resembling that of the Shepherd and Clown here: in both homely rusticity is synchronized and contrasted with storm and shipwreck. There is, however, no satire here in the rustics' talk, except for the Shepherd's opening remark on the behaviour of men between sixteen and three and twenty, always 'getting wenches with child, wronging the ancientry, stealing, fighting' (III. iii. 58–62), which recalls Thersites, whilst continuing our present obsession with birth and age; but there is no more of it. More important are the two lost sheep which he expects to find by the sea 'browsing of ivy' (III. iii. 68): it is somehow very reassuring to find the simple fellow at his homely job after our recent terrors with their appalling sense of human insecurity. Both the Shepherd and his son are thoroughly at home in this weird place; its awe-inspiring quality fades, as memory of nightmare before the heavy step and traffic of dawn. Bears are no terror to them, they know their ways: 'they are never curst but when they are hungry' (III. iii. 135). The scene wakes

into semi-humorous prose, sturdy commonsense, and simple
kindliness.

There is the usual mismanagement of words typical of
Shakespeare's clowns, but the humour soon takes a new turn
in the son's exquisite description of the wreck and Antigonus'
death, subtly veiling the horror and removing its sting. Tragedy
is confronted by comedy working in close alliance with birth:

> Heavy matters ! heavy matters ! but look thee here, boy. Now
> bless thyself : thou mettest with things dying, I with things new
> born.   (III. iii. 115)

The baby is found with a casket of gold. The Shepherd calls it
a 'changeling' and attributes his luck to the 'fairies' (III. iii.
121–2). So the craggy setting is lit by the glow of 'fairy gold'
(III. iii. 127). We have entered a new, and safer, world.

II

Time as chorus functions normally with certain obvious
apologies recalling Gower in *Pericles* (IV. iv.) and at least one
touch in Gower's style: 'what of her ensues I list not prophecy'
(IV. chor. 25). A crucial phrase occurs at the start:

> I, that please some, try all, both joy and terror
> Of good and bad, that make and unfold error,
> Now take upon me, in the name of Time,
> To use my wings . . .   (IV. chor. 1)

'Make and unfold error' links *The Winter's Tale* to the earlier
comedies which, though less deeply loaded with tragic meaning, regularly hold tragic reference in close relation to 'error',
and finally drive the action to a formal conclusion in which
mistakes are rectified.

The Winter's Tale presents a contrast of sinful maturity and
nature-guarded youth in close association with seasonal change.
But there is more to notice. Shakespeare's genius is labouring
to pit his own more positive intuitions, expressed hitherto
mainly through happy-ending romance and comedy, against
tragedy: they are to work as redeeming forces. The idyll of
Florizel and Perdita will fall naturally into place : but romance
in Shakespeare regularly enjoys the support, or at least the

company, of humour. In Leontes Shakespeare's tragic art has reached a new compactness and intensity; and now in our next scenes, he gives us a figure of absolute comedy, Autolycus.

Richest humour offers a recognition of some happy universal resulting from the carefree stripping away of cherished values: elsewhere[1] I have compared such 'golden', or sympathetic, humour, of which Falstaff is an obvious example, with humour of the critical, moralistic, Jonsonian, sort, such as that Shakespeare touches in Malvolio. Falstaff, though utterly unmoral, yet solicits our respect, and in that recognition consists the fun. The fun itself is, moreover, in essence a lark-like thing; it will sing, or dance, and may elsewhere house itself in spring-frolic and lyrical verse, such as 'It was a lover and his lass . . .' introduced by Touchstone in *As You Like It* (v. iii.). Autolycus is a blend of burly comedian and lyrical jester.

He enters singing verses redolent of spring:

> When daffodils begin to peer,
>   With heigh ! the doxy over the dale,
> Why, then comes in the sweet o' the year ;
>   For the red blood reigns in the winter's pale.
>
> (IV. ii. 1)

He is spring incarnate; carefree, unmoral, happy, and sets the note for a spring-like turn in our drama, reversing the spring and winter conclusion of Shakespeare's first comedy, *Love's Labour's Lost*. His following stanzas continue with references to country linen on the hedge (cp. *Love's Labour's Lost*, v. ii. 914), songbirds, tooth-ache, ale, the lark and jay, 'summer songs for me and my aunts', hay-merriment: it is a glorious medley of inconsequential realistic rusticity. Suddenly he comments in prose:

> I have served Prince Florizel and in my time wore
> three-pile; but now I am out of service.   (IV. ii. 13)

He interrupts himself only to drop again into song—'But shall I go mourn for that, my dear?' Like Touchstone, and Poor Tom in *King Lear*, he has seen better days, but remains happy, his thoughts slipping naturally into song. He next explains his profession of minor thief, off the high road, as 'a snapper up of unconsidered trifles' (IV. ii. 26).

---

[1] In writing of Byron in *The Burning Oracle*.

His play with the Clown is supremely satisfying, and far more convincing than most stage trickery (e.g. Iago's of Cassio, Roderigo and Othello). The Clown is presented as a thorough gull, though not inhumanly so, as is Sir Andrew or Roderigo. Every phrase tells. As the supposedly injured man is carefully lifted—'O! good sir, tenderly, O!' (iv. ii. 76)—his purse is being delicately manœuvred within reach; the victim's attention is meanwhile firmly directed away from the danger-zone—'I fear, sir, my shoulder blade is out' (iv. ii. 78); and, when the business is successfully accomplished, there is the delightful *double entendre*, 'You ha' done me a charitable office' (iv. ii. 82). Shakespeare's last work often recalls the New Testament, and here we have, in Autolycus' account of his beating, robbery and loss of clothes, a clear parody of the parable of the Good Samaritan, the pattern being completed by the Clown's continuation, 'Dost lack any money? I have a little money for thee' (iv. ii. 83), and Autolycus' hurried and anxious disclaimer, 'No, good sweet sir: no, I beseech you, sir . . . Offer me no money, I pray you! that kills my heart' (iv. iii. 85). There follows Autolycus' description of himself with some rather ordinary court-satire and finally the delightful conclusion, crying out for stage-realization:

Clown. How do you now ?
Autolycus. Sweet sir, much better than I was : I can stand and walk. I will even take my leave of you, and pace softly towards my kinsman's.
Clown. Shall I bring thee on the way ?
Autolycus. No, good-faced sir ; no, sweet sir.
Clown. Then fare thee well : I must go buy spices for our sheep-shearing. (iv. iii. 119)

'Softly' is spoken with an upward lilt of the voice. Autolycus is a sweet, smooth-voiced rogue. The Clown says his last speech to the audience with a broad grin on his vacant face. When he is gone, Autolycus takes one agile skip, then:

> Jog on, jog on, the footpath way
> And merrily hent the stile-a :
> A merry heart goes all the day
> Your sad tires in a mile-a. (iv. iii. 133)

The incident circles back to its start, enclosed in melody. It is

all utterly unmoral, as unmoral as the scents of spring. This
might well be called the most convincing, entertaining, and
profound piece of comedy in Shakespeare. Such personal
judgements are necessarily of doubtful interest, except to help
point my argument that, so far from relaxing, Shakespeare's
art is, on every front, advancing.

The sheep-shearing scene similarly sums up and surpasses
all Shakespeare's earlier poetry of pastoral and romance. It is
nevertheless—this is typical of our later plays—characterized
by a sharp realism. The Clown's shopping list has already
built a sense of simple cottage housekeeping and entertainment, with a suggestion of something out-of-the-ordinary in
his supposed sister, Perdita:

> Three pound of sugar ; five pound of currants ; rice. What will
> this sister of mine do with rice ? But my father hath made her
> mistress of the feast, and she lays it on.   (IV. ii. 40)

His following reference to psalm-singing puritans sticks out
awkwardly; more in place are the 'nosegays' and 'raisins o' the
sun' (IV. iii. 43–53), especially the last. Autolycus has already
sung of the 'red blood' reigning after winter (IV. ii. 4), and
soon our merry-makers are to be 'red with mirth' (IV. iii. 54).
We are to watch a heightening of English country festivity,
touched with Mediterranean warmth, something, to quote
Keats,

> Tasting of Flora and the country green,
> Dance, and Provençal song, and sun-burnt mirth.

So we move from spring to summer, under a burning sun.

The sun has not been so honoured before.[1] We have known
the moon-silvered encounters of Romeo and Juliet and glim-
mering tangles of the 'wood near Athens'; also the cypress
shadows of *Twelfth Night* and chequered glades of Arden; but
never before, not even in *Antony and Cleopatra*—a necessary
step, where sun-warmth was, however, felt mainly through
description, the action itself searching rather for 'gaudy' (III.
xi. 182) or moonlit nights—never before has the sun been so
dramatically awakened, so close to us, as here; and there is a

---

[1] The heavy emphasis in *Love's Labour's Lost* remains throughout imagistic, in the manner
of the Sonnets. This early play does much to define both the positive end of Shakespeare's
work and the reasons for its postponement. See my remarks in *The Shakespearian Tempest*.

corresponding advance in love poetry, compassing, though with no loss of magic, strong fertility suggestion and a new, daylight assurance:

> These your unusual weeds to each part of you
> Do give a life : no shepherdess, but Flora
> Peering in April's front. This your sheep-shearing
> Is as a meeting of the petty gods,
> And you the queen on't.   (IV. iii. 1)

So speaks Prince Florizel. But Perdita's answer witnesses both her country simplicity and feminine wisdom; she fears, as does Juliet, love's rashness and insecurity. Nearly all Shakespeare's love-heroines, following the pattern laid down by Venus' prophecy in *Venus and Adonis* (1135–64), are given tragic undertones; they have an aura of tragedy about them. Florizel's love is more confident and showy (as usual in Shakespeare), but his use of mythology, as in 'Flora' above, has a new, and finely convincing, impact. He catalogues the gods who have disguised themselves for love: Jupiter as a bellowing bull, Neptune a bleating lamb and, giving highest poetic emphasis to our play's supreme deity,

> the fire-rob'd god,
> Golden Apollo, a poor humble swain
> As I seem now.   (IV. iii. 29)

'O Lady Fortune', prays Perdita in a phrase reminiscent of *Pericles*, 'stand you auspicious' (IV. iii. 51). Though she remains doubtful, her doubts, a mixture of shyness and hardheaded feminine realism, only make the poetry more poignant. So, too, do the many homely reminders, as in the old shepherd's reminiscences of his dead wife's busy behaviour as hostess on such festival days as this, cooking, serving, and dancing in turn, bustling about, 'her face o' fire' (IV. iii. 60) with both exertion and refreshment. Now Perdita, following Thaisa at the court of Simonides (the repetition is close, both fathers similarly reminding their apparently shy daughters of their duties), is 'mistress of the feast' (IV. iii. 68; cp. 'queen of the feast' at *Pericles* II. iii. 17), and has to conquer her shyness.

There follows Perdita's important dialogue with Polixenes. She, rather like Ophelia in a very different context, is presenting posies according to the recipient's age and offers the two

older men (Polixenes and Camillo wear white beards, IV. iii.
417) rosemary and rue, which, she says, keep their savour 'all
the winter long' (IV. iii. 75): notice the recurring emphasis on
age and seasons. But Polixenes (forgetting his disguise?)
appears to resent being given 'flowers of winter' (IV. iii. 79)
and Perdita gracefully apologizes for not having an autumnal
selection:

Perdita.   Sir, the year growing ancient,
           Not yet on summer's death, nor on the birth
           Of trembling winter, the fairest flowers o' the season
           Are our carnations, and streak'd gillyvors,
           Which some call nature's bastards : of that kind
           Our rustic garden's barren, and I care not
           To get slips of them.

Polixenes.   Wherefore, gentle maiden,
           Do you neglect them ?

Perdita.   For I have heard it said
           There is an art which in their piedness shares
           With great creating nature.

Polixenes.   Say there be ;
           Yet nature is made better by no mean
           But nature makes that mean ; so, over that art,
           Which you say adds to nature, is an art
           That nature makes. You see, sweet maid, we marry
           A gentler scion to the wildest stock,
           And make conceive a bark of baser kind
           By bud of nobler race ; this is an art
           Which does mend nature, change it rather, but
           The art itself is nature.

Perdita.   So it is.

Polixenes. Then make your garden rich in gillyvors
           And do not call them bastards.

Perdita.   I'll not put
           The dibble in earth to set one slip of them ;
           No more than, were I painted, I would wish
           This youth should say, 'twere well, and only therefore
           Desire to breed by me. Here's flowers for you ;
           Hot lavender, mints, savory, marjoram ;
           The marigold, that goes to bed wi' the sun,
           And with him rises weeping : these are flowers
           Of middle summer, and I think they are given
           To men of middle age. You're very welcome.

Camillo.   I should leave grazing, were I of your flock
                And only live by gazing.
Perdita.   Out, alas !
                You'd be so lean, that blasts of January
                Would blow you through and through.   (IV. iii. 79)

Of this one could say much. Notice first, the continued emphasis on seasons at the opening and concluding lines of my
quotation; the strong physical realism (recalling Hermione's
defence) in Perdita's use of 'breed'; and the phrase 'great
creating nature' (to be compared with 'great nature' earlier, at
II. ii. 60).

The speakers are at cross purposes, since one is referring to
art, the other to artificiality, itself a difficult enough distinction.
The whole question of the naturalist and transcendental antinomy is accordingly raised. The art concerned is called natural
by Polixenes in that either (i) human invention can never do
more than direct natural energy, or (ii) the human mind and
therefore its inventions are nature-born: both meanings are
probably contained. Human civilization, art and religion are
clearly in one sense part of 'great creating nature', and so is
everything else. But Perdita takes her stand on natural simplicity, growing from the unforced integrity of her own country
up-bringing, in opposition to the artificialities of, we may suggest, the court: she is horrified at dishonouring nature by
human trickery. Observe that both alike reverence 'great
creating nature', though differing in their conclusions. No
logical deduction is to be drawn; or rather, the logic is dramatic,
made of opposing statements, which serve to conjure up an
awareness of nature as an all-powerful presence, at once con-
troller and exemplar. The dialogue forms accordingly a
microcosm of our whole drama.

There is a certain irony, too, in Polixenes' defence of exactly
the type of love-mating which Florizel and Perdita are planning
for themselves. Polixenes is, perhaps, setting a trap; or may be
quite unconsciously arguing against his own later behaviour.
Probably the latter.

Perdita next turns to Florizel:

Perdita.   Now, my fair'st friend,
                I would I had some flowers o' the spring that might
                Become your time of day ; and yours, and yours,

That wear upon your virgin branches yet
Your maidenheads growing : O Proserpina !
For the flowers now that frighted thou let'st fall
From Dis's waggon ! daffodils
That come before the swallow dares, and take
The winds of March with beauty ; violets dim,
But sweeter than the lids of Juno's eyes
Or Cytherea's breath ; pale prim-roses
That die unmarried ere they can behold
Bright Phoebus in his strength, a malady
Most incident to maids ; bold oxlips and
The crown imperial ; lilies of all kinds,
The flower-de-luce being one. O ! these I lack
To make you garlands of, and my sweet friend,
To strew him o'er and o'er!

Florizel.   What ! like a corse ?
Perdita.   No, like a bank for love to lie and play on ;
Not like a corse ; or if—not to be buried,
But quick and in mine arms. Come, take your flowers :
Methinks I play as I have seen them do
In Whitsun pastorals : sure this robe of mine
Does change my disposition.   (IV. iii. 112)

Reference to the season-myth of Proserpine is natural enough, and almost an essential. You might call Perdita herself a seed sowed in winter and flowering in summer. 'Take' = 'charm', or 'enrapture'. Though Autolycus' first entry suggested spring, we are already, as the nature of our festival and these lines declare, in summer. Note the fine union, even identity, of myth and contemporary experience, finer than in earlier Shakespearian pastorals: Dis may be classical, but his 'wagon' is as real as a wagon in Hardy. See, too, how classical legend and folk-lore coalesce in the primroses and 'bright Phoebus in his strength', a phrase pointing the natural poetic association of sun-fire and mature love (as in *Antony and Cleopatra*): the sun corresponding, as it were, to physical fruition (as the moon to the more operatic business of wooing) and accordingly raising in Perdita, whose poetry is strongly impregnated with fertility-suggestion (the magic here is throughout an earth-magic, a sun-magic), a wistful aside, meant presumably for herself. Perdita's flower-poetry reaches a royal impressionism in 'crown imperial' and 'garland' suiting the speaker's innate, and indeed actual, royalty. The contrasting suggestion of 'corse' quickly merging into a love-embrace (reminiscent of the love and death associations in *Antony and Cleopatra* and Keats) finally serves to heighten the pressure of exuberant, buoyant, life. The 'Whitsun pastorals', like our earlier puritans, though perhaps historically extraneous, may be forgiven for their lively impact, serving to render the speech vivid with the poet's, and hence, somehow, our own, personal experience.

Perdita's royalty is subtly presented: her robes as mistress of the feast have, as she said, made her act and speak strangely. Florizel details each of her graces (iv. iii. 135–43), wishing her in turn to speak, to sing, to dance—as 'a wave o' the sea'—for ever. He would have her every action perpetuated, the thought recalling Polixenes' recollections of himself and Leontes as 'boy eternal' (i. ii. 65). Florizel has expressed a delight in the given instant of youthful grace so sacred that it somehow deserves eternal status; when she moves he would have her, in a phrase itself patterning the blend of motion and stillness it describes, 'move still, still so'. Watching her, he sees the universe completed, crowned, at each moment of her existence:

> Each your doing,
> So singular in each particular,
> Crowns what you are doing in the present deed,
> That all your acts are queens. (iv. iii. 143)

As once before, we are reminded, this time more sharply, of Blake's 'minute particulars'. The royalistic tonings here and in the 'crown imperial' of her own speech (iv. iii. 126) not merely hint Perdita's royal blood, but also serve to stamp her actions with eternal validity; for the crown is always to be understood as a symbol piercing the eternity dimension. We are, it is true, being forced into distinctions that Shakespeare, writing from a royalistic age, need not actually have surveyed; but Florizel's lines certainly correspond closely to those in *Pericles* imaging Marina as a palace 'for the crown'd Truth to dwell in' and again as monumental Patience 'gazing on kings' graves' and 'smiling extremity out of act' (*Pericles*, v. i. 123, 140). Perdita is more lively; time, creation, nature, earth, all have more rights here than in *Pericles*; but the correspondence remains close.

Perdita's acts are royal both in their own right and also because she is, in truth, of royal birth:

> This is the prettiest low-born lass that ever
> Ran on the green-sward. Nothing she does or seems
> But smacks of something greater than herself,
> Too noble for this place. (IV. iii. 156)

But this is not the whole truth. Later, after Polixenes' outburst, she herself makes a comment more easily appreciated in our age than in Shakespeare's:

> I was not much afeard ; for once or twice
> I was about to speak and tell him plainly,
> The self-same sun that shines upon his court
> Hides not his visage from our cottage, but
> Looks on alike. (IV. iii. 455)

The lovely New Testament transposition (with 'sun' for 'rain') serves to underline the natural excellence and innate worth of this simple rustic community; and only from some such recognition can we make full sense of the phrase 'queen of curds and cream' (IV. iii. 161). We may accordingly re-group our three royalties in terms of (i) Perdita's actual descent, (ii) her natural excellence and (iii) that more inclusive category from which both descend, or to which both aspire, in the eternity-dimension. A final conclusion would reach some concept of spiritual royalty corresponding to Wordsworth's (in his *Immortality Ode*); with further political implications concerning the expansion of sovereignty among a people.

The lovers are, very clearly, felt as creatures of 'rare'—the expected word recurs (IV. iii. 32)—excellence, and their love, despite its strong fertility contacts, is correspondingly pure. Perdita, hearing Florizel's praises, fears he woos her 'the false way' (IV. iii. 151); while Florizel is equally insistent that his 'desires run not before his honour', nor his 'lusts burn hotter' than his 'faith' (IV. iii. 33). The statement, which appears, as in *The Tempest* later, a trifle laboured, is clearly central: Perdita, as mistress of the feast, insists that Autolycus 'use no scurrilous words in's tunes' (IV. iii. 215). Our first tragedy was precipitated by suspicion of marital infidelity; and our young lovers express a corresponding purity.

The action grows more rollicking, with a dance of 'shepherds and shepherdesses' (IV. iii. 165) in which Perdita and Florizel join. There follows Autolycus' spectacular entry as musical pedlar, preceded by a rich description (IV. iii. 191–201) of his rowdy-merry catches and tunes ('jump her and thump her', 'whoop! do me no harm, good man'). He enters all a-flutter with ribbons and a tray of good things and describes his absurd ballads to the awe-struck Mopsa and Dorcas. Though the words may not be scurrilous, the songs are ribald enough, one telling of a usurer's wife 'brought to bed of twenty money-bags at a burden'; and another sung originally by a fish representing a woman 'who would not exchange flesh with one that loved her' and had been metamorphosed in punishment (IV. iii. 265, 282). They are little burlesques of our main fertility-myth, stuck in as gargoyles on a cathedral, and the two girls' anxious enquiries as to whether the stories are true, with Autolycus' firm reassurances, serve to complete the parody. Finally Autolycus conducts and joins in a catch, followed by another dance of 'twelve rustics, habited like satyrs' (IV. iii. 354), given by carters, shepherds, neatherds, and swineherds. Here our rough country fun, heavily toned for fertility, reaches its climax.

But nature continues to provide poetry as refined as Florizel's image of winter purity (winter is also present in Autolycus' 'lawn as white as driven snow' at IV. iii. 220):

> I take thy hand ; this hand,
> As soft as dove's down, and as white as it,
> Or Ethiopian's tooth, or the fann'd snow that's bolted
> By the northern blasts twice o'er.   (IV. iii. 374)

As in Keats' 'Bright Star' sonnet, human love is compared to the steadfast gazing on earth, or sea, of heavenly light:

> He says he loves my daughter :
> I think so too ; for never gaz'd the moon
> Upon the water as he'll stand and read
> As 'twere my daughter's eyes . . .   (IV. iii. 171)

This (with which we should compare the similar love-imagery of *Love's Labour's Lost*, IV. iii. 27–42) parallels Leontes' picture of Mamilius' 'welkin eye' followed by fears for the 'centre' (i.e. of the earth), forming an association of emotional and universal stability (I. ii. 137, 139); and also his later contrast and identification of 'nothing' with 'the world and all that's in it' and the 'covering sky' (I. ii. 293–4). The universal majesty is continually imagined concretely as earth and sky facing each other, as in Leontes' 'plainly as heaven sees earth or earth sees heaven' (I. ii. 315); it is the universe we actually know and see, without the cosmic, spheral, idealizing emphasis of *Antony and Cleopatra* and (once) *Pericles*. So Florizel, questioned by Polixenes, calls the universe as witness to his love:

> . . . and he, and more
> Than he, or men, the earth, the heavens, and all . . .
> (IV. iii. 383)

Should he prove false, then

> Let nature crush the sides o' the earth together
> And mar the seeds within !   (IV. iii. 491)

Though reminiscent of nature's 'germens' in *King Lear* (III. ii. 8), those 'seeds' belong especially to this, as to no other, play. The emphasis on earth's creativeness is repeated:

> Not for Bohemia, nor the pomp that may
> Be thereat glean'd, for all the sun sees or
> The close earth wombs or the profound sea hides
> In unknown fathoms, will I break my oath
> To this my fair belov'd.   (IV. iii. 501)

The sun, as the moon before, is thought as 'seeing'; it is the 'eye' of heaven of Sonnet XVIII. The sun is constantly reverenced throughout *The Winter's Tale*, either directly (as in 'welkin eye' etc.) or 'the fire-rob'd god, golden Apollo' (IV. iii. 29) and his oracle. Nature here is creative, majestic, something of illimitable mystery and depth ('profound sea', 'unknown fathoms'); but it is never bookish. Nor is it dissolved into any system of elements. Earth, sea, sun and moon are felt rather as concrete realities of normal experience, nearer Renaissance commonsense than Dantesque or Ptolemaic harmonies, whilst housing strong classical-mythological powers.

As for Polixenes' brutal interruption, we recall Capulet, Egeus, York, Polonius, Lear: Shakespeare's fathers are normally tyrannical and Polixenes has, according to his lights, cause. His threats, excessive as Capulet's, drive home a contrast of social tyranny with rustic health, clinched by Perdita's admirable comment already noticed: there is court satire elsewhere (as at IV. ii. 94–101; IV. iii. 723–6). Of course, this contrast works within, without disrupting, the prevailing royalism: apart from the old shepherd, the country folk are mainly represented by three fools and a knave.

The pastoral interest slackens and significant passages become less dense as we become involved in the rather heavy machinery of getting everyone to Sicilia. Both Camillo's tortuous scheme and Autolycus' additions to it lack conviction, and we suffer rather as in *Hamlet* during Claudius' and Laertes' long discussion about the Norman, Lamond. There is nevertheless some purpose in the sagging action of *Hamlet*,[1] whereas here we seem to be confronted by plot-necessity alone, though Autolycus' lengthy fooling with the Shepherd and Clown has a certain interest.

The dialogue not only protracts the sagging action, but rouses discomfort, Autolycus' description of the punishments awaiting the rustics, though pictorially in tone here (involving 'honey', 'wasps', midday sun, flies: IV. iii. 16–25), being a trifle unpleasant. Resenting Autolycus' fall from his first entry, one is tempted to dismiss the incident as an error. Autolycus is, however, being used to elaborate the vein of court satire already suggested by Polixenes' behaviour; it is almost a parody of that behaviour. The pick-pocket pedlar, now himself disguised as 'a great courtier' (IV. iii. 777), becomes absurdly superior and uses his new position to baffle the Clown precisely as Touchstone the courtier-fool baffles William. His elaborate description of torments is extremely cruel; but then the court—Polixenes' harshness fresh in our minds—is cruel.

But we can still disapprove the subordination of humour to satire; and yet this very subordination serves a further purpose concerned with the essence of humour itself. Autolycus is first a composite of spring music and delightful knavery; during the sheep-shearing festival he is a source of rather ribald entertainment and catchy song. Next, he goes off to sell his wares, and on his re-entry recounts his successful purse-picking,

[1] For a discussion of this 'sagging action' see 'Hamlet Reconsidered' in the enlarged (1949) edition of *The Wheel of Fire*.

which now wins from us less approval in view of our accumu-
lated concern for the simple people on whom he battens as a
dangerous parasite. He is later by chance forced to dress as
a courtier and further looks like making a good thing out of the
two rustics and their secret. He is advancing rapidly in the
social scale; the fates assist him. As he says,

> If I had a mind to be honest, I see Fortune would
> not suffer me : she drops booties in my mouth.
>
> (iv. iii. 868)

He is now all out for 'advancement' (iv. iii. 873). After don-
ning courtier's clothes, his humour takes an unnecessarily
cruel turn. Something similar happened with Falstaff, who, a
creature of pure humour (and also robbery) in Part I of *Henry
IV*, becomes less amusing in Part II where he has advanced
socially, wears fine clothes, and is tainted by a courtier's ambition.[1] He is himself subscribing to the very values which we
thought he scorned and our source of humour to that extent
weakened. The humorous parasite cannot afford to be too successful, any more than the saint. So with Autolycus : the merry
robber-tramp, as he makes his way, becomes less merry. His
vices become less amusing as he indulges his lust for power; as
his egotism expands, a cruel strain (compare Falstaff's attitude
to his recruits and Justice Shallow) is revealed; and he is at
once recognized as inferior to the society on which, as a happy-
go-lucky ragamuffin, he formerly preyed for our amusement.
More widely, we can say that the delicate balance of unmoral
humour—and no finer examples exist than the early Falstaff
and Autolycus—must be provisional only; it cannot maintain
the pace, cannot survive as a challenge among the summery
positives here enlisted against tragedy : Falstaff was, necessarily,
rejected by Prince Hal. Moreover, just as the Falstaff of
Henry IV becomes finally the buffoon of *The Merry Wives of
Windsor*, so Autolycus' last entry, when they have all arrived
in Sicilia, and the Shepherd and Clown are rich and he a recognized knave, is peculiarly revealing : we see him now bowing

---

[1] This contrast has been well exposed by Professor J. Dover Wilson in *The Fortunes of
Falstaff*. It is, however, there one strand only in a richer, satiric, design, with Falstaff
becoming more forceful as he loses humour.

and scraping to his former gull.[1] Meanwhile, our humorous
sympathies have passed over to the Clown, rather tipsy and
talking of himself as having recently become a 'gentleman born'
(v. ii. 142–64), so providing a new and richly amusing
variation in social comment.

The long scene (iv. iii.) accordingly has a falling movement;
from exquisite pastoral and the accompanying flower-dialogue,
through robust country merriment to an all but ugly humour.
The romance is to survive; not so Autolycus, who is to lose
dramatic dignity. No one will accuse Shakespeare of lacking
humour, but it is too often forgotten that his humour works
within the limits set by a prevailing 'high seriousness'.

III

Our final summing movement takes us back to Sicilia, where
all the people foregather and the complications are resolved.

Leontes is a figure of accomplished repentance. From now
on religious phraseology is insistent, with strong Christian
tonings:

> Sir, you have done enough, and have perform'd
> A saint-like sorrow ; no fault could you make
> Which you have not redeem'd ; indeed, paid down
> More penitence than done trespass. At the last,
> Do as the heavens have done, forget your evil ;
> With them forgive yourself.   (v. i. 1)

His kingdom, as the oracle foretold, is, through his own sin,
heirless (v. i. 10). The contrast in *Macbeth* between tyranny
without issue and Banquo's descendants may assist our response
to Leontes' punishment. Both heroes offend against creation
and are accordingly themselves uncreative. Paulina stands
beside him, a perpetual reminder, referring to Hermione as
'she you kill'd' (v. i. 15):

> *Leontes.*   I think so. Kill'd !
> She I kill'd ! I did so ; but thou strik'st me
> Sorely to say I did ; it is as bitter
> Upon thy tongue as in my thought. Now, good now
> Say so but seldom.   (v. i 16)

[1] There is a deplorable stage tradition that Autolycus should again, in this late scene, start
picking the purses of the Shepherd and Clown. The comedian will, of course, get his laughs ;
but for Shakespeare's opinion of such 'pitiful ambition' see Hamlet's address to the Players
(iii. ii. 50).

Paulina is here to personify Leontes' 'thought'. Cleomenes, who cannot be expected to consider her dramatic office, rebuffs her sharply; and Dion, in a speech (v. i. 24–34) loaded with regal and religious impressions ('sovereign name', 'his highness', 'royalty', 'holy', 'holier'), urges the King to marry to beget an heir. Paulina, however, demands respect to the gods' 'secret purposes' and the oracle of 'divine Apollo', which asserted that Leontes should remain heirless till his child was found (v. i. 35–40); and he, wishing he had always followed her counsel, agrees, while further imagining Hermione's return, in accusation. His remarriage, he says,

> Would make her sainted spirit
> Again possess her corpse and on this stage—
> Where we're offenders now—appear soul-vex'd,
> And begin, 'Why to me?'   (v. i. 57)

The world of sinful men is widely conceived; but also, ever so delicately, Hermione's return is hinted. Paulina next suggests that had his dead queen 'such power' (v. i. 60) of return, she would have full 'cause' of anger. Were she, Paulina, the ghost, she would shriek, point to his second wife's eyes, calling out, like the ghost in *Hamlet*, 'Remember mine' (v. i. 67):

> *Leontes.*   Stars, stars!
> And all eyes else dead coals.   (v. i. 67)

Leontes sits almost tranced, in a state of other-worldly remembrance, all but outside the temporal dimension. Paulina continues to play with the thought of Hermione's return. Leontes is not to marry

> unless another
> As like Hermione as is her picture,
> Affront his eye.   (v. i. 73)

His new wife shall be, she says, older than the first:

> She shall be such
> As, walk'd your first queen's ghost, it should take joy
> To see her in your arms.   (v. i. 79)

Leontes enters into the grave game, willingly agreeing not to marry till Paulina bids him, and she clinches the compact, whilst further preparing for the resurrection:

> That
> Shall be when your first queen's again in breath ;
> Never till then.   (v. i. 82)

Observe how carefully we are being prepared for the conclusion, our thoughts whetted, our minds subtly habituated, if not to its possibility, at least to its conceivability.

On the entry of Florizel and Perdita our most important impressions concern Perdita herself, given the usual praise accorded these later heroines: she is 'the rarest of all women' (v. i. 112), a 'goddess' (v. i. 131), a 'paragon' (v. i. 153), or—exactly suiting our recurring impressionism of earth and sun—'the most peerless piece of earth' 'that e'er the sun shone bright on' (v. i. 94). She reminds the tactless but purposeful Paulina of that 'jewel of children', Mamilius (v. i. 117). She is a creature

> Would she begin a sect, might quench the zeal
> Of all professors else, make proselytes
> Of who she but bid follow.   (v. i. 107)

Earthly and transcendental impressions intermix in her praise. Both recur together in Leontes':

> And you, fair princess—goddess ! O, alas !
> I lost a couple, that 'twixt heaven and earth
> Might thus have stood begetting wonder as
> You, gracious couple, do.   (v. i. 131)

Children, planted between heaven and earth, beget 'wonder', a word to be used later on for miraculous events. Children are copies of their parents:

> Your mother was most true to wedlock, prince ;
> For she did print your royal father off,
> Conceiving you.   (v. i. 124)

We remember Mamilius' resemblance to Leontes and Paulina's description of Leontes' baby daughter. Children are nature's miracles, and these two as welcome 'as is the spring to the earth' (v. i. 151). So Leontes prays that 'the blessed gods' may 'purge all infection from our air' whilst their stay lasts (v. i. 168), a phrase harking back to the description of Delphos, intimations of a transfigured nature matching our sense of a transfigured humanity. Man is, at his royal best, almost divine:

> You have a holy father,
> A graceful gentleman ; against whose person,
> So sacred as it is, I have done sin.
> For which the heavens, taking angry note
> Have left me issueless . . .   (v. i. 170)

The supreme punishment here, especially for a king, is to be left without natural issue; Florizel, however, lives, to render his father 'bless'd' (v. i. 174). Through the royalistic convention the poetry touches some truth concerning man, his high worth in the creative chain, his ultimate stature, that outdistances political concepts.

This semi-divine essence is also dependent on the creative love-faith of the young pair. Disaster dogs them. After surviving 'dreadful Neptune' (v. i. 154), they hear of Polixenes' pursuit. But, though 'Heaven set spies' (v. i. 203) on them; though the 'stars', in another typical image, will first 'kiss the valleys' (v. i. 206) before they be united; indeed, though Fortune appear as a 'visible enemy' (v. i. 216), their love is to remain firm. As Leontes gazes on Perdita, the stern Paulina remarks that his eye 'hath too much youth in't' (v. i. 225), and reminds him of Hermione. 'I thought of her', he answers, softly, 'even in these looks I made' (v. i. 227).

Leontes' reunion with his daughter is presented indirectly by the Gentlemen's conversation: it has already been dramatized in *Pericles* and our present dramatic emphasis is to fall on Hermione's resurrection. These gentlemen converse in a prose of courtly formality, leaving poetry to return in full contrast later. The scene is preparatory to the greater miracle and its style well-considered, introducing us lightly and at a distance to those deep emotions which we are soon to feel with so powerful a subjective sympathy. It strikes a realistic and contemporary note, using the well-known trick of laying solid foundations before an unbelievable event: we are being habituated to impossible reunions. Moreover, the slightly ornate decorum leads on to the formal, ritualistic, quality of the later climax. There is emphasis, as one expects, on Perdita's innate and actual royalty 'above her breeding' (v. ii. 41) and a comparison of earlier events to 'an old tale' (v. ii. 30, 67; cp. v. iii. 117).

The description, plastic rather than dramatic, serves to create a *sub specie aeternitatis* effect, and so further prepare us for the statue-scene:

> . . . They seemed almost, with staring on one another, to tear the cases of their eyes ; *there was speech in their dumbness, language in their very gesture* ; they looked as they had heard of *a world ransomed, or one destroyed* : a notable passion of *wonder* appeared in them ; but the wisest beholder, that knew no more but seeing, could not say if the importance were *joy or sorrow* ; but in the extremity of the one it must needs be. (v. ii. 12)

My italicized phrases are important. With the first compare the Poet's comment on a painting in *Timon of Athens*: 'To the dumbness of the gesture one might interpret . . .' (i. i. 34): see also *Cymbeline*, ii. iv. 83–5. The watchers are, to quote Milton, made 'marble with too much conceiving'; made to share the frozen immobility of art. Leontes' reaction to Hermione's statue is to be similar. Next, notice the apocalyptic suggestion of 'ransomed' and 'destroyed': is the miracle a transfiguration of nature or wholly transcendental? Certainly it strikes 'wonder'. Last, observe the indecisive reference to 'joy' and 'sorrow', which recurs again in description of Paulina:

> But O ! the noble combat that 'twixt joy and sorrow was fought in Paulina. She had one eye declined for the loss of her husband, another elevated that the oracle was fulfilled. (v. i. 80)

Exactly such a blend of joy and sorrow is to characterize our final scene. Though we are pointed to 'the dignity of this act' performed by kings and princes (v. ii. 88), it is all carried lightly, the dialogue following on with courtly fluency:

> One of the prettiest touches of all, and that which angled for mine eyes—caught the water though not the fish—was when at the relation of the queen's death, with the manner how she came to it . . . (v. ii. 91)

And yet the easy, almost bantering, manner can, without losing its identity, handle the most solemn emotions justly, as in the account of Leontes' confession:

> Who was most marble there changed colour; some swounded, all sorrowed ; if all the world could have seen it, the woe had been universal. (v. i. 100)

As in 'ransom'd' and 'redeem'd' earlier, the drama is, as it were, on the edge of something 'universal': we watch more than a particular incident.

Now this dialogue has been leading us on very carefully to its own little climax, directly preparatory to the play's conclusion:

> No ; the princess hearing of her mother's statue, which is in the keeping of Paulina—a piece many years in doing, and now newly performed by that rare Italian master, Julio Romano ; who, had he himself *eternity* and could put *breath* into his work, would beguile *Nature* of her custom, so perfectly he is her ape : he so near to Hermione hath done Hermione that they say one would speak to her and stand in hope of answer : thither with all greediness of affection are they gone, and there they intend to sup. (v. ii. 105)

For the general thought of art imitating nature's human handi-work, compare the 'nature's journeymen' of Hamlet's address to the Players (*Hamlet*, iii. ii. 38). Here the statue is already associated with 'eternity', regarded as the creative origin;[1] 'breath' is to be important again. The implications of 'eternity' are semi-transcendental in attempt to define that unmotivated power behind the mystery of free generation in nature and in art; indeed, implicit in freedom itself. The Gentlemen next refer to the statue as 'some great matter' already suspected from Paulina's continual visits to the 'removed house' where it stands (v. ii. 117–20). We are made thoroughly expectant, attuned to a consciousness where 'every wink of an eye some new grace will be born' (v. ii. 124); a queer phrase whose courtly ease points the miracle of creation in time—there was a mysticism within Renaissance courtliness, as Castiglione's book indicates—whilst recalling the apocalyptic phrase in the New Testament about men being changed 'in the twinkling of an eye'.

Both through Paulina's dialogue with Leontes in v. i. and the Gentlemen's conversation we have been prepared for the resurrection. But there are earlier hints, not yet observed. At Hermione's death, Paulina asserted:

> If you can bring
> Tincture or lustre in her lip, her eye,
> *Heat outwardly or breath within*, I'll serve you
> As I would do the gods.　　　　　(iii. ii. 205)

---

[1] Compare the use of 'eternity' as the home of divinity in close association with power at *Coriolanus*, v. iv. 26.

A warm physical realism is regularly here felt as essential to resurrection. Paulina is suggesting that it would need a Cerimon, in Christian thought Christ, to work the miracle: the possibility at least was thus early suggested. Later Florizel referred to just such superhuman power when, after calling vast nature and all men as witness, he swore:

> That, were I crown'd the most imperial monarch,
> Thereof most worthy, were I the fairest youth
> That ever made eye swerve, *had force and knowledge*
> *More than was ever man's*, I would not prize them
> Without her love. (IV. iii. 385)

This close association of royalty ('crowned', 'imperial', 'monarch') with superhuman strength and wisdom may assist our interpretations elsewhere of Shakespeare's later royalism, whose spirituality (to use a dangerously ambiguous word) was forecast in Romeo's and Cleopatra's dreams of immortal, and therefore *imperial*, love (*Romeo and Juliet*, v. i. 9; *Antony and Cleopatra*, v. ii. 76–100). The king is, at the limit, a concept of superman status. Florizel later addresses Camillo in similar style:

> How, Camillo,
> May this, almost a miracle, be done?
> That I may call thee something more than man,
> And after that trust to thee. (IV. iii. 546)

Another clear reminiscence of Cerimon, with suggestions of some greater than human magic; white magic.

Now, as the resurrection draws near, we are prepared for it by Perdita's restoration. St. Paul once seems, perhaps justly, to consider resurrection as no more remarkable than birth (see *Romans*, iv. 17 in Dr. Moffatt's translation).[1] Certainly here the safeguarding of Perdita is considered scarcely less wonderful than the resurrection of the dead. That the child should be found, says Paulina,

> Is all as monstrous to our *human reason*
> As my Antigonus to break his grave
> And come again to me. (v. i. 41)

[1] It must, however, be noted that the birth here concerned seems to be one of an abnormal, semi-miraculous, sort ; but the Pauline doctrine of resurrection holds strong fertility suggestion elsewhere, as in the great passage on immortality at 1 *Corinthians*, xv, where the dead body is compared to a grain of wheat buried in earth.

Yet she is restored, as the Gentlemen recount, and human
reason accordingly negated. Scattered throughout are dim
foreshadowings of the miraculous. Nevertheless, death looms
large enough still, in poetry's despite: Paulina sees to that.
When a gentleman praises Perdita she remarks:

> O Hermione !
> As every present time doth boast itself
> Above a better gone, so must thy grave
> Give way to what's seen now.   (v. i. 95)

The temporal order demands that the past slip away, that it
lose reality; the more visible present always seems *superior*.
Paulina resents this; and her remark may be aligned with both
our early lines on boyhood never dreaming of any future other
than to be 'boy eternal' (i. ii. 65) and Florizel's desire to have
Perdita's every act in turn—speaking, dancing, etc.—perpetuated. All these are strivings after eternity. Paulina, moreover,
here suggests that the gentleman concerned, who seems to be a
poet, is himself at fault: his verse, which 'flow'd with her
(i.e. Hermione's) beauty once', is now 'shrewdly ebb'd' (v. i.
102). The complaint is, not that Hermione has gone, but that
the gentleman has failed in some sense to keep level. Death is
accordingly less an objective reality than a failure of the subject to keep abreast of life. This may seem to turn an obvious
thought into meaningless metaphysics, but the lines, in their
context, can scarcely be ignored. Throughout *Troilus and
Cressida* (especially at iii. iii. 145–84, an expansion of Paulina's
comment) Shakespeare's thoughts on time are highly abstruse
(see my essay in *The Wheel of Fire*); so are they in the Sonnets.
Wrongly used time is as intrinsic to the structure of *Macbeth*
as is 'eternity' to that of *Antony and Cleopatra* (see my essays on
both plays in *The Imperial Theme*). As so often in great poetry,
the philosophical subtlety exists within or behind a speech, or
plot, of surface realism and simplicity. Now *The Winter's Tale*
is hammering on the threshold of some extraordinary truth
related to both 'nature' and 'eternity'. Hence its emphasis on
the seasons, birth and childhood, the continual moulding of
new miracles on the pattern of the old; hence, too, the desire
expressed for youthful excellence perpetuated and eternal; the
thought of Perdita's every action as a 'crowned' thing, a

'queen', in its own eternal right (IV. iii. 145–6); and also of art as improving or distorting nature, in the flower-dialogue, in Julio Romano's uncanny, eternity-imitating, skill. And yet no metaphysics, no natural philosophy or art, satisfy the demand that the lost thing, in all its nature-born warmth, be preserved; that it, not only its descendant, shall live; that death be revealed as a sin-born illusion; that eternity be flesh and blood.

The action moves to the house of the 'grave and good Paulina' (v. iii. 1). The scene is her 'chapel', recalling the chapel of death at III. ii. 240, where Leontes last saw Hermione's dead body. Paulina shows them the statue, which excels anything the 'hand of man hath done' (v. iii. 17); and they are quickly struck with—again the word—'wonder' (v. iii. 22). Leontes gazes; recognizes Hermione's 'natural posture' (v. iii. 23); asks her to chide him, yet remembers how she was tender 'as infancy and grace' (v. iii. 27):

> O ! thus she stood,
> Even with such life of majesty—warm life
> As now it coldly stands—when first I woo'd her.
> I am asham'd : does not the stone rebuke me
> For being more stone than it ? O, royal piece !
> (v. iii. 34)

Sweet though it be, it remains cold and withdrawn, like Keats' Grecian Urn. Yet its 'majesty' exerts a strangely potent 'magic' (v. iii. 39) before which Perdita kneels almost in 'superstition' (v. iii. 43). Leontes' grief is so great that Camillo reminds him how 'sixteen winters' and 'so many summers' should by now alternately have blown and dried his soul clean of 'sorrow'; why should that prove more persistent than short-lived 'joy'? (v. iii. 49–53). Leontes remains still, his soul pierced (v. iii. 34) by remembrance. Paulina, however, speaks realistically of the statue as art, saying how its colour is not dry yet (v. iii. 47); half apologizing for the way it moves him, her phrase 'for the stone is mine' (v. iii. 58) re-emphasizing her peculiar office. She offers to draw the curtain, fearing lest Leontes' 'fancy may think anon it moves' (v. iii. 61). The excitement generated, already intense, reaches new impact and definition in Paulina's sharp ringing utterance on 'moves'.

But Leontes remains quiet, fixed, in an other-worldly

consciousness, a living death not to be disturbed, yet
trembling with expectance:

> Let be, let be !
> Would I were dead, but that, methinks, already—
> What was he that did make it ?   (v. iii. 61)

A universe of meaning is hinted by that one word 'already' and
the subsequent, tantalizing, break. Now the statue seems no
longer cold:

> See, my lord,
> Would you not deem it breath'd, and that those veins
> Did verily bear blood ?   (v. iii. 63)

As the revelation slowly matures, it is as though Leontes' own
grief and love were gradually infusing the thing before him
with life. He, under Paulina, is labouring, even now, that it
may live. The more visionary, paradisal, personal wonder of
Pericles (who alone hears the spheral music) becomes here a
crucial conflict, an *agon*, in which many persons share; dream
is being forced into actuality. 'Masterly done', answers Polixenes, taking us back to common-sense, and yet again noting
that 'the very life seems warm upon her lip'(v. iii. 65). We are
poised between motion and stillness, life and art:

> The fixure of her eye has motion in't,
> As we are mock'd with art.   (v. iii. 67)

The contrast drives deep, recalling the balancing of art and
nature in Perdita's dialogue with Polixenes; and, too, the
imaging of the living Marina as 'crown'd Truth' or monumental Patience (*Pericles*, v. 1, 124, 140). Paulina reiterates
her offer to draw the curtain lest Leontes be so far 'transported'
(cp. iii. ii. 159; a word strongly toned in Shakespeare with
magical suggestion) that he actually think it 'lives'—thus re-
charging the scene with an impossible expectation. To which
Leontes replies:

> No settled senses of the world can match
> The pleasure of that madness. Let't alone.
>
>   (v. iii. 72)

He would stand here, spell-bound, forever; forever gazing on
this sphinx-like boundary between art and life.

Paulina, having functioned throughout as the Oracle's implement, becomes now its priestess. Her swift changes key the scene to an extraordinary pitch, as she hints at new marvels:

> I am sorry, sir, I have thus far stirr'd you : but
> I could afflict you further.   (v. iii. 74)

She has long caused, and still causes, Leontes to suffer poignantly; and yet his suffering has undergone a subtle change, for now this very 'affliction has a taste as sweet as any cordial comfort' (v. iii. 76). Already (at v. ii. 20 and 81, and v. iii. 51–3) we have found joy and sorrow in partnership, as, too, in the description of Cordelia's grief (*King Lear*, iv. iii. 17–26). So Leontes endures a pain of ineffable sweetness as the mystery unfolds:

> Still, methinks,
> There is an air comes from her : what fine chisel
> Could ever yet cut breath ?   (v. iii. 77)

However highly we value the eternity phrased by art (as in Yeats' 'monuments of unaging intellect' in *Sailing to Byzantium*[1] and Keats' *Grecian Urn*), yet there is a frontier beyond which it and all corresponding philosophies fail: they lack one thing, breath. With a fine pungency of phrase, more humanly relevant than Othello's 'I know not where is that Promethean heat . . .' (*Othello*, v. ii. 12), a whole world of human idealism is dismissed. The supreme moments of earlier tragedy— Othello before the 'monumental alabaster' (v. ii. 5) of the sleeping Desdemona, Romeo in Capel's monument, Juliet and Cleopatra blending sleep and death—are implicit in Leontes' experience; more, their validity is at stake, as he murmurs, 'Let no man mock me' (v. iii. 79), stepping forward for an embrace; as old Lear, reunited with Cordelia, 'a spirit in bliss', says 'Do not laugh at me' (*King Lear*, iv. vii. 68); as Pericles fears lest his reunion with Marina be merely such a dream as 'mocks' man's grief (*Pericles*, v. i. 144, 164). Those, and other, supreme moments of pathos are here re-enacted to a stronger purpose. Leontes strides forward; is prevented by Paulina; we are

---

[1] A yet more relevant comparison with Yeats might adduce his drama *Resurrection*. Compare also the statue-interest of Ibsen's last play (1964: now studied in my *Ibsen*).

brought up against a *cul-de-sac*. But Paulina herself immediately releases new impetus as she cries, her voice quivering with
the Sibylline power she wields:

> Either forbear,
> Quit presently the chapel, or resolve you
> For more amazement. If you can behold it,
> I'll make the statue move indeed, descend,
> And take you by the hand ; but then you'll think—
> Which I protest against—I am assisted
> By wicked powers.   (v. iii. 85)

The 'chapel' setting is necessary, for we attend the resurrection
of a supposedly buried person; the solemnity is at least half
funereal. Much is involved in the phrase 'wicked powers': we
watch no act of necromancy. The 'magic' (v. ii. 39), if magic
it be, is a white magic; shall we say, a natural magic; the living
opposite of the Ghost in *Hamlet* hideously breaking his tomb's
'ponderous and marble jaws' (I. iv. 50). The difference is
that between Prospero's powers in *The Tempest* and those of
Marlowe's Faustus or of the Weird Sisters in *Macbeth*. The
distinction in Shakespeare's day was important and further
driven home by Paulina's:

> It is requir'd
> You do awake your faith. Then, all stand still ;
> Or those that think it is unlawful business
> I am about, let them depart.   (v. iii. 94)

The key-word 'faith' enlists New Testament associations, but
to it Paulina adds a potency more purely Shakespearian: music.
Shakespeare's use of music, throughout his main antagonist to
tempestuous tragedy, reaches a newly urgent precision at
Cerimon's restoration of Thaisa and Pericles' reunion with
Marina. Here it functions strongly as the specifically releasing
agent:

> *Paulina.*   Music, awake her : strike !
> 'Tis time ; descend ; be stone no more ; approach ;
> Strike all that look upon with marvel. Come ;
> I'll fill your grave up : stir, nay, come away ;
> Bequeath to death your numbness, for from him
> Dear life redeems you. You perceive she stirs.

Start not ; her actions shall be holy as
You hear my spell is lawful : do not shun her
Until you see her die again, for then
You kill her double. Nay, present your hand :
When she was young you woo'd her ; now in age
Is she become the suitor ?

Leontes.   O ! she's warm.
If this be magic, let it be an art
Lawful as eating.   (v. iii. 98)

'Redeems' (cp. 'ransomed' at v. ii. 16), 'holy' and 'lawful'
continue earlier emphases. The concreteness of 'fill your grave
up' has analogies in Shelley's *Witch of Atlas* (LXIX–LXXI) and
the empty sepulchre of the New Testament. Such resurrections are imaged as a re-infusing of the dead body with life.
Hermione's restoration not only has nothing to do with black
magic; it is not even transcendental. It exists in warm human
actuality (cp. *Pericles*, v. i. 154): hence our earlier emphases
on warmth and breath; and now on 'eating' too. It is part after
all of the one 'great creating nature'; no more, and no less;
merely another miracle from the great power, the master-artist
of creation, call it what you will, nature or eternity, Apollo or
the New Testament's great God of Life (*Acts*, XVII, 23–8).

The poet carefully refuses to elucidate the mystery on the
plane of plot-realism. When Polixenes wonders where Hermione 'has liv'd' or 'how stol'n from the dead', Paulina merely
observes that she *is* living, and that this truth, if reported rather
than experienced, would 'be hooted at like an old tale' (v. iii.
114–17; cp. 'like an old tale' at v. ii. 30, 67). Perdita's assistance is needed to unloose Hermione's speech; whereupon she
speaks, invoking the gods' 'sacred vials' of blessing on her
daughter and referring to the Oracle (v. iii. 121–8). Leontes
further drives home our enigma by remarking that Paulina
has found his wife, though 'how is to be question'd'; for,
he says,

I saw her
As I thought, dead, and have in vain said many
A prayer upon her grave.   (v. iii. 139)

We are not, in fact, to search for answers on this plane at

all: the poet himself does not know them.[1] Certainly our plot-realism is maintained: Paulina reminds us that her husband is gone; and we may remember Mamilius. It is the same in *Pericles*. The subsidiary persons are no longer, as persons, important: the perfunctory marrying of Paulina and Camillo to round off the ritual might otherwise be a serious blemish.

The truth shadowed, or revealed, is only to be known, if at all, within the subjective personality, the 'I' not easily linked into an objective argument. It is precisely this mysterious 'I' in the audience that the more important persons of drama, and in especial tragedy, regularly objectify. Now within the 'I' rest all those indefinables and irrationalities of free-will and guilt, of unconditioned and therefore appallingly responsible action with which *The Winter's Tale* is throughout deeply concerned; as in Leontes' unmotivated sin for which he is nevertheless in some sense responsible; with his following loss of free-will, selling himself in bondage to dark powers, and a consequent enduring and infliction of tyranny. The outward effects are suspicion, knowledge of evil and violent blame; with a final spreading and miserable knowledge of death ('There was a man dwelt by a churchyard'—II. i. 28), leading on, with Paulina's assistance, to repentance. Time is throughout present as a backward-flowing thing, swallowing and engulfing; we are sunk deep in the consciousness of dead facts, causes, death. But over against all this stands the creative consciousness, existing not in present-past but present-future, and with a sense of causation not behind but ahead, the ever-flowing in of the new and unconditioned, from future to present: this is the consciousness of freedom, in which 'every wink of an eye some new grace will be born' (v. ii. 124). Hence our poetry plays queer tricks with time, as in the 'boy eternal' passage where consciousness is confined to 'to-day' and 'to-morrow': in Florizel's dreams of immediate perfection eternalized; in thought of 'eternity' (which includes the future, being over-dimensional to the time-stream) as the creative origin; and in Paulina's annoyance at the poet-gentleman's ready submission to time

---

[1] Note that Shakespeare here purposely drives the miraculous to a limit not touched in *Pericles*. For a full discussion of the metaphysical implications of the immortality dramatized in *The Winter's Tale* and other such works I must refer the reader to Chapter X of *The Christian Renaissance*.

the destroyer. Freedom is creation, and therefore art; and hence our emphases on art, in the flower-dialogue, in notice of Julio Romano's skill, in the statue-scene; and here we approach a vital problem. It is precisely the creative spirit in man, the unmotivated and forward 'I', that binds him to 'great creating Nature', the 'great nature' by whose laws the child is 'freed and enfranchised' from the womb (II. ii. 60–1): he is one with that nature, in so far as he is free. Our drama works therefore to show Leontes, under the tutelage of the Oracle, as painfully working himself from the bondage of sin and remorse into the freedom of nature, with the aptly-named Paulina as conscience, guide, and priestess. The resurrection is not performed until (i) Leontes' repentance is complete and (ii) creation is satisfied by the return of Perdita, who is needed for Hermione's full release. Religion, art, procreation, and nature (in 'warmth', 'breath' and 'eating') are all contributory to the conclusion, which is shown as no easy release, but rather a gradual revelation, corresponding to Pericles' reunion with Marina, under terrific dramatic pressure and fraught with an excitement with which the watcher's 'I' is, by most careful technique, forced into a close subjective identity, so that the immortality revealed is less concept than experience. Nor is it just a reversal of tragedy; rather tragedy is contained, assimilated, transmuted; every phrase of the resurrection scene is soaked in tragic feeling, and the accompanying joy less an antithesis to sorrow than its final flowering. The depths of the 'I', which are tragic, are being integrated with the objective delight which is nature's joy. The philosophy of Wordsworth is forecast; for he, too, knew Leontes' abysmal 'nothing'; he too suffered some hideous disillusion, in part evil; he too laboured slowly for reintegration with nature; and, finally, he too saw man's true state in terms of creation and miracle. The response, in both Wordsworth and Shakespeare, is a reverential wonder at knowledge of Life where Death was throned.[1]

---

[1] We find a closely equivalent sense of the miraculous in the early scenes of *All's Well that Ends Well*, where Helena's mysterious art is clearly comparable with Cerimon's, and the style of speech continually takes on a rhymed formality similar to that in *Pericles*. Lafeu's excellent comment might be read as a text for *The Winter's Tale*:

They say miracles are past; and we have our philosophical persons, to make modern and familiar things supernatural and causeless. Hence is it that we make trifles of terrors, ensconcing ourselves into seeming knowledge, when we should submit ourselves to an unknown fear. (II. iii. 1.) (**Continued next page.**)

The Winter's Tale may seem a rambling, perhaps an untidy, play; its anachronisms are vivid, its geography disturbing. And yet Shakespeare offers nothing greater in tragic psychology, humour, pastoral, romance, and that which tops them all and is, except for *Pericles*, new. The unity of thought is more exact than appears: it was Sicily, at first sight ill-suited to the sombre scenes here staged, that gave us the myth of Proserpine or Persephone. The more profound passages are perhaps rather evidence of what is beating behind or within the creative genius at work than wholly successful ways of printing purpose on an average audience's, or an average reader's, mind; but the passages are there, and so is the purpose, though to Shakespeare it need not have been defined outside his drama. Meanwhile that drama, by its very enigma, its unsolved and yet uncompromising statement, throws up—as in small compass did the little flower-dialogue too—a vague, numinous, sense of mighty powers, working through both the natural order and man's religious consciousness, which preserve, in spite of all appearance, the good. Orthodox tradition is used, but it does not direct; a pagan naturalism is used too. The Bible has been an influence; so have classical myth and Renaissance pastoral;[1] but the greatest influence was Life itself, that creating and protecting deity whose superhuman presence and powers the drama labours to define.

Helena's success is 'the rarest argument of wonder that hath shot out in our latter times'; the 'showing of a heavenly effect in an earthly actor' ; 'in a most weak and debile minister, great power, great transcendence' (II. iii. 8, 28, 40). See also the many thoughts earlier on science, nature, death, 'inspired merit', 'skill infinite' and divine action at II. i. 102–89 ; with hint of a medicine 'able to breathe life into a stone' (II. i. 76). The relation of *All's Well that Ends Well* to the Final Plays deserves more attention than can be accorded it here. See also *As You Like It* (with Rosalind as magician), v. ii. 65–9. 1964: My full-length study of *All's Well that Ends Well* has now appeared in *The Sovereign Flower*.

[1] And, it would seem, Greek drama too, especially Sophocles', wherein a tyrant is punished like Leontes by the sudden loss of his son (*Antigone*) and a child exposed like Perdita (*Oedipus*).

Additional note, 1982

On p. 101 my handling of Autolycus' actions owes much to W. Lyndon Smith's admirable performance in my 1936 Toronto production.

For more thoughts on Julio Romano and Hermione's statue, see my essay 'Visual Artistry in Kyd and Shakespeare' to appear in my collection *A Shakespeare Manifesto, with supporting essays* (forthcoming).

IV

CYMBELINE
I. THEMES AND PERSONS

Prince.	I do not like the Tower, of any place :
	Did Julius Caesar build that place, my lord ?
Buckingham.	He did, my gracious lord, begin that place,
	Which, since, succeeding ages have re-edified.
Prince.	Is it upon record, or else reported
	Successively from age to age, he built it ?
Buckingham.	Upon record, my gracious lord.
Prince.	But say, my lord, it were not register'd,
	Methinks the truth should live from age to age,
	As 'twere retail'd to all posterity,
	Even to the general, all-ending day.

Richard III, iii. 1, 68.

IT would seem that *Pericles* and *The Winter's Tale* were followed by *Cymbeline*, which incorporates a re-working of themes already discussed into a more comprehensive design. *Cymbeline* is an extremely complex work: in mastery of plot-weaving it certainly has no rival. The different stories diverge, interweave and dovetail with a striking precision and the extraordinary events march smoothly to their conclusion. The consummate plot-weaving of *Twelfth Night* is re-explored to hold a greater range of serious themes; while a prevailing quietude reminiscent of such earlier romances overbroods and enriches the tougher conflicts of tragedy.

The play is not, however, easy of approach. The start appears dull and ineffective, and the people uninteresting. Emphasis seems to lie on plot and event without persons or atmosphere of sufficient glamour to arrest attention. Certain most subtle imagistic impressionisms are at work, but they are far from obvious, being split among the varying themes, and time is needed for them to accumulate mass and generate each its own particular field of meaning. *Cymbeline* strikes one as a peculiarly studied work. All is smooth, considered and correct. The mythology, the names of places and persons, the historical effects, are all considered. Even its anachronisms appear to be planned. It is, indeed, to be regarded mainly as an historical play. *Pericles* and *The Winter's Tale* blend Shakespeare's early comedy with his later tragedy; *Cymbeline* does this too, but is also concerned to blend Shakespeare's two primary historical interests, the Roman and the British, which meet here for the first time. These are close-knotted with the personal, tragic interest, together with the feminine idealism, of *Othello* and *The Winter's Tale*; recent discoveries are incorporated into a national statement; and all is subdued within a melancholic harmony distantly resembling that of *Twelfth Night*.

First, let us inspect its national interest, concentrating on Cymbeline, his Queen and Cloten.

Of Cymbeline as a man there is little to say, but he is important as king. He is accordingly comparable with the early King John. His distress under threat of invasion resembles that of John when hearing simultaneously of the French army's invasion and his mother's death (*King John*, iv. ii. 116–132):

> Imogen,
> The great part of my comfort, gone ; my queen
> Upon a desperate bed, and in a time
> When fearful wars point at me ; her son gone,
> So needful for this present : it strikes me, past
> The hope of comfort.   (iv. iii. 4)

The accent recalls Claudius in *Hamlet*, iv. v. 77–96. Cymbeline is less a man than a centre of tensions due to his royal office; persuaded, attacked, tugged asunder and finally re-established by the various themes and persons.

His Queen is more firmly realized as a 'crafty devil' (ii. i. 59) and 'mother hourly coining plots' (ii. i. 66). Her considered villainy is amazing and her only unselfishness her instinctive support of her fool son, Cloten. She is a composite of Lady Macbeth and Goneril, though without the tragic dignity of the one and the cold rationality of the other. She is cruelty incarnate. We find her (i. v.) sending a lady out for flowers, and next questioning Cornelius the physician about some poisoned drugs she has ordered for her scientific studies. Though she insists that she will only experiment 'on such creatures as we count not worth the hanging', the physician is shocked by her unwomanly hardness: 'Your highness shall from this practice but make hard your heart' (i. v. 19, 23). She gets, as she thinks, the drug and gives it to Pisanio. The lady brings her her flowers, violets, cowslips and primroses: the scene ends. Consummate villainy is framed by flowers, so consistently in Shakespeare associated with feminine sweetness; exactly as her wickedness is enclosed in a feminine, supposedly gentle, form.

The Queen seems to project some definite intuition of feminine evil running from Tamora through less tragic, but perfectly serious, examples in Adriana and Katharina the Shrew, to Lady Macbeth, the Witches, Hecate, Goneril, Regan and Dionyza, with weaker reflections in Gertrude and Cressida; which relates to the Dark Lady of the Sonnets, forms part of Cleopatra, is finally symbolized in Sycorax, and expressed here in Posthumus' distracted words:

> Could I find out
> The woman's part in me ! For there's no motion
> That tends to vice in man but I affirm
> It is the woman's part ; be't lying, note it,
> The woman's ; flattering, hers ; deceiving, hers ;
> Lust and rank thoughts, hers, hers ; revenges, hers ;
> Ambitions, covetings, change of prides, disdain,
> Nice longing, slanders, mutability,
> All faults that man may name, nay, that hell knows,
> Why, hers, in part, or all ; but rather, all ;
> For even to vice
> They are not constant, but are changing still
> One vice but of a minute old for one
> Not half so old as that. I'll write against them,
> Detest them, curse them. Yet 'tis greater skill
> In a true hate to pray they have their will :
> The very devils cannot plague them better.   (II. v. 19)

The sentiments sink deep into all those Shakespearian agonies of jealousy and distrust of which Hamlet's 'Frailty, thy name is woman!' (I. ii. 146) is a central example. The Queen throughout personifies the ugly thing Posthumus suspects in Imogen.

Her death expands the slightly etched deaths of Lady Macbeth and Goneril. She suffers from 'a fever with the absence of her son', a 'madness' endangering her life (IV. iii. 2–3), but dies with a devilish clarity of mind. Her mental disorder is commented on, like Lady Macbeth's, by the court physician, who reports her death, saying how she ended

> With horror, madly dying, like her life ;
> Which, being cruel to the world, concluded
> Most cruel to herself.   (v. v. 31)

She died confessing that her love for Cymbeline and Imogen
had been throughout a sham, and that she had horrible poisons
ready for both; how she meant her lord to die lingeringly while
she pretended to pet and nurse him; how she had planned to
make Cloten king, but grew 'shameless-desperate' at his disappearance. All this she confesses not through penitence, but
in order to spite 'heaven and men'; and so 'despairing died'
(v. v. 57–61). She is a positive ogre, worthy of Ben Jonson, on
whom Cymbeline's comment is:

>   O most delicate fiend !
> Who is't can read a woman ?   (v. v. 47)

She is a considered study of extreme, specifically feminine, evil;
a possessive maternal instinct impelling her violent life. She is
not a caricature. The study is brief, but convincing. Cymbeline has to learn painfully the worthlessness of his wife and
her, not his, son, Cloten. In the wider national reading we can
feel Britain learning to reject all for which they stand.

Cloten is a boastful fool: his name suggests clot-pole, the
term being used to jingle with his name (at IV. ii. 184); a word
also applied to Oswald by King Lear (*King Lear*, I. iv. 51).
We find him puffing and blowing after an interrupted duel,
convinced fallaciously that he would have won it (I. ii). He
loses his money and his temper, swearing and striking a
bystander, at bowls (II. i. 1–8), and nearly involving himself
in another duel. He is quarrelsome and generally obnoxious,
a blustering, high-born, fool, very conscious of his rank:

> When a gentleman is disposed to swear, it is not for any standers-by
> to curtail his oaths, ha ?   (II. i. 11)

and

> . . . A pox on't. I had rather not be so noble as I am. They dare
> not fight with me because of the Queen my mother. Every Jack-
> slave hath his bellyful of fighting, and I must go up and down like
> a cock that nobody can match.   (II. i. 21)

As a study of foolish nobility he resembles Sir Andrew Ague-
cheek and Roderigo; and yet he is at once more intelligent,

full-blooded and forceful, than those. He seems to have a genuine appreciation of Imogen (III. v. 70–4) and serenades her with taste (II. iii. 22). One cannot deny him a certain arrogant dignity that makes it easier to laugh behind his back (as his interlocutors do) than to his face. His high position alone, with his consciousness of it, itself gives him dramatic weight. When he questions Pisanio on Imogen's absence, there is force in his attack:

> Where is thy lady ? or, by Jupiter,
> I will not ask again. (III. v. 84)

and,

> Where is she, sir ? Come nearer,
> No further halting ; satisfy me home
> What is become of her ? (III. v. 91)

He will not be put off by flattering phrases, shouting 'no more of "worthy lord" ' (III. v. 96); threatens instant death; and finally wins, as he thinks, Pisanio's betrayal of Posthumus, next determining to pursue Imogen 'even to Augustus' throne' (III. v. 101). Pisanio records the incident later, saying how Lord Cloten 'came to me with his sword drawn', 'foam'd at the mouth'—a revealing phrase—and threatened him with death; how he succeeded in putting him off with a false letter; and how Cloten 'enforced' from him his master's garments (v. v. 275–82). There is power of rank in Cloten; rather as Sir John Falstaff, though a coward (of a kind) in one context, yet automatically drives off Pistol, furious at being 'braved' by such a 'rascal' (2 *Henry IV*, II. iv. 231); or as Sir Toby, a drunken sot, is on his mettle when Antonio or Sebastian turns his sport into a serious fight. Somewhat similarly, Pisanio is quelled by 'Lord Cloten'.

Cloten is certainly both ridiculous and vicious. Like Sir Andrew he is vain, comparing his figure with Posthumus' (IV. i. 7–11), and is necessarily maddened by Imogen's rejection of himself for a mere nobody. He is autocratic and insulting— witness his continued insults concerning Posthumus' low birth —and has a thoroughly nasty mind, seen in his dastardly plot to revenge himself by raping Imogen whilst wearing Posthumus' garments. There is poetic justice in his death: he who has so often been saved by well-meaning courtiers from the

consequences of his own quarrelsomeness, rashly insults as a
'robber' and 'law-breaker' (IV. ii. 74) the young Guiderius in
his mountain home and, finding his rank of little service to him
there, gets his deserts without delay. He is a fool and rash,
but no coward; and he meets his death at the hands of no less
a person than the King's son. The conception throughout
works within the limits imposed by the noble birth his very
being disgraces.

King Cymbeline supports both these bad persons, banishing
Posthumus mainly at the Queen's instigation and for Cloten's
sake. Our drama shows therefore a misguided King of Britain
fostering evil and folly near his throne.

Our main national interest concerns Cymbeline's refusal to
continue Britain's tribute to Rome. The question of Britain's
islanded integrity is clearly raised; more, it is phrased. Told
by Philario that he thinks the ambassador Caius Lucius will
succeed in getting the tribute, since Britain has cause to
remember Rome's power, Posthumus answers:

> I do believe—
> Statist though I am none, nor like to be—
> That this will prove a war ; and you shall hear
> The legions now in Gallia sooner landed
> In our not-fearing Britain, than have tidings
> Of any penny tribute paid. Our countrymen
> Are men more order'd than when Julius Caesar
> Smil'd at their lack of skill, but found their courage
> Worthy his frowning at : their discipline—
> Now winged—with their courage will make known
> To their approvers they are people such
> That mend upon the world.   (II. iv. 15)

Posthumus' thoughts are obvious and what we would expect
from him; but what we might not expect is to find precisely the
same thoughts expressed even more satisfyingly by the Queen
and Cloten. The Queen and Cloten urge on Cymbeline to
resistance rather as the Bastard urges on King John, Cloten's
wit definitely recalling the Bastard's. Lucius has said how the
tribute is 'left untender'd':

> Queen.   And, to kill the marvel,
>   Shall be so ever.

Cloten.   There be many Caesars
       Ere such another Julius. Britain is
       A world by itself, and we will nothing pay
       For wearing our own noses.

Queen.   That opportunity,
       Which then they had to take from 's, to resume,
       We have again. Remember, sir, my liege,
       The kings your ancestors, together with
       The natural bravery of your isle, which stands
       As Neptune's park, ribbed and paled in
       With rocks unscaleable and roaring waters,
       With sands, that will not bear your enemies' boats,
       But suck them up to the topmast. A kind of conquest
       Caesar made here, but made not here his brag
       Of 'came and saw and overcame' : with shame—
       The first that ever touch'd him—he was carried
       From off our coast, twice beaten ; and his shipping—
       Poor ignorant baubles !—on our terrible seas,
       Like egg-shells mov'd upon their surges, crack'd
       As easily 'gainst our rocks : for joy whereof
       The fam'd Cassibelan, who was once at point—
       O giglot fortune !—to master Caesar's sword,
       Made Lud's town with rejoicing-fires bright,
       And Britons strut with courage.   (III. i. 10)

The Queen has powerfully expressed precisely the sentiments many Elizabethan Englishmen must have felt after the failure of the Spanish Armada. She is deadly serious; Cloten witty. Though told by the King to keep quiet—as the Bastard, Falstaff and Enobarbus are rebuffed in similar circumstances—he continues :

> We have yet many among us can gripe as hard as Cassibelan ; I do not say I am one, but I have a hand. Why tribute ? why should we pay tribute ? If Caesar can hide the sun from us with a blanket, or put the moon in his pocket, we will pay him tribute for light ; else, sir, no more tribute, pray you now.   (III. i. 40)

Cloten's wit (so like the Bastard's in purpose and Enobarbus' in manner) is admirable; he for once even shows modesty. King Cymbeline continues with a speech every phrase of which raises a natural response, urging the original freedom of Britain, Caesar's insatiate and inexcusable ('colour') ambition, the compulsion on a 'war-like' people to resist slavery, and especially the Roman's 'mangling' of Britain's traditional 'laws' deriving from her first king, Mulmutius (III. i. 47–62). He reminds the ambassador that other peoples are fighting for 'their liberties' (III. i. 73–6), an example Britain must follow. The discussion, except for Cloten's interruptions, is on a high level of seriousness and chivalric courtesy, though Cloten's admirable interjections remain its high lights:

> His majesty bids you welcome. Make pastime with us a day or two, or longer ; if you seek us afterwards in other terms, you shall find us in our salt-water girdle ; if you beat us out of it, it is yours ; if you fall in the adventure, our crows shall fare the better for you ; and there's an end. (III. i. 78)

This is in line with the island-patriotism of 3 *Henry VI*, IV. i. 39–46; *Richard II*, II. i. 31–68; and *King John*, II. i. 19–31. There is no more subtle praise of British independence than Cloten's; and yet the play ends with Cymbeline's willing payment of tribute from which, he says, he was only persuaded by his 'wicked queen' (V. v. 464). How are we to read all this?

First, we can observe an impingement of the national on the more purely personal; rather as when in *King Lear* the French king is summarily recalled to France leaving Cordelia in charge of his army to avoid at once the danger and difficulty of soliciting our sympathy for an invading king on British soil. The problem is basic in the design of *King John*, where the Bastard's abhorrence at the death of Arthur is followed by his support and indeed exhortation of the King when invasion is threatened. So here, the wicked Queen and her normally repellant son are, at this moment, primarily Britons and their reaction to the Roman threat the measure of British toughness and the islanded integrity of their land. Neither speaks out of character: the Queen merely finds an occasion for the blameless exercise of her fierce and active temperament, urging the King (III. v. 26), as Elinor urges King John and Goneril Albany, to resist invasion; while Cloten, always conscious of his birth and place and a born quarreller and swaggerer, is for once in his element without being obnoxious; the national situation serving, as often in real life, to render violent instincts respectable.

A certain incompatibility, perhaps, remains, the more so as Cloten shows many of the worst qualities habitually associated

by Shakespeare with foreign travel or foreign birth; and indeed,
when Imogen asserts that Posthumus' 'meanest garment' is of
more worth to her than a number of Clotens, and Cloten
repeats and reiterates the phrase after her exit in a puerile tan-
trum (II. iii. 154–61), one is reminded of Austria in *King John*
and the Bastard's repetition of Constance's line, 'And hang a
calf-skin on those recreant limbs' (*King John*, III. i. 131, 3).
The Queen and Cloten, though British and the upholders of
Britain's integrity, are nevertheless conceived as types which
Cymbeline, that is, Britain, must finally reject. So too Richard
III, villain though he be, can under threat of invasion show a
tough patriotism not unlike the Bastard's (at *King John*, v. ii.
128–58):

> Let's whip these stragglers o'er the sea again ;
> Lash hence these overweening rags of France . . .
>
> (*Richard III*, v. iii. 328)

His whole speech forms an admirable commentary on *Cymbeline*. But we find here no scorn of the invader, for Shakespeare honours Rome almost equally with Britain, with a
respect that rings in Lucius' line, so reminiscent of the Roman
tragedies (e.g. *Antony and Cleopatra*, IV. xiii. 57), 'A Roman
with a Roman's heart can suffer' (v. v. 81). Understanding of
Shakespeare's Roman sympathy is vitally necessary. A final
solution to our difficulties is hinted by Cymbeline's remark to
Lucius earlier (in our diplomatic scene) that

> Thy Caesar knighted me ; my youth I spent
> Much under him ; of him I gather'd honour ;
> Which he, to seek of me again, perforce,
> Behoves me keep at utterance.   (III. i. 70)

In modern phraseology the speech says: 'It has been Britain's
destiny, as a nation, to spend its youth under Roman tutelage,
drawing virtue from her traditions; and yet any too forceful
assertion by Rome of her own superiority must negate the very
virtues we have learnt and be resisted to the last.'[1] That is, the

---

[1] Put Papal authority for Caesar, and the same argument could well be applied by Protestantism. Britain's relation to the Church of Rome in *King John* is very similarly developed. The
King first repudiates the Pope's interference with a fine patriotism, but later offers his submission to Pandulph, the Pope's legate. Peace with France is finally concluded through both
the Bastard's resistance and Pandulph's intercession (v. vii. 81–6). *Cymbeline* and *King John*,
except for *Henry VIII* the two most complex of Shakespeare's patriotic plays, make a fascinating
comparison.

knightly 'honour' Cymbeline has drawn from Rome's favour must be defended, if need be, against Rome herself, slavery being incompatible with the chivalric virtues. Though the phraseology enlists associations of a later age, Shakespeare is definitely envisaging the youth of Britain: careless as he often is of anachronisms, he never in *Cymbeline* allows the word 'England' to intrude.

The play's action dramatizes the only possible solution. The Romans invade and the British at first fail, Cymbeline being captured; he is afterwards saved by Belarius and his own (unrecognized) sons, whose efforts are seconded by Posthumus. Britain's integrity (symbolized by the King) is thus preserved by (i) the royal boys and (ii) Posthumus (representative, as we shall see, of British manhood). The action is given first in dumb-show (v. iii. 14), but afterwards described by Posthumus:

>   . . . These three,
> Three thousand confident, in act as many—
> For three performers are the file when all
> The rest do nothing—with this word, 'Stand ! stand !'
> Accommodated by the place, more charming
> With their own nobleness—which could have turn'd
> A distaff to a lance—gilded pale looks,
> Part shame, part spirit renew'd ; that some, turn'd coward
> But by example—O ! a sin of war,
> Damn'd in the first beginners—'gan to look
> The way that they did, and to grin like lions
> Upon the pikes o' the hunters. Then began
> A stop i' the chaser, a retire, anon,
> A rout, confusion thick ; forthwith they fly
> Chickens, the way which they stoop'd eagles[1]; slaves,
> The strides they victors made. And now our cowards—
> Like fragments in hard voyages—became
> The life o' the need . . .   (v. iii. 28)

It is a long speech, in that cramped, interjectory style variously used by Shakespeare for expression of nervous disorder; here breathless excitement and exhaustion. The disadvantages are obvious; the defence, that the poet seems to rely on a succession of impressionistic flashes, whose logic and grammar are (to a listener) obscure, to build an intentionally vague yet always

[1] A modern paraphrase would run : 'Immediately they retrace like chickens the path down which they had recently advanced like swooping eagles'.

expectant sense of something that needs time, must be strung out in length, if the experience is to be thoroughly assimilated. Something similar may occur in philosophic passages; as in the labouring of one thought, giving it various expressions, throughout Ulysses 'order' speech. Such speeches generally conclude with a very simple summing up of the meaning for which the listener's mind has been half-consciously prepared, as in Ulysses'

> To end a tale of length
> Troy in our weakness lives, not in her strength.
> > (*Troilus and Cressida*, i. iii. 136)

So here our hazy sense of a rout turned to victory is finally given clear imprint by the Lord's

> This was strange chance :
> A narrow lane, an old man, and two boys !   (v. iii. 51)

On another level, we can say that, after living in the experience and expressing it as he wishes, the poet wisely recognizes that his play fails unless the meanest member of his audience knows what has happened.

So Britain wins. But, having won, King Cymbeline learns of his Queen's wickedness and agrees, willingly, to pay tribute to Rome:

> And Caius Lucius,
> Although the victor, we submit to Caesar,
> And to the Roman Empire ; promising
> To pay our wonted tribute, from the which
> We were dissuaded by our wicked queen.   (v. v. 460)

Britain's integrity is to be no hot-headed self-assertion; it must learn to reject such influences as the Queen and Cloten; and to recognize, but freely, its Roman inheritance and obligation. So the action marches to its stately conclusion:

> Set we forward : let
> A Roman and a British ensign wave
> Friendly together ; so through Lud's town march . . .
> > (v. v. 480)

Such is the massive union, not unlike the union of lovers in a happy-ending romance, that our play dramatizes; a kind of majestic marriage, where we are to imagine that the partners 'lived happily ever afterwards'.

Interwoven with these national issues is the story of Post-humus' jealousy, redeveloping the old theme running from Ford, Claudio and Antonio (in *Twelfth Night*) through Troilus and Othello to Leontes. One is apt to tire of it; and here, at first anyway, it scarcely grips the Shakespearian student. The treatment is less glamorous than in *Othello* and less revealing than in *The Winter's Tale*, and one is apt to wonder why Shakespeare bothers to complicate what might have been a purely national play with such an already well-worked-over plot. Besides, Posthumus has, as a man, no such impact on us as Othello and Leontes; he is a colourless person being, one half suspects, put through the paces of love, jealousy, disillusion and repentance rather as a representative of something, perhaps of earlier heroes, than as a man in his own right. He is a person with no core to his personality, and hence shows something of that queer colourlessness (though not the artificial, puppet-like, movement) noticeable in Prince Hal in *Henry IV*, who, though less of a person than Falstaff and Hotspur, is yet supremely important as typifying the English temperament: the treatment there being extremely complex, involving humour, irresponsibility, sportfulness, duty, courage and something very near to treachery; with a final humility and grave, if priggish, sense of responsibility. Now Posthumous shows nothing of Hal's variety, and his more emotional rôle is convincingly developed; but he serves a not dissimilar function. He is here to typify Britain's best manhood; not royalty or princeliness, since there are others for that, but manhood. Though bound to speak blank verse by the emotional pressure of his rôle— even Othello was supposedly 'rude' in speech (*Othello*, I. iii. 81)—he is prosaically conceived. Therefore he is also, though again with many differences, comparable with the Bastard in *King John*: in both their office of generalized nationhood seems to be supported (as with Macduff too—and Aeneas) by a certain irregularity of birth.

He is introduced by the two Gentlemen's conversation in the opening scene. One calls him 'a poor but worthy gentleman' (I. i. 7), commiserating with his sorrows, and remarking, 'Alack! good man' (I. i. 18). He is defined in terms of worth but with no suggestion of splendour:

First Gentleman.   . . . a creature such
As to seek through the regions of the earth
For one his like, there would be something
                                                                failing
In him that should compare.   I do not think
So fair an outward and such stuff within
Endows a man but he.

Second Gentleman.   You speak him far.

First Gentleman.   I do extend him, sir, within himself,
Crush him together rather than unfold
His measure duly.   (I. i. 19)

The words selected ('creature', 'fair', 'stuff') are quite colour-less; and the language gets periphrastically involved in the attempt to define an extreme worth without committing itself to the high-sounding phrase. The elaborate description of him in the Vision scene (v. iv.) is precisely similar. In both scenes he is *pitied*, with an attendant loss of glamour. Throughout we are continually pointed to (i) his great merit and (ii) his com-paratively low rank. This lack of rank directly causes his banishment and his enemies make capital of it. To Iachimo he is a 'beggar' (I. iv. 24) and to Cloten a 'base wretch', 'one bred of alms and foster'd with cold dishes' (II. iii. 118), 'the low Posthumus' (III. v. 76). Cloten's peculiarly snobbish arrogance instinctively insults him. The two are dramatically opposed as rivals for Imogen's love, the one being of high birth but worth-less, the other without rank but all-worthy: much is involved in the British princess' choice of Posthumus.

A certain mystery shrouds his descent. 'I cannot', says the Gentleman, 'delve him to the root' (I. i. 28): in so far as Post-humus symbolizes British strength, Shakespeare is carefully non-committal as to its origin. For the rest, we are told that his father was Sicilius, who fought for Britain against Rome under Cassibelan and next under Tenantius, who gave him the surname 'Leonatus'; the lion, as at *King John*, II. i. 135–42 and v. i. 57, being well-suited to the national type intended. His mother having died at his birth, and his father and two brothers having fallen in the wars, he was brought up by Cym-beline, took to education naturally and, whilst still young, became a 'sample' to youth, a pattern to the 'mature', and a guide to old age (I. i. 48–50). He is generally praised and

loved (I. i. 47), especially by Imogen, who has married him;
the best proof, we are told, of his 'virtue' (I. i. 50–4). Again,
the direct and glamorous phrase is avoided: there is, perhaps,
something a trifle priggish, to our ears, in this description of
youthful gravity and solid worth, so different from the praise
accorded the true sons, as Posthumus is the adopted son, of
Cymbeline. Notice, too, that his own name and surname and
also his father's sound not British but Roman. He is imaginatively at least a composite of the British and the Roman—his
virtues are throughout pre-eminently the Roman virtues—and
as such personifies the play's main statement. During the war
his dress and supposed action (though he never fights against
Britain) vary: 'Italian,' next British, then Roman.

Against Posthumus are balanced both Cloten and Iachimo.
The one we have discussed; the other needs careful understanding.

Iachimo is to be regarded as a Renaissance Italian, quite
distinct from the Romans. As his name suggests, he is a
re-creation of Iago as a creature of Italian cunning, though with
important differences. He is, as an individual, more convincing
than either Iago, about whom one writes metaphysical essays,
or Edmund, who could scarcely exist outside the peculiar web-
texture of *King Lear*. He is more rounded out, more analysable
as a person, can stand on his own feet. As so often, Shakespeare's last work presents, if anything, an advance in human
delineation; as though the new intuition of transcendence
accompanies a newly concrete awareness of man. Iachimo
is peculiarly well done. His motivation as villain is clearly one
with his excessive self-confidence and knowledge of his own
brilliance and personal attraction. He is a born exhibitionist,
smug, suave, showy and bold as the occasion demands, or all at
once. He is, too, typically foreign. We first meet him during
the general conversation in Rome, where a courtier prose of
easy polish is the order. During the discussion before Posthumus' entry his every accent shows an easy mockery growing
to jealousy of the praise accorded the rough islander of undis-
tinguished origin who is shortly to arrive. Observe his off-
hand style in addressing poor Philario, who so desires that his
friend shall be well received in Italy: 'But how comes it he is
to sojourn with you? How creeps acquaintance?' (I. iv. 25).

'Sojourn'; 'creeps'—the last word could only be spoken by
Iachimo; spoken, I think, with a half-smile and a lift of the
eyebrows. When he joins conversation with Posthumus concerning the Britisher's faith in his lady, his manner is intended
to be subtly insulting. The argument has grown out of Posthumus' former difference with the Frenchman on an earlier
occasion when, each offering the praise 'of our country mis-
tresses' (i. iv. 65)—a national issue is involved—Posthumus
asserted his to exceed in value and virtue, whilst being 'less
attemptable' (i. iv. 68) than any in France. Iachimo attacks
him on behalf of Italy ('You must not so far prefer her, fore
ours of Italy'—i. iv. 75), being irritated by the new arrival's
islanded ignorance and priggish certainties:

> As fair and as good—a kind of hand-in-hand comparison—had
> been something too fair and too good for any lady in Britain. If
> she went before others I have seen, as that diamond of yours out-
> lustres many I have beheld, I could not but believe she excelled
> many ; but I have not seen the most precious diamond that is, nor
> you the lady.   (i. iv. 80)

The voice rises on the final phrase with telling *insouciance*.
Iachimo's words are the more infuriating for their calm rationality and smooth assurance. The argument is in part national,
as Iachimo's emphasis on 'Britain' shows, and in such terms it
continues, Iachimo suggesting that, just as a 'cunning thief'
might easily win the ring, so an 'accomplished courtier' (i.e. of
continental training and experience) would soon vanquish the
simple British girl in question. Posthumus answers:

> Your Italy contains none so accomplished a courtier to convince
> the honour of my mistress, if, in the holding or loss of that, you
> term her frail. I do nothing doubt you have store of thieves ;
> notwithstanding I fear not my ring.   (i. iv. 108)

There is an implicit contrast between the fearless, slightly
rough, Briton, keeping, as it were, his own ideals intact wherever
he journeys, and continental intrigue, showiness, and superficial refinement. Iachimo, a born seducer, is thus put on his
mettle, and the wager follows.

His behaviour at the British court is finely illustrative. When
he insinuates to Imogen that her lord is unfaithful, his words

flow out with an easy mastery and grace and a use of pause and
repetition ever-so-little tilting the balance of sincerity:

> Had I this cheek
> To bathe my lips upon ; this hand, whose touch,
> Whose every touch, would force the feeler's soul
> To the oath of loyalty ; this object, which
> Takes prisoner the wild motion of mine eye,
> Firing it only here ; should I—damn'd then—
> Slaver with lips as common as the stairs
> That mount the Capitol . . .   (I. vi. 99)

As he sees his words register, he promptly, and with most
extraordinary forwardness, suggests himself as both substitute
and means of revenge:

> Revenge it.
> I dedicate myself to your sweet pleasure,
> More noble than that runagate to your bed . . .
>   (I. vi. 135)

His advance failing, he is no whit abashed, but pretends, with
a suave assurance, that it was all merely a trial of her virtue for
Posthumus' sake; and Imogen believes him. He now gives
Posthumus the highest honours:

> He sits 'mongst men like a descended god :
> He hath a kind of honour sets him off,
> More than a mortal seeming.   (I. vi. 169)

This is just the kind of superlative praise others always deny
Posthumus, but that such a speech should be uttered by
Iachimo, at this moment, for his own purpose, preserves the
delicate contrast of Posthumus as against Guiderius and Arviragus, for whom such phrases are in order. Iachimo is more
than a skilful flatterer; he is a superficially charming person
(Imogen is clearly captivated by his mannered splendour), rich
in sex-appeal and all the graces of courtesy. He glitters.

Posthumus, honest man, is no match for his skill. Iachimo's
victimization of his quarry is far more convincing than Iago's,
partly through the higher power generated by his stage, and
stagey, personality. He shows Imogen's bracelet, given to her
by her lover:

Posthumus.   Jove !
        Once more let me behold it. Is it that
        Which I left with her ?
Iachimo.   Sir—I thank her—that :
        She stripp'd it from her arm ; I see her yet ;
        Her pretty action did outsell her gift,
        And yet enrich'd it too. She gave it me, and said
        She priz'd it once.
Posthumus.   May be she pluck'd it off
        To send it me.
Iachimo.   She writes so to you, doth she ?
                                    (II. iv. 98)

Iachimo's libertine personality breathes in his speech. Othello
is beaten by evidence and logic; Posthumus by all that, but
still more by Iachimo's living personality, and his sin lies precisely in his allowing Iachimo's Italian slickness to gain the
ascendancy. Later, Iachimo leads his own contingent in the
war. He, like Iago, is called 'bold' (IV. ii. 340; *Othello*, II. i.
75); and so he is, in more ways than one. But his immoral,
Italianate boldness meets its match, for he finds himself beaten
by Posthumus disguised as a ruffian soldier and his conscience,
pricking him for his offence against the princess, Imogen, suggests that the very 'air' of Britain 'revengingly enfeebles' him
(V. ii. 3). His later repentance, though what we expect in
Shakespeare's last period, is in character. Iachimo is no ogre,
but merely an exhibitionist ruled by a childish pride in his own
sex-appeal joined to a refusal to allow in others the more puritanical virtues that are a denial of all he lives for. His faults
are, in their way, in spite of his blasé, man-of-the-world
cynicism, those of immaturity; are superficial; and can thus be
knocked out of him.

Iachimo is superficial, though showy; Posthumus just the
reverse. His unspectacular rôle reaches its consummation in
his later disguise fighting for Britain as the *meanest possible*
soldier:

        Woe is my heart
    That the poor soldier that so richly fought,
    Whose rags sham'd gilded arms, whose naked breast
    Stepp'd before targes of proof, cannot be found.
                                    (V. v. 2)

He is, as it were, the unknown soldier, to borrow a contemporary phrase, of the war. His disguise serves, poetically, a national purpose, convincing Iachimo that, if 'this carl', this 'very drudge of nature's' can so fight, the British gentry must be 'gods' (v. ii. 4–10). Posthumus here expresses a sterling valour and patriot integrity similar to that of the Bastard in *King John*. During the battle his ironic rhymes (v. iii. 53–63) are in the Bastard's very accents; in description of his countrymen's disgrace (v. iii. 4–13) he resembles Enobarbus and Scarus in *Antony and Cleopatra* (iii. viii. 11–33); while his criticism of the 'lord' who questions him

> This is a lord ! O noble misery !
> To be i' the field, and ask, 'what news' of me !
>
> (v. iii. 64)

reminds us of the 'popinjay' who infuriated Hotspur (1 *Henry IV*, i. iii. 29–69). His words recapture the accents of past warriors. His disguise in the King's cause, too, recalls that of Kent in *King Lear* with whom, as another honest but expressly unshowy person, he has much in common. Kent's contrast with the flattering, oily Oswald ('No contraries hold more antipathy than I and such a knave', *King Lear*, ii. ii. 92; cp. also *King Lear*, ii. ii. 88–9 with *Cymbeline*, i. i. 167–9) is developed here into the contrast of Posthumus as against the somewhat different falsities (since neither are weaklings) represented by Cloten and Iachimo.

Certain strains that recur throughout Shakespeare are here found to be sorting themselves out and reweaving themselves into a new and more deeply purposeful design. First, we have the Machiavellian villain: Richard III, Don John, Iago, Edmund, variously associated with sexual appeal and conquest (in Richard and Edmund) or sexual intrigue and slander (Don John and Iago). In firm contrast is the blunt loyal man (whom Iago pretends to be on occasion): the Bastard, Kent, Enobarbus. To Shakespeare the distinction is close to that of the English as against the continental; of the Bastard against Austria in *King John*. In *Romeo and Juliet* the opposition becomes Mercutio functioning as a typical Englishman in mockery of Tybalt's continental swaggering, tricky sword-play and duellist braggadocio (*Romeo and Juliet*, ii. iv. 20–38). Though the more national distinction cannot be always, or even often, explicit, it works subtly beneath. The national hero, Henry V, adopts a rough Hotspur-like exterior, unable to flatter and wooing in 'true English' (*Henry V*, v. ii. 99–304): when warrior heroism is over and love-making in question, he is presented as a poor, because typically British, courtier. In *Othello*, too, we have a simple soldier lacking social refinement ('rude am I in my speech . . .' I. iii. 81) whose warrior simplicity is, like Posthumus', brought up against Italian cynicism and license:

> *Iago.*   I know our country disposition well.
> In Venice they do let heaven see the pranks
> They dare not show their husbands . . .
>
> *Othello*   Dost thou say so?
>
> (*Othello*, III. iii. 201)

Foreign fashions and the obnoxiousness of travellers fresh from the Continent and its ways are directly or indirectly criticized at *Love's Labour's Lost*, v. i. 15, 117; *King John*, I. i. 182–216; *Much Ado about Nothing*, III. iii. 138–51; v. i. 87–99 (in direct reference to Claudio's jealousy); *The Merchant of Venice*, I. ii. 39–113; *As You Like It*, IV. i. 11–40; v. iv. 40–114; and elsewhere. There are the Spaniard and Frenchman of the Brothel-scene in *Pericles*, IV. ii. 108–26. The contrast is simple; and yet not until *Cymbeline* do we find a clean dramatic opposition of (i) British manhood being led to (ii) sexual disintegration by (iii) foreign and especially Italianate intrigue. That the Queen and Cloten, representatives of murderous drugs (cp. 'drug-damn'd Italy' at III. iii. 15) and arrogant swaggering, are British in no sense spoils the pattern, since they are, like Richard III, shown as finally rejected by their country; and they are here for that purpose. We find two main aspects of a single hated complex: (i) the Machiavellian villain and (ii) the swaggerer, fashion-monger (e.g. Osric) or flatterer: sometimes they occur in pairs, as Don John and Claudio, Iago and Roderigo, Edmund and Oswald, Iachimo and Cloten.

The pattern in *Cymbeline* is very clear. The banished Britisher was from the start thrown among dangerous foreigners. On his arrival in Italy there were, besides Iachimo and Philario, not only the Frenchman, but also a Dutchman and a Spaniard (I. iv. direction): the intention is obvious. The simple islander

is in danger of moral ruin: he is automatically on the defensive,
the issue formerly with the Frenchman and next with Iachimo
being his lady's honour; that is, the romantic and puritanical
idealism of his country as against the license of the Continent.
Yet another nationality is involved in Posthumus' agony at
Imogen's supposed seduction:

> . . . perchance he spoke not, but
> Like a full-acorn'd boar, a German one,
> Cried 'O !' and mounted.   (II. v. 15)

The list is complete. Remembering Imogen's royal birth, we
can say that Posthumus defends not merely a single lady, but
Britain's soul-integrity, widely conceived, among foreigners
who cannot understand his idealism and resent its implications.
The phraseology throughout drives in the national contrast.
Iachimo is more than a melodramatic villain: he is called a
'slight thing of Italy' (v. iv. 64) and 'Italian fiend' (v. v. 211).
To Imogen he is a 'saucy stranger' in the British court (I. vi.
151); and later, hearing of her lord's jealousy, she concludes
that the 'drug-damn'd Italy hath out-crafted him' (III. iv. 15),
feeling sure that 'some jay of Italy' (III. iv. 51) must be
responsible. So Pisanio attributes the trouble to some 'false
Italian' (III. ii. 4). Iachimo himself ends by confessing the
villainous cunning of his 'Italian brain' (v. v. 197). Conversely,
Britain is felt as the home of honour. Imogen would not lose
the gift of her British lover 'for a revenue of any king's in
Europe' (II. iii. 148). You can see how peculiarly offensive, to
British ears, is Iachimo's studied lie, describing how Posthumus, known abroad as 'the Briton reveller' (I. vi. 61), mocks
at a Frenchman's simple love-faith:

> *Iachimo.* There is a Frenchman, his companion, one,
>   An eminent monsieur, that, it seems, much loves
>   A Gallian girl at home ; he furnaces
>   The thick sighs from him, whiles the jolly Briton—
>   Your lord, I mean—laughs from's free lungs,
>
>   cries, 'O !
>   Can my sides hold, to think that man, who knows
>   By history, report, or his own proof,
>   What woman is, yea, what she cannot choose
>   But must be, will his free hours languish for
>   Assured bondage ?'
>   (I. vi. 64)

Imogen's comment is pithy: 'My lord, I fear, has forgot Britain' (I. vi. 112). But perhaps never in all Shakespeare does Britain assume a sweeter excellence than in Imogen's wistful thoughts—recalling Mowbray in *Richard II*—of leaving it:

> Where then ?
> Hath Britain all the sun that shines ? Day, night,
> Are they not but in Britain ? I' the world's volume
> Our Britain seems as of it, but not in't ;
> In a great pool a swan's nest : prithee, think
> There's livers out of Britain.   (III. iv. 138)

A pool or pond in Shakespeare carries undertones suggestive of impurity[1] : there is a precision in the image, constituent to its beauty.

In studying the opposition here encountered of British manhood and Italian cunning in direct reference to marriage-integrity an historical reminder may be forgiven. At the Renaissance, the marriage bond becomes, for the first time in Christian history, a pressing and dominating concern of literature. No age but Elizabeth's could have produced Spenser's two bridal poems. Now this concentration, so evident in Lyly and Spenser, and so overpowering in Shakespeare, may be in particular related to the severe moral feeling, the innate puritanism, of the English temperament, rooting especially from the sixteenth century, though perhaps ingrained from an earlier date: certainly in no other literature are the dramatic implications, and reverberations, more powerful.[2] The term 'Elizabethan' fits Shakespeare's precursors, Lyly and Spenser, as it does not fit Marlowe, himself more properly than they the voice of the European Renaissance widely understood in all its unmoral extravagance: aptly, Machiavelli speaks a prologue on his stage. The Renaissance exuberance is controlled and directed in England and in her voice, Shakespeare; and this it is that prompts his continual return to themes of jealousy, that accounts for the puritanical emphasis on pre-nuptial purity in *The Winter's Tale* and *The Tempest* and the close reference of the sexual to the national in *Cymbeline*. In contrast the Continent, in both the political and the social spheres, is considered dangerous.

---

[1] As at I. iv. 103 ; also *The Winter's Tale*, I. ii. 195. See also p. 218.

[2] The especial importance of love-ritual in Lyly's plays I have discussed in an article contributed to *The Review of English Studies*, April 1939.

Shakespeare's insularity expresses a fear of continental influence natural to England during the Reformation and after. The imaginative power exerted by Italy in Shakespeare's day is witnessed by his steady reliance on Italian settings (where anti-continental satire may nevertheless, as in *Romeo and Juliet* and *Much Ado About Nothing*, be rather illogically contained). Throughout our later poetry the fascination of the Continent, and especially Italy, is variously balanced against the will to British integrity: the general situation being compactly described by Imogen's comment on Britain as 'of' the world but 'not in it' (III. iv. 141).

A sharp distinction between Roman and Italian elements in *Cymbeline* is, accordingly, demanded. Shakespeare's habitual indulgence in anachronism reaches an extreme development, whilst simultaneously becoming newly purposeful and attaining the level of artistic device. We have in a single action a distinction between ancient Rome and Renaissance Italy, the first highly honoured, the other all but equated with the devil.[1] Though their mutual relation is never stated, the moral of Roman decline is clear and involved in the separate relations of each to Britain. Posthumus is imaginatively one quarter Roman, but the antithesis of an Italian, and his sin precisely that of taking the continental taint and becoming, however indirectly, an 'Englishman Italianate' (the phrase is Ascham's). Though the overlaying of Italian on Roman in one plot is highly illogical, there is remarkably little confusion and one is never in doubt as to the response demanded. A Roman atmosphere is projected into detailed reference with considerable success. Roman mythology dominates powerfully. References to Julius Caesar and Augustus come in convincingly. Proper names are subtly used. Wales is Cambria (III. ii. 44) and France may be Gallia (IV. iii. 24), though 'Wales' occurs when the situation demands it (as at III. ii. 61). 'Frenchman', 'monsieur' and 'Gallian' are mixed up *together* when the modern Italian, Iachimo, is speaking to the ancient Briton, Imogen;

---

[1] Once only does Shakespeare admit the continuity of contemporary Italy with ancient Rome, when he speaks of Antonio as

> One in whom
> The ancient Roman honour more appears
> Than any that draws breath in Italy.
>
> (*The Merchant of Venice*, III. ii. 295.)

with, a little later, both France and Gallia at I. vi. 64–6, 189, 201. The problem is neatly handled. Ancient warfare is properly presented with Roman horses neighing at IV. iv. 17, legions at IV. iii. 24 and even chariots, when we might expect Shakespeare to think in terms only of contemporary arms, such as the 'pikes' at v. iii. 39:

> *Cymbeline.* Lucius hath wrote already to the emperor
> How it goes here. It fits us therefore ripely
> Our chariots and horsemen be in readiness ;
> The powers that he already hath in Gallia
> Will soon be drawn to head, from whence he moved
> His war for Britain.   (III. iv. 21)

'Roman' may, of course, refer to the city only and suit a Renaissance atmosphere, as in 'Roman courtezan' at III. iv. 126, or 'Romish stew'—Romish channelling modern associations—at I. vi. 152. But when a meeting of the two worlds is forced, it is done without reserve. A Roman captain says:

> The senate hath stirr'd up the confiners
> And gentlemen of Italy, most willing spirits,
> That promise noble service ; and they come
> Under the conduct of bold Iachimo,
> Sienna's brother.   (IV. ii. 337)

Note that the 'Italian gentry' are subtly considered as allies, not identified with the Romans nor automatically involved in their cause. About Caius Lucius, who functions wholly as a Roman, there is never any doubt, though there is certainly a jar when Imogen introduces herself to him as the former page of 'Richard du Champ' (IV. iii. 377). The precision is, on the whole, remarkably well maintained. When Posthumus changes over from the Roman to the British side he clearly sees himself as deserting not Romans but Italians, having come over 'among the Italian gentry'. He has joined the invaders during his fury against Imogen, but now, 'I'll give no wound to thee' he says, addressing Britain, in remorse at having, as he supposes, killed her 'mistress-piece', Imogen. Therefore,

> I'll disrobe me
> Of these Italian weeds and suit myself
> As does a Briton peasant . . .   (v. i. 22)

He prays for 'the strength of the Leonati', and proceeds to fight for Britain, for Imogen (v. i. 26), for his ancestry: the various themes are closely in-knotted. Later he redisguises himself as one of the invaders in a speech (v. iii. 73–83) carefully avoiding the word Italy and using 'Roman' only.

Enough has been said to indicate all that is involved in the opposition of Posthumus and Iachimo, to suggest how deeply it sinks back into Shakespeare's earlier work and how it is here first clarified, reaching its perfect terms of expression. But clearly much depends on the realization of Imogen as an extreme worth, both personal and national. To her we next turn our attention.

Imogen has little of Portia's strength, Beatrice's independence or Juliet's passion; she shows nothing of the tougher, uncompromising qualities of Isabella and Cordelia. Yet she is equally far from the passive acquiescence of an Ophelia. She is made of the rarest moments only of those and other former heroines: the Portia of girlish surrender (*Merchant of Venice*, III. ii. 149–75), the Viola of 'She never told her love . . .' (*Twelfth Night*, II. iv. 112), the Desdemona of the Willow-song (*Othello*, IV. iii), the Helena of 'Not my virginity yet . . .' (*All's Well that Ends Well*, I. i. 181–93; a speech in Imogen's very accents). She knows the utter loneliness experienced by Juliet after she parts company with the Nurse (*Romeo and Juliet*, III. v. 239). Her style of speech is forecast by the broken phrases, veiling a world of unuttered sorrow, of the early Julia:

Host.   How now ! are you sadder than you were before ? How do you, man ? the music likes you not.
Julia.   You mistake ; the musician likes me not.[1]
                     (*The Two Gentlemen of Verona*, IV. ii. 55)

Imogen has this same poignant gift of repetition:

Cymbeline.   Past grace ? obedience ?
Imogen.   Past hope, and in despair ; that way, past grace.
                                          (I. i. 136)

---

[1] It is important not to misread Julia's line : 'likes' = 'pleases'.

She is not, however, plaintive, or self-pitying. Her deepest sorrows are shot through with smiles, recalling the Rosalind of half-tearful, half-playful, wit (*As You Like It*, iv. i.); the Cordelia of April, sunshine, tears (*King Lear*, iv. iii. 13–26); the Cleopatra of iridescent fun at the towering moment of grief (*Antony and Cleopatra*, iv. xiii. 32, 82–3). So sighs and smiles mix in Imogen: this is stated for us (at iv. ii. 52), but you feel it in the very texture of her speech. She is patience incarnate, 'grief and patience' entwining their roots in her (iv. ii. 57), recalling those marvellous images of Patience eternally out-smiling grief in *Twelfth Night* (ii. iv. 116) and *Pericles* (v. i. 140). The poet's own comments describe for us the subtlety he has created. As with Cleopatra, so amazingly compounded a creature of varying personality, whose complexity is twice defined for us (*Antony and Cleopatra*, i. i. 49; ii. ii. 243), so here, beyond the passages just noticed, we are pointed by—of all people—Cloten to Imogen's peculiar excellence, drawing on all rarest moments of the poet's feminine perception:

> . . . from every one
> The best she hath, and she, of all compounded,
> Outsells them all. (iii. v. 72)

She is fragile and tender, with a host of pretty touches in her speech, but royal too, and brave. She rouses pity without condescension: rather a shocked indignation at her suffering.

Her sweetness of disposition signs itself on her every phrase. She would have Posthumus

> At the sixth hour of morn, at noon, at midnight
> To encounter me with orisons, for then
> I am in heaven for him . . . (i. iii. 31)

We see her in bed praying to be guarded from all 'tempters of the night' (ii. ii. 9). This scene, where Iachimo comes out of his trunk, though far-fetched in probability, is justified by its superb stage effect; and that effect draws strength from the audience's half-fascinated horror at seeing the 'yellow Iachimo' (ii. v. 14) awake and active in her chamber. He describes her sleeping, the eyes

now canopied
Under these windows, white and azure lac'd
With blue of heaven's own tinct . . .   (II. ii. 21)

and the 'mole cinque-spotted' on her breast, 'like the crimson
drops i' the bottom of a cowslip' (II. ii. 38). She is delicately,
intimately, touched by the poetry. Her ways, her figures of
speech are all her own. She had such 'pretty things' (I. iv. 26)
to say to Posthumus at parting. All she does is unique:

With everything that pretty is
My lady sweet, arise.   (II. iii. 28)

Her very thoughts are pretty. She blesses the little bees that
made the wax—her speech is full of minute things—that serve
to seal Posthumus' love-letter (III. ii. 36); and, after reading,
continues with a succession of characteristic, semi-philosophic,
semi-playful tricks of thought:

O ! for a horse with wings ! Hear'st thou, Pisanio ?
He is at Milford-Haven ; read, and tell me
How far 'tis thither. If one of mean affairs
May plod it in a week, why may not I
Glide thither in a day ? Then, true Pisanio—
Who long'st, like me, to see thy lord ; who long'st—
O ! let me 'bate—but not like me ; yet long'st,
But in a fainter kind :—O ! not like me,
For mine's beyond beyond ; say, and speak thick—
Love's counsellor should fill the bores of hearing,
To the smothering of the sense—how far it is
To this same blessed Milford ; and, by the way,
Tell me how Wales was made so happy as
T' inherit such a haven . . .   (III. ii. 49)

'Beyond beyond', 'this same blessed Milford': no one else in
Shakespeare talks quite like this. Her speech is full of evanescent, glinting things of tiny fancifulness, concerned with her
love or, later, sorrow. No one but her could have given us that
lovely image of Britain as 'a swan's nest' in the great pool of
human vice (III. iv. 142). There is, from the first, sadness in
her tragically-crossed love, and, at the lowest ebb of her endurance, a whimsical half-amused awareness, as of an object outside her, of her own suffering.

And yet the royal (III. v. 70) strain in her can be 'anger'd' (II. iii. 145). Learning of Posthumus' jealousy and command that she be murdered, she asserts herself with a typical reserve, claiming that her refusal of many 'princely' suitors in favour of a simple gentleman was, after all, 'no act of common passage but a strain of rareness' (III. iv. 94), though already beginning, characteristically, to pity his suffering when he shall realize his mistake. She forgives him before learning of Iachimo's plot; as indeed he forgives her, before learning how he has been tricked. She implores Pisanio to slay her, as his lord commands; and when he refuses, remains lost, in despair, unwanted, homeless:

> Pisanio.   If you'll back to the court—
> Imogen.   No court, no father ; nor no more ado
>   With that harsh, noble, simple nothing Cloten !
>   (III. iv. 133)

Her disjointed, weary phrases speak more than rhetoric.

Pisanio advises her to adopt a boy's disguise, putting on 'waggish courage' (III. iv. 160) like Rosalind and Portia; and she agrees, planning (like Viola) to offer her music (III. iv. 178) as a recommendation for service. In this guise she is felt as peculiarly, pathetically, attractive, more so than past heroines: witness the idyllic admiration she at once arouses in Guiderius and Arviragus. During her troubled journey towards Milford Haven—she is the first of our pathetic, road-wearied, heroines, ancestress to those of George Eliot, Hardy and other novelists —she gets lost in the wild country, and comes on the outlaws' mountain retreat, all wearied and hungry, like Orlando in *As You Like It*, eating what she finds and offering payment when discovered. They find her there, and Belarius thinks her a fairy (III. vi. 41). She is, one feels, magnetized to this, enchanted, spot, and indeed, before finding it, as though qualifying for final initiation into this sanctuary of natural royalty, to which she alone of our other persons has the right of entry, gets direction from 'beggars' and moralizes thereon, comparing them with kings and courts (III. vi. 8–14). Belarius and the boys look after their Fidele, treating her as a brother, half in love. She is at home with them; they with her.

When she falls sick, 'heart-sick' as she calls it (IV. ii. 37), her

queer disjointed phrases are shot through with a wry amusement at herself and an unwillingness to burden others:

> So sick I am not, yet I am not well :
> But not so citizen a wanton as
> To seem to die ere sick. So please you, leave me ;
> Stick to your journal course ; the breach of custom
> Is breach of all. I am ill ; but your being by me
> Cannot amend me ; society is no comfort
> To one not sociable. I am not very sick,
> Since I can reason of it ; pray you, trust me here,
> I'll rob none but myself, and let me die,
> Stealing so poorly.   (IV. ii. 7)

The boys remark on her trick of yoking sighs and smiles,

>   as if the sigh
> Was that it was, for not being such a smile ;
> The smile mocking the sigh . . .   (IV. ii. 52)

Her supposed death—found 'smiling as some fly had tickled
slumber' (IV. ii. 210)—symbolizes her life. But she preserves
throughout a certain richly spiritual force that can make her
seem 'more goddess-like than wife-like' (III. ii. 8); the boys call
her 'angel' (IV. ii. 48), a 'divine temple' (IV. ii. 55); she receives
the glistering idealization usual in *Pericles* and *The Winter's
Tale*, here denied to Posthumus and reserved for her and the
royal boys themselves. And yet, even as boy-servant, she
remains 'tender' and 'nurse-like' (V. v. 87–8). She is, one might
say, poetically happiest in her grief, as in her little oath 'Ods
pitikins!' (IV. ii. 293) when she finds, as she thinks, Posthumus
dead, and the characteristic

>   . . . but if there be
> Yet left in heaven as small a drop of pity
> As a wren's eye, fear'd gods, a part of it !   (IV. ii. 303)

But, when all discords are dissolved, she it is to whom the poet
has given his one most electric description of delight, as we see
her darting her quicksilver glances on everyone in turn to hit
'each object with a joy' (V. v. 396).

Imogen interthreads the play's action, touching all the persons (even Caius Lucius, whom she serves as a page) as does
no one else; both woman and boy, alive then dead, and then

alive again; weak but courageous, light as a feather to the winds of chance, but unswerving in her course of faith; fragile yet indestructible; loved and desired by all in turn, and wronged by most; winning her 'supreme crown of grief' (I. vi. 4) on her road to joy. It is this slip of tender royalty, made of the winnowed best of Shakespeare's other heroines—in Donne's phrase, 'like gold to airy thinness beat'—that Posthumus, type of Britain's best manhood, wins; loses through his own foolishness and the seductive wiles of Italy; but finally recovers.

The plot-construction and interweaving of themes and persons in *Cymbeline* are extraordinarily interesting; so is its impressionistic subtlety, to be reviewed later. We have, however, so far missed the imaginative density of *The Winter's Tale*, scenes where person, setting, action and imagery make one glowing ingot, anvil-hot; and not until we approach Bellarius' cave do we find a comparable creative magic. We wait for it until the third act; but then the poet's genius functions with sovereign power.

These scenes have the glow, the imaginative aura, of *The Winter's Tale*. The setting is a cave in a 'mountainous country', among the Welsh mountains. Nowhere else in Shakespeare do mountains, to become later such recurring powers in our poetry, receive a primary emphasis. The setting is rugged; we face nature in its primal grandeur.

Belarius tells his charges, the royal boys, how their cave's low entrance instructs them how to 'adore the heavens' with 'a morning's holy office'; and proceeds to contrast their wild existence with the arrogance of monarchs whose lofty gates allow them to keep their 'impious turbans on without good-morrow to the sun'. Two paganisms, grand and ignoble, are finely contrasted. 'Hail, thou fair heaven!' he cries; and the boys repeat, in turn, 'Hail, heaven!' (III. iii. 1–9). The sunlit heaven is conceived simply, as a living presence (as again later in Belarius' magnificent phrase 'It is great morning' at IV. ii. 61) in this prayer of natural piety, of devotion to the great Nature of *The Winter's Tale*, seen in all its rugged and golden works.

Belarius draws morals from the 'mountain-sport' to follow, contrasting, precisely as do the outlaws in *The Two Gentlemen of Verona* and the banished duke in *As You Like It*, this nature-fed existence with the insincerities of the court. But the boys see themselves as 'unfledg'd' eagles that have 'never wing'd from view o' the nest'—as eaglets in their mountain eyrie— and thirst for the wider life:

> *Arviragus.*   What should we speak of
> When we are old as you ? when we shall hear
> The rain and wind beat dark December, how
> In this our pinching cave shall we discourse
> The freezing hours away ?   (III. iii. 35)

Belarius recalls those wrongs that drove him to this wild calling and starts them off for their day's hunting among the mountain crags:

> But, up to the mountains !
> This is not hunter's language. He that strikes
> The venison first shall be the lord o' the feast ;
> To him the other two shall minister . . .   (III. iii. 73)

The tiny community has its own rough aristocracy to be daily reasserted and re-won. Belarius' cave reminds one of Jason and the boy-heroes under Cheiron, the Centaur, in the old Greek story: there is the same rough magic, the same boyhood glamour, in both.

When they are gone, Belarius meditates how

>   nature prompts them
> In simple and low things to prince it much
> Beyond the trick of others.   (III. iii. 84)

Of the elder, Guiderius, he tells us:

> When on my three-foot stool I sit and tell
> The war-like feats I have done, his spirits fly out
> Into my story : say, 'Thus mine enemy fell,
> And thus I set my foot on's neck' ; even then
> The princely blood flows in his cheek, he sweats,
> Strains his young nerves, and puts himself in posture
> That acts my words. The younger brother, Cadwal—
> Once Arviragus—in as like a figure,
> Strikes life into my speech and shows much more
> His own conceiving . . .   (III. iii. 89)

How admirable is this diagnosis of youthful psychology in its desire to *act*, as by sympathetic magic, what it dreams. Guiderius in this description is the more warlike, Arviragus the more sensitive, of the two; the one has the makings of a soldier, the other of an artist. Both enjoy a certain lustre outshining all Posthumus' worthiness: they are the bearers of the royal, he of, in our modern sense, the democratic, virtues. And yet 'virtue' must be read rather in its older sense, in terms of innate fineness rather than of moral choice. Each is both fierce and gentle, the emphasis lying on Guiderius' strength and Arviragus' gentleness. Guiderius wins the first place at hunting and becomes 'master of the feast' (III. vi. 28) and makes short work of Cloten (IV. ii). One feels a wild beast's ferocity in their attack; they house primal nature in its ferocious, as Perdita in its flowery, aspect; and yet they show Perdita's flower-sweetness also.

Returning from the hunt, they discover Imogen, in her boy's dress, eating She alone of our persons could enter this magic circle, and there is something inevitable in her finding her way here. More, she at once receives the poetry that *Cymbeline* so often avoids, the valuation outspacing all rational categories. Belarius thinks her a 'fairy' (III. vi. 41) and continues:

> By Jupiter an angel ! or, if not,
> An earthly paragon ! Behold divineness
> No elder than a boy !   (III. vi. 42)

Such poetry is to be subtly distinguished from the at first sight equally extreme praise of Imogen in the wager scene, where the prosaic Posthumus, though he sets no limit to her worth, sees it in terms of the ethical, rather than the poetic, judgement; and, while reverencing it as 'the gift of the gods' (I. iv. 97), remains outside it, as an 'adorer' (I. iv. 79), not quite attuned to its magic. With Belarius and his charges it is different. She no sooner enters the cave than she belongs there. She, like the boys, is crowned by the 'light that never was, on sea or land'; that touch of unearthliness burning from earth, hinted, ever so delicately, in her own phrase about finding 'gold strew'd i' the floor' (III. vii. 49; cp. the 'fairy gold' of *The Winter's Tale*, III. iii. 127) of this strangely hospitable cave. She is entertained, and shares in the hunters' feast.

The royal boys are captivated by their new friend. Guiderius is the more impulsive, Arviragus the more sensitively, more quietly and inwardly, responsive; Guiderius woos, Arviragus mothers, the boy, murmuring, when he is ill, 'poor sick Fidele' (IV. ii. 166); and it is Arviragus' music, the solemn throbs of his mournful harp from the cavern's dark recesses, as from the mouth of death itself, that announce Fidele's passing. 'Is Cadwal mad?' they ask (IV. ii. 195). He enters, the boy in his arms, murmuring 'The bird is dead' (IV. ii. 197), a phrase echoing his own wild rock-nurtured life. This 'blessed thing' (IV. ii. 206), this 'most rare boy' (IV. ii. 208) he found lying cheek on cushion and half smiling, like Keats' image of poetry 'half-slumbering on its own right arm' and Shelley's Child in *Prometheus*. Fidele seems, like Cleopatra, to be sleeping:

Guiderius.   Why, he but sleeps :
If he be gone, he'll make his grave a bed ;
With female fairies will his tomb be haunted,
And worms will not come to thee.
Arviragus.   With fairest flowers
While summer lasts and I live here, Fidele,
I'll sweeten thy sad grave ; thou shalt not lack
The flower that's like thy face, pale primrose, nor
The leaf of eglantine, whom not to slander,
Out-sweeten'd not thy breath : the ruddock would,
With charitable bill—O ! bill ! sore-shaming
Those rich-left heirs, that let their fathers lie
Without a monument—bring thee all this :
Yea, and furr'd moss besides, when flowers are none
To winter-ground thy corse.   (IV. ii. 215)

It is as though the very earthiness of death, its kinship with dank soil, flowers and cool moss, were sanctified, 'charity' breathing through the forest ritual.

Guiderius, ever practical, calls an end to fantasy and urges on the burial. Arviragus would 'sing him to the ground' (IV. ii. 236); but since Guiderius 'cannot sing' (IV. ii. 240), they intone the dirge. First the practical Guiderius remembers the death of Euriphile:

Nay, Cadwal, we must lay his head to the east ;
My father hath a reason for 't.   (IV. ii. 255)

It is not for Guiderius to tax himself with reasons; he acts first. Then follows their famous dirge:

Fear no more the heat o' the sun,
    Nor the furious winter's rages,
Thou thy worldly task hast done,
    Home art gone, and ta'en thy wages ;
Golden lads and girls all must,
    As chimney-sweepers, come to dust.   (IV. ii. 258)

The simple ritual done, Belarius strews on them, on Fidele
and the dead Cloten, 'herbs that have on them cold dew o'
the night' (IV. ii. 284). Throughout our impressions are
melancholy and dark, and smell of the earth: Imogen continues
them when she recovers, planning with Lucius to strew her
Posthumus 'with wild wood-leaves and weeds' (IV. ii. 390),
searching out, he says—for the stern Roman catches it too—
'the prettiest daisied plot we can' (IV. ii. 398). Never was the
tang of earthy burial more kind, nor sorrow itself more
friendly; as though through some foreshadowing whereby
death itself were known to draw continued sustenance from the
caress of wind and earth, like the mouldering sweetness of
autumnal leaves.

The poetic magic lies close to the prevailing conception of
royalty, of royal blood, as quite outspacing political categories,
while drawing near to the mystical or magical. When Arviragus asks Fidele, 'Are we not brothers?' she answers:

    So man and man should be.
But clay and clay differs in dignity,
Whose dust is both alike.   (IV. ii. 3)

Where 'dignity' means worth, or value. Belarius says of
Cloten:

    He was a queen's son, boys,
And though he came our enemy, remember
He was paid for that ; though mean and mighty rotting
Together, have one dust, yet reverence—
That angel of the world—doth make distinction
Of place 'tween high and low. Our foe was princely,
And though you took his life, as being our foe,
Yet bury him as a prince.   (IV. ii. 244)

The whole action is conceived to show that Cloten was, in fact,
far from 'princely'; but the key lies in 'reverence', corresponding to 'respect' in Ulysses' order-speech in *Troilus and Cressida*

(I. iii. 75), the great principle of value, of worth, of, at the limit, divinity. This principle must be guarded: it is 'the angel of the world', that is, the messenger, or link, between God and man. That is why Belarius trains the boys in service and respect, he who wins highest honour—note that it has to be daily re-won—in the day's hunting being 'lord o' the feast' (III. iii. 75; III. vi. 29), and the others serving him. The boys themselves are far from respect for superficial values. Ingrained in them is a haughty loathing for money, learnt, we may suggest, from that other cave-dweller, Timon:

> All gold and silver rather turn to dirt !
> As 'tis no better reckon'd but of those
> Who worship dirty gods.   (III. vii. 53)

That Shakespeare can visualize the highest possible as independent of rank and birth is clear at *Henry V*, IV. iii. 61–3; *All's Well That Ends Well*, II. iii. 124–51; *Pericles*, III. ii. 26–31; and *Henry VIII*, v. v. 37–9.

Here, however, the wonder is in the instinctive assertion of royal blood, apart from ceremony (cp. *Henry V*, IV. i. 250–304) and recognition. Observing their love of Fidele, Belarius remarks:

> O noble strain !
> O worthiness of nature ! breed of greatness !
> Cowards father cowards, and base things sire base . . .
>   (IV. i. 24)

His best comment is:

> O thou goddess !
> Thou divine Nature, how thyself thou blazon'st
> In these two princely boys. They are as gentle
> As zephyrs, blowing below the violet,
> Not wagging his sweet head ; and yet as rough,
> Their royal blood enchaf'd, as the rud'st wind,
> That by the top doth take the mountain pine,
> And make him stoop to the vale. 'Tis wonder
> That an invisible instinct should frame them
> To royalty unlearn'd, honour untaught,
> Civility not seen from other, valour
> That wildly grows in them, but yields a crop
> As if it had been sow'd !   (IV. ii. 169)

In terms of royal blood—of which he elsewhere recognizes the limitations—Shakespeare defines something half-magical, some excellence beyond the normal categories exemplified by Post-humus. Though gentleness is emphasized (as in 'two of the sweet'st companions in the world' at v. v. 350), though flower-thoughts blend naturally into the description, and indeed come spontaneously elsewhere to the boys' lips, yet both the rough and the gentle aspects of nature are contained; a strength, even violence, suggested, the rough beginnings of that forcefulness characterizing a born leader. And yet the words 'princely', 'royal', 'royalty', 'honour', 'civility', all witness that the primal instinct at work does not run counter to the chivalric virtues. Guiderius reacts instinctively from Cloten's arrogance, asserting that it was 'most uncivil' and 'nothing prince-like' (v. v. 294). However reached, and whatever its relation to Tudor politics, Shakespeare's conception clearly hints some high order of human being in embryo, to which the nearest analogies in our literature are the youthful heroes of Coleridge's *Zapolya* and Keats' *Otho the Great*; with one sad miscarriage of attempt in Wordsworth's *Excursion*.[1] The excellence intended is perhaps best defined as a grand potentiality in boyhood; a mature figure being always liable to fail, becoming either impractical, as are Shakespeare's philosophic rulers and Byron's Sardana-palus, or a conventional soldier, like Shakespeare's Henry V. A final elucidation is given by Nietzsche's *Thus Spake Zara-thustra*: the royal boys have not attained the integration of gentleness and power Nietzsche preaches, but they are match-less raw material for it.

When Britain is invaded, the boys, despite Belarius' advice, press to join their country's defenders; they are unwilling to remain 'hot summer's tanlings and the shrinking slaves of winter' (IV. iv. 29): in a state, that is, of natural servitude, beyond which their royal instincts prompt them. And yet it is 'by this sun that shines' (IV. iv. 34) that they swear their resolution, preserving their natural piety:

> I am asham'd
> To look upon the holy sun, to have
> The benefit of his bless'd beams, remaining
> So long a poor unknown.   (IV. iv. 40)

[1] See *The Starlit Dome*, especially p. 173 (for Coleridge); pp. 292–3 (for Keats); and p. 54 (for Wordsworth).

Nature, the 'great creating nature' of *The Winter's Tale*, itself drives them beyond their semi-savage existence. So these two, with the old Belarius, and joined by Posthumus, turn Britain's defeat to victory. They prove themselves 'the liver, heart and brain of Britain' by whom 'she lives' (v. v. 14).

Cymbeline is a vast parable, with affinities to Lyly's *Endimion*, though far more compacted and weighty and with no stiffness of allegory. A sense of destiny is pointed by two transcendental incidents: (i) the appearance of Jupiter and (ii) the Soothsayer's vision; the reference of the one being mainly personal; of the other national; though the two interests dovetail.

The action reaches a climax at Jupiter's appearance to Posthumus. This scene we shall study in detail presently. The extraordinary event cannot be properly received without full appreciation of the more-than-personal significance of Posthumus and the social and national implications of his marriage. Jupiter leaves an oracular tablet, reminiscent of the dream-book in *Endimion*,[1] foretelling in cryptic phraseology the King's recovery of his lost sons and Posthumus' union with Imogen. The King is called a 'royal cedar', Posthumus Leonatus a 'lion's whelp', and Imogen 'a piece of tender air', the phrase being derived by the Soothsayer through *mollis aer* to *mulier*, to emphasize her typifying of womanhood, at its gentle best (v. v. 436–53). So Posthumus' representative function, whereby his successful marriage becomes at once the matrimonial peace of the individual, the social integrity of the nation and the union of British manhood with the essence—Imogen is just that, an 'essence'—of royalty, which is also the union of strength with gentleness, becomes peculiarly clear:

> . . . then shall Posthumus end his miseries, Britain be fortunate and flourish in peace and plenty.   (v. v. 441)

Posthumus' happiness is one with Britain's welfare. His marriage-happiness is assured by Jupiter, in whose 'Temple' he was married (v. iv. 106); and indeed the will to preserve the marriage bond inviolate, so strong in Shakespeare's work, may well be derivative from Roman rather than Hebraic sources. So young Britain receives, through Posthumus, the blessing and protection of great Jupiter, the guardian deity of ancient Rome.

[1] See my note on p. 197.

The play's final scene, a *tour de force* of technical compression, knits our various themes together. The King recovers his sons, as Pericles recovers Marina and Leontes Perdita, though here there is the further national symbolism of royal strength return-ing to Britain (cp. 'Now these her princes are come home again . . .' at *King John*, v. vii. 115); and perhaps too of some yet greater royalty as yet unborn. Iachimo is, like Iago, un-masked, though again with a wider significance; and the dead Queen and Cloten are at last known for what they are, or were, and finally repudiated; as, in the sequence of Shakespeare's national thinking, Richard III and Macbeth (who tried to murder Britain's destiny at its source) were rejected.

Each person accordingly contributes to the national state-ment whose enveloping action dramatizes the conflict and union of Britain with Rome. This enveloping action has, too, its transcendental pointing. The Soothsayer describes his vision:

> I saw Jove's bird, the Roman eagle, wing'd
> From the spongy south to this part of the west,
> There vanish'd in the sunbeams . . .   (IV. ii. 348)

He takes it to portend Britain's defeat, but when things develop differently attempts a re-interpretation:

> . . . for the Roman eagle
> From south to west on wing soaring aloft,
> Lessen'd herself, and in the beams o' the sun
> So vanish'd : which foreshow'd our princely eagle,
> The imperial Caesar, should again unite
> His favour with the radiant Cymbeline,
> Which shines here in the west.   (V. v. 471)

The meaning need not be limited to this interpretation, though the union of Rome and Britain is, of course, central. The word 'spongy' suggests softness and also, perhaps, an enervating, clammy heat, as though the imperial eagle were leaving a soft, effete, decaying land for one more virile[1]. It underlines the precise relation within our drama of Renaissance Italy to

---

[1] Shakespeare's use of 'sponge' is elsewhere derogatory. It is associated with foreign drunken-ness at *The Merchant of Venice*, I. ii. 106, and with flattery at *Hamlet*, IV. ii. 12–23 ; while 'the poisonous damp of night *disponage* upon me' is used for retribution on treachery at *Antony and Cleopatra*, IV. ix. 13. See also *Troilus and Cressida*, II. ii. 12. A concordance might supply further examples.

ancient Rome, whilst indicating why their synchronization was forced: as the Roman virtue sinks to the level of Iachimo, the heritage of ancient Rome falls on Britain. The western, sunset emphasis may even hold a hint of Elizabethan sea-adventures. Certainly we are to feel the Roman power as vanishing into the golden skies of a Britain destined to prove worthy of her Roman tutelage.

Jupiter's blessing on Posthumus' marriage and the Soothsayer's vision thus make similar statements. Both symbolize a certain transference of virtue from Rome to Britain.

Shakespeare's two national faiths are here married; his creative faith in ancient Rome, felt in the Roman dramas from *Titus Andronicus* to *Coriolanus*, and his faith in England:

> Set we forward : let
> A Roman and a British ensign wave
> Friendly together ; so through Lud's town march :
> And in the temple of great Jupiter
> Our peace we'll ratify ; seal it with feasts.
> Set on there. Never was war did cease,
> Ere bloody hands were wash'd, with such a peace.
>
> (v. v. 480)

As *Pericles* and *The Winter's Tale* assimilate and negate tragedy, so *Cymbeline* transmutes former dramas of victorious war into a strangely paradoxical harmony of war-negating peace, wherein the victor in fine humility acknowledges the loser's right.

That our supreme national poet should have thus set himself to delve into the historic origins of his nation with a view to interpretation of its destiny is not strange. Shakespeare's own concern with Britain's Roman associations is already clear enough at *Richard III*, iii. i. 68–93, where the Tower of London's supposed relation to Julius Caesar acts as an inspiration to the Prince's English patriotism (see also *Richard II*, v. i. 2). Other writers, too, have left similar works, from Layamon's *Brut* to Milton's *History of Britain*. The legendary relation of Brut through Brutus to ancient Troy, or of Lud to Lydia cannot here receive the investigation it demands; but there seems to have been a deep interest in these legends and a desire to use them. National allegory is powerful in Spenser's *Faerie Queene* and Lyly's *Endimion*, and probably an Elizabethan would feel a Tudor reference in the royal boys' Welsh upbringing; though such enquiries into secondary meanings are dangerous and of slight value. Apart from Shakespeare's obviously historical work, the Nordic tragedies themselves idealize 'the most high and palmy state of Rome' (*Hamlet*, i. i. 113; see also v. i. 235), while also holding overtones of national prophecy, faint in *King Lear* (iii. ii. 80), and clear in *Macbeth*, with its vision of British kings stretching 'to the crack of doom' (*Macbeth*, iv. i. 117; cp. 'the general all-ending day' in our Tower of London passage, *Richard III*, iii. i. 78).

Cymbeline not only enweaves, through Imogen, the feminine transcendentalism of *Pericles* and *The Winter's Tale* into a national design, but also serves to link Shakespeare's past Histories and Tragedies to *Henry VIII*.

II. THE VISION OF JUPITER

> My son, despise not the chastening of the Lord, neither be wearied
> of his correction: for whom the Lord loveth he correcteth; even as a
> father the son in whom he delighteth.   *Proverbs*, iii, 11.

In approaching Posthumus' vision (v. iv.) it is necessary to
face the complaints of established criticism levelled against its
authenticity. On the publication of *Myth and Miracle* one
critic of high repute dismissed my central emphasis as a
critical solecism, quoting Dowden's opinion (offered tentatively
in the Arden introduction) that 'some playhouse hack or a
handy actor' 'strung' the greater number of lines together 'to
prolong a spectacular scene'; while a justly famous scholar
elsewhere observed that 'not the most hardened anti-disin-
tegrationist' would 'ascribe' the scene to Shakespeare, the
assumption being that its spuriousness was no longer a matter
of opinion. My purpose here is two-fold: (i) to show that the
Vision in its entirety must be accepted, whilst simultaneously
(ii) examining it as an example of a normal Shakespearian
technique whereby a single important unit concentrates the
massed meanings of its play.[1]

Posthumus sleeps in prison. There is solemn music—a
usual Shakespearian direction, used earlier of Cadwal's harping
(iv. ii. 186)—and then 'enter as in an apparition' Posthumus'
father and mother 'with music before them'; and then 'after
other music', his brothers. They 'circle' round the sleeping
figure (v. iv. 29). The phraseology resembles that of other
ritualistic directions in Shakespeare's final period. We find
nothing whatever in the language, here or afterwards, to question. Queen Katharine's similar vision in *Henry VIII* is also
accompanied by 'sad and solemn music', the elaborate direction
being of similar style and including the phrase 'as it were by
inspiration' (*Henry VIII*, iv. ii. 80–2).

Posthumus' vision is darker than Queen Katharine's but
precisely suits his fortunes and the whole play. It is stately,
solemn, and harmonious, using circular movement and a melo-

---

[1] Two good examples occur in *Antony and Cleopatra*: Enobarbus' description of Cleopatra
on Cydnus and Cleopatra's dream of the universal Antony; and one in *Macbeth*, where child-
apparitions rise from a work rich in child-reference. These examples are discussed in my
Imperial Theme.

dious chant: death, through these ghosts, is functioning as harmony. There could be no more vivid mark of its authenticity; for such is death throughout *Cymbeline*, so rich in sweetly sombre impressions of death; of death, as it were, softened, with a pervading atmosphere of deep but ineffectual tragedy. Death is here desired, yet merciful. Significantly, no major tempest-symbolism, outside our Vision, jars the action.

Posthumus early invokes 'bonds of death' (i. i. 117) to prevent his loving any wife but Imogen; while she, referring to their separation, remarks 'There cannot be a pinch in death more sharp than this is' (i. i. 130). Cornelius has been asked by the wicked Queen for poisons, 'the movers of a languishing death' which 'though slow are deadly' (i. v. 9), but instead supplies a potion that only makes 'a show of death' (i. v. 40). It resembles the Friar's drug in *Romeo and Juliet*, a play recalled too by Iachimo's words over the sleeping Imogen:

> O sleep ! thou ape of death, lie dull upon her ;
> And be her sense but as a monument
> Thus in a chapel lying. (ii. ii. 31)

Hearing from Pisanio that Posthumus has ordered her death, Imogen craves his obedience, herself prevented from suicide by a reminiscence of *Hamlet*:

> Against self-slaughter
> There is a prohibition so divine
> That cravens my weak hand. (iii. iv. 78)

She desires death; it is a kindly release, as when, sick in the cave, she says 'let me die' (iv. ii. 15), her pathetic longing developing into the beauty of her supposed death, found 'stark' dead, but

> Thus smiling, as some fly had tickled slumber,
> Not as death's dart, being laugh'd at ; his right cheek
> Reposing on a cushion. (iv. ii. 210)

Like all about her, Imogen's 'death' is supremely pretty, its associations sad yet reassuring. There are Arviragus' thoughts of strewing her grave—which Guiderius, saying 'he but sleeps', calls a 'bed' (iv. ii. 215–16)—with wild flowers and the following picture of the robin, continuing that office, with flowers, leaves, and moss (iv. ii. 224–9). There was Cadwal's (i.e.

Arviragus') first mournful harping (IV. ii. 186), his, to quote a
phrase from *The Phoenix and the Turtle*, 'defunctive music' and
the sweetly-solemn dirge:

> Golden lads and girls all must,
> As chimney-sweepers, come to dust.   (IV. ii. 262)

As in Hamlet's graveyard meditations, 'mean and mighty rotting together have one dust' (IV. ii. 246). Death is supreme but
musical; an embedding in earth and its earthy sweets. The
Dirge itself hymns death as the release from all mortal fears—
harsh nature, tyranny, slander—a calling home and a rewarder
(II. ii. 258–81). There is, to quote again from *The Phoenix and
the Turtle*, something peculiarly 'death-divining' in the mournful but melodious accents. Imogen's revival makes contact with
the resurrections of Thaisa and Hermione; the miraculous
element being shaded in later by Guiderius' 'the same dead
thing alive' (v. v. 124) and 'we saw him dead' (v. v. 127); and
Imogen's 'most like I did, for I was dead' (v. v. 260). When
Imogen finds Posthumus' supposed dead body, she gets Lucius
to help bury him, together searching for 'the prettiest daisied
plot' they can find (IV. ii. 398) and strewing the grave 'with
wild wood-leaves and weeds' (IV. ii. 390). The wistful sadness
of it all suits Imogen.

The repentant Posthumus likewise desires to die in battle.
Having killed, as he thinks, the thing he loved, his 'life is,
every breath, a death' (v. i. 27). But the other 'death' in battle
he cannot find (v. iii. 69). He invokes it again in prison as
'the sure physician, death' (v. iv. 7), and prays to the 'great
powers' (v. iv. 26):

> For Imogen's dear life, take mine ; and though
> 'Tis not so dear, yet 'tis a life ; you coin'd it . . .
>   (v. iv. 22)

He concludes: 'O Imogen! I'll speak to thee in silence' (v. iv.
28); he enters the death-world of sleep, to commune with the
dead. Thereupon follows the Vision, followed closely by his
dialogue with the gaoler, which, by the usual Shakespearian
process of playing a humorous variation on a serious theme,
offers some macabre fun on death as the solver of all
debts:

Gaoler. O ! the charity of a penny cord ; it sums up thousands in
a trice : you have no true debitor and creditor but it ; of
what's past, is, and to come, the discharge. Your neck,
sir, is pen, book, and counters ; so the acquittance follows.

Post. I am merrier to die than thou art to live.

Gaoler. Indeed, sir, he that sleeps feels not the toothache . . .

(v. iv. 169)

Death is less an imposition than a liberator. Our ghostly
Vision is thus enclosed and clasped firmly by speeches of
serene deathly meditation. As the play draws to its conclusion,
Cymbeline observes in the manner of *Pericles* (at v. i. 192–6)
that the gods are striking him 'to death with mortal joy' (v. v.
235).

No better masque-equivalent to these at once fearful and
fruitful impressions of harmonious death in a work concluding
with a series of miraculous survivals could be imagined than
that composed of these kindly yet piteous ghosts from the
Elysian Fields circling to 'solemn music' and demanding
Jupiter's intercession. They fit in.

Everyone is, moreover, correctly presented. Sicilius, 'old'
at I. i. 37 and 'most venerable' at II. v. 3, is, in our carefully-
worded direction, 'an old man' (v. iv. 29). Posthumus' birth
after his father's death and itself the immediate cause of his
mother's, the two brothers' death whilst serving under Tenantius, the phrase 'Leonati's seat' (v. iv. 60; cp. 'strength of the
Leonati' at v. i. 31), all is presented, in both stage direction
and speech, without a slip in strict conformity with the account
given by the Gentleman in I. i. The lines

> That striking in our country's cause
>   Fell bravely and were slain ;
> Our fealty and Tenantius' right
>   In honour to maintain   (v. iv. 71)

exactly match the heroic and warlike feeling elsewhere. A
careful interpolater might, presumably, master such details,
but he would scarcely have been skilful enough to present
Posthumus, in every reference, with exactly the kind of unspectacular honour which we have observed as his poetic lot
throughout:

> Great nature, like his ancestry,
>   Moulded the *stuff* so *fair*,
> That he deserv'd the praise o' the world,
>   As great Sicilius' heir.   (v. iv. 48)

Compare the second line with 'so *fair* an outward and such *stuff*
within' at I. i. 23. The praise is controlled and sternly limited
to natural process (cp. 'stuff', used derogatively, at *Timon of
Athens*, IV. iii. 273[1]); the third line suits a man of solid merit
winning his way; the references to ancestry suggest less a
splendid individual than a link in an heroic chain of descent.
When 'mature for man' he is a 'fruitful object' in the 'eye of
Imogen' who recognizes his 'dignity', i.e. 'worth' (v. iv. 52–7),
exactly as recounted earlier at I. i. 50–4. His worth is beyond
'compare' at I. i. 22; he is without 'parallel' at v. iv. 54. The
phrases are lustreless and diverge strongly from those applied
to Cymbeline's princely sons. Posthumus' 'worth' (I. i. 7) is
here a matter of 'hardiment' duly 'perform'd' to the King, a
subject's duty (v. iv. 75–6), a question of his 'merits' (v. iv. 79),
of which we are reminded throughout. In I. i. he is, as we
have noticed earlier, *pitied*; so he is in the Vision. 'Hath my
poor boy', asks the old Sicilius, 'done aught but well?' (v. iv.
35). 'Our son', says his Mother, 'is good' and she prays for
his 'miseries' to be relieved (v. iv. 85). Later Jupiter refers to
'Your low-laid son', and his 'affliction' (v. iv. 103, 108, 110).
Posthumus here as elsewhere is depicted as a worthy man
suffering unjustly; indeed, less as a man than member of 'a
valiant race' (v. iv. 83), the phrase exactly hitting off his typifying rôle. As for Iachimo, here called 'slight thing of Italy'
(v. iv. 64), the words directly complement 'some jay of Italy'
(III. iv. 51), 'my Italian brain' (v. v. 197), and 'Italian fiend'
(v. v. 211) elsewhere. By what conceivable stroke of genius
could an alien interpolator, obtruding his own incompetence
in another man's work, have insinuated these minute impressions with so unswerving an accuracy?

Posthumus' birth, which we have referred to the Bastard's
in *King John* and Macduff's in *Macbeth*, is described, moreover,
in terms recalling other Shakespearian plays and especially the
final group. Consider this stanza:

---

[1] The word has elsewhere a derogatory tinge in Shakespeare, as at *The Tempest*, IV. i. 236 ;
Macbeth, v. iii. 44 ; *Henry VIII*, I. i. 58.

> Lucina lent not me her aid ;
> But took me in my throes ;
> That from me was Posthumus ript,
> Came crying 'mongst his foes,
> A thing of pity !   (v. iv. 43)

For Lucina, compare *Pericles*, III. i. 10–14; for 'ript' compare Macduff's use at *Macbeth*, v. vii. 45; and for the final two lines, *King Lear*, IV. vi. 187–8. The thought and language are Shakespearian. Compare the description here of the child in the 'womb' as 'attending nature's law' (v. iv. 38) and the 'great nature' which next 'moulded' the growing child (v. iv. 48) with:

> The child was prisoner to the *womb* and is
> By *law* and process of *great nature* thence
> Freed and enfranchis'd.
>   (*The Winter's Tale*, II. ii. 59)

So vivid a recollection forces the question: how far does *Cymbeline* as a whole repeat the particular nature-emphasis of its predecessor? For only if it does so are such phrases organic.

The packed inter-knitting of themes in *Cymbeline* clearly leaves no room for the generous exploitation of natural powers in the former play, but a precisely similar impressionism recurs. The sun is again a great god, the only deity known to the royal boys: references occur at I. vi. 86; II. iii. 23; III. i. 43; III. ii. 69; III. iii. 7; III. iv. 139, 166; IV. ii. 258, 350; IV. iv. 34; IV. iv. 41; v. v. 191. Besides the rugged grandeur of the cave's mountain setting and the earth-magic of its poetry (one passage of which has been more than once well compared to the flower-passage in *The Winter's Tale*), there are many examples of scattered nature-imagery recalling the other play. The seasons are suggested when Posthumus shows himself so apt a pupil that he 'in's spring became a harvest' (I. i. 46); in Imogen's contrast of 'summer' and 'winterly' news (III. iv. 12); and by the chant (at IV. ii. 258–9). Or Arviragus':

> When we shall hear
> The rain and wind beat dark December, how
> In this our pinching cave shall we discourse
> The freezing hours away ?   (III. iii. 36)

The boys resent being always 'hot summer's tanlings and the shrinking slaves of winter' (IV. iv. 29). Imogen's

> And like the tyrannous breathing of the north
> Shakes all our buds from growing   (I. iii. 36)

is a pure *Winter's Tale* reminder. Flowers are important in key-passages concerned with the supposedly dead Imogen and Posthumus. Natural sanctity is emphatic in the 'morning's holy office' paid to the sun (III. iii. 4), the 'chalic'd flowers' filled with dew at II. iii. 25, and

> The benediction of the covering heavens
> Fall on their heads like dew !   (V. v. 351)

The lark singing at 'heaven's gate' (II. iii. 22), 'the blue of heaven's own tinct' (II. ii. 23) and Belarius' 'it is great morning' (IV. ii. 61), all make us feel, just as in *The Winter's Tale*, something beyond platitude in so ordinary a phrase as 'Twixt sky and ground' (V. v. 147). Such poetry is expanded in Iachimo's:

> What ! are men mad ? Hath nature given them eyes
> To see this vaulted arch, and the rich crop
> Of sea and land, which can distinguish 'twixt
> The fiery orbs above and the twinn'd stones
> Upon the number'd beach ?   (I. vi. 32)

This is the handiwork of that 'divine nature' that 'blazons' herself in the two 'princely boys' (IV. ii. 170). Enough has been said to show that the conception in the Vision of human birth and 'great nature' is in direct alignment with *Pericles* and *The Winter's Tale*, and no intrusion in *Cymbeline* itself.

To turn to a very different imagistic group. *Cymbeline* is rich in descriptions of metallic art. Iachimo asks Imogen to guard 'a present for the emperor':

> 'tis plate of rare device, and jewels
> Of rich and exquisite form ; their values great.
> (I. vi. 189)

In Imogen's chamber he observes a 'tapestry of silk and silver' showing 'proud Cleopatra' about to meet 'her Roman' on 'Cydnus':

> a piece of work
> So bravely done, so rich, that it did strive
> In workmanship and value . . .

'The true life' was on it (II. iv. 69–76). The final plays are
characterized by a newly vivid interest in such arts of design,
shading into thoughts of eternity, as when Iachimo sees sleeping Imogen 'as a monument thus in a chapel lying' (II. ii. 32).
To continue:

> The chimney
> Is south the chamber, and the chimney-piece
> Chaste Dian bathing ; never saw I figures
> So likely to report themselves ; the cutter
> Was as another nature, dumb ; outwent her,
> Motion and breath left out.   (II. iv. 80)

Again, we are reminded of 'that rare Italian master, Julio
Romano' and his control of 'eternity', 'nature' and 'life' (*The
Winter's Tale*, v. ii. 105–116; see also v. ii. 15). Finally:

> The roof o' the chamber
> With golden cherubins is fretted ; her andirons—
> I had forgot them—were two winking Cupids
> Of silver, each on one foot standing, nicely
> Depending on their brands.   (II. iv. 87)

It has been observed that in Antony's

> Let Rome in Tiber melt and the wide arch
> Of the rang'd empire fall !
>   (*Antony and Cleopatra*, I. i. 33)

'the wide arch' suggests both the extent and the stability of the
Roman Empire and also its engineering feats (roads, bridges,
aqueducts). Now not only does *Cymbeline*, so full of Roman
interest, present a very fair antiquarian accuracy in proper
names and other detail, but it is peculiarly fond of architectures,
especially roofs, as in 'the roof o' the chamber' in our recent
quotation. Belarius observes how their cave's low 'roof' instructs them to 'adore' the Heavens, whereas the 'gates of
monarchs' are 'arched so high' that their impiety goes un-
checked (III. iii. 1–9); but the boys' 'thoughts' nevertheless
'hit the roofs of palaces' (III. iii. 84): we have a complex of
heavens, roofs, arches, and palaces. Our most splendid nature-

reference, already observed, speaks of the 'vaulted arch' of the
sky (i. vi. 33). The lark sings at 'heaven's gate' (ii. iii. 22),
while the sun's steeds are watering at the dew held by 'chalic'd
flowers' (ii. iii. 25). Cymbeline's sons are 'worthy to *inlay*
heaven with stars' (v. v. 352). Our collection shows interesting
variations on solid workmanship, both blending with Renaissance art and contributing something to the play's solid Roman
impact; with especial emphasis on roofs; of a lady's chamber, a
cave, palaces, the roofed arch of heaven itself.

Now let us turn to our Vision. The ghosts implore Jupiter
to 'ope' his 'crystal window' (v. iv. 81) and 'peep through' his
'marble mansion' (v. iv. 87; cp. 'look through a casement' at
ii. iv. 34); after answering their prayer he returns to his
'palace crystalline' (v. iv. 113); and next Sicilius remarks:

> The marble pavement closes ; he is enter'd
> His radiant roof . . .   (v. iv. 120)

—compare 'radiant Cymbeline' at v. v. 476. The whole Vision
is weightily, sculpturally, conceived.

The Vision dramatizes a choral prayer imploring the divinity to relieve the unjust sufferings of Posthumus. We shall
next notice (i) a complex of associations involving rights,
revenge, justice and imprisonment, and (ii) the relation here
of humanity to the divine, with especial regard to prayer.

The persons assert their rights with almost querulous per-
sistence. Cloten's overweening pride is infuriated by Imogen's
slighting of him in favour of a 'base slave' (ii. iii. 127). Posthumus' confidence in his lady seems to be resented as an insult
by both the Frenchman and Iachimo. Posthumus is infuriated
at Imogen's supposed betrayal. Britain and Rome both assert
their rights regarding the tribute. Belarius originally kid-
napped the King's sons in revenge for injustice (iii. iii. 99–
103), the two royal boys assert their rights to experience a
wider world; and so on.[1] Posthumus' merit is a major theme
throughout. Perhaps most significant of all is Imogen's speech
where she, the last person to assert her own deserts, mildly, as
is her way, understates her case, saying that her refusal of
princely suitors was, after all, 'no act of common passage but

---

[1] F. J. Furnivall noted a general tendency in the persons of *Cymbeline* to act precipitately
(introduction to the Leopold Shakespeare).

a strain of rareness' (III. iv. 94); and proceeds to grieve for her unfaithful lover.

The persons tend towards a kind of rough justice, the words vengeance or revenge recurring. Iachimo's scheme is a punishment for the Britisher's overweening confidence; Posthumus' revenge on Imogen is a major, and Belarius' on Cymbeline a minor, theme; Cloten's absurd and dastardly scheme of revenge is luridly conceived (III. v. 133–51), while his vicious arrogance meets a deserved punishment at the hand of Guiderius. The Queen, broiling up evil within herself, is in the background plotting a neurotic revenge on everybody, and, when her son seems lost, takes pleasure 'in despite of'—i.e. spite towards— 'heaven and men' (v. v. 58) in promulgating her nefarious designs. The pervading vengefulness blends into more directly legal action, as when Cymbeline banishes Posthumus; and indeed, there is a queerly persistent sense of law, bondage, debt and suchlike precursors of Posthumus' final imprisonment, his long soliloquy in prison and conversation with the Gaoler concerning death's loosening of all 'bonds'—a recurring word—and debts. The scattered references, none in themselves particularly important, are, in the mass, interesting. Imogen is 'imprison'd' for her marriage (I. i. 8) and later the Queen, in supposed kindness, calls herself Imogen's 'gaoler' and she the 'prisoner', using the phrase 'lock up your restraint' (I. i. 72–4); Posthumus calls the bracelet he gives Imogen 'a manacle of love' and her a 'prisoner' (I. i. 122–3); the covenant between Posthumus and Iachimo is to be set down 'by lawful counsel' (I. iv. 185); Iachimo says that Imogen's beauty 'takes prisoner the wild motion of mine eye' (I. vi. 103). Imogen, breaking the wax on Posthumus' letter, finds in 'these locks of counsel' occasion to draw a contrast between 'lovers' and 'men in dangerous bonds', thinking of 'forfeiters' being 'cast into prison' (III. ii. 36–9). Guiderius considers his cave-life as 'a prison for a debtor' (III. iii. 34)—see also 'debtor' at I. iv. 40 and II. iv. 8—and Arviragus continues the thought with:

> our cage
> We make a quire, as doth the prison'd bird,
> And sing our bondage freely.　　　　(III. iii. 42)

Pisanio is threatened by Cloten with 'condemnation' (III. v. 98)

and Guiderius 'condemn'd' by Cymbeline to 'a hard sentence'
under the 'law' (v. v. 290–300). Cloten calls Guiderius a
'robber' and 'law-breaker' (iv. ii. 74–5), and gets promptly
killed for it with the boy's comment:

> The law
> Protects not us ; then why should we be tender
> To let an arrogant piece of flesh threat us,
> Play judge and executioner all himself,
> For we do fear the law ?   (iv. ii. 125)

Posthumus, hoping Pisanio has not obeyed his murderous
command, says:

> Every good servant does not all commands ;
> No bond but to do just ones.   (v. i. 6)

'Bond', a Shakespearian favourite, is especially emphatic in
Cymbeline. See also the important remark on the laws of Britain
having been 'mangled' by 'the sword of Caesar' (iii. i. 57);
'lawyer' and 'case' at ii. iii. 79, legal 'action' at ii. iii.
156, 'bondage' at i. vi. 73, 'voucher' and 'law' at ii. ii. 39;
and so on.

Clearly, such scatterings—my list is not exhaustive—slight
or otherwise necessitated in themselves, yet relate to the prison
scene, where the Vision occurs. They cluster thick-knotted in
Posthumus' preliminary soliloquy. The Gaoler remarks 'you
have locks upon you' (v. iv. 1) and Posthumus speaks at length
in extreme remorse. Here are some relevant phrases: 'Most
welcome, bondage, for thou art a way, I think, to liberty';
death as 'the key to unbar these locks'; 'my conscience, thou
art fetter'd more than my shanks and wrists'; 'the penitent
instrument to pick that bolt'; 'I cannot do it (i.e. repent) better
than in gyves'; the gods' mercy contrasted with 'vile men who
of their broken debtors take a third, a sixth, a tenth, letting
them thrive again on their abatement'. He concludes:

> and so, great powers,
> If you will take this audit, take this life,
> And cancel these cold bonds.   (v. iv. 3–29)

See how the imagery of bonds, law, and debt, the latter to recur
in the later dialogue with the Gaoler, leads immediately to the

Vision, wherein the Ghosts conclude their invocation by threatening to 'appeal' from Jupiter's 'justice' to the other gods (v. iv. 88–92). Thus human justice in Posthumus' soliloquy preceding and the Gaoler dialogue succeeding our Vision is variously (i) referred to death as the solver of all justice and injustice alike and (ii) lifted to the higher plane of heavenly justice and human penitence. Prayers are 'debts' to heaven at III. iii. 72. The close reference of legal terminology to semi-theological problems has precedent in the New Testament, throughout Shakespeare's own *Merchant of Venice* (especially at IV. i. 184–205)[1] and in *Measure for Measure* (II. ii. 57–66, 71–79). So much for Posthumus' soliloquy. The deity's actual appearance follows not unnaturally.

We shall next study the relation throughout *Cymbeline* of man to the divine powers.

The Vision of Jupiter certainly occurs in a work saturated with religious suggestion. The people are not only vengeful; they can also repent. There is the forgiveness of both Posthumus and Imogen of each other before they learn of Iachimo's plot. Posthumus' remorse, as in the soliloquy just noticed, is powerful and joined with the truly remarkable thought—considering Shakespeare's usual attitude—that Imogen's unfaithfulness is a mere slip (v. i. 12). We have Iachimo's summoning conscience (v. ii. 1) and later repentance, with Posthumus' finely-worded forgiveness (v. v. 418–21). Cymbeline himself finally realizes how he has been deceived, and forgives everyone, saying, 'pardon's the word to all' (v. v. 423). The main people are shown as drawing towards a more god-like understanding.

The gods are even more frequently mentioned than in *King Lear*; and, as in *King Lear*, they are entwined with meditations on human justice or injustice. When Iachimo says it is 'the office of the gods to venge' Posthumus' betrayal (I. vi. 92), the thought is a weaker version of Albany's two pronouncements on divine interposition in *King Lear* (IV. ii. 46–50, 78–80). More directly comparable is Cymbeline's comment on the death of his wicked Queen, on whom, he says, the heavens, 'in justice

---

[1] 'Bond', an important word in Shakespeare, as at *Macbeth*, III. ii. 49, reaches intense dramatic and spiritual significance throughout *The Merchant of Venice*, a play whose deeper implications are discussed in my *Shakespearian Production*.

both on her and hers, have laid most heavy hand' (v. v. 465).
The theology in *Cymbeline* is both more optimistic and more
insistent than in *Lear*. There is a belief in 'heaven's bounty'
(I. vi. 78), in gracious (I. iv. 100) powers from whom good
things come: Imogen is 'the gift of the gods' (I. iv. 97), they
made her sweet disposition (I. vi. 177), 'the gods' make Belarius
and the two boys 'preservers' of Cymbeline's throne (v. v. 1).
If things go wrong, the people accept misfortune with a stoic
faith in the guiding powers: Imogen accepts Pisanio's advice,
recognizing that it is 'all the comfort the gods will diet' her
with (III. iv. 182); 'let ordinance', says Arviragus, 'come as the
gods foresay it' (IV. ii. 145); Pisanio, baffled by many complications, contents himself with 'the heavens still must work'
(IV. iii. 41); Lucius faces death in stoic resignation to the will
of 'the gods' (v. v. 78); even men's 'bloods', that is their
physical life, are said to 'obey the heavens' (I. i. 2). Britain
would have lost 'but that the heavens fought' (v. iii. 4). Man
is here utterly dependent, more so than in *King Lear*, on the
'gods' or 'heavens' whose creature he is. That is why the
people talk so naturally to them. Imogen half speaks to 'Jove'
as to a companion (III. vi. 6); when she wakes beside a dead
body, her immediate cry is, 'O gods and goddesses!' (IV. ii.
295); there is her typical and pretty oath in misfortune ' 'Ods
pittikins' (IV. ii. 293). When she introduces herself to Caius
Lucius as the servant of 'Richard du Champ', she wryly hopes
that the gods, if they happen to hear her falsehood, will forgive
it (IV. ii. 377): the gods are always, as it were, just round the
corner, listening, likely to interrupt. The tendency is yet
stronger with Posthumus, as we shall see. Guiderius and Arviragus have an equivalent sense of divine nearness though with
them it is, aptly, felt most strongly through the sun (IV. iv. 34,
41).

This prevailing sense of heaven's nearness shapes itself
naturally into blessings and prayers, such as 'The gods protect
you' (I. i. 128), 'May the gods direct you to the best' (III. iv.
195), 'Flow, flow, you heavenly blessings on her' (III. v. 166),
and 'The benediction of these covering heavens fall on their
heads like dew' (v. v. 351). The gods are normally kind, and
susceptible to pleading. When the possibility of a second love
is suggested to him, Posthumus exclaims:

You gentle gods, give me but this I have,
And sear up my embracements from a next
With bonds of death !   (I. i. 115)

Imogen, receiving his letter, slips naturally into

You good gods
Let what is here contain'd relish of love . . .
                                             (III. ii. 29)

Or, when things are cruel:

But if there be
Yet left in heaven as small a drop of pity
As a wren's eye, fear'd gods, a part of it !
                                             (IV. ii. 303)

More formal, and Christian, prayers are involved when she
wishes she had charged the absent Posthumus

At the sixth hour of morn, at noon, at midnight,
To encounter me with orisons, for then
I am in heaven for him.   (I. iii. 31)

We see her actually praying in her chamber:

To your protection I commend me, gods !
From fairies and the tempters of the night
Guard me, beseech ye !   (II. ii. 8)

Significant, too, is Belarius' speech to the two boys as they
stoop at the cave's entrance and pay 'a morning's holy office'
to the sun, crying 'Hail, heaven !' (III. iii. 1–9), and the following contrast drawn with the impiety of civilized courts. Here,
he says, Belarius 'has paid more pious *debts*' (i.e. prayers) 'to
heaven' than in all his former life (III. iii. 72). The supposed
death of Fidele is accompanied by mournful harping, thoughts
of 'priests and fanes' (IV. ii. 242), the ritual of burial and the
concluding chant or prayer:

No exorciser harm thee !
    Nor no witchcraft charm thee !
Ghost unlaid forbear thee !
    Nothing ill come near thee !
Quiet consummation have ;
And renowned be thy grave !
                                             (IV. ii. 276)

These clustering impressions of divinity and man's reliance thereon, these prayers and chants, form a setting for our Vision with its chanted prayer of intercession imploring the Deity's too long withheld favour. The play ends on a note of prayer: 'Laud we the gods . . . bless'd altars' (v. v. 477). The Ghosts' prayer is thus an extreme instance of a general tendency.

It is, moreover, continuous with Posthumus' two important soliloquies preceding the Vision. These sum and condense our varying significances whilst preparing for, indeed all but demanding, the Deity's appearance. The gods are conceived as variously stern and kind:

> Gods ! if you
> Should have ta'en vengeance on my faults, I never
> Had liv'd to put on this ; so had you sav'd
> The noble Imogen to repent, and struck
> Me, wretch more worth your vengeance. But, alack !
> You snatch some hence for little faults ; that's love,
> To have them fall no more ; you some permit
> To second ills with ills, each elder worse,
> And make them dread it, to the doer's thrift.
> But Imogen is your own ; do your best wills,
> And make me bless'd to obey.   (v. i. 7)

He asks the 'good heavens' to 'hear patiently' his purpose (v. i. 21). One feels the divine powers very near, he is *talking* to them; he prays the 'gods' to give him the 'strength o' the Leonati' (v. i. 31), those same Leonati who in the Vision pray on his behalf. The pressure is being swiftly heightened throughout these agonized soliloquies. Next in prison he wrestles again with the powers above, praying the 'good gods' (v. iv. 9) to forward his repentance:

> Is't enough I am sorry ?
> So children temporal fathers do appease ;
> Gods are more full of mercy.   (v. iv. 11)

He proceeds to argue with them, to bargain:

> If of my freedom 'tis the main part, take
> No stricter render of me than my all . . .   (v. iv. 16)

Our massed thinking on justice, debts and law is here, as we noticed earlier, woven into a fierce, insistent plea from man to god. He ends with:

> ... and so, great powers,
> If you will take this audit, take this life,
> And cancel these cold bonds. O Imogen !
> I'll speak to thee in silence.   (v. iv. 26)

One feels the tension, which has become unbearable, about to snap. The gods have been drawing nearer and nearer; and we are prepared for the Ghosts' final invocation and the logical though startling climax of Jupiter's appearance. If he does not appear, to what do these tormented soliloquies lead?

The Vision is exactly in tone with the play's theological impressionism, which, though a continuation of normal Shakespearian thought, is, in its peculiar emphasis, new; recalling *King Lear* most, but with reminders of the religious optimism of *Pericles* and *The Winter's Tale*, though to be subtly distinguished nevertheless from the 'fortune' of the one and the nature, in association with Apollo, of the other.

But, it may be said, the many appearances of 'gods' and 'heavens' in the text must be distinguished from a mythological deity such as Jupiter. Is there, it will be asked, a soil, as it were, of classical mythology rich enough to bear this staggering *deus ex machina?* The answer is that *Cymbeline*, whose purpose is in part to emphasize the importance of ancient Rome in Britain's history, probably exceeds any other Shakespearian play in its fecundity of classical, and especially mythological, reference.

Imogen is compared to 'the Arabian bird' (i. vi. 17) or Phoenix; Iachimo sees himself as Tarquin (ii. ii. 12) and Imogen's bracelet as 'the Gordian knot' (ii. ii. 34); Imogen in bed reads the story of Philomel and Tereus (ii. ii. 45), while her tapestry shows Cleopatra on Cydnus (ii. iv. 69–72). Slander, says Pisanio, 'outvenoms all the worms of Nile' (iii. iv. 37); Imogen refers to Aeneas and Sinon (iii. iv. 60–1); 'not Hercules', says Guiderius, 'could have knocked out' Cloten's brains, since 'he had none' (iv. ii. 114); he refers later to Thersites and Ajax (iv. ii. 252). Imogen, for once stung to violence, imprecates 'all curses madded Hecuba gave the Greeks' (iv. ii. 313) on the supposed murderer of her lord. As for deities, no other play is so rich in Roman gods and goddesses: they are, moreover, presented with a peculiar feeling for their particular natures, they are *intimately* discerned. The comparison of Imogen to 'Cytherea' is vividly conceived:

> Cytherea
> How bravely thou becom'st thy bed ! fresh lily
> And whiter than the sheets.   (II. ii. 14)

Britain's coasts stand 'as Neptune's park' (III. i. 19), the roaring waters being carefully realized. Juno's irascible jealousy is assumed (as, too, in our Vision) in Pisanio's remark that Imogen's beauty 'made great Juno angry' (III. iv. 168); so is her regal dignity in the thought that Imogen's skill in cookery 'sauc'd our broths as Juno had been sick, and he her dieter' (IV. i. 51). Two aspects of the sun-god are presented: one in 'the greedy touch of common-kissing Titan' (III. iv. 165); the other, in suggestion of his resplendent chariot, 'had it been a carbuncle of Phoebus' wheel' (V. v. 190) and the thought of 'Phoebus' arising and watering his heavenly 'steeds' in Cloten's serenade (II. iii. 23). There are the 'two winking'—i.e. blind —'Cupids of silver' in Imogen's chamber (II. iv. 89), while a love-letter is called 'young Cupid's tables' (III. ii. 39). Imogen shows

> A pudency so rosy the sweet view on't
> Might well have warm'd old Saturn.   (II. v. 11)

Diana gets a recurring notice. To preserve chastity is to 'live like Diana's priest, betwixt cold sheets' (I. vi. 133); gold makes 'Diana's rangers false' (II. iii. 74); Posthumus' mother seemed 'the Dian of that time' (II. v. 7); Posthumus speaks of his lady 'as Dian had hot dreams' (V. v. 181). Imogen's chamber aptly has a carving showing 'chaste Dian bathing' (II. iv. 82). The eternity of art is well hinted in report of ladies

> . . . for feature laming
> The shrine of Venus or straight-pight Minerva,
> Postures beyond brief nature.   (V. v. 164)

The list is itself significant, but the degree of intimacy, the use of adjectives and reference to the typical behaviour or duties of the divinities concerned is even more so; mythology is felt as coming alive as we read. The Ghosts' references to Mars and Juno ('that thy adulteries rates and revenges' V. iv. 32–4) is in keeping[1]; and Sicilius' intimately realized comment later (v. iv. 114–19) on Jupiter's, and his eagle's, typical behaviour a natural culmination.

Apart from Jupiter, the deities most honoured here are (i) Diana, the goddess who actually appears in *Pericles*, and (ii) Phoebus-Apollo, who rules in *The Winter's Tale*. But in this peculiarly Roman play, the main emphasis naturally falls on Jupiter, who is, as one expects, mentioned most frequently of all, the words, 'Jove' or 'Jupiter' recurring about a dozen times outside the Vision. 'Jove' is exclamatory at III. iii. 88; and part of a tiny prayer at II. iv. 98 and III. vi. 6. 'By Jupiter' occurs twice at a central moment in the action (II. iv. 121–2; and again at III. v. 84 and III. vi. 42). Elsewhere we have 'Jove knows what man thou mightst have made' (IV. ii. 207), and 'Wert thou the son of Jupiter' (II. iii. 130). Lucius cries 'Great Jupiter be prais'd' (v. iii. 84). Imogen describes Posthumus as Hamlet describes his father:

> I know the shape of's leg, this is his hand,
> His foot Mercurial, his Martial thigh,
> The brawns of Hercules, but his Jovial face . . .
> (IV. ii. 309)

Jupiter moreover contributes dramatically to the play's unfolding purpose in the Soothsayer's earlier vision:

> *Lucius.*　　　　　　　　. . . Now, sir,
> What have you dream'd of late of this war's purpose ?
> *Soothsayer.* Last night the very gods show'd me a vision—
> I fast and pray'd for their intelligence—thus :
> I saw Jove's bird, the Roman eagle, wing'd
> From the spongy south to this part of the west,
> There vanish'd in the sunbeams ; which portends,
> Unless my sins abuse my divination,
> Success to the Roman host.　　　(IV. ii. 344)

We accordingly have Jupiter's eagle already associated with a prophecy outside our main Vision. The Soothsayer's vision forms a miniature of what is shortly to be dramatized: both are dreams; both suggest a transference of power, or virtue, in the one personal, or matrimonial, and in the other national, from Rome to Britain. Posthumus later reports his experience:

---

[1] This Euripidean remark on Jupiter's matrimonial difficulties (in order presumably to enlist his sympathies for those of Posthumus) may seem ill-judged; a rather similar use of mythological detail occurs in the Masque of *The Tempest*.

                    As I slept, methought,
            Great Jupiter, upon his eagle back'd,
            Appear'd to me, with other spritely shows
            Of mine own kindred.   (v. v. 427)

Jupiter, Rome's chief god, naturally dominates the play's
conclusion, where the Soothsayer, after remarking that 'the
fingers of the powers above do tune the harmony of this peace'
(v. v. 467), recounts and re-interprets his own dream, relating
the eagle to Rome; Cymbeline carrying on with 'Laud we the
gods' (v. v. 477) and deciding to ratify the peace 'in the temple
of great Jupiter' (v. v. 483).

No other play gives Jupiter quite such honour, but he is
Shakespeare's most frequent and most powerful god throughout; and after the parts played by the less important Diana and
Apollo in *Pericles* and *The Winter's Tale*, one surely here expects Jupiter, who seems to have been reserved for the purpose,
to do something spectacular.

Here is our stage-direction:

> Jupiter descends in thunder and lightning, sitting upon an eagle :
> he throws a thunderbolt. The ghosts fall on their knees.

Thunder and lightning are usual in Shakespeare's directions
and both are imagistically associated with Jupiter. Here we
find yet another example of the process already observed,
whereby old tragic imagery becomes new dramatic actuality,
Jupiter's appearance corresponding to Pericles' entry on a
tempest-tossed ship, the throwing of Thaisa, as a-jewel-in-a-
casket, overboard and the appearance of a bear during storm in
The Winter's Tale. One is scarcely surprised to find yet another
important tragic impression brought similarly to life. Is
Jupiter's appearance any more surprising, or technically weak,
than that of the bear? Shakespeare has made peace with one of
his two main tempest-gods, Neptune and Jupiter (compactly
presented together at *Coriolanus*, III. i. 255–6), at *Pericles*, v. i.
(direction); it is natural that he should now make peace with
the other.

But what of the eagle? The deity's position certainly sounds
precarious. The idea of a god riding on or being driven by a
bird or birds is, however, classically correct (e.g. Apollo riding
on a swan[1]; Aphrodite, or Venus, and her team of doves, as in

---

[1] As in an Attic vase-design (in the British Museum).

The Tempest, IV. i. 94), and the conception again actualizes old imagery. Angels, that is messengers from heaven to earth (in the sense already implied by 'angel' at IV. ii. 248)—and as such Jupiter here functions, like Ariel in his thunderous appearance disguised as a harpy (i.e. a blend of angel and eagle, as defined at *Pericles*, IV. iii. 47–8)—are regularly described as riding. In *Macbeth* we have Pity 'striding the blast' and 'Heaven's cherubin hors'd upon the sightless couriers of the air' (I. vii. 21–5); in I *Henry IV* Prince Hal's company are compared to 'eaglets having lately bath'd' and himself to 'feather'd Mercury', while his horsemanship suggests that of an 'angel dropt down from the clouds to turn and wind a fiery Pegasus' (IV. i. 97–110); in *Romeo and Juliet* we have 'a winged messenger of Heaven' seen as *bestriding* 'the lazy-pacing clouds' and amazing the 'upturned' eyes of mortals who 'fall back to gaze on him' (II. ii. 26–32), just as the Ghosts in our Vision 'fall on their knees' at Jupiter's appearance (V. iv. 93). Angels are *athletically* conceived, and hence Hamlet's words 'In action, how like an angel! In apprehension, how like a god!' (*Hamlet*, II. ii. 325).[1] The royal boys in the battle fight like 'angels' (V. iii. 85).

Cymbeline itself has elsewhere relevant images of Phoebus' steeds (II. iii. 24) and the wheel of his sky-chariot (V. v. 191). 'Swift, swift', prays Iachimo, 'you dragons of the night' (II. ii. 48); Imogen prays for 'a horse with wings' (III. ii. 49); 'slander's breath', we are told, 'rides on the posting winds' (III. iv. 37). With such—there is elsewhere rich volatile suggestion—the Vision is continuous. Moreover, the eagle itself is here important. Imogen compares Posthumus to an eagle (I. i. 139). The bird naturally suits the cave scenes, where Belarius contrasts the 'sharded beetle' with the 'full-wing'd eagle' (III. iii. 21), a speech followed directly by Guiderius'

> We, poor unfledg'd,
> Have never wing'd from view of the nest, nor know not
> What air's from home.   (III. iii. 27)

The boys are eaglets in their mountain-eyrie (cp. the 'aery of children, little eyases' at *Hamlet*, II. ii. 362). To the Sooth-

---

[1] The Folio reading is borne out by Shakespeare's habitual visualization of angels as active beings. See *The Wheel of Fire*, 1949; App., Note B.

sayer the eagle is both 'Jove's bird' and 'the Roman eagle'
(IV. ii. 348; V. v. 471). When Iachimo refers to the group
of Roman nobles who are buying a gift for the Emperor as
'the best feather of our wing' (I. vi. 186), the eagle is intended;
so is it when Britain's once undisciplined army is said to be
'now winged' (II. iv. 24), or when Cymbeline, his army being
broken, is 'of his wings destitute' (V. iii. 5). When the British
rout is turned to victory by Belarius and the two royal boys
the equivalence of eagle = royal strength (hence its aptitude in
the cave-scenes) shines, indirectly, through the gritty syntax:

> . . . forthwith they fly
> Chickens, the way which they *stoop'd* eagles . . .
> (v. iii. 41)

A speech our interpolator may have had in mind when, after
Jupiter's disappearance, he wrote:

> . . . the holy eagle
> *Stoop'd*, as to foot us ; his ascension is
> More sweet than our blest·fields ; his *royal* bird
> Prunes the immortal wing and cloys his beak,
> As when his god is pleas'd.   (v. iv. 115)

'Immortal wing' may further be compared to the 'invulnerable'
'plume' of Ariel's harpy-appearance (*The Tempest*, III. iii. 65).
    Jupiter's actual throwing of the 'bolt' has interesting Shake-
spearian analogies. His business is to strike awe and yet prove
merciful, his actions thus toning with the religious expectance
throughout *Cymbeline* and Shakespeare's consistent attribution
of mercy to the divine powers (*Titus Andronicus*, I. i. 117–19;
The Merchant of Venice, IV. i. 184–202; *Coriolanus*, v. iv. 25–8;
Cymbeline, v. iv. 13). Correspondences occur in *Measure for
Measure*, both at II. ii. 72–80 and in:

> Could great men thunder
> As Jove himself does, Jove would ne'er be quiet,
> For every pelting, petty officer
> Would use his heaven for thunder ; nothing but thunder.
> Merciful heaven !
> Thou rather with thy sharp and sulphurous bolt
> Split'st the unwedgeable and gnarled oak
> Than the soft myrtle . . .   (II. ii. 110)

The speech vividly assists our understanding of the Vision. 'Sulphurous' points on to the similar speech in *Coriolanus*:

> Thou hast affected the fine strains of honour,
> To imitate the graces of the gods ;
> To tear with thunder the wide cheeks o' the air,
> And yet to charge thy sulphur with a bolt
> That should but rive an oak.   (v. iii. 149)

The Vision, where Jupiter's breath is 'sulphurous' (v. iv. 115), but his words merciful, is a precise actualization of earlier poetry. *Cymbeline* itself, moreover, offers some valuable supporting phrases. In the dirge sung over Fidele we have, in description of mortality's trials:

> Fear no more the lightning-flash
> Nor the all-dreaded thunder-stone.   (iv. ii. 270–1)

There is Imogen's

> 'Twas but a bolt of nothing, shot at nothing,
> Which the brain makes of fumes.   (iv. ii. 300)

More clearly significant is Pisanio's 'the gods throw stones of sulphur on me' (v. v. 241), the image of Imogen's happy glances hitting everyone 'like harmless lightning' (v. v. 395), and Cymbeline's

> If this be so, the gods do mean to strike me
> To death with mortal joy.   (v. v. 235)

How exactly these optimistic miniatures—with, too, Iachimo's flattering description of Posthumus (for whom our Vision is enacted) as 'a descended god' (i. vi. 169)—reflect, in Shakespeare's usual manner, our central symbolism, wherein the god, descending to thunder and lightning and throwing his dreaded bolt, proceeds to announce a reversal of the hero's suffering and a general happiness.

This is, of course, precisely what one would expect. Jupiter functions here as does Diana in *Pericles*. The theophany is there less powerful, the play's most potent moments concerning the actual resurrection and reunions; the same happens in *The Winter's Tale*, where Apollo remains a background, though appallingly potent, deity. In *Cymbeline* the poet attempts to make his theophany central and dominating. You can feel a progress from the rather pale figure of Diana through Apollo to Jupiter. The description of Apollo's oracle directly forecasts *Cymbeline*:

> *Dion.*   . . . O, the sacrifice !
> How ceremonious, solemn and unearthly
> It was i' the offering !
> *Cleomenes.*   But of all, the burst
> And the ear-deafening voice o' the oracle,
> Kin to Jove's thunder, so surpris'd my sense,
> That I was nothing.
>   (*The Winter's Tale*, iii. i. 6)

Apollo's cryptic answer is of the same *genre* as Jupiter's tablet. Later we have evidence of the god's powers in the trial scene and Antigonus' account of his dream-vision of Hermione, attributed to Apollo (iii. iii. 15–45). It is natural that *Cymbeline*, whose Jupiter corresponds to Diana and Apollo in the sister-plays, should offer something even bolder to correspond to its greater stress on classical deities. *The Tempest* contains a masque where Juno, Ceres and Iris appear; while Ariel's thunderous appearance as a Harpy pronouncing judgement and conditional mercy is a close equivalent to Jupiter's appearance and actions. Finally *Henry VIII* contains Queen Katharine's vision of angels, introduced by an elaborately ritualistic direction in a style exactly recalling that in *Cymbeline*. Posthumus' and the Queen's reactions are similar. Compare

> *Posthumus.*   But—O scorn !—
> Gone ! they went hence as soon as they were born :
> And so I am awake. Poor wretches, that depend
> On greatness' favour, dream as I have done ;
> Wake, and find nothing   (v. iv. 125)

with

> *Q. Katharine.* Spirits of peace, where are ye ? Are ye all gone,
> And leave me here in wretchedness behind ye ?
>   (*Henry VIII*, iv. ii. 83)

Compare, too, Caliban's pathetic account of visionary sleep with its '. . . that when I wak'd I cried to dream again' (*The Tempest*, iii. ii. 154). The word 'celestial' accompanies these incidents with a notable regularity. We have Pericles' exclamation, directly after the theophany, 'Celestial Dian, goddess argentine . . .' (*Pericles*, v. i. 251). Directly before his remark on the 'sacrifice' at Delphos already quoted, Dion refers to

> the celestial habits—
> Methinks I so should term them—and the reverence
> Of the grave wearers.
>   (*The Winter's Tale*, III. i. 4)

Queen Katharine, just before her dream, is meditating 'on that celestial harmony I go to' (*Henry VIII*, IV. ii. 80). In *The Tempest* the word occurs in Caliban's comment on Stephano (who acts on him as these other theophanies on us): 'That's a brave god, and bears celestial liquor' (II. ii. 126). And in *Cymbeline* we have:

> He came in thunder ; his celestial breath
> Was sulphurous to smell . . .   (v. iv. 114)

Again, how intimate the approach, as in the reference to the gods' 'nostrils' at the play's conclusion (v. v. 478).

Surely the necessity of our Vision is now apparent. If we reject it, *Cymbeline* is left, alone in this group, without any striking transcendental moment. Nor is it merely a question of its conformity with the other final plays: nearly all Shakespeare's greater works have their transcendental, or semi-transcendental, scenes: the Ghost in *Hamlet*, the Cauldron-scene in *Macbeth* (with Hecate and the Apparitions), the weird tempests continually, as in *Julius Caesar* and *King Lear*, the mysterious music in *Antony and Cleopatra*.[1] *Pericles* and *The Winter's Tale* have their powerful tempests, but *Cymbeline* no active tempest-symbolism outside the Vision; its massed effect is one of sombre assurance; but surely something similar is needed. Now our Vision of Jupiter the Thunderer exactly fits our sense of purposeful, controlled tragedy. Thunder, apart from Jupiter himself, is a central symbol, as in Lear's

> Let the great gods
> That keep this dreadful pother o'er our heads
> Find out their enemies now !
>   (*King Lear*, III. ii. 49)

and the searching question later, 'What is the cause of thun-

---

[1] The analogies in *Othello* are (i) the storm and (ii) the magical handkerchief (discussed in my *Shakespearian Production*).

der?' (*King Lear*, III. iv. 159). In Jupiter's appearance and words we have a synthesis of (i) the tragic tempests and (ii) the beneficent deities of the two sister-plays: in him a new compactness is reached. Throughout Shakespeare 'tempests' are balanced against 'music', a balance peculiarly clear in *Macbeth*, where the three thunderous apparitions are set beside the show of kings passing to music. Our Vision again conforms. It is, moreover, carefully designed: Posthumus sleeps, the Ghosts enter to solemn music and lift their chant, rising to an insistent cry for justice; the Deity appears to thunder, speaks a heavier, more resonant rhymed verse, and ascends; the Leonati speak normal dramatic verse, as though waked from pain; Posthumus wakes. The movement reflects the mysterious rhythms within the swift passage from dream to waking life.

But, it may be said, the scene's poetry leaves us cold and cannot accordingly be Shakespearian. Such purely aesthetic judgements are surely irresponsible. Apart from Shakespeare's being himself an Elizabethan and Jacobean playwright, one would have, to-day, to meet our own objections with the best possible modern stage-representation; and while the scene is cut out of our performances, no advance is possible. But, to return to facts, the Vision's style, whether good or bad, is Shakespearian.

We must, of course, compare it not with Shakespeare's normal blank-verse or rhyme, nor with the semi-human speech of Oberon and Puck, the Ghost in *Hamlet*, the Weird Women in *Macbeth* and Ariel in *The Tempest*; but rather with what can more strictly be termed theophanies. Such are: Hymen in *As You Like It*, Hecate and the Apparitions in *Macbeth*, Diana in *Pericles* and Juno, Ceres and Iris in *The Tempest*. Listen to Hymen, entering to 'still music':

> Then is there mirth in heaven,
> When earthly things made even
>   Atone together.
> Good duke, receive thy daughter ;
> Hymen from heaven brought her ;
>   Yea, brought her hither,
> That thou mightst join her hand with his,
> Whose heart within her bosom is.
>
> (*As You Like It*, v. iv. 115)

Is that more poetically cogent than the chorus in *Cymbeline*? Surely, it is less so. As for Hecate, her lines have been regularly, though I suggest wrongly,[1] regarded as non-Shakespearian. The Apparitions speak a style nearer the normal, but, studied apart from its context by a critic who had never heard the lines well spoken with all the atmospheric advantage of stage-production, one may doubt whether this couplet, by itself, would pass the required test:

> Macbeth ! Macbeth ! Macbeth ! beware Macduff ;
> Beware the Thane of Fife. Dismiss me. Enough.
>
> (*Macbeth*, IV. i. 71)

The goddesses in *The Tempest* speak in rhymed couplets, of a stilted formality. And what of Diana? Here is her speech:

> My temple stands in Ephesus ; hie thee thither,
> And do upon mine altar sacrifice.
> There, when my maiden priests are met together,
> Before the people all,
> Reveal how thou at sea didst lose thy wife ;
> To mourn thy crosses, with thy daughter's, call
> And give them repetition to the life.
> Perform my bidding, or thou liv'st in woe ;
> Do it, and happy ; by my silver bow !
> Awake, and tell thy dream ! (*Pericles*, v. i. 241)

Now consider Jupiter's:

> No more, you petty spirits of region low,
> Offend our hearing ; hush ! How dare you ghosts
> Accuse the thunderer, whose bolt, you know,
> Sky-planted, batters all rebelling coasts ?
> Poor shadows of Elysium, hence ! and rest
> Upon your never-withering banks of flowers.
> Be not with mortal accidents opprest ;
> No care of yours it is ; you know 'tis ours.
> Whom best I love, I cross ; to make my gift
> The more delay'd, delighted. Be content ;
> Your low-laid son our godhead will uplift :
> His comforts thrive, his trials well are spent.
> Our Jovial star reign'd at his birth, and in

---

[1] See *The Shakespearian Tempest*, Appendix B.

Our temple was he married. Rise, and fade !
He shall be lord of Lady Imogen,
     And happier much by his affliction made.
This tablet lay upon his breast, wherein
     Our pleasure his full fortune doth confine :
And so, away : no further with your din
     Express impatience lest you stir up mine.
     Mount, eagle, to my palace crystalline.   (v. iv. 93)

Both deities conclude with a personal reference: 'my silver
bow' and 'my palace crystalline'. Their speeches show a
similar lilt: compare the rhymed quatrain in *Pericles* 'Before
the people . . . life' with Jupiter's rhymed quatrain 'Our Jovial
star . . . made', rising on the third and falling in the fourth line.
Jupiter's speech is, however, the more weighty and rounded,
and far nearer normal late-Shakespearian verse, the condensed
syntax of 'the more delay'd, delighted' being quite characteristic. In the thunderer's 'sky-planted' bolt battering 'coasts'
we have a coalescence of (i) thunderous action, as in *King Lear*,
from heaven on to earth and (ii) rough seas raging against a
shore: both are normal and their coalescence, in Shakespeare,
poetically natural. Correspondences for (i) are obvious throughout; for (ii) we may compare descriptions of Britain at *Richard
II*, ii. i. 62 and *King John*, ii. i. 24; also 'wrackful *seige* of
battering days' in Sonnet LXV. Our closest parallel to Jupiter's
line occurs in the formal rhymed inscription made for Marina,
'make raging battery upon shores of flint' (*Pericles*, iv. iv. 43),
spoken of the sea-goddess, Thetis. 'Batter' or 'battery' is a
usual word occurring in association with violent sound (as at
Antony and Cleopatra, ii. vii. 116) and with assault on a resisting
town (as at *King John*, ii. i. 446; *Troilus and Cressida*, i. iii. 206;
Cymbeline, i iv. 23).[1] Jupiter's vocabulary and imagery are
thoroughly Shakespearian. The 'shadows of Elysium' resting
on their 'never withering banks of flowers' have analogies in
Orsino's 'sweet beds of flowers' (*Twelfth Night*, i. i. 40),
Troilus' description of Elysian bliss on 'lily-beds' (*Troilus and
Cressida*, iii. ii. 12) and Antony's:

---

[1] Notice that Jupiter's line would be less appropriate in another play. In *Richard II* and *King
John* the besieging waves, to be associated with armed invasion, are sternly repelled. But here
Britain is a rebel island and the Roman god's metaphor the more reasonable. For mortal exis-
tence=island, compare *Macbeth*, i. vii. 6 ;=shores, *Pericles*, v. i. 195 ;=ship, Sonnet LXV.

Where souls do couch on flowers, we'll hand in hand,
And with our *spritely* port make the ghosts gaze ;
Dido and her Aeneas shall want troops
And all the haunt be ours.

(*Antony and Cleopatra*, IV. xii. 51)

As in our Vision (v. iv. 88), 'ghosts' is used for spirits in Elysium; for 'spritely' compare Posthumus' 'spritely shows' (in description of his vision) at v. v. 429; and for 'haunt' compare 'haunt' in the Vision at v. iv. 133. That *Antony and Cleopatra* should be recalled is further evidence of authenticity, since reminders occur elsewhere ('Arabian bird' at I. vi. 17, as at *Antony and Cleopatra*, III. ii. 12; 'all the worms of Nile' at III. iv. 37; Cleopatra on Cydnus, II. iv. 69–72). For 'cross' compare 'crosses' in Diana's speech; for 'full fortune' (= good fortune) compare *Antony and Cleopatra*, IV. xiii. 24, and the use of 'fortune' throughout *Pericles*; 'confine' is thoroughly Shakespearian; 'stir up' is used as at *Julius Caesar*, III. ii. 214. Equally authentic is the vocabulary of the Ghosts: 'mortal flies' suggesting *King Lear*, IV. i. 36; 'geck and scorn' recalling Malvolio's 'geck and gull' (*Twelfth Night*, v. i. 355); 'chide'; 'rates'; 'revenges'. But to return to Jupiter: the thoughts 'Whom best I love I cross . . . delay'd, delighted' and 'happier . . . made' are close replicas of Pericles':

. . . No more, you gods ! your present kindness
Makes my past miseries sport. (*Pericles*, v. iii. 40)

Compare also Proverbs III. 11. But Jupiter is an especially Roman divinity. The reference to Posthumus' birth under 'our Jovial star' and his marriage in 'our temple' accordingly impresses the signature of Rome's presiding deity on British manhood, and that manhood's matrimonial integrity, whilst pointing on to the ratification of the Romano-British peace 'in the temple of great Jupiter' at v. v. 483. In rhythm, vocabulary, sentiment and purpose the speech is Shakespearian.

These scenes have had a poor deal. Hymen, appearing in a 'comedy', has had no serious attention at all; Hecate has, like Jupiter, been all but liquidated by scholarship, while the same shadow has fallen over the masque of goddesses in *The Tempest*. *Pericles* as a whole has always (on more scientific grounds, since it was excluded from the Folio) been suspect, and Diana consequently not yet won the honour of a considered rejection; while the Vision of Queen Katharine occurs in one of the scenes of *Henry VIII* rashly attributed to Fletcher. Is it possible that twentieth-century scholarship is merely attributing to Shakespeare its own dislike of the visionary and the supernatural? And that its stylistic judgements merely reflect that dislike?

It is, I suppose, theoretically possible that Shakespeare always handed his theophanies over to a friend and tutored him in the relevant phraseology, sentiments and rhythms; but if so, that friend was by his side, whenever wanted, from *As You Like It* onwards, and conveniently silent when nothing of a transcendental sort was needed: the supposition approaches absurdity. It is, of course, no part of my present purpose to argue that the vision in question is a good vision or the theophany effective on the stage, though in *Cymbeline* especially music and thunder, stage grouping and dance, correct chanting and declamation, with lights, could do much. There is a possibility that Shakespeare was not himself wholly satisfied: in *The Tempest* Ariel's similar appearance is given normal blank-verse, while the goddesses are mere etceteras, called up and puffed away at Prospero's will; and in *Henry VIII* the emphasis is, except for the soft music, wholly on silent, though elaborately directed, dumb-show and ritual.

After Jupiter's exit the ghosts themselves speak pure Shakespearian blank-verse, with the almost too jagged caesuras, resulting in an addition of thoughts rather than an evolution, as at *Pericles*, III. i. 1–9. Posthumus' comment on waking is normal in style, containing the word 'rare' so important in both *Pericles* and *The Winter's Tale* and repeated throughout *Cymbeline*: 'A book? O rare one!' (V. iv. 131). Which raises another question. If the Vision is to be discarded, what of Jupiter's prophetic 'tablet'? Not only is the Vision afterwards described by Posthumus exactly as it has occurred, but the tablet itself is vital to the action, is re-read later, and given primary attention at the close. If Jupiter is to go, the tablet must surely go too; and yet, apart from its other necessity, its wording is, like that of the rest of the Vision, indisputably organic in regard to *Cymbeline* as a whole, while recalling the oracular message of Apollo in *The Winter's Tale*. Posthumus reads it on waking:

Whenas a lion's whelp shall, to himself unknown, without seeking find, and be embraced by a piece of tender air ; and when from a stately cedar shall be lopped branches, which, being dead many years, shall after revive, be jointed to the old stock, and freshly grow, then shall Posthumus end his miseries, Britain be fortunate, and flourish in peace and plenty.   (v. iv. 138)

This the Soothsayer later interprets. The 'lion's whelp' is obviously Leo-natus, that is, Posthumus: the lion is continu-ally a symbol of noble strength and it is significant that, apart from his otherwise colourless presentation, Posthumus is else-where compared to the eagle (i. i. 139). The two creatures, lion and eagle, are together present in the battle-description (v. iii. 38, 42). The stately cedar and its branches are Cym-beline and his sons, the obvious image of a tree to signify descent being thoroughly Shakespearian (as at 3 *Henry VI*, ii. vi. 46–51 and often elsewhere); and the cedar especially is a symbol of strength and high place (2 *Henry VI*, v. i. 205; 3 *Henry VI*, v. ii. 11; *Coriolanus*, v. iii. 60; *Henry VIII*, v. v. 54). Other tree-images in *Cymbeline* occur at iii. iii. 60–4; iv. i. 57–8; iv. ii. 59, 175.[1]

There remains the strange equation of Imogen with 'a piece of tender air'. *Cymbeline* is rich in volatile and aerial images, either used by, or associated with, Imogen, or spoken in the cave-scenes, mainly by Arviragus. Imogen speaks of the 'crow' (i. iv. 15) and 'puttock' (i. i. 140); the lark occurs in the dawn-song sung for her (ii. iii. 22); she herself calls Britain 'a swan's nest' (iii. iv. 142), reads the story of Philomel in bed (ii. ii. 46), and suspects 'some jay of Italy' has wronged her (iii. iv. 51). She also uses a pretty image, to be noticed again, of a 'wren's eye' (iv. ii. 305). Arviragus thinks of the 'ruddock with charitable bill' strewing her grave (iv. ii. 224); she is, in his lovely phrase, herself a bird: 'the bird is dead' (iv. ii. 197). The cave-scenes naturally tend to produce such imagery, as in Arviragus' 'the night to the owl and morn to the lark less welcome' (iii. vi. 93) and

> our cage
> We make a quire, as doth the prison'd bird,
> And sing our bondage freely.   (iii. iii. 42)

[1] Compare the account of Endimion's dream in Lyly (*Endimion*, v. i. 104–8). In this dream an old man offers a book in which are described the political dangers threatening a 'princely eagle' ; that is, Queen Elizabeth, who is elsewhere (ii. i. 93) compared to a 'stately cedar'. For 'princely eagle' see *Cymbeline*, v. v. 474. Both phrases are accordingly duplicated.

The boys are, in Guiderius' more masculine phraseology, 'unfledg'd' birds, probably eaglets, who 'have never winged from view of the nest' (III. iii. 28), a thought coming soon after Belarius' mention of a 'crow' (III. iii. 12) and contrast of the 'sharded beetle' and 'full-wing'd eagle' (III. iii. 20–1). There is Iachimo's 'bare the raven's eye' (II. ii. 49) and his innuendo about 'strange fowl' that 'light upon a neighbouring pond' (I. iv. 102); and also the other eagles already discussed. Apart from these, birds seem to be mainly associated with the delicate royalty of Imogen and the music-loving Arviragus.

Imogen is also associated with other types of aerial impression. She cries for 'a horse with wings', wishing to 'glide' to Milford in one day to meet her lover (III. ii. 49, 53), and it is suggested later that she has 'flown' to him 'wing'd with fervour of her love' (III. v. 61). 'Slander's breath', Pisanio tells her, 'rides on the posting winds' (III. iv. 37). Posthumus' 'soul' sails 'slow', but the ship bearing him from Imogen is all too 'swift' (I. iii. 13). Regarding Iachimo's quick return as a proof of her loyalty (II. iv. 30), Posthumus remarks:

> The swiftest harts have posted you by land,
> And winds of all the corners kiss'd your sails,
> To make your vessel nimble.   (II. iv. 27)

Imogen sees her father's anger as 'the tyrannous breathing of the north' which 'shakes all our buds from growing' (I. iv. 36). Arviragus, talking of her smiles and sighs, says how a sigh goes out 'from so divine a temple to commix with winds that sailors rail at' (IV. ii. 55); while the royal boys themselves are compared to 'zephyrs, blowing below the violet' without disturbing it; or, angered, to a violent wind (IV. ii. 171–6). Both Imogen and the boys are conceived aerially, an angelic essence being hinted. Iachimo, apologizing for his rudeness to Imogen, says how it is only his own love for Posthumus that 'made me to fan you thus' (I. vi. 177): that is, awake her temper. In the bed-chamber he observes how 'her breathing' perfumes the room, noticing how 'the flame of the taper bends towards her' (II. ii. 18), presumably, if a realistic explanation is sought, controlled by an air-current. Thus when Iachimo comes to fight in Britain, with the guilty knowledge that he has belied 'the princess of this country', he appropriately finds that 'the air on't revengingly enfeebles me' (v. ii. 2). There is also Imogen's 'were you but riding forth to air yourself' (i. i. 110) and Guiderius' complaint that he and his brother have never learn'd 'what air's from home' (iii. iii. 29).

Such impressionism aims to define something peculiarly indefinable and invisible, concerning Imogen in particular, but also the royal boys, and on occasion Posthumus too; something to do with innate, instinctive royalty or nobility. That is why Posthumus is said to have received education 'as we do air, fast as 'twas minister'd' (i. i. 45), and Belarius so emphasizes the evidence of 'invisible instinct' in his charges' royal behaviour (iv. ii. 177). It is this pervading sense of evanescent, intangible quality in Imogen that prompts those strange, very feminine, images of minuteness so evident in her language. Distance makes the departing Posthumus 'as little as a crow'. The image is developed:

> I would have broke mine eye-strings, crack'd them, but
> To look upon him, till the diminution
> Of space had pointed him sharp as my needle,
> Nay, follow'd him, till he had melted from
> The smallness of a gnat to air, and then
> Have turn'd mine eye, and wept.   (i. iii. 17)

No one else in all Shakespeare talks quite like that. Notice again 'air'; and the two references to eyes. She would like to see Posthumus and Cloten fight out their rivalry, with herself standing by 'with a needle' to 'prick the goer-back' (i. i. 168). Here is another:

> 'Twas but a bolt of nothing, shot at nothing,
> Which the brain makes of fumes.   (iv. ii. 300)

Again:

> But if there be
> Yet left in heaven as small a drop of pity
> As a wren's eye, fear'd gods, a part of it !   (iv. ii. 303)

She blesses the bees that made the wax for Posthumus' love-letter (iii. i. 36). Belarius in the mountain eyrie has one of a more normal kind:

> Consider
> When you above perceive me like a crow,
> That it is place that lessens and sets off . . .
>   (iii. iii. 11)

As before, we find a minor reflection of the Imogen-association
in the cave. When Imogen is found dead, says Arviragus, she
was smiling 'as some fly had tickled slumber' (iv. ii. 210).
When she is called a 'fairy' (iii. vi. 41) or an 'angel' (ii. ii. 50;
iii. vi. 42; iv. i. 48), or the princes called 'angels' at v. iii. 85—
or talks of herself as being 'in heaven' for Posthumus at
prayer-time (i. iv. 33), the phrases hold a more than obvious
precision. Twice she becomes, once in Iachimo's flattery and
once in the ecstasy of joy, a visible radiance:

> Had I this cheek
> To bathe my lips upon ; this hand, whose touch,
> Whose every touch, would force the feeler's soul
> To the oath of loyalty ; this object, which
> Takes prisoner the wild motion of mine eye
> Firing it only here . . .   (i. vi. 99)

and

> See,
> Posthumus anchors upon Imogen,
> And she, like harmless lightning, throws her eye
> On him, her brothers, me, her master, hitting
> Each object with a joy . . .   (v. v. 393)

How important and how subtle in both is the characterization
of eyes and sight, as too in Imogen's thought of cracking her
eye-strings recently quoted (i. iii. 17). 'Eyes' are continual in
Cymbeline, as at i. i. 90; i. iii. 9; i. vi. 32, 39; ii. ii. 20–1;
ii. ii. 49; ii. iii. 27; ii. iv. 107; iii. iv. 104; iv. ii. 301, 305;
v. iv. 56 (during the Vision); v. iv. 183; and v. v. 169; besides
other more subtle images of sight (e.g. iii. iii. 12). The emphasis on eyes, 'the most pure spirit of sense' (*Troilus and
Cressida*, iii. iii. 106; see also ii. ii. 63; v. ii. 104–5, 119), may,
indeed, relate to the two major visions, those of the Soothsayer
and Posthumus.

But to return to Imogen and our bird, volatile, and aerial
impressions. They suggest a certain indefinable spirituality
touching the Shakespearian royalty; a certain royal, immaterial,
essence; a spiritual royalty, as in Imogen's 'supreme crown of
grief' (i. vi. 4). Though it be 'tender' and 'nurse-like' (v. v.
87–8), the royal boys, themselves so tender to Imogen and
gentle as zephyrs (iv. ii. 171), have it too. This royal essence
it is, reminiscent of Marina and Perdita, that the rougher,

though highly meritorious, Posthumus, the man of solid, almost stolid, merit, symbol of British manhood, wins. To announce that destiny the Vision is composed; and so in the prophecy he is said to 'find without seeking' (i.e. perhaps 'to win honour for which he has no conscious ambition') and be 'embraced by a piece of tender air'. Our various imagery is thus interpreted for us. Notice that, when this, with the restoration to King Cymbeline of his royal sons, who themselves contain both elements, strength and gentleness, of the Posthumus-Imogen union (cp. *King John*, 'Now these her princes are come home again', v. vii. 115), comes about, 'then shall Posthumus end his miseries, Britain be fortunate, and flourish in peace and plenty'. Posthumus' fortunes are one with Britain's. The tablet renders explicit a reading demanded by the whole tenour of the action.

The Vision is, indeed, purest Shakespeare, from whatever aspect we regard it. Here is a miniature of its main associations neatly compacted in Shakespeare's early work:

> Thus yields the *cedar* to the axe's edge,
> Whose arms gave shelter to the *princely eagle*,
> Under whose shade the ramping *lion* slept,
> Whose top branch over-peer'd *Jove's* spreading tree,
> And kept low shrubs from winter's powerful *wind*.
>
> > (3 *Henry VI*, v. ii. 11)

The Final Plays, with great consistency, rely on an expansion of earlier imagery and attendant symbolism as a basis for dramatic action; and what truth they reveal is accordingly a truth lying near to the heart of poetry.

Therefore our acceptance or rejection of this crucial scene is of primary importance. More even is at stake than our understanding of Shakespeare's reading of his country's destiny. We have regarded Jupiter as pre-eminently the Romans' god; but he is, throughout Shakespeare, more than that, and may often be best rendered 'God', a word Shakespeare was diffident of using on the stage, though it occurs at *King Lear*, v. iii. 17. The puritanical Malvolio thanks 'Jove' for his good fortune (*Twelfth Night*, ii. v. 195); and at *Measure for Measure*, ii. ii. 111, the Deity serves powerfully (in passages already noted) to extend some of Shakespeare's purest and most fervent passages of Christian doctrine, explicitly referring, through the pronoun 'He' (ii. ii. 74–6), to the Christian God. We may practically equate Shakespeare's Jove with Jehovah, whilst also observing that, since representation of the supreme deity cannot be completely successful (as Milton also found), Shakespeare probably gains rather than loses in *Cymbeline* by reliance on a semi-fictional figure allowing a maximum of dignity with a minimum of risk. So, within a plot variously concerned with the building up and dispelling of deceptive appearance, we find, at its heart, this vivid revelation of a kindly Providence behind mortality's drama. Our apocalypse accordingly stands central among Shakespeare's last plays; study of it radiates out first into *Cymbeline*, next into the final group, and lastly into the mass of Shakespeare's work. It is our one precise anthropomorphic expression of that beyond-tragedy recognition felt through the miracles and resurrections of sister-plays and reaching Christian formulation in *Henry VIII*.

The defence here presented must be faced by Shakespearian scholarship. The methods hitherto used for deciding the authenticity of suspected passages are patently insufficient. A purely personal reaction unaccompanied by the labours of exact investigation *within the art-form itself* is necessarily unreliable. Stylistic judgement is only too apt to vary according to the critic's like or dislike of the subject-matter expressed; and it is probable that, now that our Vision is reclaimed, critics will come forward to show, on purely 'literary' considerations, that in both plan and execution it is, as I personally think it, worthy of Shakespeare. But the importance goes further. The Vision's authenticity is easy to defend; indeed, it would be hard to find an example that was easier. But there remains a yet more serious problem. Shakespeare's last play, *Henry VIII*, is still in part suspect; and the grounds for suspicion are as baseless as those that have hampered the understanding of *Cymbeline*. Only through a careful study of the harmonies, minute and massive, of Shakespeare's world can the full authenticity of these crowning works be established.

1964: My remarks on staging on p. 192 have been borne out by a recent Stratford presentation, in which the Vision proved outstandingly powerful.

THE SHAKESPEARIAN SUPERMAN: AN ESSAY ON *THE TEMPEST*

As Zarathustra thus discoursed he stood nigh unto the entrance of his cave ; but with the final words he slipped away from his guests and fled for a brief while into the open air.

O clean odours around me ! he cried. O blessed stillness around me ! But where are my beasts ? Draw nigh, mine Eagle and my Serpent !

Tell me, my beasts—all these Higher men, smell they, perchance, not sweet ? O clean odours around me ! Now only do I know and feel how I love you, my beasts !

Thus Spake Zarathustra, The Song of Melancholy.

I

WE have seen how these final plays tend to refashion old imagery into some surprising dramatic incident; of which the most striking examples are the jewel-thrown-into-the-sea, Thaisa in her casket-coffin; Pericles on board his storm-tossed ship; the co-presence of actual storm and bear, an old poetic association, in *The Winter's Tale*; the appearance of Jupiter the Thunderer in *Cymbeline*. In these we find a variation of a normal Shakespearian process; for Shakespeare is continually at work splitting up and recombining already used plots, persons, and themes, weaving something 'new and strange' from old material. Much of his later tragedy and history is contained in *Titus Andronicus* and *Henry VI*; much of later comedy in *Love's Labour's Lost* and *The Two Gentlemen of Verona*. The opposition of cynic and romantic in *Romeo and Juliet* gives us Mercutio and Romeo; the same opposition— with what a difference!—becomes Iago and Othello; and again, Enobarbus and Antony. Prince Hal and Hotspur together make Henry V; and as for Falstaff, his massive bulk contains in embryo much of the later tragedies in their nihilistic, king-shattering, impact; though, as comedian, he stands between Sir Toby and Autolycus. One could go on, and on.

The last plays are peculiar in their seizing on poetry itself, as it were, for their dominating effects; and in doing this also find themselves often reversing the logic of life as we know it, redeveloping the discoveries and recognitions of old comedy into more purposeful conclusions, impregnated with a far higher order of dramatic belief. The finding of Aemilia as an abbess in *The Comedy of Errors* forecasts the finding of Thaisa as priestess of Diana in *Pericles*; the recovery of Hero, supposed dead, in *Much Ado about Nothing* that of Hermione; Juliet and Imogen endure each a living death after use of similar potions. What is first subsidiary, or hinted by the poetry itself, as when Romeo or Cleopatra dream of reunion beyond, or within, death (*Romeo and Juliet*, v. i. 1–9; *Antony and Cleopatra*, v. ii. 75–100), is rendered convincing later.

This tendency *The Tempest* drives to the limit. For once, Shakespeare has no objective story before him from which to create. He spins his plot from his own poetic world entirely, simplifying the main issues of his total work—plot, poetry, persons; whittling off the non-essential and leaving the naked truth exposed. *The Tempest*, patterned of storm and music, is thus an interpretation of Shakespeare's world.

Its originating action is constructed, roughly, on the pattern of *The Comedy of Errors* and *Twelfth Night*, wherein wreck in tempest leads to separation of certain persons and their reunion on a strange shore; the plots being entwined with magic and amazement, as in Antipholus of Syracuse's comment on Ephesus as a land of 'Lapland sorcerers' (*The Comedy of Errors*, iv. iii. 11), and Sebastian's amazement at Olivia's welcome (*Twelfth Night*, iv. iii. 1–21; see also Viola's pun on Illyria and Elysium at i. ii. 2–3). There is an obvious further relation of *The Tempest* to *A Midsummer Night's Dream*, both plays showing a fairy texture, with Puck and Ariel, on first acquaintance, appearing as blood-brethren, though the differences are great. The balance of tempests and music, not only in imagery but in plot too, throughout the Comedies (including *A Midsummer Night's Dream* and *The Merchant of Venice*) here reaches its consummation; but the Tragedies, wherein tempests and music are yet more profoundly important, are also at work within our new pattern of shipwreck and survival.

Prospero is a composite of many Shakespearian heroes; not in 'character', since there is no one quite like him elsewhere, but rather in his fortunes and the part he plays. As a sovereign wrongfully dethroned he carries the overtones of tragic royalty enjoyed by Richard II. Ejected from his dukedom by a wicked brother—'That a brother should be so perfidious' (I. ii. 67)—he is placed, too, like the unfortunate Duke in *As You Like It* and as Don Pedro might have been placed had Don John's rebellion succeeded in *Much Ado about Nothing*. Clarence, Orlando and Edgar suffer from similar betrayals.

Now Prospero's reaction is one of horror at such betrayal of a 'trust' and a 'confidence sans bound' (I. ii. 96) by 'one whom', as he tells Miranda, 'next thyself of all the world I lov'd' (I. ii. 69). So Valentine suffers from Proteus' betrayal in *The Two Gentlemen of Verona* and Antonio, as he thinks, from Sebastian's in *Twelfth Night*. King Henry treats the faithless lords in *Henry V* to a long tirade of withering blank-verse on ingratitude and betrayal comparable with Richard II's scathing denunciation of his betrayers. Ingratitude generally is basic to the emotions, speeches, and songs of *As You Like It*; and in *King Lear* we have a 'filial ingratitude' (III. iv. 14), corresponding to Prospero's viewing of himself as 'a good parent', too kindly begetting in his child (meaning his brother) a corresponding 'falsehood' (I. ii. 94; cp. *King Lear*, 'Your old kind father whose frank heart gave all' at III. iv. 20). Loyalty to king, master, friend, wife, husband, is a continual theme. It is basic in *Julius Caesar*, in Brutus' relation to Caesar, in Portia's to Brutus, in the friendship of Brutus and Cassius: it vitalizes the whole of *Antony and Cleopatra*, with the subtly defined, personal, tragedy of Enobarbus—'a master-leaver and a fugitive' (IV. ix. 22). There are the loyal friends: Antonio to Sebastian; Horatio to Hamlet; or servants—the Bastard in *King John*, Adam, Kent; Gonzalo here winning a corresponding honour. The extensions into sexual jealousy are equally, or more, important; as in *The Merry Wives of Windsor*, *Much Ado about Nothing*, *Troilus and Cressida*, *Hamlet* (felt on the father's behalf by the son), *Othello*, *Antony and Cleopatra*, *The Winter's Tale*, *Cymbeline*.

There is a recurring sense of desertion, of betrayal, very strong in *Troilus and Cressida*; and also in *King Lear*, the old man's age underlining his helplessness. In *King Lear*, and often elsewhere, the result is a general nausea at human falsity; the poet continually driving home a distinction of falsehood, and especially flattery, and true, unspectacular, devotion (as in

Theseus' words to Hippolyta, *A Midsummer Night's Dream*, v. i. 89–105). This disgust tends to project the action into wild nature, conceived, as in *The Two Gentlemen of Verona, As You Like It*, and *King Lear*, as an improvement on the falsities of civilization. In *King Lear* the return to nature is acted by Edgar and endured, for his purgation, by Lear on the tempest-torn heath; while many variations are played throughout on the comparison and contrast of human evil with the beasts and elemental forces. The pattern of *The Winter's Tale* shows a similar movement from falsehood through rugged nature to an idealized rusticity. Of all this the great prototype, or archetype, is *Timon of Athens*, where the princely hero, conceived as a sublime patron and lover of humanity, is so thunder-struck by discovery of falsehood and ingratitude that he rejects man and all his works and in uncompromising bitterness retires in nakedness to a cave by the sea-shore, where he denounces to all who visit him the vices of civilization and communes, in savage solitude, with all of nature that is vast and eternal; his story finally fading into the ocean surge. *The Tempest* shows a similar movement. Prospero, like Timon and Belarius—for Belarius is another, driven to the mountains by the ingratitude of Cymbeline—lives (presumably) in a cave; like Timon, by the sea.

He is akin, too, to all princes whose depth of understanding accompanies or succeeds political failure: to Hamlet, Brutus, Richard II, Henry VI. Hamlet, like Timon, is an archetypal figure, being a complex of many heroes. He is out of joint with a society of which he clearly sees the decadence and evil. Through his ghostly converse and consequent profundity of spiritual disturbance, he is unfitted for direct action, while nevertheless doing much to control the other persons, indeed dominating them, half magically, from within. Hamlet is a student and scholar; and in this too, as in his surface (though not actual) ineffectuality and his revulsion from an evil society, he forecasts the learned Prospero, whose dukedom was

> reputed
> In dignity, and for the liberal arts,
> Without a parallel.   (I. ii. 72)

Such enlightenment was bought at a cost:

> these being all my study,
> The government I cast upon my brother,
> And to my state grew stranger, being transported
> And rapt in secret studies.   (I. ii. 74)

Prospero is in straight descent from those other impractical governors, Agamemnon in *Troilus and Cressida*, whose philosophic attitude to his army's disaster (I. iii. 1–30) calls forth Ulysses' famous speech on order; and Vincentio, Duke of Vienna, in *Measure for Measure*, whose depth of study and psychological insight make execution of justice impossible. All these are in Prospero; while the surrounding action, both serious and comic, condenses the whole of Shakespeare's political wisdom.

He is also a recreation of Cerimon in *Pericles*. Listen to Cerimon:

> I hold it ever,
> Virtue and cunning were endowments greater
> Than nobleness or riches ; careless heirs
> May the two latter darken and expend ,
> But immortality attends the former,
> Making a man a god.   (*Pericles*, III. ii. 26)

And to Prospero:

> I, thus neglecting worldly ends, all dedicated
> To closeness and the bettering of my mind
> With that which, but by being so retir'd,
> O'erpriz'd all popular rate . . .   (I. ii. 89)

The lines set the disadvantage of the monastic life against the supreme end it pursues. Duke Prospero was, like Lord Cerimon (also a nobleman), a religious recluse on the brink of magical power; and may be compared with those earlier religious persons, Friar Laurence in *Romeo and Juliet*, whose magic arts control the action (and who speaks, like Prospero, of his 'cell'), and Friar Francis in *Much Ado about Nothing*, who negotiates Hero's death and reappearance. These are people of spiritual rather than practical efficiency; like Duke Vincentio and Hamlet (who so mysteriously dominates his society, by play-production and otherwise), they are plot-controllers; Duke Vincentio, disguised as a Friar, organizing the whole action, and being directly suggestive of 'power divine' (*Measure for*

Measure, v. i. 370). So, too, Prospero manipulates his own plot like a god. He is a blend of Theseus and Oberon.

Prospero is a matured and fully self-conscious embodiment of those moments of fifth-act transcendental speculation to which earlier tragic heroes, including Macbeth, were unwillingly forced. He cannot be expected to do more than typify; there is not time; and, as a person, he is, no doubt, less warm, less richly human, than most of his poetic ancestors. But only if we recognize his inclusiveness, his summing of nearly all Shakespeare's more eminent persons, shall we understand clearly what he is about. He, like others, Vincentio and Oberon pre-eminently, is controlling our plot, composing it before our eyes; but, since the plot is, as we shall see, so inclusive an interpretation of Shakespeare's life-work, Prospero is controlling, not merely a Shakespearian play, but the Shakespearian world. He is thus automatically in the position of Shakespeare himself, and it is accordingly inevitable that he should often speak as with Shakespeare's voice.

Ariel incorporates all those strong picturizations of angels aerially riding observed in our recent analysis of the Vision in *Cymbeline*.[1] To these we may add the Dauphin's humorous but poetically revealing comparison of his horse to a Pegasus in *Henry V*:

> When I bestride him, I soar, I am a hawk : he trots the air ; the earth sings when he touches it ; the basest horn of his hoof is more musical than the pipe of Hermes. . . . It is a beast for Perseus ; he is pure air and fire ; and the dull elements of earth and water never appear in him but only in patient stillness while his rider mounts him ; he is indeed a horse. . . . It is a theme as fluent as the sea.
>
> (III. vii. 11–44)

Precisely from this complex of air, fire, music and lightly apprehended sea in contrast to the duller Caliban-elements of earth and water Ariel is compounded. He personifies all Shakespeare's more volatile and aerial impressionism (he is called a 'bird' at IV. i. 184, 'chick' at v. i. 316, and 'an airy spirit' in the *dramatis personae*), especially those images or phrases involving 'swift' (i.e. either intuitional or emotional) thought (a vein of poetry discussed in *The Shakespearian*

[1] See p. 187.

Tempest, Appendix A, particularly pp. 308–11). A good example occurs in the association of thought's swiftness and 'feathered Mercury' at *King John*, IV. ii. 174. Ariel is mercurial and implicit in both the agile wit and Queen Mab fantasies of the aptly-named Mercutio; compare his definition of dreams, 'as thin of substance as the air' (*Romeo and Juliet*, I. iv. 100), with Prospero's 'thou, which art but air' (v. i. 21), addressed to Ariel. Ariel is implicit often in Shakespeare's love-poetry: though he is not an Eros-personification, yet, wherever we find emphasis on love's lightning passage, as at *Romeo and Juliet*, II. ii. 118–20 or *A Midsummer Night's Dream*, I. i. 141–9; on its uncapturable perfection, as throughout *Troilus and Cressida* (with strong emphasis on volatility and speed at III. ii. 8–15 and IV. ii. 14); on its spiritual powers, as in the aerial imagery and energy of *Antony and Cleopatra*, with Cleopatra at death as 'fire and air' (v. ii. 291); or on its delicate and tender sweetness, as in the 'piece of tender air', Imogen (*Cymbeline*, v. v. 436–53); wherever such elusive and intangible excellences are our matter, there Ariel is forecast. He is the spirit of love's aspiration 'all compact of fire' in *Venus and Adonis*, 149. He is made of Biron's speech of elaborate love-psychology with its contrast of 'slow arts' and the quicksilver swiftnesses of love's heightened consciousness, its new delicacy of perception and increased power, all entwined with fire, thoughts of mythology, poetry and music, and the ability (shown by Ariel's music in *The Tempest* at III. ii. 136–55 and IV. i. 175–8) to

> ravish savage ears
> And plant in tyrants mild humility;

while at the limit touching, as does Ariel (at v. i. 19), 'charity' (*Love's Labour's Lost*, IV. iii. 320–65). Closely similar is Falstaff's speech on sherris-sack, which makes the brain 'apprehensive, quick, forgetive, full of nimble, fiery and delectable shapes which, deliverer'd o'er to the voice, the tongue, which is the birth, becomes excellent wit' (2 *Henry IV*, IV. iii. 107). Ariel is also forecast by other passages on wit (in the modern sense), so often, as is Mercutio's, levelled *against* love; as when the shafts of feminine mockery are compared to the swiftness of 'arrows, bullets, wind, thought' at *Love's Labour's Lost*, v. ii. 262. Ariel exists in a dimension overlooking normal categories of both reason and emotion: he is the 'mutual flame' in which the winged partners of *The Phoenix and the Turtle* transcend their own duality.[1]

Since, moreover, he personifies these subtle and overruling powers of the imagination, he becomes automatically a personification of poetry itself. His sudden appearance depends, precisely, on Prospero's 'thought' (IV. i. 163–5; cp. 'the quick forge and working-house of thought', *Henry V*, v. chor. 23). He is the poetic medium, whatever the subject handled, his powers ranging over the earthy and the ethereal, tragic and lyric, with equal ease. As a dramatic person, he certainly descends from Puck and also, in view of his songs and trickery— he is a 'tricksy spirit' (v. i. 226; a word associated with Launcelot Gobbo in *The Merchant of Venice*, III. v. 75)—from the jesters Feste, Touchstone, even Lear's Fool; all of whom enjoy a share of the poet's own, critical, awareness, as in certain of Puck's generalized speeches and his final epilogue, the philosophic detachment of Feste's and Touchstone's wit, and the Fool's perceptual clarity. Ariel likewise is apart: he is emotionally detached, though actively engaged, everyone and everything, except Prospero and Miranda, being the rough material of creation on which the Ariel-spirit of poetry works; an opposition seen most starkly in his piping to Caliban.

Ariel is accordingly shown as the agent of Prospero's purpose. He is Prospero's instrument in controlling and developing the action. Through him Prospero raises the tempest, Ariel (like mad Tom in *Lear*) being part of it, acting it (I. ii. 195– 215). He puts people to sleep, so tempting the murderers, but wakes them just in time (II. i.), thunderously interrupts the feast, pronouncing judgement and drawing the moral (III. iii.). He plays tricks on the drunkards (III. ii.), hears their plot and leads them to disaster (III. ii; IV. i. 171–84). His music leads Ferdinand to Miranda (I. ii.). He puts the ship safely in harbour (I. ii. 226) and later releases and conducts the mariners (v. i.). He is Prospero's stage-manager; more, he is the enactor of Prospero's conception: Prospero is the artist, Ariel the art. He is a spirit of 'air' (v. i. 21) corresponding to the definition of poetry as 'airy nothing' in *A Midsummer Night's Dream* (v. i. 16). His powers range freely

[1] See also my note on p. 240.

over and between the thunderous and the musical, tragic and lyric, extremes of Shakespearian drama.

Caliban condenses Shakespeare's concern, comical or satiric, with the animal aspect of man; as seen in Christopher Sly and the aptly-named Bottom (whose union with Titania drives fantasy to an extreme), Dogberry, writ down 'an ass' (*Much Ado about Nothing*, iv. ii. 75–93), Sir Toby Belch; and Falstaff, especially in *The Merry Wives of Windsor*, where his animality is punished by fairies (that Falstaff should show contacts with both Ariel and Caliban exactly defines the universal nature of his complexity). Caliban also symbolizes all brainless revolution, such as Jack Cade's in 2 *Henry VI*, and the absurdities of mob-mentality in *Julius Caesar* and *Coriolanus*. So much is fairly obvious; but there is more.

Caliban derives from other ill-graced cursers, a 'misshapen knave' and 'bastard' (v. i. 268–73) like the deformed Thersites ('bastard begot, bastard instructed, bastard in mind, bastard in valour, in everything illegitimate', *Troilus and Cressida*, v. vii. 17) and bitter as Apemantus; from the 'indigest deformed lump', 'abortive rooting hog', 'poisonous bunch-back'd toad' and 'cacodemon', Richard III (3 *Henry VI*, v. vi. 51; *Richard III*, i. iii. 228, 246, 144; cp. Caliban as 'demi-devil' at v. i. 272); and from all Shakespeare's imagery of nausea and evil expressed through reptiles or, since we must not forget Sycorax (who may be allowed to sum all Shakespeare's evil women), creatures of black magic, as in *Macbeth*. He derives from all bad passion, as when Lear and Coriolanus are called dragons (*King Lear*, i. i. 124; *Coriolanus*, v. iv. 14). He combines the infra-natural evil of *Macbeth* with the bestial evil of *King Lear*, where man's suicidal voracity is compared to 'monsters of the deep' (*King Lear*, iv. ii. 50). He is himself a water-beast, growing from the ooze and slime of those stagnant pools elsewhere associated with vice, being exactly defined by Thersites' description of Ajax as 'a very land-fish, languageless, a monster' (*Troilus and Cressida*, iii. iii. 266). But he has a beast's innocence and pathos too, and is moved by music as are the 'race of youthful and unhandled colts' of *The Merchant of Venice* (v. i. 71–9; cp. the comparison of the music-charmed Caliban to 'unback'd colts' at iv. i. 176–8). He sums up the ravenous animals that accompany tempest-passages, the boar, bull, bear; especially the much-loathed boar of *Venus and Adonis*. In him is the ugliness of sexual appetite from *Lucrece* onwards, and also the ugliness vice raises in those who too much detest it, the ugliness of hatred itself and loathing, the ugliness of Leontes. Man, savage, ape, water-beast, dragon, semi-devil—Caliban is all of them; and because he so condenses masses of great poetry, is himself beautiful. He is the physical as opposed to the spiritual; earth and water as opposed to air and fire. That he may, like Ariel, be considered in closest relation to Prospero himself is witnessed by Prospero's admission: 'This thing of darkness I acknowledge mine' (v. i. 275).

These three main persons present aspects of Timon. Besides Prospero's resemblance already observed, Ariel's thunderous denunciation (at III. iii. 53) recalls Timon's prophetic fury, both addressed to a society that has rejected true nobility for a sham, while Caliban reproduces his naked savagery and the more ugly, Apemantus-like, affinities of his general hatred. This especial inclusiveness marks Timon's archetypal importance.

To turn to the subsidiary persons. Alonso and his party present a varied assortment of more or less guilty people. We have, first, a striking recapitulation of *Macbeth*, Antonio persuading Sebastian to murder the sleeping king in phrases redolent of Duncan's murder:

> What might,
> Worthy Sebastian ? O ! what might ?—No more :
> And yet methinks I see it in *thy face*,
> What thou should'st be. *The occasion speaks thee* ; and
> My strong imagination sees a *crown*
> Dropping upon thy head.   (II. i. 212)

We remember 'Your face, great thane, is as a book . . .'; 'Nor time, nor place, did then adhere and yet you would make both; they have made themselves . . .'; and 'all that impedes thee from the golden round . . .' (*Macbeth*, I. v. 63; I. vii. 51; I. v. 29). Antonio's

> O !
> If you but knew how you the purpose cherish
> Whiles thus you mock it . . .   (II. i. 231)

is a crisp capitulation of Lady Macbeth's soliloquy on her husband's divided will (I. v. 17–30). *Macbeth* is resurrected in both phrase and verse-texture:

> And by that destiny to perform an *act*
> Whereof what's past is *prologue*, what to come
> Is yours and my discharge.   (II. i. 260)

Compare Macbeth's 'happy *prologues* to the swelling *act* of the imperial theme' and Lady Macbeth's 'Leave all the rest to me' (*Macbeth*, I. iii. 128; I. v. 74). Death and sleep are all but identified in both (II. i. 268–70; *Macbeth*, II. ii. 54). Antonio's attitude to conscience ('Ay, sir, where lies that?' at II. i. 284) parallels Lady Macbeth's, while her 'Who dares receive it other?' (*Macbeth*, I. vii. 77) is expanded into Antonio's scornful certainty that 'all the rest' will

>   take suggestion as a cat laps milk ;
> They'll tell the clock to any business that
> We say befits the hour . . .   (II. i. 295)

—where even the cat, a comparatively rare Shakespearian animal, harks back to 'the poor cat i' the adage' (*Macbeth*, I. vii. 45). In both plays the victim's weariness is brutally advanced as an assurance of sleep: compare Duncan's 'day's hard labour' which shall 'invite' him to sound sleep (*Macbeth*, I. vii. 62) with 'now they are oppressed with travel' (III. iii. 15). That *Macbeth* should be singled out for so elaborate a re-enactment is not strange, since, standing alone in point of absolute and abysmal evil, it shares only slightly (via Sycorax) in the general recapitulation covered by Caliban, whom Prospero specifically acknowledges. Thus poetic honesty leaves Antonio's final reformation doubtful.

Alonso is less guilty, nor is there here any so vivid correspondence to be observed. Sebastian blames him for insisting on marrying his daughter Claribel against her and his subjects' will to an African (II. i. 130–42); and, since Gonzalo partly sanctions the criticism, we must, it would seem, perhaps with some faint reference to Desdemona's ill-starred marriage, regard Alonso's action as a fault. He was also a silent accomplice to Antonio's original treachery, and Ariel later asserts that he is being punished for it by his son's loss (III. iii. 75).

As one of Shakespeare's many autocratic fathers and also as a king rather pathetically searching for his child, he is a distant relative of Lear. Both are purgatorial figures: he realizes his 'trespass' (III. iii. 99).

The faithful and garrulous old lord Gonzalo is a blend of Polonius, Adam and Kent. The courtiers Adrian and Francisco are not particularized. The wit of Antonio and Sebastian on their first entry needs, however, a remark.

It is cynical and cruel. The points made are of slight importance except for the extraordinary reiteration of 'widow Dido' (II. i. 80–107). There is presumably a sneer at an unmarried woman who has been deserted by her lover being given the status of 'widow'; and this we may tentatively relate to *Antony and Cleopatra*, wherein 'Dido and her Aeneas' are once compared to the protagonists (IV. xii. 53) and which in Cleopatra's phrase 'Husband, I come!' (V. ii. 289) reaches a compact self-interpretation in direct answer to such cynicism as Antonio's. The whole dialogue, starting with criticism of Gonzalo's and Adrian's insistence on the isle's fertility (the island varies mysteriously according to the nature of the spectator) and leading through ridicule of Gonzalo's phrase 'widow Dido' and his identification of Tunis and Carthage, to a final flowering in his Utopian dream, serves very precisely to define an opposition of cynic and romantic.[1] The points at issue are less important than the points of view:

> Antonio.   He misses not much.
> Sebastian. No. He doth but mistake the truth totally.
>
> (II. i. 59)

That is cynical keenness in good form; and our dialogue takes us accordingly to the threshold at least of *Antony and Cleopatra*, the supreme answer of romanticism, wherein human love, though criticized as filth, wins through to glory. There is further corroboration: not only do the phrases 'such a paragon to their queen', 'miraculous harp' and 'impossible matter' (II. i. 79, 90, 93) raise, ironically or otherwise, suggestion of the marvellous harking back to *Antony and Cleopatra*, but we have one direct reminder:

[1] According to Vergil Dido was widowed before Aeneas' arrival at Carthage and Gonzalo here, as in his identification of Tunis and Carthage, is correct. The cynic's sneer is based on lack of information.

Sebastian.   I think he will carry this island home in his *pocket*, and give it his son for an apple.

Antonio.   And, sowing the kernels of it in the sea, bring forth more *islands*.   (II. i. 95)

Compare Cleopatra's dream, with its 'realms and *islands* were as plates dropt from his *pocket*' (*Antony and Cleopatra*, v. ii. 91). We find the romantic extreme, whether in jocular cynicism or in visionary earnest, reaching definition in similar terms. Certainly one expects some trace of the earlier play, some honest facing in this austere work of its golden sexuality; and perhaps the easiest way to honour it was through the self-negating cynicism of an Antonio.[1]

To return to the marriage of Claribel to the King of Tunis. Any further correspondences (outside *Othello*) may again be sought in *Antony and Cleopatra*, where a west-east conflict in relation to marriage is strongly developed; and again in the Prince of Morocco, in *The Merchant of Venice* (see also *The Winter's Tale*, v. i. 156–67). Criticism of the marriage originates from Sebastian, the cynic being naturally hostile, as in *Othello*, to the eastern glamour; while Gonzalo changes his view later, regarding it as part of the general happiness (v. i. 209). To Shakespeare Africa and the Orient are at once glamorous and dangerous (Sycorax came from Argier), with something of the disturbing magic wielded by the Indian fairies in *A Midsummer Night's Dream*: perhaps that is why Antonio seems to regard Tunis as an *infinite* distance from Milan.

The central experience of this group is the offering and sudden withdrawal of the mysterious banquet, with Ariel's appearance as a harpy and speech of denunciation.

Feasts are regularly important throughout Shakespeare, but are so obvious that one accepts them without thought. It is the mark of greatest literature to play on such fundamentals of human existence and we must remember their importance in Homer and the New Testament; in the one direct, in the other, in event, miracle and parable, carrying symbolic overtones. Shakespeare ends his two morality farces, *The Taming of the Shrew* and *The Merry Wives of Windsor*, with feasts, acted or announced, to convey a sense of general good-will succeeding

[1] My suggestion must remain tentative; but it has at least some confirmation from my brother's reading of Vergil's poetic methods (see *Roman Vergil*, by W. F. Jackson Knight).

horse-play. In *Romeo and Juliet* a feast and dance relate neatly to the family feud, raising questions of daring, adventure and hospitality. There is the rough feasting in Arden and Belarius' cave, both characterized by hospitality. Eating and drinking are continually given dramatic emphasis, with various ethical implications: they are important throughout *Antony and Cleopatra*, with one gorgeous feast-scene celebrating union after hostility, though nearly ruined by treachery. An elaborate banquet occurs in *Pericles*, with Thaisa as 'queen of the feast' (II. iii. 17) pointing on, as we have seen, to Perdita as 'mistress of the feast' (IV. iii. 68) in *The Winter's Tale*. Important examples occur in *Timon of Athens* and *Macbeth*. In *Timon* there are two: the first (I. ii) conceived as a sacrament of love and friendship (with New Testament reminiscence at line 51), crowned by Timon's speech and negatively underlined by Apemantus' cynicism; the second (III. v.), planned as a deadly serious practical joke, in which Timon, after raising his false friends' hopes, speaks an ironic grace, overturns (probably) their tables, and douses them with luke-warm water. In *Macbeth*, we have first the irony of the feasting of Duncan (I. vii), and later on (IV. i) the *inverted* good of the 'hell-broth' brewed by the Weird Women; and, in between (III. iv), the feast to which Banquo has been carefully invited and which he attends as a ghost, smashing up the conviviality and social health so vividly emphasized in the text, and thus denying to Macbeth's tyrannous and blood-stained rule all such sacraments of brotherhood.[1] These two *broken* feasts in *Timon of Athens* and *Macbeth*, related to the two main Shakespearian evils of unfaithfulness and crime, are key-scenes; and their shattering stage-power derives precisely from the simplicity of the effects used, planted squarely as they are on fundamentals.

The meaning of the feast offered but denied to Alonso, Sebastian and Antonio will now be clear; and also its relevance to the Shakespearian world.

The 'solemn and strange music' (III. iii. 17) of the feast is followed by Ariel's appearance as a Harpy to 'thunder and lightning' (III. iii. 53). The sequence recalls the Vision in

[1] It may be worth recording that my understanding of this feast's importance as discussed in *The Imperial Theme* developed from a search for something in the Tragedies to correspond with the banquet in *The Tempest*, to which my attention had been called by Colin Still's study. See p. 226.

Cymbeline, and Ariel's harpy-appearance drives home the similarity. Like Jupiter, he enters as a figure of overruling judgement, speaking scornfully of the lesser beings who think to
dispute the ordinances of 'fate' (III. iii. 61; cp. 'How dare you
ghosts . . .' *Cymbeline*, v. iv. 94). Both epitomize the Shakespearian emphasis on thunder as the voice of the gods, or God.
So Ariel acts the more awe-inspiring attributes of Shakespeare's
tempest-poetry before our eyes, and in a long speech drives
home its purgatorial purpose.

Besides Alonso and his party, we have the comic group of
Stephano and Trinculo, in association with Caliban. The
comedy is delightful, but scarcely subtle. Stephano the butler
is an unqualified, almost professional, drunkard, with nothing
of the philosophic quality of Falstaff or the open if unprincipled
bonhomie of Sir Toby. Both those are, in their way, gentlemen,
and yet their new representative (as drunkard) is of a low type
socially; as are Dogberry, Bottom and the Gravediggers, though
Stephano is a poor equivalent, lacking natural dignity. Trinculo
is an equally poor successor to Touchstone, Feste, Yorick and
Lear's Fool. Note that their representative quality is nevertheless emphasized by their joint embodiment of the two main
sorts of clown: the natural and the artificial.

The Tempest is an austere work. The poet, while giving his
clowns full rein in comic appeal, allows them no dignity. In
writing of Autolycus we have observed Shakespeare's tendency
there, as with Falstaff, earlier, to show his humorist as disin-
tegrating; both as losing dignity and revealing ugly tendencies.
So, too, with Sir Toby: in spite of his admirable 'cakes and ale'
(*Twelfth Night*, II. iii. 125) he is carefully made to lose dignity
towards the play's conclusion, the balance of conviviality and
reproof being carefully held.

Both Falstaff and Autolycus, as their glow of humour pales,
show themselves as rather cheaply ambitious: whilst bearers of
the comic spirit, they are, for a while, the superiors of kings;
but when they, in their turn, ape the courtier, join in the vulgar
scramble for show, they fall lower than their meanest dupes.
Falstaff in 2 *Henry IV* is enjoying his advance, ordering new
clothes, being the grand man.[1] Here the distinction is subtle;

[1] For my earlier remarks on the change in Falstaff, with an acknowledgement, see p.
112.

but the way is open for his final disintegration in *The Merry Wives of Windsor*. So, too, with Autolycus: he dresses as a courtier, apes a courtier's grandiosity and trades sadistically on the Shepherd's and Clown's anguish. He is finally shown as cringing to his former dupe. Now, remembering, too, Hamlet's disgust at the heavy drinking of Claudius' court, observe what happens to our comic trio, especially Stephano.

First, he drinks and sings maudlin songs. Next, he becomes a petty tyrant and engages in a bloody plot, aiming to make himself lord of the island. He is a burlesque of the power-quest, with all the absurdity of a barbaric despotism, having his foot licked by Caliban and posing as king, resembling Marlowe's Tamburlaine and the Macbeth of

> Now does he feel his title
> Hang loose about him, like a giant's robe
> Upon a dwarfish thief.   (*Macbeth*, v. ii. 20)

Stephano parodies the essential absurdity of tyrannic ambition. Now he and his companions are lured by Ariel to a filthy pool:

> at last I left them
> I' the filthy-mantled pool beyond your cell,
> There dancing up to the chins, that the foul lake
> O'erstunk their feet.   (iv. i. 181)

Stagnant water occurs regularly to suggest filth and indignity. Poor Tom in *King Lear* has been led by the foul fiend 'through fire and through flame, through ford and whirlpool, o'er bog and quagmire'; and an utmost degradation is suggested by his eating 'the swimming frog, the toad, the tadpole, the wall-newt and the water' and drinking 'the green mantle of the standing pool' (*King Lear*, iii. iv. 50; 132, 137). The lascivious Falstaff is ducked in *The Merry Wives of Windsor*; in flowing water, certainly, but the dirty-linen basket supplies the rest. There is also the final entry of the absurd braggart, Parolles, in *All's Well that Ends Well*, bedraggled, with filthy clothes, and admitting that he is 'muddied in Fortune's mood' and smelling 'somewhat strong of her strong displeasure'; with a developed dialogue on bad smells, an 'unclean fish-pond', 'carp', etc. (v. ii. 1–27). Notice that (i) lust—there is direct association of pools to sexual vice at *The Winter's Tale*, i. ii. 195

and *Cymbeline*, I. iv. 103—and (ii) braggadocio are involved. Stephano, the would-be tyrant, meant to possess Miranda after murdering Prospero; Caliban has already tried to rape her; and all three are accordingly left in the 'filthy-mantled pool'.

Our buffoons are next tempted, like Autolycus, by an array of 'trumpery' (IV. i. 186), of 'glistering apparel' (IV. i. 194). Rich clothes were a more pressing masculine temptation in Shakespeare's day than in ours. One of Faustus' ambitions was to clothe Wittenberg's students in silk, and *Macbeth's* power-quest is characterized in terms of 'a giant's robe' (*Macbeth*, v. ii. 21; cp. *The Tempest*, II. i. 280). Shakespeare reiterates his scorn for the latest (usually foreign) fashions, for all tinsel of clothes, speech, or manners, in play after play; as with Claudio, Sir Andrew and his 'flame-colour'd stock' (*Twelfth Night*, I. iii. 146), Kent's 'a tailor made thee' (*King Lear*, II. ii. 59), Osric, and many others. The prim Malvolio is fooled in his yellow stockings; Christopher Sly dressed absurdly in a nobleman's robes; Katharina the Shrew tormented with finery. This vein of satire beats in our present symbolic incident: the two fools are ensnared by a tinsel glitter, though Caliban, being closer to nature, has more sense (the temptation is perhaps slightly out of character for the others too, whose job here is, however, to parody their social superiors). All three are next chased off by Prospero's hounds. The pool and the show of garments will be now understood, but what of the hounds? Hounds are impregnated with a sense of healthy, non-brutal, and (like Shakespeare's horses) man-serving virility, occurring favourably at *Venus and Adonis*, 913–24; *Henry V*, III. i. 31; and *Timon of Athens*, I. ii. 198. Hunting is a noble sport, though sympathy can be accorded the hunted hare (at *Venus and Adonis*, 679–708, and 3 *Henry VI*, II. v. 130). Courteous gentlemen, such as Theseus and Timon, necessarily hunt, especially important being the long description of Theseus' *musical* hounds, with reference also to those of Hercules, baying the bear in Crete (*A Midsummer Night's Dream*, IV. i. 112–32). Hounds are adversaries to the bear and (in *Venus and Adonis*) the boar, both 'tempest-beasts', and, though the fawning of dogs is used satirically, hounds, as such, may be musically, almost spiritually, conceived: hence their picturesque names in *The Tempest*: 'Mountain', 'Silver', 'Fury' and

'Tyrant'.[1] They are spirit-essences directed against the bestial Caliban and his companions.

So, too, the fleshly and 'corrupt' Falstaff was punished by fairies or supposed fairies in *The Merry Wives of Windsor* by pinching (v. v. 96–108), conceived as a punishment of 'sinful fantasy', 'lust' and 'unchaste desire' by spirits (v. v. 96–108). Here Caliban regularly (I. ii. 325–30, 368–9; II. ii. 4), and now Stephano and Trinculo, too, are thoroughly *pinched* and given cramps and aches (IV. i. 261–4).[2]

Such is Shakespeare's judgement on drunkenness, sexual lust and braggart ambition. Such evils have, variously, held dignity, as in Falstaff's speech on sherris-sack (2 *Henry IV*, IV. iii. 92), the riotous love of Antony and Cleopatra and, for the power-quest, *Macbeth*; but it is a tight-rope course; one slip and the several vices appear in their nakedness. That naked essence, in all its lewd and ludicrous vulgarity, is here emphasized.

There remain Ferdinand and Miranda. These are representative of beautiful and virtuous youth as drawn in former plays (Marina, Florizel and Perdita, Guiderius and Arviragus), though lacking something of their human impact. Our new pair illustrate humility (as in Ferdinand's log-piling), innocence, faith and purity; their words being characterized by utter simplicity and sincerity. They are whittled down to these virtues with slight further realization, and in comparison with earlier equivalents must be accounted pale. As elsewhere, essences are abstracted and reclothed. Except for Prospero, Ariel and Caliban, the people scarcely exist in their own right. The real drama consists of the actions and interplay of our three major persons with the natural, human and spiritual powers in which their destiny is entangled.

Prospero, who controls this comprehensive Shakespearian world, automatically reflects Shakespeare himself. Like Hamlet, he arranges dramatic shows to rouse his sinning victims' conscience: the mock-feast (whose vanishing, as we have seen, recalls Macbeth's ghost-shattered banquet), brought in by

---

[1] The use of such names as 'Tyrant' and 'Fury' does not lower the animals' status, since the implied humanizing serves as an idealization ; as with battleships, where the names H.M.S. *Furious* or H.M.S. *Venomous*, by attributing living status to a machine, witness a respect not usually offered to ill-temper and snakes.

[2] Compare the fairies' song 'Pinch him black and blue' in Lyly's *Endimion*.

a 'living drollery' of 'shapes' (III. iii. 21); and the masque of goddesses and dancers (IV. i), which, like the Final Plays themselves (of whose divinities these goddesses are pale reflections), is addressed to the purer consciousness (Ferdinand's). This tendency, as in *Hamlet*, reflects some degree of identification of the protagonist with the playwright, whose every work is a parable. Prospero himself delivers what is practically a long prologue in Act I, and in his own person speaks the epilogue. He is, even more than the Duke in *Measure for Measure*, a designer of the drama in which he functions as protagonist. We have seen how many of Shakespeare's tragic themes are covered by him; and that his farewell might have been spoken by Shakespeare is a correspondence demanded by the whole conception.

He addresses (v. i. 33–57) the various powers (drawn from folk-lore and called, with a grand humility, 'weak') by whose aid he has 'bedimm'd the noontide sun' (as 'the travelling lamp' is strangled in *Macbeth*, II. iv. 7) and loosed the 'mutinous winds' to 'set roaring war' between sea and sky, thereby recalling such tempests throughout the great tragedies, in *Julius Caesar*, *Othello*, *Macbeth*, *King Lear*, with their many symbolic undertones of passionate conflict here crisply recapitulated in thought of war betwixt 'sea' and 'sky'. He has used 'Jove's own bolt' to blast (as at *Measure for Measure*, II. ii. 116, and *Coriolanus*, v. iii. 152) Jove's tree, the oak, recalling Jupiter the Thunderer in *Cymbeline*. From such images the speech moves inevitably to:

> Graves at my command
> Have wak'd their sleepers, op'd, and let them forth
> By my so potent art. (v. i. 48)

The statement, with its parallel in the resurrections of *Pericles* and *The Winter's Tale* and the less vivid restoration of Imogen in *Cymbeline*, may seem to apply more directly to Shakespeare than to Prospero; though the miraculous preservation of the ship and its crew must be regarded as an extension of earlier miracles. Prospero's speech, ending in 'heavenly' or 'solemn' (v. i. 52, 57) music, forms a recapitulation of Shakespeare's artistic progress from tempest-torn tragedy to resurrection and music (cp. the 'music of the spheres' at *Pericles*, v. i. 231, and the resurrection music of *Pericles*, III. ii. 88, 91; and *The*

Winter's Tale, v. iii. 98) corresponding to its forecast in *Richard II*.[1]

Prospero uses his tempest-magic to draw his enemies to the island, and there renders them harmless. He wrecks and saves, teaches through disaster, entices and leads by music, getting them utterly under his power, redeeming and finally forgiving. What are the Shakespearian analogies? The poet himself labours to master and assimilate that unassuaged bitterness and sense of rejection so normal a lot to humanity (hence the popularity of *Hamlet*) by drawing the hostile elements within his own world of artistic creation; and this he does mainly through tragedy and its thunderous music; and by seeing that, in spite of logic, his creation is good. By destroying his protagonists, he renders them deathless; by expressing evil, in others and in himself, he renders it innocent. And throughout this tumult of creative activity, turning every grief to a star, making of his very loathing something 'rich and strange', there is a danger: a certain centre of faith or love must be preserved, this centre at least kept free from the taint of that rich, wild, earthy, lustful, violent, cursing, slimy yet glittering thing that is creation itself, or Caliban; that uses cynicism (born of the knowledge of lust) to ruin Desdemona, though not Othello's love for her; that tries in vain, but only just in vain, to make of Timon an Apemantus. Therefore Prospero keeps Miranda intact, though threatened by Caliban, just as Marina was threatened in the brothel of Mitylene. Alone with her he had voyaged far to his magic land, cast off in a wretched boat,

> To cry to the sea that roar'd to us ; to sigh
> To the winds whose pity, sighing back again,
> Did us but loving wrong.   (i. ii. 149)

What an image of lonely, spiritual, voyage, like that of Wordsworth's Newton 'voyaging through strange seas of thought, alone'; while echoing back, through the long story of Shakespearian 'sea-sorrow' (i. ii. 170), to the Nordic origins of our literature in *The Wanderer* and *The Seafarer*. Prospero, unlike Lear, Pericles and Leontes, guards his Miranda, and with her survives on his island of poetry, with Ariel and Caliban. Who are these? The one, clearly, his art, his poetry in action; the

[1] See my 'Note on *Richard II*' in *The Imperial Theme*.

other, the world of creation, smelling of earth and water, with the salt tang of the physical, of sexual energy, and with, too, all those revulsions and curses to which it gives birth. Prospero finds both Ariel and Caliban on the island, releasing the one (as genius is regularly characterized less by inventiveness than by the ability to release some dormant power) and aiming to train the other; and both must be strictly controlled. Prospero, Ariel, Caliban, Miranda: all are aspects of Shakespeare himself. Prospero, corresponding to the poet's controlling judgement, returns to Milan, uniting his daughter, his human faith, to his enemy's son; and Shakespeare's life-work, in *Henry VIII*, draws to its conclusion.

It is, indeed, remarkable how well the meanings correspond. Prospero has been on the island for twelve years (I. ii. 53); and it is roughly twelve years since the sequence of greater plays started with *Hamlet*. Before that, Ariel had been prisoned in a tree for another twelve years (I. ii. 279); again, roughly, the time spent by Shakespeare in his earlier work, before the powers of bitterness and abysmal sight projected him into the twilit, lightning-riven and finally transcendent regions; rather as Herman Melville passed from *Typee* and *White Jacket* to *Moby Dick*, *Pierre* and his later poetry. And now, as the end draws near, Ariel cries (as does Caliban too) for freedom from ceaseless 'toil':

Prospero.	How now ! moody ?	
	What is't thou canst demand ?	
Ariel.		My liberty.
Prospero.	Before the time be out ? No more !	(I. ii. 244)

Prospero dominates Ariel and Caliban with an equal severity: as Shakespeare may be supposed to have willed, sternly, the safe conclusion of his labour in *Henry VIII*.

That labour is not all easy. Prospero, though still, is not static. Like Hamlet's, his very centrality is dynamic, drawing others to him, like Timon in his retirement, radiating power; or rather those earlier spiritual radiations are here given appropriate, symbolic, action, just as, according to Shelley's definition, poetry itself holds, in its very reserve, its stillness, a myriad radiations.

II

Our study does not involve us in those close references to the author's imagery which Shakespeare's work normally demands; and for a precise reason. Here the poetry is pre-eminently in the events themselves, which are intrinsically poetic. Now just as in Dante a visionary conception is expounded, as Mr. T. S. Eliot has observed, by an unmetaphoric and 'transparent' style, so *The Tempest* will be found peculiarly poor in metaphor. There is the less need for it in that the play is itself metaphor. Shakespeare's favourite imagery of storm and wreck cannot powerfully recur as descriptive comparison since the whole play, as its title announces, revolves round that very conception[1]; and so, in their degree, with other favourite imagery (e.g. the sounds of tempest-animals, bulls and lions bellowing heard by Gonzalo at II. i. 320; the hounds already noted at IV. i. 258; the oak, pine and cedar, old favourites, now part of the story, at I. ii. 277, 294; v. i. 45, 48). Usually Shakespeare's tricks of pictorial suggestion can be felt as playing over and interpreting a story, though too rigid a distinction is dangerous; here there is no interpretation; the story is, or is supposed to be, self-explanatory; the creative act is single. It might be called Shakespeare's 'purest work of art'; though whether purity, in art or in moral doctrine, itself so severe in *The Tempest*, is the whole of wisdom remains arguable. There is usually something ego-centric about it, as with Isabella. And yet, though *The Tempest* can be considered as Shakespeare's artistic autobiography, it certainly does not incur the charge made by Swift in *The Battle of the Books* against the moderns whose self-nurtured egotism he contrasts with the creative freedom of the ancients settling like bees on this or that in the objective world, and making therefrom honey and wax; that is, 'sweetness and light'.

Though Shakespeare writes from his own poetic world, that

[1] This suggests a warning concerning Caroline Spurgeon's work on Shakespearian imagery. Her study is severely limited to certain kinds only of minor imagery, with an intentional exclusion of major effects. Shakespeare shows little 'imagery' from warfare; not that he is uninterested, but rather since his plots are usually warlike. Hence, though her positive contribution is of unquestionable value, her negative results are misleading (e.g. she concludes that *Julius Caesar*, being barren of 'imagery', was coldly conceived; and yet no play of Shakespeare is more rich in a startling and fiery impressionism made variously of nouns, such as 'fire', and description of events).

world is itself peculiarly objective. Like all great poets, he has written regularly with strict respect for historical persons and events, well-worn mythology, thought-schemes not his own, sources of all sorts, sometimes an old play. This tendency marks not weakness but strength, and the resulting wholes become through that very self-loss constituent to his properly artistic realization; and it is precisely this selfless artistic world that *The Tempest* reduces to simplicity. Nor need we confine the argument to plot and persons. Poetic language is itself an incarnation, not a transcription, of thought; it is a seizing on truth beyond the writer's personal thinking through submission to the object; and hence its high proportion of concrete impressions drawn from objective phenomena. Such submission conditions the deepest self-realization, since what normally passes for thought is merely a cheap currency drawn from and touching the mental centres only; and in its terms no deeply-felt subjective emotion or knowledge can be handed on. But poetry works to render fully objective the deepest 'I'-intuition; as in Hamlet, himself so much the 'I' of every spectator or reader. In his concentration on objective, especially natural, phenomena the poet expresses, as in a mirror common to all, his most intimate dreams and sorrows, while similarly in-reading subjective existence, the 'I' quality (no normal thought-currency gets the distinction) into the supposedly inanimate world. So, whether in plot or person, imaginative description and atmosphere, or in the minutest details of imagistic impression; in words themselves handled as rounded and worthy things well-charged with meaning; in all this the literary artist, in either verse or prose, attains the highest realization, something more real than either philosophy or science. This realization is, moreover, superpersonal and therefore universal. What is generally called a man's spiritual autobiography is accordingly less important than his artistic autobiography. Such an autobiography is *The Tempest*, isolating and intensifying the grand objectivity that characterizes the life-work it reduces to simplicity; for ever witnessing that the depths of personality blossom impersonally and that finest self-penetration is one with universal statement in the creative order where subject and object are felt as twin aspects of the more rounded, indescribable, whole.

8

The Tempest is accordingly no mere subjective record. Its more autobiographical meanings have another aspect; and, looked at from this angle, it reveals a wide range of universal meanings. Shakespeare has objectified, not merely his created world, but himself as creator; and yet Prospero, one person in a play of many, cannot finally be equated with the author whose self-reflection is necessarily, at the time of composition, the whole play. The total result is nearer self-transcendence than self-reflection; while, in throwing himself as creator on to the screen, and showing himself at work in creative activity and control, the poet constructs a myth of creation in its wholeness and universality.

The most careful and important study of *The Tempest* hitherto is undoubtedly Colin Still's *Shakespeare's Mystery Play* (Cecil Palmer, 1921; revised and reissued under the title *The Timeless Theme*, Nicholson & Watson, 1936). His reading is, very roughly, this: Prospero = God, Ariel = the Angel of the Lord, Caliban = the Devil, Miranda = the Celestial Bride. Of the human persons, the comedians are the lowest led on by the Devil, the 'Court Party' of purgatorial status, while Ferdinand attains to Paradise; the scheme being, very roughly, Dantesque. The thesis is supported by a reference of nearly every event to something in ancient ritual or myth, while offering psychological or spiritual equivalents to the elements of earth, mud, water, mist, air, fire. Still's mass of material (to which my summary does slight justice) clearly breaks new ground. The argument must, of course, be read as a deliberate thesis, pushing the particular reading to the limit. Therein lies its value; we can make our own reservations. The book has, on the whole, had a cold reception, though there should, once my own reading of *The Tempest* is accepted, be nothing particularly surprising in its argument. A myth of creation woven from his total work by the most universal of poets is likely to show correspondences with other well-authenticated results of the racial imagination.

The human imagination finds expression not only through accepted thought-forms of legend and history, but also through a hierarchy of semi-esoteric symbols drawn mainly from natural phenomena, with strangely consistent meanings throughout the centuries and across the globe. Fundamental verities of nature, man, and God do not change; nor will their mirror, the imagination, in the Shelleyan sense, produce a series of discrepancies. There is accordingly a certain common language of symbol exploited by mythology, ritual and poetry from age to age. The development of the Attic stage from the worship of Dionysus and the Elizabethan playhouse from the mystery and morality plays is well-known; and yet what is equally important, and here even more significant, is the sharp break between the medieval and Shakespearian drama. The dominating ritual of the Middle Ages was the Mass; it was the one supreme drama, to which other forms existed in strict subservience. The medieval system losing its hold, the way was at once opened for a far more richly varied drama, with manifold dangers but also new possibilities of illumination. The plays of Marlowe, Shakespeare, Webster and Jonson could not have been written and acted in the age of Chaucer and Dante; still less in that of Francis of Assisi, or Augustine. The modern tendency to emphasize the Elizabethans' reliance on medieval thought, itself a reaction against a former over-statement, in no sense disposes of a sharp distinction: human drama becomes autonomous; the age-old importance of ritual moves from the altar to the playhouse; and this drama of the humanistic imagination is newly wealthy in crowned kings and lovely heroines. A common store of racial wisdom for centuries untapped is now released, as Prospero releases Ariel; and the highly responsible artist has himself to explore and exploit the wide areas of imaginative truth apparently excluded (though perhaps in some sense surveyed and transcended) by Christian dogma.

Here lies the danger of a scholarship over-concerned to find rational, easily understood, 'reasons' or 'sources' for every Shakespearian detail. Among his many historical blunders, Shakespeare has a queer knack of getting things right that could not reasonably be demanded of him. When Cleopatra, in describing her dream of the universal Antony, says

> His face was as the heavens, and therein stuck
> A sun and moon, which kept their course and lighted
> The little O, the earth . . . (*Antony and Cleopatra*, v. ii. 79)

Shakespeare uses an image from ancient Egypt identifying the sun and moon with the eyes of Horus. Are we to suppose he was relying on some book or picture? It is conceivable, but unlikely. Prospero, Ariel and Caliban recall Plato's description in the *Phaedrus* of the soul as a charioteer driving two steeds, the one fiery and excitable, the other sluggish and unwilling. Was Plato's the cause of Shakespeare's conception? or was there not rather a single cause behind both?

A still more vivid analogy is presented by a fascinating Chinese story of the sixteenth century, recently translated by Mr. Arthur Waley under the title *Monkey*, in which a hero-saint, Tripitaka, is accompanied on a pilgrimage by two servants, Monkey and Pigsy; the one, according to Mr. Waley, standing for 'the restless instability of genius', and the other symbolizing physical appetite, brute strength, and a kind of cumbrous patience. The analogy to Ariel and Caliban is clear. Correspondences bristle. Both Monkey and Ariel are found by their future masters; they are not just subjective symbols; each has had an independent past, Monkey's being most lurid, for he has, like Milton's Satan, caused trouble in Heaven and been imprisoned under a mountain for five centuries to do penance for riotous behaviour (compare the story of Prometheus as handled by Aeschylus and Shelley). On hearing his cries, Tripitaka at first fears he may prove 'an unruly monster who would discredit his undertaking' (p. 127); but, though scarcely respectable, Monkey has considerable powers and is known as the 'Great Sage Equal of Heaven'. The thoughts invite reference to human genius, especially of the Renaissance era. Clearly, too, we can compare Prospero's hearing of Ariel's groans (i. ii. 287) and his subsequent release through Prospero's 'art' (i. ii. 291); a comparison especially fruitful if we allow Ariel to typify man's free, and as yet suspect, imagination liberated after centuries of penance under ecclesiastical control. Ariel's tree-imprisonment suggests, moreover, a potential life, power and even personality to be tapped within nature, and to be variously related to ancient myth, modern science and the assertions of romantic poets. In the Chinese Monkey was prisoned under the Mountain of the Five Elements (pp. 76, 126); so, too, Ariel is practically identified with 'the elements' (v. i. 317), into which he finally dissolves. Monkey's release is easy. Tripitaka has only to *want* to release him, but he cautiously first makes certain that it is Heaven's will (p. 127);

compare Shakespeare's repudiation of black magic, in *The Winter's Tale* and, as we shall see, *The Tempest*.

Tripitaka's new 'disciple' is, like Ariel, adept at changing his shape; he can root armed opposers to the ground, as do Ariel and Prospero, with 'a magic pass' (p. 203); he plays every trick conceivable, with many repetitions of miraculous survival (mainly his own), such as we have in *The Tempest*. Compare 'not a hair of my body was hurt' (p. 155) with 'not so much perdition as a hair . . .' at I. ii. 30. He is at home in the higher elements, shooting about like lightning, swooping up to heaven, and fond of loosing extraordinary tempests:

> 'Now, Thunder God', screamed Monkey, 'do your work ! Strike down all greedy and corrupt officials, all disobedient and surly sons, as a warning to the people !' The din grew louder than ever . . .
>
> (p. 231)

He can also dive like Ariel (I. ii. 191, 252–3) to the waters' depths, though preferring to relegate such tasks to Pigsy, who, like Caliban, is partly a water-monster, formerly 'Marshal of the River of Heaven' (pp. 161, 267). Pigsy is brainless, strong and used, like Caliban, as a labourer; and, like Caliban, only more good-humouredly, a grumbler. He joins the party after Monkey rescues a farmer's daughter from his monster-embraces: we may compare Caliban's attempt to violate Miranda.

Tripitaka needs Monkey as surely as Prospero needs Ariel, without whom and his other spirits and 'books' he is—if we are to believe Caliban—but a 'sot' (III. ii. 104). Tripitaka's whole adventure is a quest for certain sacred 'scriptures'. Monkey uses 'the spirits of the mountain and the local deities', commanding the '*little* divinities' (pp. 184, 206) just as Prospero enlists 'elves of hills, brooks, standing lakes, and groves' (referred to as 'weak masters' at v. i. 41), as necessary to his purpose. Both masters rule their disciples with a similar firmness. When Monkey proves insubordinate Tripitaka uses a heaven-given spell that rolls him on the ground, his head splitting in agony, until he promises to behave[1]; compare

---

[1] 'You've been putting a spell upon me', he said. 'Nothing of the kind', said Tripitaka. 'I've only been reciting the Scripture of the Tight Fillet.' 'Start reciting again,' said Monkey. When he did so, the pain began at once. 'Stop ! stop !' screamed Monkey. 'Directly you begin the pain starts ; you can't pretend it's not you that are causing it.' 'In future, will you attend to what I say ?' asked Tripitaka. 'Indeed I will,' said Monkey. 'And never be troublesome again ?' said Tripitaka. 'I shouldn't dare,' said Monkey. (P. 136.)

Prospero's use (already observed) of internal cramps, aches, stitches, etc., to control Caliban and his equally severe treatment of Ariel, with the latter's promise to be 'correspondent to command' and do his 'spiriting gently' (I. ii. 297).

There are, necessarily, many divergences, some of Caliban's attributes occurring in Monkey and some of Ariel's in Pigsy, but the main allegory of man dependent on, yet having to control, a wayward genius, not exactly of him, yet used by him, emerges clearly. Did Shakespeare read Chinese?

To return to Colin Still's study. Though his main thesis appears basically sound, its detailed application often leads to a certain forcing, and even where there is legitimate analogy, the correspondence is likely to be inexact, leaving a heavy overplus unaccounted for in the poetry. His comparisons scarcely hold the validity of those just noticed from Monkey: Prospero is, like Tripitaka, a man, not God, and talks like a man of 'Providence', 'fortune' and so on (I. ii. 159, 178).[1] Ariel only once (in his denunciation) functions properly as 'the angel of the Lord'; while Caliban, though admittedly a tempter and often called 'devil' by Prospero, is too clearly a thing of nature for so uncompromising a definition. Still's centre of reference is less in the poetry than in a rigid system of universal symbolism deliberately, but quite legitimately, applied to it. The faults are, therefore, mostly implicit in the attempt and the book's argument could probably be modified to a precision almost as satisfying as that which matures from the autobiographical reading already examined. But neither in isolation is wholly satisfactory. Just as the poetic act exists through the fusion of subject with object (so carefully heralded by Wordsworth), so The Tempest, perhaps (in the sense already defined) the purest, though not necessarily the greatest, example of poetic action on record, must finally be studied from a view overlooking both aspects, while limited by neither: some events yielding most from the one treatment, some responding better to the other, while in some, in fact many, the coincidence is exact.[2] It is that coincidence, wherein Pros-

---

[1] Still was aware of the discrepancy and neatly observed that Prospero carefully *removes his magic mantle* whilst telling Miranda of his arrival on the island (I. ii. 25, 169), as though to suggest that here his symbolic function must be ignored. (I see no better reading of Prospero's action.)

[2] For a similar approach to the New Testament see my *Christian Renaissance*, Ch. IV.

pero is somehow more than poet yet less than God, which must form the basis of a comprehensive interpretation. We will next see, in briefest outline, what such a study shows.

III

We open with a ship being dashed on to the rocks by a terrible storm. The night is cut by zig-zag lightnings leaping from spar to spar, while thunder cracks and the ocean roars and the winds whine in their fury. On the little ship are people in mortal fear, faced by the uttermost fury of elemental nature; men shrieking, praying, doing their shipmen's job, hindering, jesting, conscience-stricken, cursing; half-mad in frenzy and plunging overboard; a crisp shorthand of mortality set among the terrors of natural existence. It is merely a flash: you can hardly take it in, it is so brief.

And next, we are on firm ground. Silhouetted against dawn, on a rugged coast, stands Prospero, a tall figure, with robe and staff, in calm control. To him comes Miranda, imploring his mercy, as to a god, on these sufferers and their ship. He re-assures her, somewhat as Christ reassures those who fear the waves:

> Be collected :
> No more amazement. Tell your piteous heart
> There's no harm done.   (I. ii. 13)

Nothing is lost; 'not so much perdition as a hair' (I. ii. 30) has touched the people in the wreck. Even their garments are unsoiled:

> Not a hair perish'd ;
> On their sustaining garments not a blemish,
> But fresher than before.   (I. ii. 217)

Where in the uncharted regions of higher imagination are we to get our axes of reference? In the Gospels, certainly; else-where, perhaps only in the raising of Thaisa from her sea-burial and the resurrection of Hermione. 'Fresher than before . . .': it is as though one were to die and find oneself no dis-carnate spirit, but with one's own body, yet newer, stronger, more comely. Such is Prospero's art; and all this he is doing for her; for Miranda (I. ii. 16).

Who is Prospero? Cerimon has already described him, saying how highest virtue and wisdom are greater than rank and wealth; those are uncertain, and mortal; but the others immortal, through which man becomes a god (*Pericles*, III. ii. 31—see also the relevant phrases in *The Winter's Tale*); that is, a god-man. Such is Prospero, formerly a student-prince, who made his court famous for 'the liberal arts' (I. ii. 73), but was less happy in the routine of government, and therefore supplanted and rejected by his own kindred and subjects, and cast adrift with his daughter. But he has established himself on his island where in loneliness he, with Miranda by his side, has slowly perfected his art. He has been weathered by suffering, but we scarcely speak of his 'character'. He is scarcely a man in that way; he strikes one as being all mind. Nor can we speak properly of his dramatic situation, since he is not the slave of circumstance, but rather creates his own circumstances, himself still, in grave repose, yet radiating power, like art itself; but fully purposeful, like religious ritual; and yet more than these, direct action being his concern.

He has on his island, beside Miranda, two creatures, Ariel and Caliban, representing respectively those aspects of life seen most clearly by Shelley and Swift. Prospero holds a Shake-spearian balance, Caliban being as necessary to him as Ariel, while Miranda is called a 'thrid', or third, of his life, although 'the whole of that *for* which' he lives (IV. i. 3).[1]

Before Prospero's arrival Ariel had been imprisoned by Sycorax' black magic in a pine; a 'delicate' (I. ii. 272; IV. i. 49) spirit shrieking in agony, transfixed, riveted, helpless, until Prospero's wisdom released him from his frozen immobility. But now Ariel is again himself; a lightning, fiery, penetrating thing, ready 'to fly, to swim, to dive into the fire, to ride on the curl'd clouds' (I. ii. 190), like man's darting intelligence; a being whose work, says Prospero, is

> To tread the ooze
> Of the salt deep,
> To run upon the sharp wind of the north,
> To do me business in the veins o' the earth
> When it is bak'd with frost.   (I. ii. 252)

---

[1] Later, Miranda's future assured, Prospero's 'every third thought' is his grave (V. i. 311).

Though he himself may be compacted of 'air' and 'fire', his range of activity is unlimited; he interpenetrates all elements alike. He is defined in Shelley's *Prometheus*,[1] where the spirit of liberated nature is felt as splitting into, diving within, hard matter; and is further reincarnated in the hermaphrodite of *The Witch of Atlas* (like Ariel to be provisionally equated with poetry) who guides the Fairy's boat in its streaming upward course. Ariel is, it seems, a boy-figure in whom grace and power blend, resembling Goethe's 'boy-charioteer', symbolizing poetry, in *Faust*; and yet his two disguises (as nymph and harpy) are feminine. He is bisexual, like Shelley's hermaphrodite, or perhaps rather sexless, with the indeterminacy of art. He is, too, fluid; again, like Keats' idea of the poet, 'always in and for something else'; always ready for self-loss and self-identification. He first is, or acts, the tempest, a thing of fierce delight, everywhere at once, pre-eminently fire:

> I boarded the king's ship ; now on the beak,
> Now in the waist, the deck, in every cabin,
> I flam'd amazement : sometime I'd divide
> And burn in many places ; on the topmast,
> The yards, and boresprit, would I flame distinctly,
> Then meet and join . . . (I. ii. 196)

He challenges—indeed is—'Jove's lightnings', while his power dominates 'mighty Neptune' (I. ii. 201–6). In him the Shakespearian tempest—like that in *Julius Caesar*, lurid and spectacular—becomes personal: the ship is 'all a-fire' (I. ii. 212) with his electric, ubiquitous, presence.[2] But soon after, we have him disguised as a 'nymph of the sea' (I. ii. 301), charming tragic passion (I. ii. 390) with a song of dance and kisses; and next piping and singing of pellucid Shelleyan depths, wherein death works ceaselessly to enrich the mortality it devours. Then again he appears as an angel of judgement, an officer of 'Destiny' itself (III. iii. 53), pronouncing judgement on 'three men of sin' (III. iii. 53):

---

[1] For my comparisons from Shelley, see the relevant passages in *The Starlit Dome*.

[2] This, Ariel's only association with fire, is tragic and tempestuous ; hence there is a certain danger in relating him too precisely to 'air and fire' as necessarily the higher, more serene, elements. Such philosophic patterns are too rigid. They are, however, provisionally useful.

                   You fools ! I and my fellows
            Are ministers of fate ; the elements
            Of whom your swords are temper'd, may as well
            Wound the loud winds, or with bemock'd-at stabs
            Kill the still-closing waters, as diminish
            One dowle that's in my plume . . .   (III. iii. 60)

He is the instrument of never-forgetting 'powers' who have
'incens'd' all nature against the 'peace' of sinful man (III. iii.
72–5); and warns them of divine wrath to come, calling them
to 'heart-sorrow' and a new life (III. iii. 76–82). His repertory is
as inexhaustible as that of nature; or of poetry. He touches the
soul of Caliban with a throbbing music. He plays vastly
amusing tricks—for he is, after all, 'a tricksy spirit' (v. i. 226)—
on Stephano and Trinculo. In him rather than Trinculo we
have the true descendant of Feste's melody and wisdom playing
over human folly; and of the plaintive Fool in *King Lear*, for Ariel
can feel compassion. Though he is mainly unmoved and cold
in his vivid activity, performing Prospero's commands with
the uninvolved precision of a child, like poetry itself, always so
dispassionately vivisectional (as Ishak in *Hassan* tells us), yet,
like poetry too, which takes us to the brink of grace, Ariel
touches charity:

Ariel.   . . . your charm so strongly works them,
            That if you now beheld them, your affections
            Would become tender.
Prospero.   Dost thou think so, spirit ?
Ariel.   Mine would, sir, were I human.
Prospero.   And mine shall.
            Hast thou which art but air, a touch, a feeling
            Of their afflictions, and shall not myself,
            One of their kind, that relish all as sharply
            Passion as they, be kindlier mov'd than thou art ?
                                            (v. i. 17)

He who rides the storm talks a pert, pretty, inconsequential
boy-talk, breaking off a lyric with—'Do you love me, master—
no?' (IV. i. 48); or again, sings a butterfly song of summer
and fruit-blossom, of how he, recently thunderous bearer of
Jehovah's wrath, will hide in a cowslip from the owl's flight.
He is nature in its ceaseless variety and poetry alike in its
thunderous reverberations and in its shifting, glinting, irides-

cent tints; he is nature as it would be were its prisoned personality released, or poetry as it would be were its melodies to step
from literature into life. He is all these, and yet a boy too,
with a boy's silvery voice; and he is music incarnate; music
soft, haunting, barbaric, solemn, heavenly.

And then there is Caliban. He is an ugly creature, growing
out of our images of brine-pits, ooze, and earthy woodland: he
is Shakespeare's imagery of stagnant pools personified. You
can't tell whether he is a gorilla or a reptile-dragon. He is a
'puppy-headed monster' (II. ii. 168). Prospero calls him a
tortoise (I. ii. 316). He is at least half a fish (II. ii. 26–33; III. ii.
31; v. i. 266; see the association of 'fish' and 'flesh' at *Pericles*,
II. i. 26–7, and *The Winter's Tale*, IV. iii. 277–84; also the
'land-fish, languageless, a monster' at *Troilus and Cressida*, III.
iii. 266.) But he is human too; strong, useful as a labourer (I. ii.
310–13), but an unwilling creature, a grumpy yahoo (cp. the
'angry ape' of *Measure for Measure*, II. ii. 120). Sometimes he
is considered a kind of devil (II. ii. 106; IV. i. 188; v. i. 272).
His mother was Sycorax, a foul witch, guilty of hideous 'sorceries' (I. ii. 264). All of pagan superstition, black-magic and
infra-human, infra-natural evil, is in her suggested; and when
he first enters, the taint of Sycorax is strong on him. Listen to
his curses:

> As wicked dew as e'er my mother brush'd
> With raven's feather from unwholesome fen
> Drop on you both ! a south-west blow on ye,
> And blister you all o'er !   (I. ii. 321)

and

> This island's mine, by Sycorax my mother,
> Which thou tak'st from me . . .   (I. ii. 331)

and

> All the charms
> Of Sycorax, toads, beetles, bats, light on you !   (I. ii. 339)

We are close to the unholy life-forms and black-magic of the
witches in *Macbeth*. So Caliban is called 'hag-seed' (I. ii. 365).
But he is a pathetic figure, remembering how he was at first
'stroked' and made much of and taught the names of sun and
moon; his eyes opened to the world of thinking beings; and
how he, in return, put his half-animal, half-savage, knowledge
of 'springs', 'brine-pits', barren and fertile spots, at Prospero's

service (I. ii. 332–8), until his attempted rape of Miranda put an end to friendly intercourse. He is close to nature, though earth-locked, and called 'thou earth' by Prospero, who also refers to Sycorax' commands as too 'earthy' and 'abhorred' (I. ii. 273, 314) for Ariel's obedience. Sycorax' sorceries are themselves closely concerned with nature. Prospero calls her

> One so strong
> That could control the moon, make flows and ebbs,
> And deal in her command without her power.   (v. i. 269)

She could apparently force nature to her will without possessing its full powers, her art controverting natural law, whereas Prospero's fulfils it (note the identification of Prospero's will with that of 'Destiny' and the greater 'powers' at III. iii. 53, 73). Sycorax can imprison Ariel, but is unable to perform his release, which had to wait for Prospero's more creative, liberating rather than constricting, art (I. ii. 291). So, though Sycorax' magic is itself in part a nature magic, it is most naturally associated with creatures of evil repute and is rather akin to the horrible inversions of nature in *Macbeth*. The dominating tone is therefore disease-ridden and infra-natural:

> You taught me language, and my profit on 't
> Is, I know how to curse ; the red plague rid you
> For teaching me your language !   (I. ii. 363)

The scene ends with Caliban's:

>   . . . his art is of such power
> It would control my dam's god, Setebos,
> And make a vassal of him.   (I. ii. 372)

The contrast drawn resembles that of Christianity and devil-worship; of white and black magic.

We next meet him bringing in wood. He curses in his heavy, stammering spits, as though speaking were hard[1] :

> All the infections that the sun sucks up
> From bogs, fens, flats, on Prosper fall, and make him
> By inch-meal a disease !   (II. ii. 1)

But now, though he speaks of Prospero's 'spirits' and 'urchin-shows' (II. ii. 3, 5), there is no thought of black-magic, nor of

---

[1] Professor Mark Van Doren has already observed this quality in Caliban's language.

Sycorax, nor of specifically ill-omened creatures; rather of
nature, or spirits in natural guise, all round him: apes chatter-
ing and biting, hedge-hogs pricking his feet, adders winding
round him (II. ii. 9–13). His bottomless evil is being tormented by nature, by animals; is being dragged painfully up
creation's stair. There is a move of emphasis, as his first line
shows, from the infra-natural to the natural.

Soon after he is fired by Stephano's drink which rouses his
wonder: 'That's a brave god and bears celestial liquor' (II. ii.
126). Certain that he has 'dropped from heaven' (II. ii. 147),
Caliban prays him to be his 'god', wishing to abase himself and
kiss the foot of this 'wondrous man' (II. ii. 160–177). The
situation is exploited in gorgeous phrases by Stephano's 'kiss the
book' and Trinculo's 'puppy-headed monster' (II. ii. 153, 168),
but there is a serious under-current, the bottle being, indeed,
at this moment Caliban's Bible, and awaking in him a delight
that makes Stephano, logically, as 'wondrous' and god-like as
Prospero is to us. The next grade in any evolutionary ascent
always is, or must seem, divine. What glamorous worlds are
compacted in Caliban's 'for the liquor is not earthly' (II. ii. 135).
Now his nature-poetry pours out. He will discover for
Stephano the springs, pluck berries, fish, get wood (II. ii. 173).
His excitement grows:

> I prithee, let me bring thee where crabs grow ;
> And I with my long nails will dig thee pig-nuts ;
> Show thee a jay's nest and instruct thee how
> To snare the nimble marmoset ; I'll bring thee
> To clustring filberts, and sometimes I'll get thee
> Young scamels of the rock . . .   (II. ii. 180)

He is now savage man revelling in earthy kinship and the
powers of huntsmanship and wood-lore that it gives; for he has
now an object of devotion, something to serve, to worship, the
deepest need of man or even, perhaps, of beast. And yet he
remains pitiful in his new advance: savage and idolatrous, the
prototype of all bad revolution, he sings in drunken ecstasy of
his new freedom, not realizing that it is an absurd foot-licking
self-abasement such as Prospero would never ask; calls his new
slavery freedom and riots in exultant, stuttering, drunken joy:
'Ban, 'Ban, Ca-Caliban . . . (II. ii. 197).

On their next entry Caliban is at first silent, but soon we have him detailing his plan for Prospero's murder. The talk is thickly scattered with military and political phraseology: 'the state totters', 'thou shalt be my lieutenant', 'subject', 'mutineer' (III. ii. 1–48); and meanwhile Ariel plays his tricks, casting dissension into this burlesque of statesmanship. Here Caliban moves from natural savagery to political intrigue; it is both advance and fall, associated, as is the fall in *Paradise Lost*, with intoxication. By a normal inversion he sees Prospero as 'tyrant' and 'sorcerer', though there is some justice in his complaint of being robbed of the island; or there would be, if all levels of existence had equal rights (III. ii. 49). Caliban regards Stephano as a hero and Trinculo as a nonentity, with a heavy concentration on bravery: 'he's not valiant', 'my valiant master', 'I know thou dar'st, but this thing dare not' (III. ii. 28, 54, 64). Caliban's plot is starkly brutal:

> I'll yield him thee asleep,
> Where thou may'st knock a nail into his head
> (III. ii. 70)

and

> . . . there thou may'st brain him,
> Having first seiz'd his books ; or with a log
> Batter his skull, or paunch him with a stake,
> Or cut his wezand with thy knife. Remember
> First to possess his books . . .   (III. ii. 99)

Though brutal, he is cunning. He tells lies about the hatred borne to Prospero by his spirits and whets Stephano's appetite with descriptions of Miranda, comparing her with Sycorax, whom she so far surpasses: note that Sycorax is mentioned here to define, by contrast, the higher intuition. Caliban is now the typical incendiary, unprincipled, lying, lustful, bound on destruction of the hated superior; the very prototype of Nietzsche's revolutionary, skilled in the art of 'making mire to boil'. So Stephano and Miranda are to be 'king and queen' and Trinculo and Caliban 'viceroys' (III. ii. 118–19): fortunately there will be no subjects to complain. Caliban, having projected his will to power, is 'merry' (III. ii. 128).

But he has shown critical sensibility in his assessment of Miranda's beauty; and now Ariel's music sounds. The others are afraid, but Caliban would reassure them, speaking for all time of the music inter-threading our world of stupidity, lust and blood-shed, the unearthly music luring creation on, and up, with dreams and disillusion:

> Be not afeard : the isle is full of noises,
> Sounds and sweet airs, that give delight, and hurt not.
> Sometimes a thousand twangling instruments
> Will hum about mine ears ; and sometime voices,
> That, if I then had wak'd after long sleep,
> Will make me sleep again : and then, in dreaming,
> The clouds methought would open and show riches
> Ready to drop upon me ; that, when I wak'd,
> I cried to dream again.   (III. ii. 147)

To Caliban the best harmony is naturally a twangling, barbaric music, sounding of hot jungle, whose sobbing tones reverberate down his earthy soul and fill his greedy eyes with sparkling gems: it is simple, savage, wonderful and pathetic. But Caliban is not sentimentalized. Stephano's remark on the prospects of free entertainment calls him back from dreamland to the rasping rejoinder: 'When Prospero is destroy'd' (III. ii. 158). Caliban is at the stage of (i) lustful evil and (ii) aesthetic appreciation: that is, man.

There follows the filthy pool, the 'trumpery', where, to do him justice, Caliban curses his companions for their delay; the hounds; the torments. But at the play's close he attains a higher wisdom. Recognizing the grandeur and dignity of Prospero in his ducal robes, he remarks:

> O Setebos ! these be brave spirits indeed.
> How fine my master is ! I am afraid
> He will chastise me.   (v. i. 261)

The suitability of 'Setebos' at this final stage is easier to recognize than define. It acts as a reminder, both harking back to his start and contrasting with his new humility:

> I'll be wise hereafter,
> And seek for grace. What a thrice double ass,
> Was I to take this drunkard for a god,
> And worship this dull fool !   (v. i. 294)

He has moved from black magic, through nature and man, to grace.

True, he remains monstrous and savage; but the potentiality is there, though Prospero's remark on his retrogression, suggesting that 'as his body uglier grows, so his mind cankers' (IV. i. 188–92) reminds us that such progress may, perhaps must, function through a series of falls; certainly Caliban's does so. The manner of Prospero's annoyance at *his own* creature —'a devil, a born devil!'—suggests that it holds the validity of a self-accusation only; while later he admits that Caliban is only a 'demi', because 'bastard', devil (V. i. 272). Caliban's deformity symbolizes—resembling the Weird Sisters in *Macbeth*—the anomalous, and therefore provisional, ascent of evil within the creative order. Caliban need not, of course, be supposed as actually passing through the evolutionary stages we have observed in these few hours; but he is conceived as reflecting the process. Eternal qualities are before us. Just as Antonio and Sebastian, being bad, are shown as at their crimes, not merely as having committed past crimes, and Stephano is always drinking, so Caliban is, far more subtly, process incarnate. He is more, expressing the *eternal quality* of creation, of time itself, as is hinted by the circling back of his final 'Setebos'. He is heavily weighted down on rails of time, and cannot move from them. Ariel's chameleon changes are discontinuous; he is potentially everything and everywhere at once, functioning, like intuition itself, in terms of the unconditioned and causeless. But Caliban is a *sub specie aeternitatis* study of creation's very inertia and retrogression in laborous advance, growing from slime and slush, slug and furry beast, to man in his misery and slavery, though shot through with glory; and learning, in his own despite, the meaning of lordship and grace.[1]

Our drama shows a wrestling of flesh and spirit, the earthy and the aerial. Tempest, thunder and strange music are together balanced against crime and lust. But the evil is

---

[1] For a further elucidation see Sonnets XLIV and XLV, which develop a careful comparison of 'slight air' and 'purging fire' respectively to the lover's (i) thought and (ii) desire. 'Thought' can overleap 'land and sea', and 'large lengths of miles' to meet the absent friend. Such 'swift' 'ambassadors of love' are contrasted with 'earth and water' and their train of 'time', 'death' and 'melancholy'. The lover is, however, made of *all four* and has to be content that the duller elements be revivified by the love-visit and speedy return of these 'sweet messengers'. The contrast of Ariel and Caliban is implicit. Especially does the paradoxical compound 'present-absent' (used for the lighter elements) fit Ariel's ubiquitous, discontinuous, space-negating quality.

given slight autonomy; it is reduced from the high Satanism of *Macbeth* (where the ultimate symbol is Hecate; see *The Shakespearian Tempest*, Appendix B) to the level of human wickedness, the only upholders of evil's autonomy being (i) the doubtfully reformed Antonio and (ii) the background figure of Sycorax; and even she, perhaps for this very reason, was not all evil (I. ii. 267). The implied system is monistic: both tempests and music are included in Prospero's art; as, too, in Shakespeare's, where tempests themselves are major elements in a cathartic whole.

Prospero's magic is both magic and art in the old sense, including science and art in ours, and to be sharply differentiated from the infra-natural and exclusive sorceries of a Sycorax. The distinction will be clearer from a comparison of *The Tempest* with Marlowe's *Faustus*, both reflections of the boundless possibilities opening at the Renaissance dawn. Faustus' will is egocentric and concerned with sexual lust, extravagant show, rich clothes for Wittenberg students, engineering feats (such as the defensive walling of Germany with brass), while sinking to the vulgarity of practical jokes on the Pope. These one can place; but the gifts of Marlowe's devil also include Helen (as romantic ideal) and Greek literature ('Have I not made blind Homer sing to me . . .'). A vast complex of human instincts, good and bad, is condemned wholesale. Finally Faustus, in noble prose, speaks lines that come home to us after three hundred years of doubtful advance; cries out for Christ; is damned. The opposition, which Milton endured later, is at once stark and unsatisfying; and yet Marlowe reads the Renaissance correctly from the standpoint of a medieval theologian, since the inroads of aesthetic delight and mental craving were not readily distinguishable from devil-worship. A Prospero's 'liberal arts' were accordingly suspect and the release of man's constricted imagination no light responsibility. In Shakespeare, however, Ariel was imprisoned by Sycorax; and, though we need not suppose that *The Tempest* equates (as did Milton) the medieval Church with sorcery, yet, from the more liberal and inclusive understanding, the contesting powers of *Faustus* are ultimately akin, as necessary partners to a single conflict; and it is that whole conflict, as a conflict of absolutes, that the Shakespearian art rejects, or perhaps transmutes. Wherever man's spontaneous imagination, which nevertheless brings with it an inner discipline of its own, is fettered by alien authority, there is tyranny and thence super-stition and black magic, or talk of it; in however sacred a name it is done, the fruits are similar. The replacing of outward by inner authority has, certainly, its dangers—Prospero admits his personal responsibility for Caliban (v. i. 275)—and Shake-speare's reading of continental license regularly takes them into account. Prospero symbolizes the Renaissance as it takes form in alliance with Puritan instinct and under Elizabethan guid-ance; the Renaissance of Lyly and Sidney, not that of Machia-velli and Marlowe. So Ariel is released.

What are the characteristics of this Shakespearian Renais-sance? It has much to do with nature, with elemental forces: Prospero does not invert theology, mumbling prayers back-wards, but returns to the source of God's creation. His art is pietistic and naturalistic, as naturalistic as Christ's, as Ceri-mon's, as Paulina's, and to nature he returns it, burying his staff and drowning his book (v. i. 55–7): we may remember Paulina's assertion that there is no black magic in her art, and the amazing discovery of Hermione's breathing warmth, with the embrace 'lawful as eating' (*The Winter's Tale*, v. iii. 111; cp. here 'their words are natural breath' at v. i. 156). We have a Gospel reminiscence in Prospero's abrupt 'No' at Antonio's suggestion that his art is devil-inspired (v. i. 129); moreover, Prospero, unlike Faustus, regards finery not as an ambition, but as a way of tempting fools. Nor is he out for defensive measures—walling Germany with brass—but rather draws his enemies to him; though stern to excess, he shows a steady will to inclusion. He has slight respect for the metallic and war-like: his art renders swords futile (I. ii. 463; III. iii. 60–8). The once impractical governor, with one wave of his wand, a phrase from his book, leaves his supplanters helpless.[1]

Prospero is well-named. He is a god-man, or perhaps the god-in-man, causing yet negating tragedy for his purpose as he draws man towards vision despite inertia and retrogression. He is no literary enigma, but a logical conception, implicit in that textbook of contemporary idealism, Castiglione's *Il Cortegiano*, wherein humanism grades by Platonic ascent into the divine.

[1] Compare the contrast of Armed Head and Tree-bearing Child in *Macbeth*.

He is the accomplished personification of that super-state hinted in *Hamlet*, but which Hamlet himself never attains. True, when given, as here, direct personal reference and dramatic pointing, the result is rather disconcerting. Prospero's matured art is like nothing we have as yet experienced, though we have had glimpses of it, in the wonder of exploration, in science, in music and in poetry. In Prospero is both the adventure of Renaissance discovery and the majesty of Renaissance intellect, the intellect of Bacon, of Newton and of Einstein; and the other majesty of art, of Bach and Beethoven, of Shakespeare himself and of Goethe. He is the eternal artist rejected by the society his art redeems. But he is more than discoverer or scientist or artist, since he houses their joint wisdom in full incarnate flower. Prospero is the great composer whose implements are natural forces and whose music is the music of creation. With the elements and their creatures he is at home and in royal control; and among men walks as a god. He is labouring, not for himself, but for Miranda; for the newness not yet matured, for new worlds as yet unborn.

Later penetrations of a similar precision and sublimity are in Wordsworth (*Recluse* fragment; Preface to *The Excursion*, 1814), in Blake, and Nietzsche: all glimpse the same divine potentiality. Wordsworth sees in the marriage of man's mind with nature the inevitable creation of a greater man in whom all myths and paradisal dreams become incarnate. Goethe defined his own art in terms of a myriad spirits, anxious to serve and crowding round, saying 'Master, here we are!' like Ariel:

> All hail, great master ! grave sir, hail ! I come
> To answer thy best pleasure . . .   (1. ii. 189)

So Ariel 'and all his quality' (the word underlining the equation Ariel = dramatic art: see *Hamlet*, 11. ii. 371, 461) come to Prospero's 'strong bidding' (1. ii. 192). Nature was to Blake personal; a hierarchy of angelic beings; and the divine to be sought in 'a human face'.

But the clearest later equivalent is Nietzsche's *Thus Spake Zarathustra*,[1] wherein the Renaissance imagination is given its sharpest definition and detonation. In it we learn what Pros-

---

[1] My original note here expressed a doubt as to the likelihood of this equivalence proving generally acceptable. I can now point to the analysis of *Thus Spake Zarathustra* in *Christ and Nietzsche*, which should go far towards clarifying my meaning (1952).

pero thought, how he developed his art, wherefrom he derived his magic powers, during his twelve years on the island. Nietzsche's cave-recluse has, like Prospero, his two beasts, Eagle and Serpent, corresponding to Ariel and Caliban. Like Prospero, his consciousness is already half in eternity, set beyond man's horizon. The Renaissance is not over; it has scarcely begun; we are all, to-day, its children. Science, litera-ture and music are, at the best, but stammering blunders to-wards what shall be; and it is that 'shall be' of which Shake-speare and Nietzsche write; of the compulsion on man to super-humanity, drawing man, in his own despite, to god-in-man.

Prospero is stern. The responsibility of Ariel's release in-volves a continual pressure and discipline. Ariel and Caliban are firmly controlled; so, too, are Alonso, Sebastian and Antonio; and Stephano and Trinculo. And what of Ferdinand? Prospero charms him from futile sword-action; next acts harshly and 'austerely' (iv. i. 1), makes him labour at a menial task; and lastly, his kindly purpose revealed, is nevertheless careful to warn Ferdinand of the consequences of breaking Miranda's 'virgin knot' before the 'holy rite' of marriage, with stern hints of matrimonial discord and infertility (iv. i. 13–23) that serve to relate our present incident to the long story of Shakespearian jealousy. Prospero is a puritanical—I use the word advisedly—father, warning Ferdinand, after the manner of certain passages in *Hamlet* (i. iii. 44, i. iii. 115, iii. ii. 198–227, iii. iv. 40–88), that 'the strongest oaths are straw to the fire i' the blood' (iv. i. 52). Ferdinand answers with many asseverations of his honour and an almost crudely em-phatic definition of true love's purity:

> The white-cold virgin snow upon my heart
> Abates the ardour of my liver.   (iv. i. 55)

Ferdinand and Miranda are conceived in terms of a purity and a humility in severe contrast to the ambitions and lusts of Pros-pero's other pupils. There is no repudiation of sexual instinct, but rather, to crown a work already deeply involved in prob-lems of true and false sovereignty, a most subtle doctrine of psychological governance. At the final point of perfection our chosen pair are thus warned against the usurpation of 'our worser genius' (IV. i. 27) as a possible barrier to marital felicity and fertility.

This doctrine is expanded in the following Masque, in which Iris and Ceres come to honour the marriage. Iris, the first to enter, well fits *The Tempest*'s watery, ethereal, palely colourful quality, as though all were being seen through a mist or water; delicate and aerial, yet arching firmly across earth and heaven. She addresses Ceres in a speech of thin sounds and rhymes and a coldly sweet imagery ('leas', 'peas', 'sheep', 'keep', 'pionéd and twilléd brims', 'betrims'), with thoughts of 'cold nymphs', 'chaste crowns', the 'dismissed bachelor' seen as 'lass-lorn', and a 'sea-marge, sterile and rocky-hard' (IV. i. 60–75). Ceres' answer is richer and fecund, referring to Iris's 'saffron wings' on 'flowers', diffusing 'honey-drops' and 'refreshing showers'; and to 'bosky acres' as the 'rich scarf to my proud earth' (IV. i. 76–83). Each associates the other with her own qualities, driving home the interdependence of sky and earth with, on the human plane, purity and fertility: that is the purpose.

But there is more. Ceres fears the marriage celebration may be interrupted by Venus and Cupid, who have stolen her own daughter and married her to 'dusky Dis' (IV. i. 89: an interesting sidelight on the marriage of Claribel to an African, completing the association of Africa with barbaric sex, as in *Antony and Cleopatra*; and did not Sycorax come from Argier?). So Ceres has 'foresworn' their company (IV. i. 86–91). But Iris allays her fears. Though they had indeed planned 'some wanton charm' on the lovers, things have of late gone badly with 'Mars' hot minion' and her 'waspish-headed' son, who in peevish anger has broken his arrows (IV. i. 91–101). Venus and Cupid are accordingly excluded. Juno enters and there are more rhymes on marriage fertility, heavily supported by nature-images from Ceres. Then Iris, as messenger, calls 'temperate nymphs' from their cool channels (recalling Milton's *Comus*, as does the poetry of the Masque throughout) and a company of 'sun-burnt sicklemen', redolent of *The Winter's Tale*, to celebrate this 'contract of true love' (IV. i. 127–138). These dance, symbolizing a union of chastity with virility. Though the play is, as a whole, sunless, we have here a miniature of that union of the puritanical with Renaissance naturalism, of purity and fertility, so emphatic in Spenser and Lyly.

To Ferdinand the visionary masque 'makes this place Paradise' (IV. i. 124); but Prospero remembers the nearing threat of Caliban's revolution. This, in rough burlesque, illustrates the psychic dangers recently outlined: note the phrase 'thought is free' in the song Stephano sings for Caliban (III. ii. 134). Prospero's abrupt dismissal of the Masque makes a neat comment on the limitations of paradisal speculation in a brutal world. The dismissal is nevertheless followed, as though to answer the questions it raises, by a repudiation not only of fantasy, but of human fabrication at its grandest (towers, palaces, temples), driving home a yet deeper contrast with Faustus' materialistic ambitions; and even of 'the great globe itself' and all its children, themselves but fantasies, called from not-being and returning thereto (IV. i. 148–58). And yet it is Prospero, the man, who holds this supernal consciousness, wherein no negation, but rather some supreme positive, is mysteriously defined; through whose summary dismissal of creation's marvels some great otherness, some Nirvana of which all these are but transient symbols, is conjured into momentary possession. Our best approach to the paradox is through Nietzsche's Zarathustra, at once a despiser of poetry and poetry incarnate. Such universes of contemplation swirling through that tiny globe, the human skull, tax the master who endures them:

> A turn or two I'll walk
> To still my beating brain.   (IV. i. 162)

So, too, Zarathustra is shown as suffering through a consciousness set on an icy infinitude.

A work so deeply rooted in the soil of Shakespeare's life-labour, forming so many contacts with the myth and ritual of antiquity and vehicle for so subtle and yet so vast a wisdom, must necessarily be more than pantomime. What, we may ask is, in an objective interpretation, Prospero's island? What can be made of the more extreme events that occur there? They are symbolic certainly; but in what sense? Our great world, as Prospero tells us, is itself no more; while the strangest fictions, as Theseus has it,[1] are no less.

---

[1] *A Midsummer Night's Dream*, v. i. 215-7. 'Shadows' as used here covers 'symbol' in our sense ; see *Richard II*, IV. i. 297.

The island is, to start with, nature. Caliban talks of berries, crab-apples, pig-nuts, the jay, marmozet, filberts, rock-scamels. In no other play of Shakespeare do such natural objects stand out with so rounded a clarity. Caliban's own earthiness seems to lend them bodily weight, bring them nearer to us, as in his 'jay's nest' (II. ii. 182) and

> Pray you tread softly, that the blind mole may not
> Hear a foot-fall.   (IV. i. 194)

The country is part-English and part-foreign, with not only adders but apes 'that mow and chatter' (II. ii. 9), the 'pard' and 'cat-o'-mountain' (IV. i. 264): though some be Prospero's spirits in disguise and others merely mentioned by him, that makes slight difference here. One feels the island as semi-tropical, but much that happens in it recalls Nordic folk-lore, as when Caliban is tormented by urchin-shows and decoyed in darkness by a 'fire-brand' (II. ii. 5–6); while he and his companions are given a rough passage by Ariel through 'tooth'd briars, sharp furzes, pricking goss and thorns' (IV. i. 180), as Puck's victims are misled in *A Midsummer Night's Dream*, where there is a rather similar blend of homely tradition with jungle beasts and Indian fairies. Prospero's renunciation draws heavily on folk-lore, with 'elves of hills, brooks, standing lakes and groves'; spirits of the sea-shore dancing on sands with 'printless foot' (a picture conjured up too by Ariel's song at I. ii. 375) and varying with the tides; and 'demi-puppets' making moonlight 'ringlets' on the woodland sward (V. i. 33–57). These are nature-spirits, essences of nature's life, expressions of its laws and habits, its inruling, guiding ministers, such as Shelley's 'spirit of the earth' in *Prometheus*.

The visitors' reactions vary. The island sets Gonzalo dreaming of a Utopia, saying that, were he 'king' of it, he would create a 'commonwealth' without business competition, law, class distinction, property, work, sexual impurity or, to cap the satire, 'sovereignty' (II. i. 152–163). The speech, filled in by Sebastian's ironic comment 'and yet he would be king on't', serves to repeat the satire on Jack Cade's rebellion in 2 *Henry VI*. Though Gonzalo's rejection of all implements of war and reliance on nature's 'foison' and 'abundance' in the manner of Marvell's *Bermudas* (II. i. 166–71) expresses an admirable

yearning, while his dream of a new 'golden age' (ii. i. 175)
both introduces and supports our central action, yet the boun-
ties of nature and freedom are not to be had on terms so easy;
certainly not by sinners; nor can they be described in categories
so simple. As though to prove it, as soon as the opportunity
occurs, two villains with evil in their hearts start to plot for this
same sovereignty; and old Gonzalo is made aware, through a
bellowing as of lions and bulls (ii. i. 320), of the eternal beast,
in nature and man, awake. Our party is next brought up
sharply against symbolic creatures functioning in a fantastic,
ludicrous, insane world having nothing in common with Gonzalo's naturalistic Utopia.

It is strange and terrible. The show of 'monstrous' creatures
with strangely 'gentle-kind' behaviour (iii. iii. 31–2) that bring
in the banquet is described in non-committal and paradoxical
terms:

> I cannot too much muse,
> Such shapes, such *gesture*, and such sound, expressing—
> Although they want the use of tongue—a kind
> Of excellent *dumb* discourse.   (iii. iii. 36)

The phraseology suggests that they hold the life of symbol, of
art, as in 'To the *dumbness* of the *gesture* one might interpret'
at *Timon of Athens*, i. i. 34, spoken of a painting; or of sculpture,
as in the characterization of the artist in *Cymbeline* who 'was,
as another nature, *dumb*', drawing level with her in all but
'motion' and 'breath' (ii. iv. 83), like Julio Romano as described in *The Winter's Tale* at v. ii. 109 in a scene which, among
other eternal premonitions, contains a description of people so
struck with wonder that 'there was speech in their *dumbness*,
language in their very *gesture*' (v. ii. 14). These 'shapes' are
plastic or pictorial art incarnate, at once inanimate and alive.
Theirs is the potent dumbness of nature, conceived in our
Cymbeline passage as a positive quality. Ariel's Harpy-appearance follows, in condemnatory accents accusing our people of
their central sin against Prospero's ducal sovereignty; a universal crime of sovereign denial, here denial of the very sovereignty
of wisdom, something in excess even of the desecration of
royalty in *Richard II* and of princely generosity in *Timon*, for
which the 'powers' above have incensed all creation against
their peace (iii. iii. 74), as in the Fall of Genesis. An opacity
has fallen between man and the living universe.

This opacity is being removed, even as we watch. Human weapons, says Ariel, may as well attempt to wound the very air or waters as seek to damage 'one dowle that's in my plume' (III. iii. 65); for Ariel is himself those very elements; he is the elemental life, and power, acting under Prospero's guidance. That is why Alonso describes the accusation in natural terms:

> O, it is monstrous ! monstrous !
> Methought the billows spoke and told me of it ;
> The winds did sing it to me ; and the thunder,
> That deep and dreadful organ-pipe, pronounc'd
> The name of Prosper : it did base my trespass.
> Therefore my son i' th' ooze is bedded ; and
> I'll seek him deeper than e'er plummet sounded
> And with him there lie mudded.   (III. iii. 95)

Sense-perception is elsewhere confused, rather as in the great passage of Shelley's *Prometheus*. So, too, Gonzalo heard Ariel's rhyme as a bellowing of beasts. You cannot here properly distinguish animals from spirits. From the start, the island varied, as Colin Still observed, with the subject's spiritual status, being fertile to Gonzalo but barren to Antonio. Caliban and the Clowns have a tempest whilst Ferdinand and Miranda enjoy good weather; and so we cannot readily distinguish subject from object and the resulting medium is, as in poetry (in spite of Wordsworth's life-long attempt), less natural—in the ordinary sense—than symbolic. Hence our richly grotesque action.

Travellers' tales have clearly contributed to *The Tempest*. We have direct reference to accounts of 'mountaineers dew-lapp'd like bulls' and of men with heads in their breasts (III. iii. 44), like those of Othello's wanderings. There is Gonzalo's 'each putter out of five for one' (III. iii. 48), Stephano's talk of the 'dead Indian' as a business proposition (II. ii. 35) and again of 'savages and men of Ind' (II. ii. 62); while some authorities have, rather illogically, used Ariel's remark on 'the still-vex'd Bermoothes' (I. ii. 229) to place our island in Bermuda, the only spot in the world it cannot be. The opening up of Renaissance exploration certainly contributes, as it contributes later to *Robinson Crusoe* and *Gulliver's Travels*; but we are not therefore, now that the globe is mapped, to suppose that we possess the relevant meanings, which as readily find expression through mythology:

Now I will believe
That there are unicorns ; that in Arabia
There is one tree, the phoenix' throne ; one phoenix
At this hour reigning there.   (III. iii. 21)

See how closely our 'willing suspension of disbelief' is depen-
dant on a sense of geographical mystery; even on geographical
ignorance. Such emblematic creatures as phoenix and unicorn
(both = immortality) and such classical hybrids as the harpy
(defined as a composite of eagle and angel at *Pericles*, IV. III.
46–8) were more imaginatively potent in Shakespeare's day
than in ours. They hint states of being transcending normal
categories, as Shakespeare's remarkable poem, *The Phoenix and
the Turtle*,[1] suggests; and it is precisely such transcension with
which *The Tempest* is concerned, whether in mythology, newly-
fabricated symbol, or travellers' tales. It is therefore the revelatory quality of travel, the opening of vistas unguessed, not
any particular location, that is here important, dropping a queer
reflection in Sebastian's emphasized assertion that Tunis is an
infinite distance from Milan (II. i. 254–8), though both had
been safely within the circle of the mapped world for centuries.
To-day we have lost contact with mystery, as well in symbol as
in geography, and the two losses are related; but meanwhile,
having lost discovery, wonder and humility, we have lost
windows to highest wisdom.[2]

We are accordingly as lost as Alonso's party, while they, in
their turn, are baffled as we among the higher visions of
literature, of Blake and Nietzsche. Their terror, extending
that of the lovers in the 'wood near Athens', is emphatic:

All torment, trouble, wonder and amazement
Inhabits here : some heavenly power guide us
Out of this fearful country !   (V. i. 104)

[1] My reading of the poem as a transcending of antinomies is given in *The Shakespearian
Tempest*, Appendix A, and *The Christian Renaissance*, Ch. XII. My failure (in the former study)
to equate the 'bird of loudest lay' *with the Phoenix itself* was an inexcusable blunder to which
I would call attention. That the bird should herald his own marriage is quite in tune with what
follows. 1964: And see now my extended study in *The Mutual Flame*.

[2] Robert Sencourt in his study of St. John of the Cross notes that San Juan 'sees farther
into the ways of God through the Indies discovered by the navigators'. San Juan says that God
is regularly compared to such islands, because of their aloofness from men and strangeness. God
has 'the strangeness of undiscovered islands' (*Carmelite and Poet*, p. 159).

They suffer as from an intoxication:

> You do yet taste
> Some subtilties of the isle. (v. i. 123)

It is less an island than some new dimension of awareness; but 'dimension' is not to suggest any bloodless mathematical precision in a work where all is so naturalistically realized, flowering from the depths of physical actuality. Nor must we be forced towards any mind-pictures of the vertical: *The Tempest* is, except for Gonzalo's one remark that the play's action deserves to be eternalized 'with gold on lasting pillars' (v. i. 208), throughout horizontal, eschewing images of height, and indeed specifically slighting man's grandest architectural fabrications. Hence our peculiar difficulties; we are as in a maze (iii. iii. 2; v. i. 242), with comparatively little hint of any overlooking beings, without theology, the only divine references being vast and general (as in 'destiny' and 'the powers delaying, not forgetting' at iii. iii. 53, 73). The arts of design, with all their eternal reminders, are themselves, as we have seen, given physical vitality in the mysterious 'shapes' of the banquet scene. It is precisely this lack of vertical, or other immobile, emphasis that has most precluded our reception of the transcendence explored. *The Tempest* is dominated by sound[1] rather than by sight, as is to be expected in this tight concentration of Shakespeare's world, itself aural rather than visual in its major effects (see my *Principles of Shakespearian Production*, Ch. I. ii.). Here, as in much else, *The Tempest* makes a Wordsworthian contact, though Romantic poetry as a whole is characterized by an opposition of architectural or other elevations as against flat nature (e.g. rivers) to point the contrast projected in Shakespeare through music and thunder-tempests. But, though eminently horizontal and naturalistic, the statement, compacted of an indeterminate and expansive nature and of symbols rooted in all ages of human experience, is at once fantastic and cogent. The wonder of myth and magic of ritual collaborate to produce a consummation 'more than nature was ever conduct of' (v. i. 243; see also v. i. 227); and yet the very agents of the miraculous are natural elements. Nature and miracle become one.

[1]This has already been noted by Caroline Spurgeon.

Though man's efforts are rendered nugatory, the seas prove strangely 'merciful' (v. i. 178), and, above all wonders, the sufferers' very clothes are fresh. The sheen of garments glistens everywhere; in Prospero's magic mantle and his ducal robes; in Ariel's disguises; in the 'trumpery' laid out for the buffoons; in Caliban's 'gaberdine' (ii. ii. 41), whatever that may have been; and, above all, in the emphasized fresh garments of the travellers:

> On their sustaining garments not a blemish,
> But fresher than before.   (i. ii. 218)

As though death were found to have left the body as well as soul intact. The ship is likewise found 'tight and yare and bravely rigg'd' (v. i. 224). Is this all a life after death? Or this same life newly understood:

> O wonder !
> How many goodly creatures are there here !
> How beauteous mankind is ! O brave new world,
> That has such people in't !   (v. i. 181)

Whatever it be, the conclusion is revelation, forgiveness[1] and safety; all find themselves, mysteriously, 'when no man was his own' (v. i. 213). Therefore:

> Look down, you gods,
> And on this couple drop a blessed crown,
> For it is you that have chalk'd forth the way
> That brought us hither.   (v. i. 201)

And, having found themselves, they return; return to Milan.

Prospero's final purpose, so unlike that of Faustus, includes the voluntary renunciation of his art:

> . . . this rough magic
> I here abjure.   (v. i. 50)

In so far as his art is poetry—and surely it is not far distant—the renunciation is natural, since all art stirs man to the beyond-art consummation. Therefore the ceremonial appearance of Prospero in his ducal robes is no weak return, but a triumphant climax symbolizing the establishment of wisdom as the crown

---

[1] Such appears to be the aim, though there is little sign of any real forgiveness of Antonio; nor, indeed, any sign of his deserving it.

of life. So, having perpetuated his advance by offering it back to man, Prospero, with Miranda married to his enemy's son, resumes his dukedom and re-engages in practical affairs, though with a consciousness whose 'every third thought' is set now on death, the 'grave', eternity (v. i. 311): for he, at the command of whose 'so potent art' graves have released their dead (v. i. 48), is necessarily passing beyond man. Prospero is a close replica of Christ, with similar miraculous powers and the same comparative scorn of miracle, though with a certain lingering bitterness nearer to Timon than to Christ.

IV

We have considered *The Tempest* as an expression of the Renaissance imagination under pressure from British puritanism. What, then, is its relation to Shakespeare's national work? Is there such a relation?

The enquiry has its dangers. The use of such terms as 'Renaissance', 'Elizabethan', 'puritanism', runs the risk of reducing the visionary whole to historical concepts—not to history, for what is greater than that? God Himself is part of history—but to the historical concept, which is a different matter. There is a danger of using our own twentieth-century abstractions, which too easily masquerade as guarantees of historical truth, to label and render nugatory, because docketed, the romantic statement; of using Elizabethan scholarship, of one sort or another, to shrivel Shakespearian power to the stature of an academic understanding; while forgetting that the super-state shadowed is as far beyond our realization, or even comprehension, as Blake's, or Shelley's, or Nietzsche's; or that of the New Testament itself. Each age in turn formulates its own expression; while the vision, existing in its own right, persists.

However, with these reservations, it can be said that *The Tempest* at no point contradicts the essence of English history, widely viewed; and can, very generally, be considered as reflecting the destiny of Shakespeare's land, then young.

The background action is, as usual with Shakespeare, political. This strong political reference distinguishes the Shakespearian statement from our other examples of visionary literature, whilst also enabling it to reflect the wider history of

Great Britain, itself so largely concerned with the attempt to fuse Christianity and politics. Prospero is Plato's philosopher-king betrayed by a Machiavellian 'policy'; and Ariel's denunciation of his betrayers is an indictment of the second-rate, or third-rate, in government, so criminally opposed against the first-rate, arduous, idealism. Prospero himself, against whose magic swords are futile, is now at least no impractical dreamer. He curtly dismisses his masque to meet Caliban's revolution; which, though it seem trivial, is yet, its implications understood, far otherwise, symbolizing that bestial retrogression and drunken worship of a Stephano as 'wondrous man' (II. ii. 177) in place of a Prospero, that utter miscarriage of all true valuation, which lurks within every denial of highest sovereignty. Prospero's story is set between an impractical idealism on the one side and political villainy and lust on the other; while dramatizing the attainment of a practical idealism negatively pointed by the satire on Gonzalo's Utopian dream. *The Tempest* accordingly falls into alignment with Shakespeare's massed statements elsewhere in definition of true sovereignty and, directly or indirectly, of British destiny; the 'liberal arts' (I. ii. 73) of Renaissance Europe are here shaped firmly into an Elizabethan mould; while Britain has, since Shakespeare's day, laboured with varying success towards the middle course suggested.

The inclusiveness of Prospero's art illustrates a British tendency. The building up of our island population by continental invasion produced a blend of unbending integrity and wide catholicity properly reflected in Prospero. Since Shakespeare's day the drawing to our island of other peoples has, as was prophesied in Queen Elizabeth's prayer before the Armada, more than once characterized our history. But this implied equation of Prospero's island with Great Britain remains a momentary analogy that could bear no stress.[1]

Prospero's magic is largely a sea-magic; his island story is sea-rooted (his description of his lonely voyage with Miranda faintly recalling, as we have suggested, the old English poems, *The Wanderer* and *The Seafarer*), and ends with a voyage home;

[1] Compare, however, John Cowper Powys, *Mortal Strife*, ch. IV, p. 156: 'There is a story that the old gods, hunted from Europe, took refuge in these Islands. Well, let us hope that the hunted human soul, the mother of all the gods, has done the same!'

in the interim, he has been gradually mastering the sea-powers. Similarly Great Britain has laboured at ocean-mastery; the 'ocean' being both the actual ocean and those oceanic instincts, or forces, within man which it so consistently throughout the ages symbolizes. British colonization from the start went hand in hand with Puritanism; the early colonizers, not unlike Prospero, being impelled by political or religious tyrannies to follow their soul-cravings across the sea and there work out the controlled magic of personal integration.

Suppose that Britain's contribution were being assessed some ten thousand years hence by an enlightened historian. He would probably point to (i) her in-ruling severe, yet inclusive and tolerant, religious and political instincts, of which her first colonial adventures and the Puritan revolution were active examples; (ii) her inventive and poetic genius variously concerned with the tapping and use of natural energy; and (iii) her colonizing, especially her will to raise savage peoples from superstition and blood-sacrifice, taboos and witchcraft and the attendant fears and slaveries, to a more enlightened existence. Little ingenuity is needed to find correspondences with Prospero, Ariel, and Caliban. Especially we may equate the king who is yet no tyrant, the student-prince un-at-home with forceful action, who yet, under pressure of his island existence, gains power to control armed opposition, with the dimly apprehended pacifism inspiring Great Britain's history and the implied liberalism of her constitutional monarchy; only gestures as yet, but gestures that speak 'an excellent dumb discourse'. As for Miranda, what of her? Without her, perhaps, our ten-thousand-years-hence historian would not have been born; or, at least, been in no position to write his book.

It is, perhaps, inevitable that Shakespeare, whose work from *Henry VI* and the Histories, through the Tragedies to *Henry VIII*, is so saturated with the spirit of his land, should, in such a summation of that work in *The Tempest*, have outlined, among much else, a myth of the national soul.

Additional note, 1982
For a discussion of *The Tempest* in relation to colonialism, see my essay 'Caliban as a Red Man' in *Shakespeare's Styles: Essays in Honour of Kenneth Muir*, Cambridge, 1980.

VI

HENRY VIII AND THE POETRY OF CONVERSION

Though I speak with the tongues of men and of angels, and have not charity, I am become as sounding brass, or a tinkling cymbal. And though I have the gift of prophecy and understand all mysteries and all knowledge ; and though I have all faith, so that I could remove mountains, and have not charity, I am nothing.   1 Corinthians xiii. 1.

I will discase me and myself present
As I was sometime Milan.
                                        The Tempest.

I

THE TEMPEST would scarcely have been quite satisfying as Shakespeare's last play, since despite its many subtle recapitulations, it might yet seem to dissolve the stern political and national interest of earlier works into a haze of esoteric mysticism. One expects, from such a poet, a less visionary and enigmatic conclusion.

Shakespeare seems continually to have been forced backwards as his historical interest developed and plots became exhausted. Starting with the three parts of *Henry VI* and continuing through *Richard III* to the establishment of the Tudor monarchy, he quickly brings his story too near home for a further advance. So, retracing his steps, he writes, with a developing insight, the sequence from *Richard II* to *Henry V* with, at some period hard to specify, the richly compacted *King John*. *Henry V*, the culmination, stands as a landmark: it is his finest accomplishment in national poetry to date and, within its limits, final. But the great Tragedies make no absolute break with the Histories, being concerned (see 'This Sceptred Isle' in *The Sovereign Flower*) with a reworking of old interests under a more profound handling. A Greek setting is clearly used in *Troilus and Cressida* and *Timon of Athens* to mark a contemporary satire, the balance of Trojan and Greek in the former probably suggesting, in view of the traditional association of Britain and Troy, a contrast of England as the upholder of a medieval chivalry as against Renaissance decadence. The Roman plays, however, stand throughout in their own right, ancient Rome being too cogent and, paradoxically, too near for fiction. *King Lear*, *Macbeth*, and *Cymbeline*, deliberately handle British history with variously precise messages for Shakespeare's day, *Macbeth* being a study of tyranny in attempt to annihilate England's destiny at its root and *Cymbeline* showing the Roman eagle melting into the sun-beams of Britain. There is profound examination throughout the Tragedies and Final Plays of such ever-vital and contemporary matters as state-order, warrior honour, kingship and tyranny; many of which are worked, as we have seen, into *The Tempest*. Finally the poet, copying his analogue Prospero, returns deliberately to a national and contemporary theme, and writes *Henry VIII*. He may have originally purposed such a conclusion, holding it in reserve for his crowning work.

The difficulties would appear great. After *The Tempest*, the poet cannot well be content with anything less comprehensive. The tenour of his recent work precludes, moreover, war, enthusiasm for which was, as it were, scotched by the noble conclusion to *Cymbeline* and the general statement of *The Tempest*. Something at least of a corresponding serenity is demanded. As for the visions and recognitions, the eternal whisperings and thunderings, all such wondrous things as Cerimon, Apollo's oracle, Hermione's resurrection, Jupiter, Prospero's white magic, what comparable themes can be elicited from a realistic and near-distance story? Can a Christian mythology be impregnated with the necessary dramatic force without sacrilege or bathos? Can the more tragic facts of this well-known plot be rendered worthy successors of *Hamlet* and *King Lear*? And what of comedy? Finally, Shakespeare has of late tended more and more to rely on symbol and ritual, ending with *The Tempest*, a play made throughout of such substance. Can this be continued? Are there any possible analogies?

I hope to show how *Henry VIII* meets all these difficulties with ease, whilst adding excellences of its own. We may start by observing how it roughly incorporates certain major features of earlier Histories. It is as massively conceived and constructed as the peculiarly massive *Richard III*, while showing correspondences in pageant and group-work to the other play's theatric formalism of lamenting women and fatalistic ghosts. Both plays are concerned with the punishment of inordinate ambition. We have reminders of the royalism of *Richard II* and much, as we shall see, of its sense of fallen greatness followed by religious mysticism. *Richard II* contains one of Shakespeare's two lengthy passages of national praise; *Henry VIII* contains the other. The balance of humour against law, of Falstaff and the Lord Chief Justice, in the two parts of *Henry IV*, finds here not merely expression, but synthesis. *Henry V*, the patriotic play crowning the earlier sequence, is clearly analogous to *Henry VIII* the patriotic play crowning the second, the prologues of both being couched in a vein of humble reverence for the high themes to follow, with

> Think when we talk of horses that you see them
> Printing their proud hoofs i' the receiving earth
> > (*Henry V*, I. chor. 26)

balanced by

> Think ye see
> The very persons of our noble story
> As they were living . . .   (*Henry VIII*, pro. 25)

The grand actions of both dramas work up to studied eulogies on peace. But our clearest parallel is *King John*. Here, as in *King John*, we have a central figure whose supreme status as king of England is variously related (i) to his own character and (ii) to Papal control (Cardinals being in both plays important). Yet more interesting is the similarity in structure, whereby the tragic endurance of fine people, Constance and Arthur in the one and Buckingham, Wolsey and Queen Katharine in the other (Katharine confronted by Wolsey and Campeius closely resembling Constance by the side of Pandulph), is firmly juxtaposed to the King's, or England's, advance, with the same seemingly inhuman faculty shown by the poet in so indulging his sympathies without losing the national perspective. The pattern is more symmetrical and purposeful in *Henry VIII*, and here the concluding national prophecy—both end with a prophecy—is more elaborate. *Henry VIII* is thus a recapitulation of earlier Histories, though itself more sober and more substantial, at once modulated and enriched by the wisdom garnered during intermediate works.

In spite of its greatness, *Henry VIII* has, however, for long been suspected as, in part, non-Shakespearian; and we must give a brief preliminary notice of the main argument. Individual commentators have made lists of so called 'weak' or 'feminine' endings, calculated percentages and made their private allotments of this or that scene to Fletcher, Massinger, or some author unknown. The process has gone so far that popular editions are found to state, without qualification or reserve, that the play *is* the work of Shakespeare and Fletcher. This is surely inexcusable.[1]

The various allotments cannot possibly be answered in detail; and it is really less any one specific argument that is nowadays our obstacle than a certain vague conviction that the play is largely spurious. At the risk therefore of labouring a proof that concerns a scene not necessarily regarded as inauthentic, but which nevertheless serves as a useful opening, we shall first consider a passage from Queen Katharine's defence:

> Sir, I desire you do me right and justice ;
> And to bestow your pity on me ; for
> I am a most poor woman, and a stranger
> Born out of your dominions ; having here
> No judge indifferent, nor no more assurance
> Of equal friendship and proceeding. Alas ! sir,
> In what have I offended you ? what cause
> Hath my behaviour given to your displeasure,
> That thus you should proceed to put me off
> And take your good grace from me ? . . . Sir, call to mind
> That I have been your wife in this obedience
> Upward of twenty years, and have been blest
> With many children by you : if, in the course
> And process of this time, you can report,
> And prove it too, against mine honour aught,
> My bond to wedlock, or my love and duty,
> Against your sacred person, in God's name
> Turn me away ; and let the foul'st contempt
> Shut door upon me, and so give me up
> To the sharp'st kind of justice.   (II. iv. 11)

Feminine endings and run-on lines abound, precisely as with Hermione's very similar defence in *The Winter's Tale*, in style and sentiment a neat precursor:

[1] Important exceptions are the late Edgar I. Fripp and Professor Peter Alexander (see *Shakespeare; his Life and Art*, 1938).

You, my lord, best know—
Who least will seem to do so—my past life
Hath been as continent, as chaste, as true,
As I am now unhappy ; which is more
Than history can pattern, though devis'd
And play'd to take spectators. For behold me,
A fellow of the royal bed, which owe
A moiety of the throne, a great king's daughter,
The mother to a hopeful prince, here standing
To prate and talk for life and honour 'fore
Who please to come and hear. For life, I prize it
As I weigh grief, which I would spare : for honour,
'Tis a derivative from me to mine,
And only that I stand for. I appeal
To your own conscience, sir, before Polixenes
Came to your court, how I was in your grace,
How merited to be so ; since he came,
With what encounter so uncurrent I
Have strain'd, to appear thus : if one jot beyond
The bound of honour, or in act or will
That way inclining, harden'd be the hearts
Of all that hear me, and my near'st of kin
Cry fie upon my grave !

                    (*The Winter's Tale*, III. ii. 33)

In stress-variation, pause, run-on and feminine, sometimes
monosyllabic, endings, the two styles are closely similar expressions of an almost identical argument. Or listen to Volumnia:

                    For myself, son,
I purpose not to wait on Fortune till
These wars determine : if I cannot persuade thee
Rather to show a noble grace to both parts
Than seek the end of one, thou shalt no sooner
March to assault thy country than to tread . . .

                    (*Coriolanus*, v. iii. 118)

The Tempest provides relevant examples continually.
    The use of such a style in *Henry VIII* forms of itself no
argument whatsoever for suspicion. The style has great force.
Weak final words and a strong run-on give sense of logic overruling metre in an argumentative and expostulatory speech.
Consider the lifted energy of the run-on in 'For life, I prize
it . . .' in Hermione's words, and the stress of 'if I cannot

persuade thee . . .' in Volumnia's. Compare the expostulatory emphasis in Queen Katharine's

> It is not to be *quest*ion'd
> That they had gather'd a wise counsel to them
> Of every realm, that did debate this business,
> Who deem'd our marriage lawful.   (II. iv. 48)

You can hear the voice, see the pursed lips or impatient little gesture, in the verse's lilt. Such touches grow more frequent in Shakespeare's late plays. In *Henry VIII* they are used to give a sharp, lilting, upward spring to a merry dialogue in a manner certainly new but as successful as our other examples:

> You would swear directly
> Their very noses had been counsellors
> To Pepin or Clotharius, they keep state so.   (I. iii. 8)

The scene is regularly handed over to Fletcher; but compare the stress on '*state* so' with that on '*both* parts' in Volumnia's lines. Again:

> the sly whoresons
> Have got a speeding trick to lay down ladies ;
> A French song and a fiddle has no fellow.   (I. iii. 39)

The line rises to a laugh: there is no harm in that.

It may be felt that we have not yet touched the peculiar uneasiness felt by scholars reading *Henry VIII*. Here, perhaps, are more relevant lines:

> All good people,
> You that thus far have come to pity me,
> Hear what I say, and then go home and lose me . . .
>> (II. i. 55)

and

> Vain pomp and glory of this world, I hate ye !
>> (III. ii. 366)

and

> And when I am forgotten, as I shall be,
> And sleep in dull cold marble, where no mention
> Of me more must be heard of, say, I taught thee . . .
>> (III. ii. 433)

and

> His overthrow heap'd happiness upon him . . .
>> (IV. ii. 64

and

> The last is, for my men : they are the poorest,
> But poverty could never draw 'em from me ;
> That they may have their wages duly paid 'em,
> And something over to remember me by.   (IV. ii. 149)

and

> Truth shall nurse her,
> Holy and heavenly thoughts still counsel her . . .
> (V. v. 29)

These are from scenes regularly repudiated. And do we not sense something strange? Is it the queer play on *personal pronouns* weakly, or strongly, falling? or on other small words, sometimes a long string of monosyllables? an absence of metaphor, and colour? The most characteristic rhythms do not involve a run-on: the lines are units; falling units. And yet these very sequences build some of the most heart-searching passages in all Shakespeare. Their meaning we shall study: but first, a further objection may be raised. Whatever their 'meaning', is it natural for Shakespeare to change within a single play from the packed and metaphoric style of I. i., which is normal Shakespeare of the purest sort, not only to the feminine endings and run-on of the expostulatory style, but to these other, yet more emphatic, mannerisms? Does his earlier work show any precedent for such stylistic variation?

Compare, in *Hamlet*, the complexity of syntax in Horatio's narrative explanation of the political situation at I. i. 79 and Hamlet's somewhat similarly placed 'dram of eale' speech at I. iv. 13, both involved, complex and, to put it bluntly, a trifle boring, with the gripping lucidity of Horatio's and Hamlet's addresses to the Ghost and any of Hamlet's later star-speeches, especially his 'To be or not to be . . .' (*Hamlet*, III. i. 56). There is a clear contrast of complicated factual report and analysis with some simple rhetorical flow. The same happens in *Antony and Cleopatra*: compare the speeches of Caesar in I. iv., or Ventidius in III. i.; indeed, any of the more purely political and historical stuff, with Enobarbus' description of Cleopatra on Cydnus (II. ii. 198) or Cleopatra's death speech (V. ii. 282). In *The Winter's Tale* we have the sharp change from Leontes' first divided consciousness and complexity of expression to an emotional simplicity following conversion (as at III. ii. 233); while in *The Tempest* Prospero's long but often tediously involved account of his brother's wickedness (in I. ii.) is likewise balanced by the lucidity of his 'Cloud-capp'd towers' speech (IV. i. 148) and his final renunciation (V. i. 33). Now in *Henry VIII* compare the extreme complexity of Buckingham's account of Wolsey's machinations at I. i. 168 or the King's story of his troubled conscience at II. iv. 153 with the simplicity of Buckingham's, Wolsey's or Katharine's speeches *after* their respective falls. We may conclude that Shakespeare regularly employs a complicated syntax for the rough and tumble of actual life, and those divisions of consciousness it awakes; but automatically uses a simple expression where the speaker functions as a unit; and, further, that it is these latter, not the former, that give us our generally recognized set-pieces of supreme poetry. Moreover, in *The Winter's Tale* and *The Tempest* the contrast is respectively that of (i) sin and conversion and (ii) the closely related move from bitterness to renunciation; and it is precisely such a contrast that we meet, expanded, in *Henry VIII*.

The most authoritative voice so far lifted on behalf of the play's complete authenticity is probably Swinburne's. Here is his central conclusion:

> The speech of Buckingham, for example, on his way to execution, is of course at first sight very like the finest speeches of the kind in Fletcher ; here is the same smooth and fluent declamation, the same prolonged and persistent melody, which if not monotonous is certainly not various ; the same pure, lucid, perspicuous flow of simple rather than strong and elegant rather than exquisite English; and yet if we set it against the best examples of the kind which may be selected from such tragedies as *Bonduca* or *The False One*, against the rebuke addressed by Caratach to his cousin or by Caesar to the murderers of Pompey—and no finer instance of tragic declamation can be chosen from the work of this great master of rhetorical dignity and pathos—I cannot but think that we shall perceive in it a comparative severity and elevation which will be missed when we turn back from it to the text of Fletcher. There is an aptness of phrase, an abstinence from excess, a 'plentiful lack' of mere flowery and superfluous beauties, which we may rather wish than hope to find in the most famous of Shakespeare's successors.

(Quoted by C. Knox Pooler, Introduction to the Arden
edition of *Henry VIII*, p. xxxiv)

It is significant that the main defence of the play's authenticity
since suspicion was first aroused during the mid-Victorian era
should come from a writer who was at once poet, dramatist, and
Elizabethan scholar; and that his arguments should be based
not on statistics or collections of phrase-resemblances but on
the poetic status of the passages concerned.

Let us turn to the two plays Swinburne selects. The passages
he himself mentions are (as the Arden editor agrees) satisfactorily judged by his own comment; but there are others of
greater interest. Here is one, forming a curious replica in
parody of Wolsey's great speech of repentant counsel in *Henry
VIII* (at III. ii. 432):

Septimius.   O good soldiers
          You that have Roman hearts, take heed of falsehood ;
          Take heed of blood ; take heed of foul ingratitude.
          The gods have scarce a mercy for those mischiefs.
          Take heed of pride, 'twas that that brought me to it.
2 *Soldier.* This fellow would make a rare speech at the gallows.
3 *Soldier.* 'Tis very fit he were hang'd to edify us.
Septimius Let all your thoughts be humble and obedient,
          Love your commanders, honour them that feed ye :
          Pray that ye may be strong in honesty
          As in the use of arms ; labour, and diligently,
          To keep your hearts from ease, and her base issues ;
          Pride and ambitious wantonness, those spoil'd me.
          Rather lose all your limbs, than the least honesty;
          You are never lame indeed, till loss of credit
          Benumb ye through : scars, and those maims of honour
          Are memorable crutches, that shall bear
          When you are dead, your noble names to eternity.
1 *Soldier.* I cry.
2 *Soldier.* And so do I.
3 *Soldier.* An excellent villain.
1 *Soldier.* A more sweet pious knave I never heard yet.
                              (*The False One*, IV. iii.)

The correspondences to Wolsey's lines are obvious; but so,
too, is the incomparability in value. True, the speaker is being
satirized; but, the real weakness of the verse is scarcely a
studied weakness. Even if it were, is it conceivable that anyone capable of writing Wolsey's words would be also capable

of this fatuous burlesque? Is this the kind of ridiculing we expect from a serious poet of his own greatest work? Consider how different is Pyramus' tragic bombast in *A Midsummer Night's Dream* from the serious tragic poetry of *Romeo and Juliet*; or Chaucer's *Sir Thopas* from *Troilus and Criseyde*. Are these lines not rather a lesser poet's semi-humorous variation on another's famous passage, probably well known to the audience?

In reading Beaumont and Fletcher, say *The Maid's Tragedy* or *Philaster*, one is continually made aware of some well-worn Shakespearian emotional theme being used, as here (e.g. 'beware of foul ingratitude'), for a temporary purpose, and next curtly dismissed, with scant respect to the depths involved in the Shakespearian statement, to make way for some new attraction. Each piece, out of its context, may quite often seem as good as Shakespeare; but where in Shakespeare a whole play's impact is behind his greater passages, enforcing them far beyond themselves, Beaumont and Fletcher so aim at getting the maximum of poetic thrill out of each incident in turn irrespective of the rest that no reservoir of significance can accumulate and even the finest separate pieces fail of a maximum effect. Power leaks out into the wide areas of second-rate event and sentiment. Here, for example, is a remarkably fine unit, a far better example, it would seem, for the Fletcherian cause than those chosen by Swinburne:

> Thou hallow'd relique, thou rich diamond
> Cut with thine own dust ; thou for whose wide fame
> The world appears too narrow, man's all thoughts,
> Had they all tongues, too silent ; thus I bow
> To thy most honour'd ashes : though an enemy,
> Yet friend to all thy worths ; sleep peaceably ;
> Happiness crown thy soul, and in thy earth
> Some laurel fix his seat, there grow, and flourish,
> And make thy grave an everlasting triumph.
> Farewell all glorious wars, now thou art gone,
> And honest arms adieu : all noble battles
> Maintain'd in thirst of honour, not of blood,
> Farewell for ever.   (*Bonduca*, v. i.)

That for a brief while holds a serenity of sentiment and perfection of technique comparable with Cranmer's prophecy in

Henry VIII; but it remains rather solitary and brief. A line
or two later, moreover, it changes from a note again resembling Cranmer's speech (at its opening) to loose rhythms that
never occur in *Henry VIII*, though usual enough in Fletcher:

> This worthy Roman
> Was such another piece of endless honour,
> Such a brave soul dwelt in him : their proportions
> And faces were not much unlike, boy. Excellent nature!
> See how it works into his eyes, mine own boy.
>
> (*Bonduca*, v. i.)

Notice, too, our line (recently quoted) from *The False One*:
'When you are dead, your noble names to eternity'. You get
such lines often. Here are some others: 'Shall be thy prisoner,
the day yours without hazard', 'What do I ail, i' the name of
heaven? I did but see her', 'Or lose my life i' th' purchase; good
gods comfort thee' (*Bonduca*, iii. ii.; v. ii.; v. iii.). Now, though
the main 'Fletcherian' rhythms in *Henry VIII* can be paralleled
regularly from Shakespeare's earlier work, such limping lines,
almost the main hall-mark of Fletcher's looser manner (and it
is with that manner we are concerned), *never* occur in our suspected scenes. After this fine blank-verse threnody in *Bonduca*
they drop the poetic dignity sadly. It would, of course, be easy
to select Fletcher's finest efforts, and argue that they must have
been inserted by Shakespeare; but it is safer to suggest that,
whereas Fletcher's greatest things come in haphazardly,
Shakespeare writes from that higher dimension of artistic control that not only composes a supreme passage but knows precisely how to place it, maintain its dignity and channel its
worth.

But the most important argument of all concerns the
strangely reiterated use of feminine endings falling on monosyllables and, especially, pronouns. Here the style of *Henry
VIII* is, though certainly Fletcherian, not precisely Fletcher's.
Consider an example of Fletcher's use:

> I am thine,
> Thine everlastingly, thy love has won me,
> And let it breed no doubt ; our new acquaintance
> Compels this, 'tis the gods' decree to bless us.
> The times are dangerous to meet ; yet fail not,

By all the love thou bear'st me I conjure thee,
Without distrust of danger to come to me,
For I have purpos'd a delivery
Both of myself and fortune this blest day
Into thy hands, if thou think'st good.

(*Bonduca*, III. ii.)

In *Henry VIII* we find a similar employment of falling rhythm, with cadences dwelling similarly on prepositions and personal pronouns, especially ' 'em', 'ye', and the ending of line or sentence on 'on me' or 'upon me', rising to so striking an emphasis as

                  where no mention
Of *me* more must be heard of. . . .   (III. ii. 434)

In Shakespeare such turns of speech are limited, roughly, to a certain psychic state; in Fletcher they occur normally, at all times. An ear attuned to the Shakespearian usage will find even this pleading speech from *Bonduca*, where the rhythms accompany a purpose as near as may be to Shakespeare's in *Henry VIII*, peculiarly dry. Normally, they contribute little or nothing; as though Fletcher were not understanding his own rhythms and what they should be doing. Besides, how do we know that Fletcher is not copying Shakespeare?

Now in *Henry VIII* this particular mannerism is used with strong dramatic point. When a speaker is ambitious and aspiring to play his part in affairs, he speaks normal Shakespearian verse, packed, metaphoric, allusive, complex; when arguing for himself, or herself, against a hostile community, as with Katharine at her trial, the weak-endings occur with run-on and mid-line pause, in what I have called an 'expostulatory' style; which, though not to be limited to expostulation, is probably most potent when used for such a purpose, as was witnessed by our comparisons from *The Winter's Tale* and *Coriolanus*. But *Henry VIII* shows yet a third style: when the speaker's cause is lost and he is severed from all worldly ambition, the run-on ceases, the lines are simple, falling, units with a delicate but reiterated stress on personal pronouns in collaboration with feminine endings. It is, very roughly, the speech of lonely souls, of persons rejected, thrown back on themselves, concentrating on their own, or someone else's, individual selves, what might be called the essential 'I' or 'thou' of human personality. Though a bitter self-concentration may be involved, it is most naturally used for the language of renunciation and acceptance.

This manner is not new to Shakespeare. In *The Tempest* it recurs continually in the speech of that rejected, though bitter, soul, Caliban, always so turned inward on his own pathetic self. His very first speech has the supposedly Fletcherian ending on 'ye' and his second gives us 'my dinner', 'which thou tak'st from me', 'Thou strok'dst me, and mad'st much of me; would'st give me', 'and then I lov'd thee', 'light on you', 'and here you sty me', 'whiles you do keep from me' (*The Tempest*, I. ii. 321–44): the emphasis is, naturally, transferred to similar endings on 'thee' when, recognizing his god, Stephano, he finds the sudden release of a 'thou'-consciousness. There are other earlier examples. We have Lear's 'do not mock me' and 'do not laugh at me', both occurring at that dramatic moment of conversion or reorientation, his reunion with Cordelia, at *King Lear*, IV. vii. 59, 67. Pericles' similar reunion with Marina (in sackcloth and unshaven, i.e. in a state of repentance) offers 'I do think so. Pray you, turn your eyes upon me', 'Recount I do beseech thee. Come, sit by me', and 'Lest this great sea of joys rushing upon me' (V. i. 102, 143, 194). Leontes in *The Winter's Tale* uses a sparse sprinkling of such endings involving 'him' and 'thee' until his conversion, when, at his final exit after the disastrous trial, the more typifying note at once occurs on 'me', as in

> . . . which I receive much better
> Than to be pitied of thee. Prithee, bring me . . .
> (III. ii. 234)

concluding on

> . . . so long as nature
> Will bear up with this exercise, so long
> I daily vow to use it. Come and lead me
> Unto these sorrows. (III. ii. 241)

This sudden fall after the gathering up-sweep of the play's first movement precisely forecasts the dramatic rhythms of *Henry VIII*. One is not surprised to find Leontes' remorse during the resurrection housing itself in a similar style: 'when first I woo'd her', 'does not the stone rebuke me', 'let no man mock me', 'for I saw her' (V. iii. 36, 37, 79, 139). But perhaps our

most interesting analogy occurs at the poignant moment of
Enobarbus' repentance in *Antony and Cleopatra*. Hitherto he
has spoken normal verse. Now his single, short, speech starts:

> O sovereign mistress of true melancholy,
> The poisonous damp of night disponge upon me . . .
>
> (IV. ix. 12)

There precisely is the note to be sounded by Shakespeare in
Buckingham's farewell. I point less to numerical facts than a
poetical quality. My arguments are not statistical, and must
remain subject to many reservations. But clearly there is in
such passages a certain detectable rhythm concerned variously
with a poetic self-pity or self-accusation; a turning inward from
the community to the individual soul, of oneself or another;
and this it is which gives us that peculiar music of prepositional
and pronominal endings that has caused so much trouble
in *Henry VIII*.

This music we scarcely, I think, detect in Fletcher. Even
supposing that Shakespeare (long before the composition of
Henry VIII) had caught the trick from his junior contemporary
—or perhaps from Massinger, or some other—we shall observe
that he has turned it to a use to them unknown; he has recognized and released the dormant potentiality, the soul-principle,
in these little rhythms, and set them softly burning.

It is, indeed, too little recognized that genius consists less
in inventing things unheard of than in recognizing and releasing, as Prospero releases Ariel, a prisoned magic in things well-
known and well-worn. That is Shakespeare's method with his
plots and old-plays. Though 'evidence' is also adduced by the
Fletcherian apologist concerning the presence of certain words
or phrases in *Henry VIII* not elsewhere observed in Shakespeare, we can, if we wish, readily suppose some earlier text
behind Shakespeare's. It is not unlikely that other plays on
the subject had already appeared, and passages from them may
well show through, as, very probably, passages of older works
show through in *Hamlet* and *King Lear*. Or again, Shakespeare,
who must have known Fletcher's plays well, may have found
some fine lines of his attractive and, recognizing instinctively a
value for his immediate purpose, may conceivably have tuned
himself in once or twice to the Fletcherian vocabulary. Being

deliberately engaged in a peculiarly new adventure—how peculiar I hope to show—he may even have asked a friend to make some rough drafts for him to work on, in order to transcend his earlier manner, to get, as it were, outside his own universe and see that universe afresh. But we are here perilously near fantasy, and a return to hard fact, the hard fact of the Folio and its editors' claims, would be wise. And there is yet another hard fact: that of *Henry VIII* itself, the living work, in all its intricate detail and massive impact.

The arguments for spuriousness are really quite untenable; for, though the suspected scenes may contain some minor phrase-reminiscences from Fletcher's work, they offer many reminders, of far greater force and importance, from Shakespeare's. The Arden editor shows an intimate knowledge of the works of Beaumont and Fletcher; but his acquaintance with Shakespeare is less obvious.[1] We shall shortly observe how closely the 'Fletcherian' parts re-work favourite Shakespearian themes; as in the fall of Buckingham, with its sense of personal betrayal; the Lords' sharp conversational satire on foreign fashions; Wolsey's feast, both in management and in detail an exact successor to others; Queen Katharine's Desdemona-like retirement to domestic solitude, accompanied by song and music, so invariably used hitherto for just such backwater moments in a tragic movement; her vision of Paradise, corresponding to the visions of other late plays; the stress on the faithfulness of both Wolsey's and Katharine's servants; and finally, the concluding prophecy, in which a life's work of national poetry, more than once already given prophetic form,[2] culminates. Can the Fletcherian supporters adduce correspondence of a like nature *at every turn*? Is it not strange that *all* these supposedly Fletcherian incidents, both in their selection and treatment, should conform choicely to Shakespearian tradition? Can these scenes, so rich in generation of the

---

[1] His notes to the text are scattered with parallels from the works of Beaumont and Fletcher with whom rather than Shakespeare he appears anxious to establish its relation : thus his note to 'piece' at v. v. 26 adduces a distant Fletcherian analogy whilst ignoring obvious Shakespearian comparisons (for which see the Oxford glossary).

[2] See *Richard II*, ii. i. 31–68; *King John*, v. vii. 112–8; *Macbeth*, iv. i. 112–24; and also the prophecies in *Cymbeline*. Even more directly relevant, however, is the 'prophecy' spoken over 'England's hope', the boy Richmond, as future inaugurator of the Tudor peace ; a pleasing miniature of Cranmer's prophecy over the child Elizabeth in *Henry VIII* (3 *Henry VI*, iv. vi. 68–76 ; 92).

typically Shakespearian atmosphere, that weighted and most un-Fletcherian imaginative consistency more important even than 'style' or 'character', though made, in part, from them, be without a miserable incongruity transplanted to the comparatively infertile tracts of the lesser poet from that rich soil where we find them already so naturally flowering?

Moreover, certain recurring thoughts, images,[1] and themes will be found richly sprinkled throughout, whatever the style used, both the Shakespearian and the 'Fletcherian' parts being crammed with similar matter contributing equally to the whole.[2] Lines or images of unquestionably Shakespearian calibre are apt to start up within suspected scenes. Where a certain telescoping of dramatic development is demanded by the design, as with our rapid change from a preliminary hostility towards Wolsey to sympathy for his fall, a long 'Fletcherian' scene forms the necessary link, supplying precisely the necessary gradation; while the complex personality of the King himself is stabilized at all his appearances, with the same characterizing touches of speech. An understanding of the whole design and the interweaving of its themes and persons, though it cannot prove Shakespeare to have written every word (who can prove that of *Hamlet*?) must quickly remove all cause for suspicion. Contenders for spuriousness themselves fall back regularly on arguments concerned with the play's supposed looseness, pageantry, and lack of concise dramatic statement; and even Swinburne, though sure of the poetry's merit, admitted (in a passage not quoted by the Arden editor) that the play, as a whole, baffled him. That is no reason why we, to-day, should remain baffled. A complete defence would, however, demand a treatment at least as long as that to be devoted here to a pure interpretation. To that interpretation we shall now advance, with the reminder that, even were *Henry VIII* proved to have been composed by two, three, or any number of separate authors writing independently, the interpretation here offered would remain substantially no less true than if the play were

---

[1] The test of 'imagery' must not, however, be applied with rigidity : any change in blank-verse rhythm necessarily corresponds to some change in the experience expressed ; and this will tend to dictate some variation also in choice, and amount, of imagery.

[2] My rough notes for this essay included six page-references for one of the recurring key-words, 'charity'. An investigation as to their proportion in Shakespearian and 'Fletcherian' scenes revealed, in order, this pattern: Shakespeare, Fletcher, Shakespeare, Fletcher, Shakespeare, Fletcher. I am considering III. ii. 204–350 as 'Shakespeare'.

incontrovertibly known to be the child of Shakespeare's
undivided and unprompted invention.

My remarks on authorship have been necessarily sketchy:
they indicate directions, no more; and it is my hope that no
more will be necessary.

II

The prologue announces that we are to attend something
'weighty' and 'serious', full of both 'state' and 'woe'. There
will be room for 'pity', and those who want 'truth' will find it.
As for 'show', there will be plenty of that. But there is to be no
sheer fooling, nor any mock warfare: it is to be a work of
'chosen truth', that is, a choice and real thing, which to reduce
to 'fool and fight' would be sacrilege. Though the prologue,
concentrating on what might appear a purely morality doctrine of the fall of princes, scarcely covers the whole action, it
serves nevertheless to define those elements which we, following its emphasis, are to discuss first. Thereafter we shall
examine a wider pattern not precisely envisaged by the
prologue itself.

We shall now follow three stories: those of Buckingham,
Wolsey, and Queen Katharine.

Buckingham is a fine gentleman, proud in his birth, who is
infuriated by the upstart Wolsey's scheming:

> No man's pie is free'd
> From his ambitious finger.   (I. i. 52)

As Wolsey passes they fix each other with looks of 'disdain'
(I. i. 115). Afterwards Buckingham fumes in aristocratic im-
potence: 'A beggar's book outworths a noble's blood' (I. i.
122). He has evidence of Wolsey's treachery: 'this holy fox,
or wolf, or both' has been plotting with the Emperor Charles
to arrange a split between England and France for his own
ends and profit (I. i. 158–93). He speaks in the cramped and
crammed parenthetical style so usual for speeches of excitement or description, or both; or perhaps to lend excitement to
what is itself undramatic, non-immediate and factual, with, as
is usual, a curt and direct summing up so that expectation is
finally satisfied:

> Let the king know—
> As soon he shall by me—that thus the cardinal
> Does buy and sell his honour as he pleases,
> And for his own advantage.   (I. i. 190)

The justice of his comment is witnessed later; but now Brandon
and a Serjeant-at-Arms enter for the arrest. It is sudden and
unexpected. Buckingham is a strong stage personality; he has
spoken vigorous and upstanding Shakespearian language, fiery
in resentment, innuendo and sarcasm, and ranging wide over
affairs of state. But the lines of force he has been radiating are
now suddenly quenched. There is a moment's deathly silence.
Then:

> Lo you, my lord,
> The net has fallen upon me ! I shall perish
> Under device and practice.   (I. i. 202)

'The net has fall'n upon me': it lilts gently, softly, and drops
on the personal pronoun: even at a mid-line, the note is
unmistakeable. Again:

> It will help me nothing
> To plead my innocence, for that dye is *on me*
> Which makes my whit'st part black. The will of heaven
> Be done in this and all things ! I obey.   (I. i. 207)

The resentments of pride and ambition give place to resignation, humility and a supervening peace, with a religious phrase
automatically enthroned. *At this exact moment of conversion the
supposedly Fletcherian touch is first heard:* 'fall'n upon me',
'that dye is on me', showing the precise use of rhythm and
phrase (recalling Enobarbus' repentance) on which the main
argument for spuriousness has been based. This first scene—
there is none finer in Shakespeare—arches up swiftly, gathers
sweep and fire, towers, and drops (not unlike the whole first
movement of *The Winter's Tale*): this movement is to be
reiterated and expanded throughout.

Buckingham's 'treason' is left as vague as the rights and
wrongs of Antony's and Caesar's disagreement in Act III of
Antony and Cleopatra. The evidence appears to be in itself
unconvincing. Buckingham's Surveyor is clearly being
prompted by Wolsey, and when haled before the King shows
a preliminary diffidence, growing in confidence as he finds his

story accepted. The speeches lend themselves to such a development, building a stage personality of an insidious, shifty, bribed rascal, while the accumulation of reported evidence gives us a dramatic miniature of high intensity.

The King has already deplored the fall of so gifted a gentleman, whom he describes as 'learn'd and a most rare speaker' (I. ii. 111), as a man

> so complete
> Who was enroll'd 'mongst wonders, and when we,
> Almost with ravish'd listening, could not find
> His hour of speech a minute . . .   (I. ii. 118)

Buckingham's eloquence is again referred to by the Gentleman's description of his trial, where we hear how he argued 'learnedly' for life; and how, when sentenced, he spoke first 'in choler, ill and hasty', but after, coming to himself, 'sweetly' showed 'a most noble patience' (II. i. 28–36). The general emphasis on his eloquence prepares us for his farewell oration, while the Gentleman's description further outlines our basic rhythm from pride to humility.

Buckingham's farewell is our first long unit in the style of falling rhythms. He starts by addressing the 'good people' who have pitied him, calling 'heaven' to witness his innocence, though refusing to blame the law itself for his condemnation, while 'heartily' forgiving his enemies, whom, however, he 'could wish more Christian', provided they (i.e. Wolsey) do not continue to persecute 'great men' (II. i. 55–68). The opening shows a quiet dignity and Christian charity. He continues in a yet sweeter strain, embracing in brotherhood of nobility those following crowds who have proved faithful, rather as King Henry V in his Crispin speech attributes royal brotherhood to the meanest soldier who sheds blood on the field of battle:

> You few that lov'd me,
> And dare be bold to weep for Buckingham,
> His noble friends and fellows, whom to leave
> Is only bitter to him, only dying,
> Go with me, like good angels, to my end ;
> And, as the long divorce of steel falls on me,
> Make of your prayers one sweet sacrifice
> And lift my soul to heaven. Lead on, o' God's name.
>
>   (II. i. 71)

The lines are spoken from that deeper, spiritual, aristocracy that underlies all Shakespeare's noblest thought. Buckingham shows here a sweetness and serenity distilled from the finest essence of nobility, courtesy, suffering and religious faith, on which the lilting rhythms, as of a boat lifting and falling on a vast sea, sit strangely appropriate. Each line is a rhythmic unit, and yet mysteriously uncompleted; each has, in Orsino's words, a 'dying fall' (*Twelfth Night*, I. i. 4), each is sweet as 'the setting sun and music at the close' (*Richard II*, II. i. 12); each faints away, an uncompleted, broken, music,[1] dissolving into infinitude.

Buckingham has won his spiritual victory and would pass on in peace. But, just as he starts, Lovell delays him, asking for the 'charity' of his whole-hearted forgiveness. Buckingham pauses; remembrances, perhaps, crowd back; the strain is telling. But, mastering himself with an effort, he lays his hand on Lovell's shoulder, and next includes the whole world of 'numberless offences' in his embracing 'peace': 'I forgive all'. For is he not already 'half in heaven'? That is how he wishes Lovell to report him to the King, for whom his 'vows and prayers' are strong as ever (II. i. 82—94). There is something a trifle over-ambitious and artificial in these last phrases of universal forgiveness: he is aiming not merely at the Christian, but at the Christ-like. And this taint of *hubris* meets a corresponding *nemesis*. When Vaux gives orders for the proper equipment, suited to his rank, of the Duke's barge, he is attacked, as it were, from within. He can forgive whilst he forgets; but this cruelly jolts his remembrance of that worldly greatness and pride sullied for ever by his betrayal and condemnation:

> Nay, Sir Nicholas,
> Let it alone ; my state now will but mock me . . .
> (II. i. 100)

Recently 'Lord High Constable and Duke of Buckingham', he is now mere 'Edward Bohun'. He recounts the story of his unhappy father under Richard III, how his own honours were restored under Henry VII, only to be again withdrawn:

---

[1] See my remarks on Shakespeare's use of 'broken music' in the wider patterns of tragedy in *The Shakespearian Tempest*.

> Now his son,
> Henry the Eighth, life, honour, name, and all
> That made me happy, at one stroke has taken
> For ever from the world.   II. i. 115)

During this historical account the verse has maintained a normal Shakespearian, this-worldly, force, the only exception being the significant phrase 'God's peace be with him' (II. i. 111). But the falling rhythms soon return, accompanying a great bitterness, that bitterness surging throughout Shakespeare; the anguish of Antonio (in *Twelfth Night*), of Richard II, Troilus, Lear, the cold anger of Henry V and Timon, at ingratitude, at betrayal; the thing which even Prospero, one feels, could only go through the form of forgiving. But no earlier hero has left such scalding tears on Shakespeare's page as Buckingham's, the more burning for that universal forgiveness we had thought established in his soul, and the religious faith that still lights it:

> I had my trial,
> And, must need say, a noble one; which makes me
> A little happier than my wretched father.
> Yet thus far we are one in fortunes; both
> Fell by our servants, by those men we lov'd most:
> A most unnatural and faithless service!
> Heaven has an end in all; yet, you that hear me,
> This from a dying man receive as certain:
> Where you are liberal in your loves and counsels
> Be sure you be not loose; for those you make friends
> And give your hearts to, when they once perceive
> The least rub in your fortunes, fall away
> Like water from ye, never found again
> But where they mean to sink ye.   (II. i. 118)

See how the pronominal emphasis attains a sudden stab-like force in 'ye', as earlier with Caliban (*The Tempest*, i. ii. 323) and often elsewhere in *Henry VIII*. Like Timon, Buckingham has been at once 'liberal' and 'loose', that is, incautious; he has already been described by phrases recalling Timon, when we heard how the commons 'love and dote on' him, calling him 'bounteous Buckingham, the mirror of all courtesy' (II. i. 52); 'mirror' also recalling 'the glass of fashion and the mould of form' applied by Ophelia to Hamlet (*Hamlet*, III. i. 162). But

see what has happened. Buckingham's very virtues, his trust-
fulness, his generosity, have come back charged with remembrance to refuse entrance to the Christ-like power that was, or
seemed, lodged in his heart. Buckingham is successor to many
past heroes, their aura is on him, in him they are all but lifted
to a nobler status; and yet in him they are, for the first time,
accused. Timon scorns to forgive; Prospero forgives, coldly,
knowing it 'the rarer action' (*The Tempest*, v. i. 27). But
Buckingham, I think, fingers in his convulsive passion a cross
worn on his breast; and it is this that accuses not only him, but
all his predecessors in passion, Richard II, Hamlet, Troilus,
Lear, Othello, Timon, Prospero—of what? Of wounded pride.
There is silence, as he realizes his new, and deeper, fall. Then,
after a pause:

<blockquote>
All good people
Pray for me.   (II. i. 131)
</blockquote>

There is now no fine Christian posture, no spiritual pride, left;
but merely the humility of a broken, and ordinary, man:

<blockquote>
I must now forsake ye : the last hour
Of my long weary life is come upon me.
Farewell :
And when you would say something that is sad,
Speak how I fell. I have done ; and God forgive me.
                    (II. i. 132)
</blockquote>

'Fell', of course, applies to his obvious disgrace, though the
final phrase of prayer may be best related to his recent bitterness.
This is Shakespeare's one explicitly Christian play; but its
Christianity is defined not by theological speculation nor any
personification of abstract qualities, but rather by the sharp
dramatic confronting of the Shakespearian nobility at its best
with the yet nobler ideal. Christianity is not treated as an intellectual scheme: it is brought, through drama, to the bar of life.
Can the Shakespearian hero live the Christian way, to the end?
The presence of Christ Himself is thus realized through His
absence.

Here Shakespeare's genius attains a spiritual sensitivity, a
fine point of Christian penetration, beyond anything so far
attempted. That alone should answer arguments of spuriousness. Is not every phrase infused, saturated, barbed with

Shakespearian feeling? Does Buckingham's passionate out-burst not lie in direct descent from *The Tempest*, *Timon of Athens*, and the rest? Does not the whole structure of semi-Christian resignation, desire to conclude a painful ordeal, mad-dening interruption and consequent reversal of the original acceptance and releasing of a bitterness formerly controlled, exactly recall the deposition scene in *Richard II*? There the effects are more lurid, the Christ-comparison explicit, Nor-thumberland's interruption plainly intolerable and the hero's remembrance concerned with his kingly status: but the move-ments are basically similar, both hinging on the Shakespearian sense of personal betrayal. Does not Buckingham's 'and when you would say something that is sad' precisely recall Richard's 'In winter's tedious nights sit by the fire . . .' (v. i. 40–50)? Surely these are the things for which to look? Words, metrical rhythm, syllables, imagery, phraseology are nothing in them-selves:

> Say that again.
> The shadow of my sorrow ! Ha ! let's see :
> 'Tis very true, my grief lies all within ;
> And these external manners of laments
> Are merely shadows to the unseen grief
> That swells with silence in the tortur'd soul.
>
> (*Richard II*, IV. i. 293)

On that 'unseen' reality, those depths of spiritual experience, our judgements must, finally, be based; not on words, phrases, images, rhythms in unhappy abstraction from their purpose.

To turn to Wolsey. Our first scene characterizes him as an upstart of low birth 'not propp'd by ancestry', winning his way by cunning and ambition to 'a place next to the king' and associated with 'hell' and the 'devil' (I. i. 52–72); a 'butcher's cur' (I. i. 120) intriguing for his own gain and becoming proud and wealthy. He is also called revengeful (I. i. 109). He is thus given a poor introduction to our sympathies. When the King shows disapproval of the new taxation, Wolsey cunningly and coolly denies any personal respon-sibility, though the Queen's plain-speaking does more than suggest a doubt; his elaborate defence, describing the criticism that necessarily attends all statesmanship, is specious and unconvincing; and, when the King remains firm, his neat arrangement for it to be 'nois'd' that the decree has been rescinded by his own 'intercession' (i. ii. 1–108) leaves no question of his duplicity. He succeeds better in planting the charge against Buckingham, his comments during the Surveyor's disclosures revealing a disguised malice which elicits another sharp rebuke from the Queen (i. ii. 143), who clearly distrusts him from the start. So do others, the choric Gentlemen later emphasizing his responsibility for Buckingham's fall, whilst remarking on his consistent policy of removing anyone 'the king favours' (ii. i. 47), and the hatred he arouses among the common people (ii. i. 39–51).

But the banquet-scene shows him in another guise, as a free and kindly host, and an appreciator of female beauty. We are carefully pointed to admire the Timon-like generosity of his 'bounteous mind'; 'his dews' we hear 'fall everywhere' and he gives a great example of liberality (i. iii. 55–62). The King's facetious innuendo on this galaxy of loveliness gathered under a churchman's roof may also be referred to later criticisms of his private life (iii. ii. 296; iv. ii. 43). To this Wolsey answers drily:

> I am glad
> Your Grace is grown so pleasant   (i. iv. 89)

and has his revenge shortly after in:

> Your Grace,
> I fear, with dancing is a little heated,   (i. iv. 99)

referring to the King's obvious response to Anne Bullen's attractions. His opposition to the King's interest in Anne is already at this early stage hinted.

Wolsey's attitude to the King's matrimonial adventures is left vague. Our main interest, after Buckingham's fall, centres on the divorce of Katharine. We are introduced to three lords talking of Wolsey as 'the king-cardinal', 'this bold bad man', 'this imperious man' (ii. ii. 20, 44, 47), and suggesting that he is directly responsible for arousing the King's conscience concerning the marriage (ii. ii. 22–37). Probably, however, the lords' rising jealousy of Wolsey is more dramatically important than any such specific charge. Two of them, attempting to visit the King, get a violent rebuff, though Wolsey and Cam-

peius, asking for 'an hour of private conference' (II. ii. 80), are
readily admitted, one of the slighted lords remarking sarcastically, 'This priest has no pride in him' (II. ii. 82): the emphasis
on pride is important. As for Wolsey's following interview
with the King, he seems to be at pains to support the divorce
whilst nevertheless appearing merely dutiful, and indeed particularly interceding on the Queen's behalf in the matter of
legal assistance (II. ii. 110–13). More important, for our study
of Wolsey, is his quite shameless aside-dialogue with Campeius on the King's secretary Gardiner, admittedly put
there by himself because the former secretary's integrity
hampered his own schemes.

During the trial at Blackfriars Queen Katharine asserts that
he has inspired the whole business and refuses to allow his and
Campeius' right to act as judges. Though his defence, deliver-
ered with calm dignity, calling the King as witness and relying
on the backing of 'the whole consistory of Rome' (II. iv. 91),
appears impregnable, the Queen's answer also carries conviction, asserting how she, but a woman, is helpless before his
learned and specious phraseology:

> You're meek and humble-mouth'd;
> You sign your place and calling, in full seeming,
> With meekness and humility; but your heart
> Is cramm'd with arrogancy, spleen and pride.
>
> (II. iv. 105)

Nevertheless the King, whom we must believe, convincingly
exonerates Wolsey, asserting that he has actually hampered the
divorce (II. iv. 161–3). The extent of his responsibility is
accordingly left vague; and when he and Campeius visit the
Queen later (III. i.) there is a subtle change. The suave cardinals' speeches contrast strongly and not altogether unfavour-
ably with Katharine's impassioned and distraught replies; with
her, we distrust them; and yet, with her, we come under their
influence. When Wolsey assures her of his honest and charitable purposes we feel, at the very least, that the trouble out-
reaches the responsibility of any one man, while she herself
begins to appear a solitary and prejudiced individual confronted by a pair of statesmen burdened with an unpleasant
duty:

> Why should we, good lady,
> Upon what cause, wrong you ? alas ! our places,
> The way of our profession is against it :
> We are to cure such sorrows, not to sow them . . .
>
> (III. ii. 154)

It is dramatically impossible, or at least most unwise, to read insincerity into such a speech. It is all very skilfully done, and we are led delicately on until the Queen ends by apology for her behaviour. After all, she is only a 'woman' and they pillars of state:

> Come, reverend fathers,
> Bestow your counsels on me . . .   (III. ii. 180)

She is humbled, while they seem no longer the hypocrites we feared. A careful technique is at work to increase Wolsey's moral stature in preparation for subsequent developments; but we are faced also by a necessary complexity, as with the quarrels in the first and last acts of *Richard II* and that already referred to in *Antony and Cleopatra*. Drama cannot afford to waste time working out the exact rights and wrongs of quarrels where its specific purpose is to avoid any final allotment of blame. So the strong asseverations of rival parties are left to speak for themselves in contrapuntal opposition. Here the antagonisms are all softened and we are left with a feeling of the subdued uncertainties of actual life.

The fairest comment on Wolsey is the Queen's charge that he takes more thought for his persons 'honour' than his 'high profession spiritual' (II. iv. 114). He is a skilful and ambitious politician, with a craving for wealth and power; generous on occasion, but over-proud. He is no criminal like Richard III, though the faults developed to prodigious proportions in the hypocrisy and ruthlessness of the tyrant are here more realistically presented, at once more softened and more subtle, rather as the flamboyances of Richard II are given a reserved presentation in Buckingham. As a man Wolsey ranks high; but—and the contrast resembles that already observed in Buckingham— he fails when judged by the standard of his priestly calling. The valuation throughout *Henry VIII* is specifically Christian.

Wolsey's fall is carefully dramatized. First, the three lords, Norfolk, Suffolk, and Surrey, are shown discussing him with the Lord Chamberlain. Some of Wolsey's schemes have come to light and they revel in thought of the royal displeasure. The atmosphere is one of scandal and gossip and the lords, as a group, lack dignity; nor does their dramatic status rise when, on Wolsey's entrance, they draw aside, to watch and whisper during his worried meditations on Anne Bullen and the rise of Cranmer.

The King enters, telling of more discoveries concerning the amassing of wealth by a man whose thoughts were supposedly set on 'spiritual' objects (iii. ii. 133), and, when the Cardinal realizes his presence, continues in the same vein heavily loaded with sarcastic reference to his calling; Wolsey replying with a little essay on temporal and spiritual responsibility which, in its careful balancing of divine, political and recreational values, forms, at this pivotal moment, a quite remarkable condensation of our whole play's statement. When questioned directly as to his loyalty, his assurances of sense of 'duty' and devotion to the King's 'good' ring true enough, since he probably does not distinguish between his own ambition and public service. Suddenly the King reveals his recent discoveries, throws the incriminating papers on the table, and stamps out. The lords follow.

Wolsey's following words (iii. ii. 204–28) admit his guilt; that is, his accumulation of wealth to help him to the popedom; and as the full implications of the miscarried letter become clear, his speech glows with a new tragic power, not quite in Buckingham's idiom of falling units, but in a related, pro-nominal, style relying on vivid imagery of fall:

> Nay then, farewell !
> I have touch'd the highest point in all my greatness;
> And from that full meridian of my glory,
> I haste now to my setting : I shall fall
> Like a bright exhalation in the evening,
> And no man see me more . . .   (iii. ii. 223)

Though pictorial, as Buckingham's tragic style was not, there is a similar lucidity and simplicity, reaching expression in obvious metaphor only and, even more characteristically, simile. The language of conversion, or reorientation, accompanies the moment of disaster; is to be withheld at the lords' re-entry and during the subsequent argument; and is to attain full flower in

Wolsey's famous concluding speeches. Commentators, disregarding *the precise reason for the change*, have here actually split the scene, handing the pre-conversion part to Shakespeare and the great tragic set-pieces to Fletcher.

But first the lords troop back, glorying, with cheap triumph, in delivery of the King's displeasure, while Wolsey remains superb in restraint and dignity, calling them 'officious lords' of 'coarse metal', only eager to follow his own 'disgraces', and hinting, in the tradition of *Richard II* (III. ii. 132; IV. i. 170, 240) and *Timon of Athens* (I. ii. 48–51), their similarity to Christ's betrayers (III. ii. 237–46). We tend to agree; for his short tragic soliloquy has already insinuated our sympathies into that natural identification with ourselves that every tragic hero solicits and through which Hamlet, from one view so impossible and dangerous a person, remains the soul-prince of the average spectator. Wolsey accordingly radiates power beyond his attackers, though the balances are well preserved, each side calling the other, with some justice, 'proud' (III. ii. 253–4). Surrey further loads the attack with remembrance of his kinsman, Buckingham, whom this 'scarlet sin' in 'holy pity' absolved 'with an axe' (III. ii. 255–65); Wolsey basing his answer on the process of 'law' by which Buckingham was condemned. Surrey's language suggests that the lords' hostility is, as was Buckingham's, that of a feudal aristocracy against an upstart:

> My lords,
> Can ye endure to hear this arrogance ?
> And from this fellow ? If we live thus tamely,
> To be thus jaded by a piece of scarlet,
> Farewell nobility . . . (III. ii. 278)

He tells Norfolk to retail the list of Wolsey's misdemeanours, concluding with a peculiarly mean thrust:

> I'll startle you
> Worse than the sacring bell, when the brown wench
> Lay kissing in your arms, Lord Cardinal !
> (III. ii. 295)

His bullying enjoyment of a sudden ascendancy recalls the thoroughly unpleasant Gratiano in the trial scene of *The Merchant of Venice*.

Wolsey remains quiet and scornful, until his enemies,
gathering round him like dogs round a bear, volley separate
charges whose accumulation beats down his defence. The
Lord Chamberlain alone is pitiful:

> O my lord !
> Press not a falling man too far ; 'tis virtue :
> His faults lie open to the laws ; let them,
> Not you, correct him. My heart weeps to see him
> So little of his great self.   (III. ii. 333)

How typical of our play's charity; and, too, as we shall see, of
its concentration on law. Observe how, with the charitable
note, the falling rhythm returns in 'to see him'. The other
lords remain cruel. Norfolk's final words phrase the naked
truth in the surest way to antagonize us:

> And so we'll leave you to your meditations
> How to live better.   (III. ii. 346)

Precisely what is to happen; and with a last 'So fare you well,
my little good Lord Cardinal' (III. ii. 350), they troop out.
Their bullying vulgarity forms the best possible preparation
for Wolsey's grand speeches—which show grandeur rather
than the simple sweetness of Buckingham's—in the falling
idiom. It is here especially that the commentators, misunder-
standing the whole nature and purpose of these speeches, have
suspected the hand of another author.

Wolsey's fall is generalized. We watch, as in *Timon of Athens*
and *Pericles*, not a particular disaster merely, but a reading of
human disaster as such, exactly recalling *Richard II*, III. ii,
160–70:

> So farewell to the little good you bear me.
> Farewell ! a long farewell, to all my greatness !
> This is the state of man : to-day, he puts forth . . .
>   (III. ii. 351)

The following lines (III. ii. 354–73) show the limp, pronominal,
rhythms: 'and then he falls, as I do', 'and now has left me',
'that must for ever hide me'. These are accompanied by purest
Shakespearian imagery, comparing man's life to the seasonal
budding of a tree, its summer blossoming, and final wintry
ruin (cp. Sonnet LXXIII; *Timon of Athens*, IV. iii. 260–7; *Cymbeline*, III. iii. 60–4; *Richard III*, I. i. 1; *Macbeth*, V. iii. 22;

and, for other relevant winter-imagery, *A Midsummer Night's Dream*, II. i. 106–14 and Sonnets xcvII and cIV). Next, we pass to 'wanton boys' (cp. 'wanton boys' at *King Lear*, IV. i. 36) and 'a sea of glory' (cp. the 'tide of blood' flowing 'proudly' and 'in vanity' for a while, but returning in repentance to the 'state of floods' at 2 *Henry IV*, v. ii. 129; great kingship as an ocean at *King John*, v. iv. 49–57; and 'the tide of pomp that beats upon the high shore of this world' in the King's 'ceremony' speech at *Henry V*, IV. i. 284; see *The Shakespearian Tempest*, pp. 49–51); and last, to the usual tragic impression of unruly, disorderly, ugly violence in 'a rude stream, that must for ever hide me' (cp. the examples of such torrential imagery quoted in *The Shakespearian Tempest*, pp. 23–6). All Shakespearian tragedy of greatness in decline, summed up in the Poet's allegory in *Timon of Athens* (I. i. 43–95), is here rendered newly purposeful in the countering strength, rising against the falling music, of

> Vain pomp and glory of this world, I hate ye !
>
> > (III. ii. 366)

'Pomp' recalls Henry V's line just noticed and Apemantus'

> Hoy-day ! what a sweep of *vanity* comes this way . . .
> Like madness is the *glory* of *this life*,
> As this *pomp* shows to a little oil and root.
> > (*Timon of Athens*, I. ii. 139)

See how Wolsey's one line, with 'hate' corresponding to the whole emotional field of *Timon of Athens*, compacts Apemantus' three and sharpens them into the fiery pin-point of the concluding 'ye'. (Cp. also the association of 'pomp' and 'glory' at *Timon of Athens*, IV. ii. 30–6). There is a pause; his expression changes; and his voice too, for:

> I feel my heart new-open'd.   (III. ii. 367)

What has happened? We watch the act of repentance, conversion (in the proper sense of turning, of new orientation); the seeing things afresh, as when convalescent or following some 'mystic' experience. Wolsey's conversion is profounder than Buckingham's in proportion as his fault is greater. He has nothing left, no possible worldly pride or hope, nor any excuse for bitterness. He merely observes that dependance on the

insecure favour of princes is a state of wretchedness, and compares his fall—he is to do so again—to that of Lucifer.

But he receives the dramatic honour of Cromwell's entry
and their deeply moving conversation:

> *Cromwell.*   How does your Grace ?
> *Wolsey.*   Why, well ;
> Never so truly happy, my good Cromwell.
> I know myself now ; and I feel within me
> A peace above all earthly dignities,
> A still and quiet conscience.   (III. ii. 377)

Wolsey embraces with full understanding that self-knowledge
to which past heroes, such as Richard II (at *Richard II*, III. ii.
98, 175; v. v. 49), Macbeth, Lear, Enobarbus, Coriolanus and
Leontes were unhappily forced; a deep religious content like
that of Richard II or Henry VI·

> My crown is in my heart, not on my head ;
> Not deck'd with diamonds and Indian stones,
> Nor to be seen : my crown is called content,
> A crown it is that seldom kings enjoy.
> (3 *Henry VI*, III. i. 62)

The King has relieved Wolsey's 'ruin'd pillars', his shoulders,
of their load of honour (III. ii. 383; cp. Timon's 'ruin'd house',
Timon of Athens, IV. ii. 16). Cromwell now functions as the
Groom in *Richard II* (v. v.), bringing bitter news to his fallen
master from the outer world. Wolsey accepts Sir Thomas
More's appointment as the new Lord Chancellor, with prayers
that he continue long in favour, doing justice 'for truth's sake
and his conscience', and finally rest in peace, universally loved;
defining precisely that virtue and its reward to which he himself can no longer aspire (III. ii. 395–400). He is, however,
disturbed by the advancement of Cranmer to the See of Canterbury, and staggered by the news of the King's secret marriage,
which he recognizes as the true cause of the King's disfavour:

> There was the weight that pull'd me down. O Cromwell !
> The king has gone beyond me : all my glories
> In that one woman I have lost for ever.
> No sun shall ever usher forth mine honours,
> Nor gild again the noble troops that waited
> Upon my smiles.   (III. ii. 408)

'Pull'd me down' continues the Shakespearian thought of sinking already found in 'a load would sink a navy' at III. ii. 384
and Buckingham's 'but where they mean to sink ye' at II. i. 131.
Wolsey's last lines exactly recall the lustre of Timon's patronage. He, like Timon, has been generous:

> That churchman bears a bounteous mind indeed,
> A hand as fruitful as the land that feeds us ;
> His dews fall everywhere.   (I. iii. 55)

That both he and Buckingham should be conceived as Timon-
like figures of bounty shows how closely Shakespeare is re-
embodying his favourite tragic theme; and that both, so bitterly
opposed as they were, should be shown as basically similar
alike in their greatness and in their fall, makes a neat comment
on all such personal rivalries. And now, when Wolsey, like
Buckingham at the end of his 'long weary life' (II. i. 133), is
merely 'a poor fall'n man' (III. ii. 414), 'weary and old with
service' (III. ii. 364), recommending Cromwell to the King's
'noble nature' (III. ii. 419), Cromwell's loyalty, like that of the
Groom in *Richard II*, of Kent, of Timon's servants, recrowns
for us the fallen master:

> Must I then leave you ? must I needs forego
> So good, so noble and so true a master ?
> Bear witness all that have not hearts of iron
> With what a sorrow Cromwell leaves his lord.
> The king shall have my service, but my prayers
> For ever and for ever shall be yours.   (III. ii. 423)

So Timon's servants ask, 'Are we undone? cast off? nothing
remaining?'; exclaim 'So noble a master fall'n!'; and, murmuring 'Yet do our hearts wear Timon's livery', part in 'sorrow'
(*Timon of Athens*, IV. ii. 1–29). Vocabulary and sentiment recur.
Wolsey is 'left naked' to his 'enemies' (III. ii. 458) just as
Timon, recently a phoenix, is 'left' a 'naked gull' (*Timon of
Athens*, II. i. 31). Wolsey's story sums up Timon's and the
many heroes Timon himself includes; and yet it quietly also
includes the power-quests of *Richard III* and *Macbeth*. Wolsey
has been proud and ambitious; at the best he has served his
king, for whose good he still prays, better than God (III. ii.
364, 416, 456–7; cp. *Richard II*, III. i. 98). So we pass to his
concluding counsel, channelling more firmly still the religious

wisdom to which all our tragic persons are at the last subdued. The speech (III. ii. 432–50) moves from monumental death to the usual imagery of a sea of glory involving wreck, and thence to religious doctrines on ambition, 'by that sin fell the angels' balancing 'Lucifer' earlier (III. ii. 372), with thought of man as 'the image of his Maker' (III. ii. 441–3):

> Love thyself last : cherish those hearts that hate thee ;
> Corruption wins not more than honesty.
> Still in thy right hand carry gentle peace,
> To silence envious tongues : be just, and fear not.
> Let all the ends thou aim'st at be thy country's,
> Thy God's, and truth's ; then if thou fall'st, O Cromwell !
> Thou fall'st a blessed martyr.   (III. ii. 444)

It is Shakespeare's supreme and final counsel to individual man, relating the religious inwardness of *Richard II* ('I'll give my jewels for a set of beads . . .' III. iii. 147) and the best of later Christian feeling (as at *The Merchant of Venice*, IV. i. 184; *2 Henry IV*, IV. i. 41–52; IV. ii. 4–30; *Measure for Measure*, II. ii. 73) to the tragic sequence which is, in Wolsey, at the last crowned, as in Prospero it was not, by humility, with only the merest tremor of remaining bitterness (III. ii. 457).

We hear later of Wolsey's death, in peace and repentance. Katharine recalls his faults; his pride, duplicity and hardness; and also the moral laxity of his personal life (IV. ii. 43). But the prevailing spirit here, to which the people have painfully to adjust themselves, will not leave it thus. So Griffeth speaks in reply of his scholarship and gentleness, his sweetness to all who 'sought' him, and his princely, Timon-like patronage:

> Ever witness for him
> Those twins of learning that he rais'd in you,
> Ipswich, and Oxford ; one of which fell with him,
> Unwilling to outlive the good that did it ;
> The other, though unfinish'd, yet so famous,
> So excellent in art, and still so rising,
> That Christendom shall ever speak his virtue.
> His overthrow heap'd happiness upon him ;
> For then, and not till then, he felt himself,
> And found the blessedness of being little :
> And, to add greater honours to his age
> Than man could give him, he died fearing God.
>   (IV. ii. 57)

'The blessedness of being little'; that very blessedness is in the lines themselves, warming the falling syllables, and lending to Griffeth's quiet accents a strength outlasting many more striking Shakespearian splendours.

Our third tragic figure is Queen Katharine. We meet her first soliciting the King to relieve his people from an unjust taxation for which she practically accuses Wolsey of being, as he clearly is, responsible. During the questioning of Buckingham's Surveyor she shows judgement and acuity, rebuffing Wolsey's insinuation with 'My learn'd Lord Cardinal, deliver all with charity' (i. ii. 142), while recognizing the Surveyor himself as a man previously dismissed from service by the master he is accusing. She appears, however, to be finally convinced, though with a charitable 'God mend all' (i. ii. 201). She is a woman of perception, showing a humble but helpful concern in matters of government, the equal of her husband in understanding and probably his superior in Christian feeling.

As we have seen, her defence at Blackfriars recalls Hermione's. Both are good women half-stunned by a totally unexpected and undeserved disgrace. Both rely on precision of statement and force of question in an expostulatory style of metrical freedom, enjambment and pause. Both refer similarly to their years of faithful wifehood in contrast to their present unmerited dishonour; to their entertainment of their husbands' friends; and to their own royal though foreign birth, being daughters respectively of the Emperor of Russia and the King of Spain (*The Winter's Tale*, iii. ii. 120; *Henry VIII*, ii. iv. 46, 70). Queen Katharine expands all that was discovered and created in Hermione, while also recalling more distantly such wronged women as Constance in *King John* and the various lamenting women of *Richard III*. Nearly all Shakespeare's Histories show the suffering of woman under the march of man's political or warlike ambition; and though in the Tragedies what might be called a feminine force does much to challenge and overturn such masculine values (a pattern explicit in *Antony and Cleopatra* and *Coriolanus*), the women, as persons, are, normally, trodden under too. This conflict is epitomized in the trial of Katharine, whose appeal will clearly be overruled and whose enemies have high-sounding defences for their every move, and indeed may well be, to a final judgement, justified, though in terms whose validity no woman can be expected to admit.

Her direct accusation of Wolsey is in the grand manner (recalling *Antony & Cleopatra*, v. ii. 171):

Q. *Katherine.*   Lord Cardinal,
                    To you I speak.
Wolsey.   Your pleasure, madam ?
Q. *Katharine.*   Sir,
                    I am about to weep ; but thinking that
                    We are a queen—or long have dream'd so—certain
                    The daughter of a king, my drops of tears
                    I'll turn to sparks of fire.
Wolsey.   Be patient yet.
Q. *Katharine.* I will, when you are humble . . .   (ii. iv. 66)

Charging him with deliberate malice, she refuses him for her judge, repelling all his suave statecraft with:

                              My lord, my lord,
                    I am a simple woman, much too weak
                    To oppose your cunning . . .   (ii. iv. 103)

Finally, she lays her cause before the Pope, as Hermione appeals to the Oracle. She will suffer no abrogation of her queenly dignity:

Griffeth.   Madam, you are call'd back.
Q. *Katharine.* What need you note it ? pray you, keep your way.
                When you are call'd, return. Now, the Lord help !
                They vex me past my patience. Pray you, pass on :
                I will not tarry ; no, nor ever more
                Upon this business my appearance make
                In any of their courts.   (ii. iv. 125)

Notice the womanly petulance of 'Now, the Lord help !' Katharine is superbly feminine, rich in a good woman's pride and duty, as the King admits, calling her 'the queen of earthly queens' (ii. iv. 139). Next, she enters the 'Fletcherian' world.

There we find her at work with her attendant ladies, solacing herself, like those other wronged women, Mariana in *Measure for Measure* and Desdemona in *Othello*, with music and a song (iii. i. 3–14) rich in Shakespearian memories, telling how Orpheus' music charmed the frozen 'mountain tops' (cp. *The*

Merchant of Venice, v. i. 80) and made 'even the billows of the
sea' to droop their 'heads' and lie still (cp. Ariel's 'the wild
waves whist', *The Tempest*, i. ii. 378):

> In sweet music is such art,
> Killing care and grief of heart
> Fall asleep or hearing die.   (iii. i. 12)

This song explicitly interprets Shakespeare's general use of
music, especially its use in the falling, backwater, fourth-act,
moments of tragedy (see *The Shakespearian Tempest*, pp. 57,
61, 187, 216–17).

Hearing of the two cardinals' presence, Katharine shows
surprise, referring to herself as 'a poor weak woman' and supposing that, after all, they 'should be good men' bound on
'righteous' business, though with an afterthought of suspicion
(iii. i. 19–23). Notice that we are carefully being prepared to
feel her rejection by the King as a state necessity, while keeping
intact our sympathies for a wronged woman, un-at-home with
state affairs:

> Your Graces find me here part of a housewife.
>
>   (iii. i. 24)

The synchronization of plaintive song with an especial domesti-
city has closely resembled Desdemona's willow-song and her
talk with Emilia ('prithee unpin me', *Othello*, iv. iii. 21). In
mood and purpose the two scenes are analogous. But, though
Katharine is presented now as pre-eminently a simple woman,
there is no break in the conception; she can still dominate, as
before; will not withdraw to a private room, nor hear Wolsey's
message in Latin, her simple and proud integrity brushing
aside such suspect formalities. Her words are nevertheless
disjointed, they come from a tired, almost a broken, woman,
fully, even humbly, conscious that her own 'weak wit' cannot
answer—she said as much at the trial but there is now less
irony than genuine humility in her phrase—'such men of
gravity and learning' (iii. i. 72):

> I was set at work
> Among my maids ; full little, God knows, looking
> Either for such men or such business . . . (iii. i. 73)

Her old greatness is slipping from her, and her style of speech

is now more thickly sprinkled with weak rhythms and feminine
endings. She is 'a woman, friendless, hopeless' in an alien land;
no one in England, even did they wish to, *dare* help her (iii. i.
79, 82–6). And then from the ashes of her greatness a last
flame leaps:

> Ye tell me what ye wish for both ; my ruin.
> Is this your Christian counsel ? out upon ye !
> Heaven is above all yet ; there sits a judge
> That no king can corrupt.   (iii. i. 97)

Notice that Katharine, who from the start enjoys that more
charitable, religious consciousness elsewhere giving rise to the
pronominal rhythms, has, as it were, the right to make a more
positive, attacking use of them, both here and elsewhere, in the
stabbing 'ye' than any other person, though the monosyllable
is generally charged with hostility (as when spoken by Buckingham at ii. i. 130; by Campeius at iii. i. 95; by Wolsey at
iii. ii. 240–4; by Gardiner at v. iii. 81; by Suffolk at v. iii. 103;
by Cranmer at v. iii. 113; and by the Lord Chamberlain at
v. iv. 76, 84; all following Gloucester's manner at 3 *Henry VI*,
v. vi. 72 and Caliban's at *The Tempest*, i. ii. 323). The word is,
however, used gently by Katharine directly after her vision of
Paradise (iv. ii. 83–4) and both by Cranmer and the King at
the play's conclusion (v. v. 9–14); where the contrasting sweetness may be allowed to suggest a relaxation of earlier tensions.[1]

Katharine for a while maintains this height of righteous
anger, bitterly accusing her visitors of 'cardinal sins and hollow
hearts', while forbearing in 'charity' to wish them her own
sufferings (iii. i. 101–10); she again asseverates her wifely
loyalty and unjust reward, speaking from a moral rectitude that
relies on such fine understatement as "Tis not well, lords';
and in just pride—and how subtly we are made to remember
that it *is* pride, however just—swears that 'nothing but death
shall e'er divorce my dignities' (iii. i. 124–41). Turning, as
does Cleopatra, to her girls, she pities them, 'ship-wracked'
with her, like Timon's servants (*Timon of Athens*, iv. ii. 19–21),
upon a hostile shore; and sinks to a lovely pathos blossoming
from *The Winter's Tale*, or the Gospels, or both:

---

[1] Though the word can occur non-committally, as in the Prologue, there certainly appears
to be some artistic consistency in the fire struck from 'ye' in *Henry VIII* that does not tally
with Fletcher's unpurposive and random use.

> Like the lily,
> That once was mistress of the field and flourish'd,
> I'll hang my head and perish.   (III. i. 150)

That marks the end of her royal self-assertion. Her concluding speech shows her willing again to admit that 'a woman
lacking wit' may have answered in 'unmannerly' fashion to
such high persons; she appears lost, in a world of statecraft
meaningless to her, that talks a different language from her
simple woman's understanding. She prays, as do all our tragic
persons, for the King, and asks the Cardinals, in all humility,
for counsel (III. ii, 181).

At Kimbolton she is nearing death, attended by Griffeth and
Patience; and how appropriate that name (recalling the fine
passage in *Pericles*) to Katharine's own Christian endurance.
Katharine's words come with difficulty, yet each phrase laden
with her sweetly-noble personality, deeply enduring, sad, at
times bitter, and yet ever, in her way, charitable. She asks
after her old enemy, 'the great child of honour' (IV. ii. 6), lately
dead, appearing interested, though beyond passion, in a lucid
consciousness remembering her wrongs but able to overlook
them, as from a height. Hearing how, in his last illness, he was
unable even 'to sit his mule', she murmurs, 'Alas! poor man';
and receives the news of his peaceful passing with 'So may he
rest; his faults lie gently on him!' (IV. ii. 11–31). She offers to
speak of his character, 'and yet'—typically of her, and the
whole play—'with charity' (IV. ii. 33); and proceeds to characterize his failings. When Griffeth asks leave to speak correspondingly of his virtues, she answers, 'I were malicious else'
(IV. ii. 48), and, after hearing him through, applauds his
account:

> Whom I most hated living, thou hast made me
> With thy religious truth and modesty
> Now in his ashes honour. Peace be with him !
>   (IV. ii. 73)

Notice how the pronominal toning in the third person assists,
as elsewhere, a charitable emphasis. Katharine experiences no
sudden conversion, since she has throughout shown a fine
balance of charity and righteous anger. But a sterner sacrifice
is asked of her: she has to conquer even righteous anger, not
as an emotional duty, but through clear sight of its limitations,

since, as Griffeth shows, Wolsey was a great man. So she learns
to transcend her own, personal, cause; and, from a wider view,
her casting off, so apparently unjust, is, as the drama unfolds,
shown as necessary. Christian charity is thus found to be no
more than is dictated by widest reason. So Katharine wins the
vision of Paradise, and has the honour of linking *Henry VIII*
to the visions and miracles of earlier works.

As she listens to 'sad and solemn music' (iv. ii. 81) and falls
asleep, the Vision rises, with six angels circling round her,
offering her an immortal crown and wafting her to her heavenly
peace; at which she makes 'signs of rejoicing'; and when she
awakes, as Pericles and Posthumus before her, she is baffled;
and, like Caliban after his dream of gaudy heaven, or the Wanderer in the Old English poem, feels sad and homesick:

Q. Katharine. Spirits of peace, where are ye? Are ye all gone
              And leave me here in wretchedness behind ye?
Griffeth.   Madam, we are here.
Q. Katharine.   It is not you I call for:
              Saw ye none enter since I slept?
Griffeth.   None, madam.
Q. Katharine. No? Saw you not, even now, a blessed troop
              Invite me to a banquet; whose bright faces
              Cast thousand beams upon me, like the sun?
              They promis'd me eternal happiness,
              And brought me garlands, Griffeth, which I feel
              I am not worthy yet to wear: I shall assuredly.
                                          (iv. ii. 83)

Griffeth's 'None, madam' echoes Helicanus' 'My lord, I hear
none'. Katharine is treated gently, humoured, just as Pericles
is humoured about his 'music of the spheres' (*Pericles*, v. i.
228–33). The phrase 'spirits of *peace*' is important, being one
link in a chain of emphasis. Now Katharine tires (in the usual
Shakespearian manner, as at *Twelfth Night*, i. i. 7 and *Richard
II*, v. v. 61) of the music: she is again peevish and old, and
altering swiftly, her face 'drawn' and 'pale', and 'of an earthy
cold'. 'She is going, wench', says Griffeth, 'Pray, pray' (iv.
ii. 96).

What dramatist would fail to leave her here? To let her
dissolve, as it were, into the radiance she has so deservedly
won. But there follows a typically Shakespearian reminder. A

messenger rushes in, and fails to kneel. The dying and rejected Queen revives:

> You are a saucy fellow :
> Deserve we no more reverence ?   (IV. ii. 101)

She is as abrupt as York addressing Northumberland on a similar occasion (*Richard II*, III. iii. 7). The messenger apologizes, pleading haste, as did Northumberland, as an excuse and announces the presence of Capucius. The Queen mutters:

> Admit him entrance, Griffeth : but this fellow
> Let me ne'er see again.   (IV. ii. 108)

She who can forgive Wolsey proves adamant, in her old-lady, peevish, irritability—even after her late vision—to an underling who slights her dignities. The superlative Christian spirit which breathes through our persons is the more vividly defined by their weak and pride-ridden humanity.

She gives Capucius her last message to the King, speaking of her daughter, her women-servants, her men, remembering their 'wages':

> As you wish Christian peace to souls departed,
> Stand these poor people's friend, and urge the king
> To do me this last right.   (IV. ii. 157)

For her servants, like Timon's, could never be drawn from her by her 'poverty' (IV. ii. 150): how high in Shakespeare is such service always rated. She would have the King know that 'his long trouble now is passing out of this world' (IV. ii. 163), and that she blessed him at her death. Recalling Desdemona and her wedding-sheets (*Othello*, IV. ii. 104), she gives orders for her burial:

> When I am dead, good wench,
> Let me be us'd with honour : strew me over
> With maiden flowers, that all the world may know
> I was a chaste wife to my grave : embalm me,
> Then lay me forth ; although unqueen'd, yet like
> A queen, and daughter to a king, inter me.
> I can no more.   (IV. ii. 168)

The words come with an effort; there are heavy pauses; and the old rhythm falls on the reiterated pronouns.

Queen Katharine is one of Shakespeare's most striking feminine creations. She is not a 'character' study like the Nurse in *Romeo and Juliet*, nor, to take another extreme, a great emotional force as is Constance in *King John*; nor a sublime hypothesis, like Lady Macbeth; nor just a creature of dignity and virtue, and not much else, like Hermione. She has the power of forceful heroines woven with the warm, domestic, virtues of a Desdemona, the integrity of Cordelia, and the spiritual worth of Imogen. Katharine is made of all the better qualities—not just the best moments, as is Imogen—of earlier women. They present aspects of womanhood; she seems, more than anyone but Cleopatra (whose very *tour de force* complexity renders her rather literary in this comparison), a real woman. Her every phrase comes direct from her woman's soul, her typical woman's plight. She is universalized, not by abstraction, but rather by an exact realization of a particular person only lately dead. As with Cleopatra and Imogen, Shakespeare knows precisely what he is doing and gives us his own definition, as when Wolsey describes her 'charity' and 'disposition gentle' together with a 'wisdom o'ertopping woman's power' (ii. iv. 83–6); and Henry himself characterizes her even more perfectly as a blend of sovereignty, wifehood and saintliness; one 'obeying in commanding' and thus 'the queen of earthly queens' (ii. iv. 134–9).

There is nothing in Shakespeare more remarkable than these three similar falling movements, of Buckingham, Wolsey, and Queen Katharine. The two first conform to the two main types of Shakespearian tragedy involving (i) betrayal and (ii) the power-quest; while the Queen sums all Shakespeare's feminine sympathies. The Tragedies culminating in *Timon of Athens* and *The Tempest* (for man) and *Antony and Cleopatra* and the remaining Final Plays (for woman) have developed the Shakespearian humanism to its limit, though with no severing of Christian contacts. Here we face the limits of even that, purified, humanism.[1]

---

[1] The sequence is forecast in Richard II's soliloquy in prison, which defines very neatly this move from tragic self-assertion or 'ambition' (*Richard II*, v. v. 18 ; see also Nestor's speech at *Troilus and Cressida*, i. iii. 33–54) to humility and music. The soliloquy and its implications are discussed fully in 'A Note on *Richard II*' in *The Imperial Theme*.

III

These events are, however, countered by others of a different tone, showing variously a gaiety, romantic warmth, and robust humour most strangely juxtaposed to their sweetly-sombre atmosphere. There is, nevertheless, a relation. Here tragedy is characterized by a prevailing softness, at once a charity in the persons themselves and a lack of bitterness in the poet, showing nothing comparable to the ugliness of Leontes, the villainy of Cymbeline's queen, or even Prospero's severity in forgiveness. Now the comedy shows similarly a new kindliness. While avoiding the chief persons, it refuses to degrade anyone: there is no serio-comic satiric creation like Cloten, no reversals of stage dignity like Autolycus', no burlesque as with Stephano and Trinculo. That 'high seriousness' of late in such stern control of both humour and the intimately related matter of sexual approach, is relaxed. It is as though the puritanical severity, gaining so strongly up to *The Tempest*, is given a holiday; as though the return from individualistic, Nietzschean, assertion and adventure to a national and contemporary subject, with a corresponding use of a Christian mythology, were in itself an act of humility dethroning the innate strictness of the individual's power-quest, and not only allowing to the poet all his old freedom,[1] but even letting new warmth stream in.

First, we have three lords discussing the invasion of court life by French fashions. Though the conversational speech-rhythms are new, they as certainly ring true, both to the speakers and to the occasion. In thought reference the dialogue is, moreover, thoroughly Shakespearian.

The 'spells of France' are called 'strange mysteries', both 'ridiculous' and 'unmanly', leading to an absurdity in behaviour and dress crisply hit off by the phrase 'fool and feather' (I. iii. 1–4, 25). Shakespeare's long-held dislike of continental travel, the most elaborate speech being the Bastard's in *King John* (I. i. 189–216), is alive here: all that the English seem to have

---

[1] I say 'old freedom', though Shakespeare's humour was from the start sternly controlled: see my remarks on *Love's Labour's Lost* in *The Shakespearian Tempest*; also on Falstaff and Autolycus earlier in this volume. Notice, however, that Falstaff and Autolycus at their best somehow exist in their own right, irrespective of what the poet may do to them; and something very similar happens with Milton's Satan. It is therefore likely that the 'romantic' approach to both will continue to challenge the less sympathetic readings.

gained by their foreign voyage is 'a fit or two o' the face' and clothes of so 'pagan' a 'cut' that you would think Christendom were worn out (I. ii. 7, 14–15: for the use of 'pagan' cp. *Hamlet*, III. ii. 37), England being aligned with the traditions of Christendom. So we hear of a proclamation out for

> The reformation of our travell'd gallants
> That fill the court with quarrels, talk and tailors.
>
> (I. iii. 19)

A life-work of comedy and satire on new-fangled fashions in dress, speech and duellist-braggadocio is hit off by the second line: Armado the 'peregrinate' (*Love's Labour's Lost*, v. i. 15), Tybalt, Pistol, Sir Andrew, Claudio, Touchstone and his 'seventh cause' (*As You Like It*, v. iv. 52), Osric, Oswald ('a tailor made thee', *King Lear*, II. ii. 59), Cloten—but these references have been given already. The proclamation, indeed, serves as a final comment on a mass of earlier material. Behind the satire lies that same strong faith in Britain's simple manhood inspiring Henry V's blunt wooing of Katharine of France and Kent's loathing of Oswald: it is no use these travel-mongers abusing 'better men than they can be' out of 'a foreign wisdom' (I. iii. 28), and they must learn to 'understand again like honest men', that is, in plain English. 'Tennis'—remember the Dauphin's insult to Henry V—'tall stockings' (and Malvolio too) and 'blister'd breeches' are taboo (I. iii. 28–32).

Though satire be keen, the outspoken sentiments are carried lightly and without bitterness. Besides, the ladies will—remember Iachimo—certainly lose by these 'trim vanities':

> There will be woe indeed, lords ; the sly whoresons
> Have got a speeding trick to lay down ladies ;
> A French song and a fiddle has no fellow.   (I. iii. 39)

Now an 'honest country lord' like Lord Sands may again stand some chance (I. iii. 44), and then follows a brisk dialogue on his abilities as a lover. The free treatment of a *risqué* matter is noticeable; but in thought and reference there is nothing un-Shakespearian, and many comparisons, beyond those noticed, could be observed: e.g. for 'colt's tooth' at I. iii. 48 compare the association of 'colt' with virility at *The Merchant of Venice* I. ii. 43; and for 'fireworks' as part of foreign extravagance in enter-

tainment at 1. iii. 27 compare *Love's Labour's Lost*, v. i. 122.
The conversation turns next to Wolsey's feast to which the
lords are invited and for which it serves as an introduction.

Wolsey's entertainment is characterized by carefree hospitality and feminine beauty:

> None here, he hopes,
> In all this noble bevy, has brought with her
> One care abroad ; he would have all as merry
> As, first, good company, good wine, good welcome
> Can make good people.   (1. iv. 3)

'The very thought of this fair company' (1. iv. 8) has given
wings to Sir Harry Guildford. Sexual warmth reaches bold
expression in Lord Sands'

> Sir Thomas Lovell, had the cardinal
> But half my lay-thoughts in him, some of these
> Should find a running banquet[1] ere they rested,
> I think would better please 'em : by my life,
> They are a sweet society of fair ones.   (1. iv. 10)

Broad-speaking marks an occasion of convivial unrestraint:

> *Sands.* If I chance to talk a little wild, forgive me ;
>   I had it from my father.
> *Anne.*   Was he mad, sir ?
>   (1. iv. 26)

The wit-combat ends with a kiss. There is a neat balancing of
sexual-romantic enjoyment against religion, as in our reference
(1. iii. 55) to Wolsey as a 'churchman', and the suggestion
that the Gentlemen will have to do 'penance' if they fail to
entertain the ladies (1. iv. 32). Wolsey himself continues the
emphasis on merry-heartedness, with especial reference to the
ladies. Things are warming up when the interruption of drums,
trumpets and cannon arouses excitement:

> Nay, ladies, fear not ;
> By all the laws of war you're privileg'd.   (1. iv. 51)

The ladies, 'this heaven of beauty' (1. iv. 59), remain our centre
of attention.

---

[1] For 'running banquet' cp. v. iv. 71. The term was apparently usual to denote 'hasty
refreshment'. See the Oxford glossary and the Arden notes on both passages ; though the innuendo
appears to go further than the editor indicates.

The masquers, first announced as 'great ambassadors from foreign princes' (i. iv. 55), enter dressed like shepherds and pretend that, hearing of Wolsey's 'fair assembly', they have left their flocks to pay their devotions to 'beauty' (i. iv. 65–70). Then follows the dance, the game of Wolsey discovering, no doubt to roars of applause, the King, and the King's interest in Anne Bullen. The sexual badinage is maintained:

> *King Henry.* You are a churchman, or, I'll tell you, Cardinal,
>   I should judge now unhappily.
> *Wolsey.*   I am glad
>   Your grace is grown so pleasant.   (i. iv. 88)

The prevailing suggestion, here and in our earlier conversation, has been carefully created to prepare for the King's meeting with Anne Bullen, an atmosphere of sexual freedom being exactly appropriate for what it would have been an error to regard as a profound romance. But we are to feel it as a privileged occasion, and the encounter escapes an adverse criticism. The King is actually given a devotional phrase reminiscent, perhaps a trifle incongruously so, of *Romeo and Juliet*:

> The fairest hand I ever touch'd ! O beauty,
> Till now I never knew thee.   (i. iv. 75)

Compare Romeo's:

> . . . And, touching hers, make blessed my rude hand.
>   Did my heart love till now ? Forswear it, sight!
>   For I ne'er saw true beauty till this night.
>   (i. v. 55)

Elsewhere his attitude is lightly appraising rather than devotional, as in 'By heaven, she is a dainty one' (i. iv. 94), though he realizes a possible danger when, Wolsey pointedly suggesting that he is a 'little heated', he answers 'I fear too much' (i. iv. 101); with which we might compare Romeo's rather similar, 'I fear too early' and 'Ay, so I fear' at *Romeo and Juliet*, i. iv. 107, i. v. 124.

The scene follows closely Shakespeare's usual manipulation and even vocabulary. Wolsey's reference to a 'broken banquet' (i. iv. 61) recalls the more violently broken banquets in *Macbeth*, *Timon of Athens*, and *The Tempest*, while his wishes for his guests' 'good digestion' (I. iv. 61–2) are an obvious reminder of *Macbeth*, III. iv. 38. The nearest equivalent is, however, the first feast in *Timon of Athens*, similarly interrupted by a masque. Compare Wolsey's 'What are their pleasures?' at I. iv. 64 with the masquers' forerunner come to 'signify their pleasures' at *Timon of Athens*, I. ii. 127; and Wolsey's 'they have done my poor house grace' (I. iv. 73) with Timon's 'You have done our pleasures much grace, fair ladies' (I. ii. 153). Wolsey's final offer of a banquet (i.e. probably desert) in another room follows Timon's and Capulet's at *Timon of Athens*, I. ii. 162, and *Romeo and Juliet*, I. v. 126. The attribution of the scene to Fletcher appears, as elsewhere, quite unwarranted. The conversational tone—one must remember that Shakespeare is presumably aiming at a contemporary idiom—closely resembles that in *Timon of Athens*; while the scene's purpose within the pattern of *Henry VIII* is both obvious and successful. A strong sexuality, of which Anne is the centre, is shown in contrast to our darker, more religious, events; rather as the two halves of *Timon of Athens* are in contrast.

Our richest humour occurs in the scene between Anne and the Old Lady. Anne is pitying Katharine, while the Old Lady shakes her head and makes conventional rejoinders, agreeing with Anne's remark on the advantages of a simple life with the platitudinous, 'Our content is our best having' (II. iii. 22): the words come as a stock response. But suddenly, on Anne's assertion that she herself would never be a queen, the Old Lady comes out with a grand piece of broad honesty reminiscent of Juliet's Nurse and Emilia in *Othello* (IV. iii. 65–88):

> Beshrew me, I would,
> And venture maidenhead for't ; and so would you,
> For all this spice of your hypocrisy.   (II. iii. 24)

Anne, she says, is fair, and so she must needs have a woman's 'heart' (II. iii. 28). As Anne gets deeper in denial, the Old Lady's hits grow more telling:

> 'Tis strange : a three-pence bow'd would hire me,
> Old as I am, to queen it. But, I pray you,
> What think you of a *duchess* ? Have you limbs
> To bear *that* load of title ?   (II. iii. 36)

You can hear the voice's insinuating lilt on 'duchess' and 'that'. The Lord Chamberlain brings news that the King is making Anne Marchioness of Pembroke with an income attached: she is breath-taken, abashed, tendering thanks 'as from a blushing handmaid' (II. iii. 72). On his exit, there is a moment's electric silence; then, instead of what we expect—the scene is full of little surprises—the Old Lady breaks out in a fury, saying how she, after begging at court for sixteen years, has accomplished nothing, whereas Anne, 'a very fresh-fish here', drops into fortune without an effort (II. iii. 81–8). Anne just sits in a trance, murmuring, 'This is strange to me', while her skies tinge with promise of a golden dawn. But now the Old Lady has her revenge:

> How tastes it ? Is it bitter ? Forty pence, no.
> There was a lady once—'tis an old story—
> That would not be a queen, that would she not,
> For all the mud in Egypt : have you heard it ?
>
> (II. iii. 89)

The voice is not harsh. It is a rich, playful, kindly-cruel badinage. No Shakespearian play shows a language so variously and exactly suited to its feminine persons; Queen Katharine, Anne in her bashfulness, the Old Lady's worldly-wise cynicism, their phrases define their personalities. One surely recognizes the long-drawn-out 'for-ty pence, no', the lilt in 'that would she not', the twinkle of the eye in 'have you heard it?' Anne flares up, blushes, is at a loss, while the old woman goes on, mightily enjoying herself, with 'Say—are you not *stronger* than you were?' (II. iii. 99). Finally Anne cuts her short with a curt statement of her sincerely anxious premonition: 'it faints me to think what follows' (II. iii. 103). She would go and comfort the Queen; but adds, as an afterthought: 'Pray, do not deliver what here you've heard to her'. The remark is necessary, with no hidden subtlety; and yet what a wealth of innuendo lies crammed in the Old Lady's capping of it at their exit with: 'What do you think me?' (II. iii. 106–7).

The short scene speaks volumes: the comedy is profound without any sacrifice of human warmth; the dramatic purpose is central. Never was Shakespeare's human insight more consummately used.

The Old Lady returns once, when she rushes in irrespective of 'manners' (v. i. 161) to announce the birth of the King's child, with a smiling, flattering, greeting, to which he replies anxiously:

> Is the Queen deliver'd ?
> Say, ay ; and of a boy.   (v. i. 164)

Taking him at his word, the irritating old woman only succeeds in tantalizing him:

> Ay, ay, my liege;
> And of a lovely boy ; the God of heaven
> Both now and ever bless her ! 'tis a girl,
> Promises boys hereafter . . . 'tis as like you
> As cherry is to cherry.   (v. i. 165)

Listen to the drawled emphasis on 'lovely', the alteration in voice at ''tis a girl', the irritating optimism of 'hereafter' and playfulness, out of tune, at 'cherry'. The King's hopes are raised, and dashed. With a curt 'Give her a hundred marks', he hurries out, leaving her alone:

> A hundred marks ! By this light, I'll ha' more.
> An ordinary groom is for such payment :
> I will have more or scold it out of him.
> Said I for this the girl was like to him ?
> I will have more, or else unsay't ; and now
> While it is hot, I'll put it to the issue.   (v. i. 173)

She alone in the play stands up to the King. She is a miniature of the Nurse in *Romeo and Juliet*, only with more dignity.

Lastly, we must notice two important incidents introducing us to the crowds of London. The rough hurly-burly of boisterous, sweating, seething common people so unsympathetically handled in the Jack Cade incidents of 2 *Henry VI*, *Julius Caesar*, *Antony and Cleopatra*, and *Coriolanus*, is here warmly apprehended. We hear how, at the public appearance of Anne after the coronation, there was a noise like a sea-tempest, composed of many notes, while 'hats', 'cloaks', and even 'doublets' were thrown in the air; and so, too, would 'faces' have been, had that been possible. Though non-satiric the description is strongly, even violently, physical, noting how 'great-bellied women that had not half a week to go' charged like rams, making the crowd 'reel' before their onset (iv. i. 70–81). There is heavy emphasis on physical procreation. In this extraordinary passage, to which we shall return, individuals are described as being so dissolved into the molten mass that personal, and especially sexual, relationships cease within this super-sexual commonalty. Such is the effect of Anne's appearance as Queen.

The crowd is yet more potent at the christening of her child, Elizabeth. There is a burly master and his man, a battered weakling with a sadly broken stick. The crowd have already broken into the palace yard and the blustering red-faced porter curses heartily, while his defeated assistant shakes his head, muttering, 'We may as well push against Paul's as stir 'em' (v. iv. 17):

> Porter. How got they in, and be hang'd ?
> Man.   Alas, I know not ; how gets the tide in ?
>   As much as one sound cudgel of four-foot—
>   You see the poor remainder—could distribute,
>   I made no spare, sir.
> Porter   You did nothing, sir.
> Man.   I am not Samson, nor Sir Guy, nor Colbrand
>   To mow 'em down before me . . .   (v. iv. 18)

The crowd is meanwhile shouting lustily. Our sexual, fertility, theme has already been subtly balanced against religion. Here the Porter mixes religious reference with a bawdy broad-talk concentrating heavily, as did both Wolsey's feast and our recent crowd passage, on the women, with violent sexual and procreative suggestion:

> Is this Moorfields to muster in ? or have we some strange Indian with the great tool come to court, the women so besiege us ? Bless me, what a fry of fornication is at door ! On my Christian conscience, this one christening will beget a thousand : here will be father, god-father, and all together.   (v. iv. 34)

Notice the reminder of Caliban, felt as an Indian at *The Tempest*, ii. ii. 35; and compare his 'I had peopled else this isle with Calibans' ' (i. ii. 350). Now these women and the crowd's fertility-impact are directly referred to the central event, to which *all* our humorous and sexual scenes point, of the christening of Anne's child. The imaginative patterning is nevertheless unobtrusive and realism is not offended, the Porter's phrases well characterizing the raw mass of humanity seething outside. The man, too, gives a superbly comic account of his stalwart defence:

> *Man.* There is a fellow somewhat near the door, he should be a brazier by his face, for, o' my conscience, twenty of the dog days now reign in's nose : all that stand about him are under the line, they need no other penance. That fire-drake did I hit three times on the head, and three times was his nose discharged against me : he stands there, like a mortar-piece, to blow us. There was a haberdasher's wife of small wit near him, that railed upon me till her pinked porringer fell off her head, for kindling such a combustion in the state. I missed the meteor once, and hit that woman, who cried out, 'Clubs !' when I might see from far some forty truncheoners draw to her succour, which were the hope o' the Strand, where she was quartered. They fell on ; I made good my place ; at length they came to the broom-staff to me : I defied 'em still ; when suddenly a file of boys behind 'em, loose shot, delivered such a shower of pebbles, that I was fain to draw mine honour in, and let 'em win the work. The devil was amongst 'em, I think, surely.
>
> *Porter.* These are the youths that thunder at a playhouse, and fight for bitten apples . . .   (v. iv. 41)

We are back in the world of *Henry IV*, with reminiscences of Bardolph's nose and Falstaff's description of his heroism at Gadshill. Here, however, contemporary London is put to a contemporary theme; Shakespeare's dream-world has come to earth, and all is newly *close*. That raw substratum of London was rejected by Prince Hal at his coronation; here it all but dominates both coronation and christening. At Anne's corona-tion the crowd was conceived as a mystical and physical com-munion, or unity; here, in the 'mortar-piece' of the man's nose, the truncheoners and 'loose shot', it is an almost terrifying physical force; the whole forming a gigantic, gargantuan, thoroughly Rabelaisian, burlesque of warfare. Here humour itself, and all that basic, physical humanity which breeds it, may be felt as challenging state officialdom (in the Lord Chamberlain), and even as winning, as in *Henry IV* it did not, for the King's very last words, addressed to the Mayor, and through him to the whole concourse of people, are:

> This day, no man think
> He has business at his house ; for all shall stay :
> This little one shall make it holiday.   (v. v. 75)

The end is merry-making. Shakespeare's comedy was never more ably used and superbly placed: all the associations of this jostling, fecund, crowd are carried into the concluding ceremonial and prophecy.

Our humour is throughout kindly; it is also characterized by sexual freedom; all, from the lords' conversation on the way to Wolsey's feast, through that feast, its merriment and gay talk, the Old Lady and her willingness to 'venture maidenhead' for a crown, to these seething crowds at coronation and christening, all cluster round Anne. Herself a bashful, modest, sensitive girl, she is crowned with the gold of boisterous and comely fun, of broad human understanding, of seething fertility and enthusiastic crowds.

We have accordingly a series of warmly conceived humanistic scenes countering our three falling movements. Those were moralistic, on the pattern of medieval stories of the falls of princes; these are eminently Elizabethan. Effects are deliberately got by juxtaposition, as when Buckingham's execution follows Wolsey's feast and the death of Katharine the coronation of Anne We attend diversely two views of human existence; the tragic and religious as opposed by the warm, sex-impelled, blood; the eternities of death as against the glow and thrill of incarnate life, of creation. These two themes meet in the person of the King.

King Henry is the one king in Shakespeare in whom you cannot dissociate man from office. In Henry VI, Richard II, Richard III, King John and Prince Hal there are clear divergences; while Henry V shows as king an idealized literary heroism as national hero followed by an equally literary bluffness as a private person; nor do the national heroism and the bluffness quite coalesce.[1] Claudius is a baffling example of resolute kingship backed by crime. In the tragedies temporal kingship pales before the advance of spiritual powers; and we have our impractical governors of philosophic insight. King Cymbeline is scarcely a personal study at all. Now Henry VIII

---

[1] Both Vergil's Aeneas and Milton's Messiah (in *Paradise Lost*) suffer from a similar dislocation. All three poets are up against the same difficulty. See also p. 140.

shows something of the rough manliness, the tough royal essence, of Coeur de Lion's son, the Bastard (and Richard III, too, in his oration), together with the official lustre of Richard II; and here the identity is always exact. He has, if not spiritual understanding, yet clear spiritual sympathies. He is all Shakespeare's more practical royalty rolled into one, and is thus kingliness personified. But it is an eminently human kingliness. He is neither faultless, nor austere: his is not quite the kingliness in whose name Henry V rejects Falstaff—he has almost as much of Falstaff in him as of Hal—nor has he the remote austerity of Prospero. He is to be aligned more nearly with our humour than with our religious inwardness. He is, like everyone here, religious, but his personality is not subdued to religion, he takes it, as it were, in his stride.

It will be clear that old conflicts of state order as against both humour (in *Henry IV*) and tragic inwardness (in the Tragedies), and the many other variations played on earthly and spiritual, or poetic, sovereignty, tend in Henry's person to at least a provisional resolution.

His position as king is questioned by no one. All the persons, including Buckingham, Wolsey, and Queen Katharine, pray for his good. We may take sides with these great persons against each other, but only in so far as our allegiance to the King is undisturbed. He dominates absolutely.

At his first appearance he is a grand gentleman, thanking Wolsey for discovering Buckingham's supposed conspiracy in a heavy, dignified manner, or courteously telling the Queen not to kneel. Hearing of the taxation he is roused: he shows a testy, irascible tendency coming not from his personal character alone, nor just from his official place, but rather from his *personal-character-as-king*:

> Taxation!
> Wherein ? and what taxation ? My Lord Cardinal,
> You that are blam'd for it alike with us,
> Know you of this taxation ?   (1. ii. 37)

He is not all under the influence of Wolsey, whose arguments he dismisses curtly with the remark that right action need fear no criticism, but that this is 'without precedent'. He would not have 'our laws' made servant to his 'will', and orders the decree to be rescinded (1. ii. 91–4). He is autocratic, but constitutionally-minded and just.

Though his admiration for Buckingham is finely phrased, he is convinced by the Surveyor's evidence and, as it piles up, his rotund irascibility, as of a man born to authority, in whom ruling is no studied profession, but has become one with his most instinctive virtues or vices, breaks out:

> Ha ! what, so rank ? Ah, ha !
> There's mischief in this man. (1. ii. 186)

'Ha' is characteristic: his whole, testy, personality is in the sound.[1] 'A giant traitor!' he cries (1. ii. 199), asserting his conviction that Buckingham plans 'to sheathe his knife in us' (1. ii. 210). He orders the arrest, saying that, if the law have mercy, well, but, if not:

> Let him not seek 't of us : by day and night!
> He's traitor to the height. (1. ii. 213)

He has here, as elsewhere, a grand exit; he is in fact very largely characterized by the peculiar impact of his entrances and exits.

He goes to Wolsey's feast as a carefree masquer, showing a robust enjoyment and an appraising eye. He is genuinely attracted by Anne Bullen and has a foreboding of consequent troubles. His sudden infatuation is of a sort that such a man may be supposed to find a normal part of his social life and is to be regarded with tolerance.

He is deeply feared. An amusing incident occurs when the Lord Chamberlain has left the King 'full of sad (i.e. serious) thoughts and troubles' (11. ii. 16) and next engages in a conversation with Norfolk and Suffolk, who signify their intention of breaking into the King's privacy. The Lord Chamberlain's reply, especially its final phrase, is delightful:

> Excuse me ;
> The king hath sent me—otherwhere: besides,
> You'll find a most unfit time to disturb him :
> Health to your lordships. (11. ii. 59)

The dignified statesman seems like a schoolboy. The others

---

[1] The interjection is used for Cloten's regal bluster (*Cymbeline*, 11. i. 13).

fail to take the hint, and approach, interrupting the King at his devotional meditations:

> *King Henry.* Who is there, ha ?
> *Norfolk.*   Pray God he be not angry.
> *King Henry.* Who's there, I say ? How dare you thrust yourselves
>   Into my private meditations ?
>   Who am I, ha ?   (II. ii. 64)

and

>   Ye are too bold.
>   Go to ; I'll make ye know your times of business :
>   Is this an hour for temporal affairs, ha ?   (II. ii. 71)

He talks to them like ill-mannered children, but changes his tone on the cardinals' arrival to discuss the divorce, greeting 'my Wolsey' as the quiet of his 'wounded conscience' and dismissing the others with a curt 'We are busy: go' (II. ii. 74–5, 81). A certain doubt as to the validity of that 'conscience' has already been hinted when, in answer to an assertion that the King's questionable marriage 'has crept too near his conscience', Norfolk replied that 'his conscience hath crept too near another lady' (II. ii. 17–19). But the King is throughout gracious and shows a characteristic good-heartedness when Wolsey suggests the Queen's right to legal assistance:

>   Ay, and the best she shall have ; and my favour
>   To him that does best.   (II. ii. 114)

His natural reaction to such a request is to pooh-pooh any suggestion of unfairness; though one feels it would be a rash man who proved the marriage lawful. His dubious sincerity is dramatically underlined by his deploring the necessity of leaving so sweet a wife, with the conclusion:

>   But, conscience, conscience !
>   O ! 'tis a tender place, and I must leave her.   (II. ii. 143)

One is to respond with an amused tolerance. He is a most human king: kindly, irascible, warm-blooded, noble by turns, and yet all these qualities are aspects of a single rough integrity paradoxically the more convincing for his ill-concealed insincerity. Probably he deceives himself. His desire for Anne is not, really, the whole cause of his conscientious doubts, as we shall see. Moreover it marks dramatically his self-alignment away from our sombre religious and tragic themes towards those warm with robust joys and physical sensation: and therefore we, being human, condone it, rather as we condone Antony's love for Cleopatra.

At the trial, he, like Leontes, is shown as a contestant before the supremacy of law, being officially commanded to 'come into the court' (II. iv. 6); though, as king of England, he sits above the Cardinals, whose judicial authority derives from Rome. However, the Queen refuses to admit the court's authority and appeals direct to the Pope.

Henry's behaviour is characteristic. After her exit, he speaks a warm-hearted eulogy of Katharine ('Go thy ways, Kate . . .' II. iv. 131), commenting on her perfect wifehood, and next proceeds to a careful exoneration of Wolsey, describing the origin of his doubts. His semi-colloquial, easy and confidential speech springs clearly from an honest simplicity. His account of how his doubts suggested that his lack of a male heir was to be referred to Providential displeasure makes a convincing blend of conscientious scruple and practical expediency which rings true. His assurance of his readiness to take back Katharine should his marriage be proved lawful may well be, at least at the moment of utterance, genuine; while his repudiation of any dislike 'against the person of the good queen' (II. iv. 221) is convincing. In the description of his conscience attacking 'with a splitting power' and making tremble 'the region (i.e. sky) of my breast' (II. iv. 181–2), this favourite and respected image can scarcely be supposed to empower a definitely false statement; nor can 'the wild sea of my conscience' at II. iv. 198. There was, after all, nothing to prevent the King having an 'affair' with Anne Bullen, had he wished; but his infatuation happens to synchronize with the other business. The play is not really concerned, nor even interested, in subtle apportioning of blame, but rather with the major events, the clash of persons and the unfolding of a design; and, too, with the uncertainty that necessarily exists as regards personal responsibility in state affairs. We are, normally, to take our people's main asseverations as, within limits, true. No one is a rank liar.

The King's resentment at the Cardinals' procrastination is used for an illuminating comment:

> I may perceive
> These cardinals trifle with me : I abhor
> This dilatory sloth and tricks of Rome.
> My learn'd and well-beloved servant Cranmer,
> Prithee, return : with thy approach, I know,
> My comfort comes along. Break up the court.
> I say, set on.   (II. iv. 233)

The speech makes some important emphases, showing the
gradual divergence between the King and Wolsey, as Rome's
representative, to make way for the entry of Cranmer. As
elsewhere (e.g. at II. i. 147–69), the new theme is hinted, in
Shakespeare's normal manner, in good time. The King finally
dismisses the court as peremptorily as Prospero his Masque.
The rest appear as puppets in comparison.

The fall of Wolsey is preluded by the lords' gossiping
enjoyment of the King's approaching anger:

> *Suffolk.*   . . . I do assure you
>   The King cried Ha ! at this.
> *Lord Chamberlain.*   Now God incense him,
>   And make him cry Ha ! louder.
>
>   (III. ii. 60)

We next watch the King's most uncompromising exercise of
power. As he speaks of Wolsey's unprincipled self-aggrandise-
ment, he at least appears genuinely shocked, showing a firm,
though mainly conventional, respect for those spiritual realities
that contrast with the worldly wealth Wolsey has been amassing
(III. ii. 133). He plays with his former favourite at a cat-and-
mouse questioning, in order to elicit the professions of spirituality and loyalty which he means to overturn, concluding:

>   'Tis nobly spoken.
> Take notice, lords, he has a loyal breast,
> For you have seen him open 't. Read o'er this ;
> And after, this : and then to breakfast, with
> What appetite you have.   (III. ii. 200)

He stamps out, 'frowning' upon the Cardinal: this is his finest
of many fine exits and entrances. How far his shocked sus-
ceptibilities are genuine and how far we are to read Wolsey's
opposition to Anne Bullen as the real cause of his overthrow, is
left vague. Though himself simple, the King's actions result

from a variety of tensions concerned with personal desire, conventional religion, and political expediency. As a man, he is far from faultless; and yet 'as a man' he does not exist. He is raised above our criticism, as a grown-up above the criticism of children, who see the all-too-human failings, while recognizing them as outside their sphere. Hence Wolsey, who has cause for bitterness at the repayment of his service, yet refers, at the last, to Henry's 'noble nature' (III. ii. 419).

So the King has his way, divorcing, remarrying, and getting a child. Others rise and fall, but he remains, rock-like and impregnable; and beneath all subtleties and superfluities, the action's steady drive towards his marriage with Anne Bullen and the birth of Elizabeth asserts itself.

We find him in anxiety (in a scene reminiscent of the birth-scenes in *Pericles* and *The Winter's Tale*) during his wife's labour:

> What sayst thou, ha?
> To pray for her? What! is she crying out?
> (v. i. 66)

He tells Suffolk to pray for her. Meanwhile, Cranmer has been sent for, and comes in, a mild man, and, though Archbishop of Canterbury, fearful of his king, his

> 'Tis his aspect of terror'   (v. i. 89)

recalling Wolsey's

> He parted frowning on me as if ruin
> Leap'd from his eyes.   (III. ii. 206)

The King speaks half-reprovingly, telling Cranmer, as though he were a schoolboy, of certain bad reports; warning him of his enemies, growing paternal, moved by his tears, comforting him, as a mother her child. He counters the other's submissive spirituality by his own burly talk:

> Now, by my holidame,
> What manner of man are you?   (v. i. 117)

and

> Look! the good man weeps;
> He's honest, on mine honour. God's blest mother!
> I swear he is true-hearted; and a soul
> None better in my kingdom.   (v. ii. 153)

The King's own speech grows steadily richer in sacred reference as the action flowers to its conclusion, though his bluff
manner is maintained. Though far from spectacular, there is
no subtler scene, defining, as it does, the inclusive nature of the
King's temporal responsibility and wisdom. The rather over-
simple, perhaps—or perhaps not?—Christ-like Cranmer, has
to be reminded of how Christ Himself (and how often Shakespeare's art reminds us of it) was betrayed:

> Ween you of better luck,
> I mean in perjur'd witness, than your master,
> Whose minister you are, whiles here he liv'd
> Upon this naughty earth ?   (v. ii. 136)

It is a strange heart-to-heart talk this, between the King and
his first churchman. The King is, more than ever, the kindly,
wise, realist, with all the rough experience and cool sanity
of long experience, guiding, mothering, the man of spiritual
wisdom.

And when Cranmer is in trouble before the Council, he
produces suddenly the ring given him by the King, who had
nevertheless sanctioned, and even for his own purposes ordered,
the enquiry; and in so doing demands that his cause be
taken 'out of the gripes of cruel men' to 'a most noble judge,
the king my master' (v. iii. 100). Like Hermione and Katharine, Cranmer, in his turn the victim of injustice, cries to a
higher authority; but now not to one divine, but to a human
king who over-arches ecclesiastical rivalries and settles their
disputes as from a higher order of wisdom. Cranmer's
accusers are thoroughly frightened; and the King himself
enters, 'frowning on them' (v. iii. 114). Impervious to Gardiner's flattery, he charges him with having 'a cruel nature and
a bloody' (v. iii. 129), and warns them all not to trouble
Cranmer more. They are thoroughly quelled:

Surrey.   May it please your Grace—
King Henry   No, sir, it does not please me.
           I had thought I had had men of some understanding
           And wisdom of my council . . .   (v. iii. 134)

They are prompted, he says, less by 'integrity'—one of our
key-words—than by 'malice' (v. iii. 145). He ends by commanding them all to be friends, giving, as a final reason for

Cranmer's acquittal, that he himself is in his debt (v. iii. 155–7). So ends the disturbance, and the King passes on to the more important matter of his child's christening, desiring Cranmer's services as god-father, answering his humble diffidence with a heavy joke, and hurrying things up with, 'I long to have this young one made a Christian' (v. iii. 178).

At the christening ceremonial he is shown as a deeply religious sovereign humbly entrusting his child to God, and next addressing the god-parents in a lighter, more typical, vein:

> I thank ye heartily : so shall this lady
> When she has so much English.   (v. v. 14)

He is gladdened by Cranmer's long prophecy, and concludes by pronouncing a general holiday.

It is a striking and unusual study. The King appears as a tower of strength and sanity above intrigue and theological subtlety. He functions in contrast to the religious inwardness of our tragic themes rather as Theseus in *A Midsummer Night's Dream*, himself a thumbnail sketch of the perfect ruler, responsible, kindly, wise and with feet set firmly on earth, contrasts with the fairy imaginings of which he so uncompromisingly (at v. i. 2–22) disposes. Henry VIII is, however, a more inclusive and realistic study: he has a genuine religious understanding, but also the instincts of a very ordinary man, his main fault being a fault natural to warm-blooded humanity. He has something in common with Antony. He is, like Antony, a superb animal as well as being, what Antony was not, a wise ruler. He is contrasted with our tragic heroes and heroine rather as Claudius is contrasted with Hamlet; and it is because of the importance of this particular robustness in contrast to a death-shadowed mysticism that one must recognize a certain merit in Claudius that Hamlet never wins.[1] In Henry we have a strength of life, a social sanity and commonsense, set against the profundities of tragedy and overruling the subtleties of religious disquisition. The conception corresponds clearly to the Crown as head of the Church in England: for Christianity, itself a religion pre-eminently of incarnation, cannot allow

---

[1] Shakespeare's clear-sighted sense of the limitations of the purely contemplative man has often been recognized. In *Hamlet* the contrast of spiritual depth and human normality is stark. *Henry VIII* serves to illuminate the earlier play.

man's private and personal spiritual adventures, whatever their eternal import, to govern. For that we must have worldly experience, width of sympathy, common sense, and humour. These are the qualities which Shakespeare shows his king as possessing.

We are also to feel British Protestantism rising in Cranmer, his advance contrasting with the fall of Wolsey, whose intrigues are partly to be associated with Rome. The King mutters his annoyance at 'the dilatory sloth and tricks of Rome' (II. iv. 235) when he feels the Cardinals are trifling with him. Wolsey seems to be only half-heartedly in favour of the divorce, certainly wanting to run the whole affair and especially the new marriage, himself:

> It shall be to the Duchess of Alencon,
> The French King's sister ; he shall marry her.
> Anne Bullen ! No ; I'll no Anne Bullens for him :
> There's more in't than fair visage. Bullen !
> No, we'll no Bullens.   (III. ii. 86)

He sees Anne, significantly, as 'a spleeny Lutheran' (III. ii. 101) and proceeds to characterize Cranmer:

> Again, there is sprung up
> A heretic, an arch one, Cranmer ; one
> Hath crawl'd into the favour of the king,
> And is his oracle.   (III. ii. 102)

Wolsey's position is clear; but others, functioning as chorus, welcome Cranmer, saying how he has satisfied the King concerning the divorce with opinions gathered from the most famous colleges in Christendom, calling him a 'worthy fellow' who has taken 'much pains in the King's business' and who is likely to be made an archbishop (III. ii. 64–74). Cranmer is, pre-eminently, the King's loyal servant; whereas Wolsey's ambitions were divided.

Cranmer is humble. We have watched the fall of three noble but variously, and emphatically, proud persons; the last movement shows the rise of a man excessively, almost absurdly, humble. At his first entrance he is timid, afraid of the King's anger; and next thanks the King 'humbly', calls himself 'a poor man' suffering under calumny, wishes God and the King to protect his 'innocence' and finally weeps (v. i. 88, 109, 114, 142). And yet he is also fearless, having a clear conscience (v. ii. 122-7). When insulted by being made to await, like a servant, the Council's pleasure, he patiently answers 'So', and wishes God to 'turn the hearts' of his enemies (v. ii. 6, 14). When charged before the Council with spreading 'new opinions' and 'heresies' related to disorders in 'upper Germany', he answers that no man more hates 'defacers of a public peace' (v. iii. 17, 18, 30, 41). He is a simple enough study of Christian 'love and meekness' (v. iii. 62) to be contrasted with the 'cruel' man of 'ambition'—ambition suggesting earlier important persons—'guilty of daily wrongs', Gardiner (v. iii. 129, 63, 68). The theological issue finds expression in personal terms. Though there is a stiff intellectual debate, it remains brief and the emphasis lies on personality and character, Cromwell suggesting that Gardiner wins men's 'fears' rather than 'prayers' (v. iii. 83), and to such a comparison questions of theological soundness are here subordinate. In modern phraseology we can say that Shakespeare throughout *Henry VIII* regards his main issues as human rather than ideological. In watching the King, Buckingham, Wolsey, Katharine and Cranmer we are aware of creatures being themselves and acting as they must, however they deceive themselves with arguments and reasons; in those they appear tangled; while the play shows the untangling, which is also the untangling of England from Continental domination. But little of this is said: the emphasis is on men and women, with the King central and the final rise of a Christian purity and simplicity in Cranmer, who thus becomes a voice for the prophecy of Elizabeth's reign.

One must therefore think clearly about Anne Bullen. She grows from the soil of rich humour and humanism already examined, though she is herself, like Cranmer, reserved and humble, with a sense of honour, sympathetic to Katharine and half-unwilling to be advanced. Choric passages clearly direct us to rejoice in the King's new marriage. The Lord Chamberlain's statement is greeted with delight: 'All my joy trace the conjunction', 'My Amen to 't', 'All men's' (iii. ii. 42-5). She is 'a gallant creature' in both 'mind' and 'feature' from whom

> Will fall some blessing to this land, which shall
> In it be memoris'd.
>   (iii. ii. 51)

Even Wolsey admits her 'virtuous' (III. ii. 98). England's future is being determined by the King's choice. The new Queen's beauty receives a glamorous poetic acceptance:

> Heaven bless thee !
> Thou hast the sweetest face I ever look'd on.
> Sir, as I have a soul, she is an angel ;
> Our king has all the Indies in his arms,
> And more and richer, when he strains that lady :
> I cannot blame his conscience. (IV. i. 42)

Our key to the whole play's morality is in that last touch of humour; for the difficulty lies too deep for any other elucidation. That is why the King's romance develops through a succession of humorous scenes. We are to forgive the King, rather as we forgive Antony: that superb play comes back into its own, at the last.[1] Henry shares in the golden quality of Antony's sin; and that that sin and the saintly Cranmer should form a natural alliance is the less strange when we remember our earlier hint that the very graciousness which characterizes our tragic heroes, and of which Cranmer is the extreme exponent, is, in the depths, one with the generosity inspiring our humour. Looking yet deeper, we can remark that Shakespeare's persons are seldom more than half responsible for what they do: chance or destiny does the other half, pushing Macbeth and his wife towards crime and forcing Cleopatra, in her own despite, to a noble sacrifice. So here, only through a sympathetic humour and that most difficult of humilities, intellectual charity, that wide trust in creation which our raucous crowd scenes so clearly assert, and of which such humour is a reflection, can we forgive the King what is a grave lapse causing terrible suffering to the good Katharine, whilst recognizing that his fault is somehow a virtue; that men, or at least kings, cannot live by morals alone; that all ethical rules and religious doctrines are, in the last resort, provisional; that only in creation itself and its inscrutable glories, the glistering might of its purposes and wonder of its achievement, is God finally revealed; in life itself as a sacrament, love its medium and the King its symbol.

An almost oriental magnificence dominates, relating closely

[1] Observe the delicate association of Anne with the Nile at II. iii. 92.

to the King who is naturally compared with the sun (as at III.
ii. 416; or, for royalty in general, II. iii. 6) and receives such
adulation as the Old Lady's flattering:

> Now, good angels
> Fly o'er thy royal head, and shade thy person
> Under their blessed wings !   (v. i. 161)

Our finest example, occurring in description of the Field of the
Cloth of Gold, will be examined later. References to India (I. i.
21) and Indies (IV. i. 45) are thoroughly organic. Something of
this lustre is shared by Wolsey, speaking of the 'sun' never more
to 'gild' the 'troops' of his followers (III. ii. 411); and by Queen
Katharine on whom a 'thousand beams' were cast, as by a great
'sun,' in her vision (IV. ii. 89). Anne at her coronation is
described as of priceless, illimitable worth. This strain of impression rules: other typical Shakespearian imagery, as of tor-
rents (III. ii. 198–9), storm (I. i. 90; II. iv. 181–2), sea-tempest
(II. iv. 198; IV. i. 72), wreck (III. i. 148), sinking (II. i. 131;
III. ii. 384), trees (I. ii. 95–8; III. ii. 353–9; IV. ii. 2) is, on
the whole, subdued to it; indeed, the sea itself, as in *Henry V*
and *Antony and Cleopatra*, is calm, as a setting for human glory
(III. ii. 361). What, more precisely, is this glistering wonder
to which all our values, even our religious idealism, pay
artistic homage? The King? He is too human for it; true, he
is man and symbol in one, but the man remains too earthly for
the splendours with which he and his play are crowned. It is
something greater, of which the man-king is shadow; it is the
nation, England; and England at a particular time and looking
forward to a particular future, the future of Elizabeth. For
this the noble people suffer, the humble Cranmer is advanced;
this it is that all dimly recognize in their prayers for the King,
that makes the King supreme arbiter of doctrines, and that
sanctifies his marriage. Toward this the whole massive work
labours; and to understand the ceremonial and prophecy of its
conclusion, we must glance at a new series of events, more
weighty than imagery and more important than persons.

IV

All the Final Plays show a tendency to make of art itself
their subject matter; as in the arts of design in *Pericles*, the

flower-dialogue and statue, with preliminary comments on a Renaissance artist, in *The Winter's Tale*; the elaborate stage-directions for the Vision in *Cymbeline*, with its choric chant, and for the visionary appearances in *The Tempest*. *The Tempest* is made throughout of poetic stuff, its events and persons being drawn less from life than from art, and showing affinities with the main rituals and mythologies of the ancients. Art and religion are more and more actualized, while this actualization affects the human themes presented, giving us new emphases on forgiveness, peace-making, prophecies, resurrections and visions. Human drama is aspiring to a more than human unity. How will all this affect *Henry VIII*?

It is remarkable that a play so un-melodramatic, so un-Aeschylean and un-heroic, should succeed in housing such high themes. *Henry VIII* is peculiarly true to the normality of human business. Things develop, rather as in *Antony and Cleopatra*, smoothly; men rise and fall, and the comic spirit functions; but all is done with charity, and without violence. One recalls Hamlet's definition of art (*Hamlet*, III. ii. 1–17), the 'smoothness' and 'temperance' there counselled here characterizing not only manner but, as far as may be, matter too. The chief persons are themselves shown as moving within the limits imposed by a charity analogous to the balanced serenities of art; as is clear in the careful weighing of Katharine's and Griffeth's judgements on Wolsey from which a final forgiveness matures. The prevailing spirit faces what Berdyaev calls the 'thou' of the other, his own peculiar 'I', whereby all ultimate hostility becomes meaningless; a tendency reflected throughout in the 'Fletcherian' speeches with their use of personal pronouns. The chief persons here show regularly a certain graciousness, expressing, as persons, a more than personal repose.

The language of such self-transcending is poetry and its active expression ritual; at the lowest, just 'manners', but elsewhere rising to some communal drama in which the ego is, as it were, willingly and intentionally lifted beyond itself to share in and contribute to some wider life, not necessarily understood. Ritual is an attempt to *live* for a while the higher, more inclusive, life of poetry and drama, and therefore in its essence religious. Now *Henry VIII* is even more intensely concerned with ritual than its predecessors,[1] though, the ritual being modern, one is apt to pass it over as meaningless show, which it certainly is not. On the contrary, the pageantry of *Henry VIII* is an extension of Shakespeare's earlier reliance on thunder and lightning, other natural phenomena, order and disorder symbolisms of various kinds, battle-sounds, ordnance, trumpets, music and visions. Here, however, the effects presented are realistic and more directly social. Shakespearian drama normally avoids emphasis on the raw mass of common people, as a mass, though as individuals he is liable to give them sovereign rights; communal reference is nevertheless throughout implicit in his kings and symbolisms. Here the crowds are themselves important,[2] while both the royalism and the related symbolisms attain new proportions.

We shall next observe a series of ceremonials concerned in turn with international amity, internal law, social entertainment, religion, and royalty: the key-thought binding them being 'peace'.

We open with Norfolk's glowing description of The Field of the Cloth of Gold in answer to Buckingham's remark that he himself was sick when

> Those suns of glory, those two lights of men,
> Met in the vale of Andren.   (I. i. 6)

Here is the description:

> Then you lost
> The view of earthly glory ; men might say,
> Till this time, pomp was single, but now married
> To one above itself. Each following day
> Became the next day's master, till the last
> Made former wonders its. To-day the French
> All clinquant, all in gold, like heathen gods,
> Shone down the English ; and to-morrow they
> Made Britain India : every man that stood
> Show'd like a mine. Their dwarfish pages were

---

[1] For Shakespearian drama and ritual see my *Principles of Shakespearian Production* (*Shakespearian Production*, 1964). Here a distinction is needed. To the producer the whole play may often be called ritualistic ; and certain plays show a peculiar formality of design or, as does *Pericles*, speech ; but in *Henry VIII* I am to emphasize events which are ritual *to the persons themselves* ; actions, that is, that can be imagined as rehearsed, or at least planned, by them.

[2] The transference is neatly pointed by the association of crowds and violent storm or sea at I. i. 90–2, IV. i. 72 and V. iv. 19.

As cherubins, all gilt : the madams, too,
Not used to toil, did almost sweat to bear
The pride upon them, that their very labour
Was to them as a painting. Now this masque
Was cried incomparable ; and the ensuing night
Made it a fool, and beggar. The two kings,
Equal in lustre, were now best, now worst,
As presence did present them ; him in eye,
Still him in praise ; and, being present both,
'Twas said they saw but one ; and no discerner
Durst wag his tongue in censure. When these suns—
For so they phrase 'em—by their heralds challeng'd
The noble spirits to arms, they did perform
Beyond thought's compass ; that former fabulous story,
Being now seen possible enough, got credit,
That Bevis was believ'd.   (I. i. 13)

The long story of Franco-British rivalry from *Henry VI* onwards reaches its consummation in amity; in Shakespearian
terms, we are pitched into a beyond-war world. Hence it is as
a heaven on earth ('the view of earthly glory'), and the description glitters. All normal excellence is surpassed and duality
transcended into a *higher* unity ('pomp', formerly 'single', is
now 'married to one *above* itself', so that people 'saw but one'):
on which the best commentary is Shakespeare's own *The
Phoenix and the Turtle*. As so often in his later work, we find
normal categories exhausted in attempt to characterize some
actualization of the indescribable. The thing is 'beyond
thought's compass'; the actuality, as Norfolk says later, outran
all description, being thoroughly 'royal' and given perfect
'order' (I. i. 39–45): note that the emphasis refers back to
Shakespeare's habitual emphasis on (i) kings (ii) order-sym-
bolism. The general conception of a superlative beyond-
thought excellence within the natural order is akin to and
makes contact with Cleopatra's account of her miraculous
dream, while Norfolk's use of 'beggar' recalls 'it beggar'd all
description' in the description of Cleopatra on Cydnus (*Antony
and Cleopatra*, v. ii. 75–100; II. iii. 198–226). We meet a
similar attempt to realize a transcendental humanism to that in
other late plays, though in terms of contemporary and national
symbolism rather than individual persons, and with an expansion of romantic love to international amity (already heralded

in *Cymbeline*). As once in *The Tempest*, we are pointed to a reality compared to which old fictions are no longer unbelievable.

That the amity here celebrated was shortly after disrupted only underlines our speech's purely introductory purpose. Buckingham, at first—while it is required of him—an enthralled listener, soon after takes a cynical view of such 'fierce vanities' of Wolsey's fabrication (I. i. 54). The cost, we are told, has been excessive; and, directly after, disruption came in 'a hideous storm', and every man was next 'a thing inspir'd', breaking out into 'prophecy' and so ruining the temporary 'peace' (I. i. 89–93). The incident is conceived as a reversal of the Babel-Pentecost sequence in the Bible, the massed unity breaking up into a tumult of individuality; but both states are mystically apprehended, and the crowd, as elsewhere in *Henry VIII*, a thing of almost terrifying power. Such is Shakespeare's ceremonial introduction to his first historical play made throughout of non-warlike material. 'Peace' is to dominate.

The step beyond war involves the ritual of law; since conflicts of some sort there must be, and since law with its ceremonial replaces armed contest, our play is loaded with legal thought and ritual.

Legal concepts are pervasive. Wolsey claims that his taxation is sanctioned 'by learned approbation of the judges', but the King argues that it is without 'precedent', refusing to replace the 'laws' by a despotic 'will' (I. ii. 71, 93). Buckingham's Surveyor is warned against perjury by the Queen and the King orders the trial with the remark that he may win mercy if he can find it 'in the law', but not else (I. ii. 173–6, 211). The Gentlemen describe Buckingham's behaviour at his trial, bringing 'many sharp reasons to defeat the law', with reference to the evidence, the court's finding and the sentence (II. i. 11–36). In his farewell Buckingham asserts that he bears the 'law' no 'malice', since it has, on the 'evidence', done 'justice', while taking pride in having had a 'noble trial' (II. i. 62, 119).

To pass to the divorce. Wolsey tells the King that things have been so well arranged that even Spain must regard the Queen's trial as 'just and noble', since Rome, 'the nurse of judgement', has been invited to send so 'just and learned' a man as Campeius for 'the impartial judging of this business'; though he asks that the Queen should, according to 'law', have 'scholars' to argue for her (II. ii. 92–113). During the trial the text is naturally full of relevant concepts, the Queen being willing to undergo 'the sharpest kind of justice' if anything be proved against her, and asserting that the marriage was originally ruled as 'lawful' by the best brains of Europe (II. iv. 42, 51). Wolsey disclaims any guilt of 'injustice', the trial being supported by the opinion of 'the whole consistory of Rome' (II. iv. 87, 91). When the Queen claims that her cause be 'judged' by the Pope, she is called 'stubborn to justice' (II. iv. 119, 120). After her exit, the King takes pains to show that Wolsey is 'justified', and recounts the story of his conscience and fears of heavenly 'judgement' (II. iv. 160, 192). Later the Queen claims that all her actions may be 'tried' freely by any eye, tongue, and opinion, but is urged by the Cardinals to submit lest more indignities fall on her through the 'trial of the law' (III. i. 35, 95). Here she makes her magnificent fling:

> Heaven is above all yet ; there sits a judge
> That no king can corrupt. (III. i. 99)

The action, of course, forces many of these concepts; but the emphasis remains heavy; besides, it is the action we are studying. The concepts are not all necessarily impregnated with dramatic belief. Buckingham's guilt was most uncertain, Wolsey's attitude is throughout suspect, the Queen's generalized attack has cogency. But whatever the failings of earthly courts, it is 'justice' on which everyone, indeed the whole play, largely concentrates.

So when the lords are gossiping about Wolsey they are anxious for God's 'justice' to overtake him; he later on defends himself by asserting that Buckingham met his death 'by law'; and when he is beaten down by the volley of charges, the Lord Chamberlain remarks that his faults, being now 'open to the laws', should be left to legal procedure (III. ii. 94, 267, 335). In his conversation with Cromwell Wolsey expresses the hope that Sir Thomas More, the new Lord Chancellor, may long 'do justice' and in his speech of counsel urges Cromwell to 'be just and fear not' (III. ii. 447). The Coronation procession in IV. i. is preceded by 'two judges'.

In Katharine's dying scene, which includes the charitable judgements on Wolsey, the concept is significantly silent: the tone here is religious, and beyond justice. But with the entry of Cranmer it returns. Warning him of his enemies, the King points out that 'the justice and the truth' of a question does not necessarily direct the 'verdict' (v. i. 131–2); during the enquiry the Lord Chancellor accuses Cranmer of offending against the 'laws'; while Cranmer, after referring to 'this case of justice', sarcastically suggests that Gardiner means to be 'both judge and juror', finally appealing 'to a most noble judge, the King, my master' (v. iii. 15, 46, 60, 101). Though not mentioned, the concept burns within Cranmer's final prophecy.

This heavy insistence on justice, in alliance with other key-words 'truth' and 'integrity', is the culmination of a long Shakespearian obsession. Legal phraseology is sprinkled throughout Shakespeare: Hamlet's graveyard meditations are symptomatic. *The Merchant of Venice* and *Measure for Measure* are specifically constructed round problems of earthly justice; while in *King Lear* and *Cymbeline* legal thought and phraseology expands to question and probe the justice of Providence. Justice is a root-concept in Ulysses' order-speech in *Troilus and Cressida*. The various limitations and necessities of human government are dramatically examined over and over again (as in *The Winter's Tale*), until Prospero, the student prince, returns to his ducal office. Especially relevant are the two parts of *Henry IV*, when Prince Hal is set delicately between Falstaff and the Lord Chief Justice, the story showing his gradual rejection of the one and self-alignment with the other, with a final speech of judicial wisdom.[1] Now, among its many syntheses, *Henry VIII*, completing Shakespeare's life-work as the story of Hal and Henry V complete his first Histories, might be said to show a coalescence of Falstaff and the Chief Justice, since King Henry is tangentially at least to be associated with Falstaff in point of buoyancy, bluff humour and physical appetite. Shakespeare's two main challenges to neat schemes of ethic and government, the humour of Falstaff and the potent sexuality of *Antony and Cleopatra*, are accordingly placed;

---

[1] See *The Sovereign Flower*, pp. 36, 52, note ; together with Professor Dover Wilson's more explicit emphasis in *The Fortunes of Falstaff*.

though no finally satisfying synthesis can be expressed in personal terms alone.

To pass now to the more ritualistic expressions. A trial is a conscious dramatization of conflict with a recognized centre of control. In *Henry VIII* we have three trials.

The conflict of Wolsey and Buckingham is introduced by a typical piece of formality at i. i. 114:

> Enter Cardinal Wolsey, the Purse borne before him ; certain of the Guard, and two Secretaries with papers. The Cardinal in his passage fixeth his eye on Buckingham, and Buckingham on him, both full of disdain.[1]

There follows the dramatic arrest and questioning of the Surveyor, itself a miniature trial; and later description of Buckingham's behaviour at the bar, his rebuttal of the evidence and plea for life. His entry is given exact, ritualistic, direction:

> Enter Buckingham from his arraignment ; tipstaves before him ; the axe with the edge towards him ; halberds on each side : with him Sir Thomas Lovell, Sir Nicholas Vaux, Sir William Sands, and common people. (II. i. 54)

Ceremonious exactitude characterizes our play everywhere; as again, when Vaux gives command for the preparation of a ducal barge (II. i. 97).

The trial at Blackfriars necessarily receives elaborate attention, the order of the various entries being noted, to give that gradual building up so important in massed pageantry, with full details of furniture and properties:

> Trumpets, sennet and cornets. Enter two Vergers, with short silver wands ; next them, two Scribes, in the habit of doctors ; after them, the Archbishop of Canterbury, alone . . .
> (II. iv.)

and then more bishops, gentlemen and officers, with the purse, seal and cardinal's hat; 'a silver mace', 'two great silver pillars', 'swords and mace'; also priests with silver crosses. The long direction is meticulous in detail, even noting distances and positions. The general effect is one of weight and lustre corre-

[1] Such visual flashes occur often in directions, as in the King's entry 'leaning on the Cardinal's shoulder' at I. ii. 1 and 'reading a schedule' at III. ii. 107 ; his exit 'frowning' upon Wolsey at III. ii. 204 and entry 'frowning' on the Council at V. iii. 113. See, too, the vivid visual description of Wolsey's behaviour at III. ii. 112–20.

sponding to the majesty of state and sanctity of law. The two cardinals sit under the King as judges, the King under 'the cloth of state'. Though the King dominates positionally, the proceedings are formally opened by the Scribe and next the court-crier calls on Henry and Katharine to 'come into the court'. The relations of King and Cardinals to each other and of both to the vague presence of ecclesiastical law is precise, though the issues raised by them are difficult enough: they are the issues raised by the play itself. The ceremonial poses our central problems.

Our third legal scene, at v. iii., when Cranmer is brought before the Council, is more purely ecclesiastical. This is an enquiry only, but the direction, though shorter, is again careful, with notice of positions. The Archbishop is kept waiting and finally allowed entrance by the Keeper in such a way as to insult him: as so often, the formality is itself of central importance. Ritual is our true protagonist.

So much for our main conflicts and their semi-subjection to legal ritual and control. These are nevertheless countered throughout by the pervading charity, so strongly emphasized already that little more attention is here needed. But a word on Shakespeare's earlier work may assist. Human and divine justice are continually balanced, the balance reaching fine expression in *The Merchant of Venice* and *Measure for Measure*: Wolsey's speech of counsel, indeed our whole play, is designed from the consciousness of Portia's 'mercy' speech. Shakespeare's impractical governors, of whom Duke Vincentio is the prototype; his strong satire against human justice (as at *King Lear*, iv. vi. 162–73, and *Timon of Athens*, iv. iii. 60, 430–56); his balancing of tragic mysticism against order in *Troilus and Cressida* (i. iii. 1–137); his tragic assertion throughout, together with his good friars and many noble passages of Christian doctrine; all witness a strong sense of human limitation and distrust of earthly governance brought to a fine point of verbal precision in Katharine's

> Heaven is above all yet : there sits a judge
> That no king can corrupt.   (iii. i. 99)

Katharine is the finest, because the most sorely tried and yet, except for Cranmer himself, the most consistent, voice for the 'charity' in *Henry VIII*. For her accordingly is arranged a ritual of vision, summing Shakespeare's finest other-worldly intuitions:

> The Vision. Enter, solemnly tripping one after another, six Personages, clad in white robes, wearing on their heads garlands of bays, and golden vizards on their faces; branches of bays or palms in their hands. They first congee unto her, then dance; and, at certain changes, the first two hold a spare garland over her head . . . (iv. ii)

The gesture is repeated by the others, while the Queen shows 'signs of rejoicing', after which there is more dancing. It is a long and complicated direction. This silent ritual is probably Shakespeare's most satisfying projection of that visionary intuition already found emphatic in recent works.

Ritual characterizes not only our tragic, but also our more buoyant scenes. There is Wolsey's feast. Feasts in *The Taming of the Shrew*, *Romeo and Juliet*, *Macbeth*, *Timon of Athens*, *Antony and Cleopatra*, *Pericles* and *The Tempest* are regularly conceived as rituals with strong social undertones. The poetic detail makes of the greatest something more than social; almost a sacrament of brotherhood. Now Wolsey's entertainment is directly in the tradition of these earlier feasts. The Masque of Shepherds and their dance merely carry on the ritual, in a usual (and of course thoroughly contemporary) manner variously reminiscent of (in addition to the plays just noted) *Love's Labour's Lost*, *Much Ado About Nothing*, and *The Winter's Tale*. This feast and dance, at which the King meets Anne Bullen, clearly play a romantic-sexual part of vital importance.[1]

We pass now to the greater, at once communal, religious, and royal rituals that crown our sequence.

First, we have careful direction for 'The Order of the Coronation' of Anne (iv. i.). This includes judges, the Lord Chancellor, singing choristers, the Mayor of London, Garter, various other lords, all described in detail; Garter with 'coat of arms' and 'gilt copper crown', others with 'sceptre of gold', 'demi-coronal of gold', 'the rod of silver with the dove', a 'robe of estate', the high-steward's 'long white wand', a 'rod of marshalship', etc. The Queen follows under a canopy borne

---

[1] Cp. For revels, dances, masks and merry hours
Forerun fair love, strewing her way with flowers.
(*Love's Labour's Lost*, iv. iii. 379.)

by four of the Cinque-ports, 'her hair richly adorned with pearl', her train borne by the 'old Duchess of Norfolk' whose gold coronal is 'wrought with flowers' and other ladies following in plain circlets. The detail of the ceremony is considered of major importance.

The actual coronation is, moreover, described for us, with the new Queen's behaviour carefully characterized. We hear of the 'holy oil', the insignia of Edward the Confessor's crown (recalling the strong national interest of *Macbeth*), the rod, the bird of peace, 'and all such emblems' laid on her by the Archbishop of Canterbury (IV. i. 86–90). Especially notice the 'rod' and 'bird of peace'. The emphasis is at once royalistic and Christian.

We must here carefully note the emphasis laid on crowds, on the common people. Already (besides the crowds at the Field of the Cloth of Gold) we have met them following Buckingham to his death; we have heard how they worshipped him and distrusted Wolsey. As the pattern unfurls, their importance, which is one with our ritual, grows. For now occurs that extraordinary description of a crowd's murmuring and massed incorporation, through excitement, into a supernormal, personality-dissolving, whole:

> Believe me, sir, she is the goodliest woman
> That ever lay by man : which when the people
> Had the full view of, such a noise arose
> As the shrouds make at sea in a stiff tempest,
> As loud, and to as many tunes : hats, cloaks—
> Doublets, I think—flew up ; and had their faces
> Been loose, this day they had been lost. Such joy
> I never saw before. Great-bellied women,
> That had not half a week to go, like rams
> In the old time of war, would shake the press,
> And make 'em reel before them. No man living
> Could say, 'This is my wife', there ; all were woven
> So strangely in one piece.   (IV. i. 69)

This clearly carries further the suggestion of our opening piece on the Field of the Cloth of Gold and the seething, tempestuous and prophetic individualism of the crowd following its rupture. That earlier tempest is now felt as making a varied yet single music through the shrouds of some victorious and undisturbed ship; for the crowd is now a single, mystic, body, wherein all those stern moral and possessive sexual severities that have for so long tormented the Shakespearian universe are, momentarily, dissolved, with no man able to claim his own wife, all personal relationships being annihilated. Here is our opposite extreme to the poetry of individuality, of personality, of the 'I'; instead we face a greater communal 'we', with direct New Testament analogies. We are in a beyond-war, beyond-ethic, millenium, the 'old time' of human antagonisms having passed. The moral problem posed by the King's marriage is thus involved. Notice how rawly the crowd is conceived, the strong physical impact being directly referred to human fertility. The coronation of Anne is firmly embedded, as is the christening of Elizabeth later, in the molten mass of common human fecundity and creation for which it, and she, exists.

V

Peace dominates our rituals and our thought. We start with the Field of the Cloth of Gold and thenceforward find at least the desire to resolve conflicts by a general recognition of majestic law. Both social warmth and communal unity receive an emphasis directly contrasted with war, as in the interruption of the feast by cannon and the light comment thereon (I. iv. 44–52); the contrast of Anne's coronation with 'the old time of war' (IV. i. 78); and the burlesque war-imagery in the crowd speech of the Porter's man (V. iv.). Peace is itself a recurring concept: in Buckingham's farewell (II. i. 85, 111), in Wolsey's 'Still in thy right hand carry gentle peace' (III. ii. 446), in Katharine's 'Spirits of peace, where are ye?' (IV. ii. 83), in the emblematic 'bird of peace' at the coronation (IV. i. 89). As the action draws to its conclusion, peace becomes yet more real to us; at the coronation ceremony; in Cranmer, conceived as its personal embodiment; in the King's insistence on a general friendliness in the Council scene; and, finally, in the christening ceremonial and Cranmer's prophecy.[1]

---

[1] In all this *Henry VIII* exploits a sensibility ardent in earlier plays : as when Richard accuses Bolingbroke and Mowbray of aiming

> To wake our peace, which in our country's cradle
> Draws the sweet infant breath of gentle sleep (*Richard II*, I. iii. 132.)

or Westmoreland addresses the Archbishop of York in a fine passage relating 'the dove and very blessed spirit of peace' (2 *Henry IV*, IV. i. 46) to his sacred office. See also Burgundy's long speech at *Henry V*, V. ii. 23–67.

This last, and greatest, ritual is gradually built up, starting
with our porters and crowds, who now come closer to us, here
functioning as a vast sea (v. iv. 19), with a grand procession
forming into a massively deployed ceremonial.[1] The direction
resembles that for the coronation, with trumpets, noblemen
and officials, and, for furniture, 'great standing bowls for the
christening gifts', the Child herself, 'richly habited in a
mantle', being carried by the Duchess of Norfolk. The
procession moves round the stage and then stops, while the
Garter King-at-Arms speaks:

> Heaven, from thy endless goodness, send prosperous life, long, and
> ever happy, to the high and mighty Princess of England,
> Elizabeth !   (v. v. 1)

This, our culminating ceremonial, is of all the most richly
conceived. Too often commentators have dismissed the greater
part of *Henry VIII* as 'pageantry': it is that, but the mistake
lies in ranking it among Hamlet's 'inexplicable dumb shows'
(*Hamlet*, iii. ii. 14) instead of observing the great architecture
of sequent pageants and their deeper meanings. Here our
whole action is rendered newly purposeful; the balancing of
religious spirituality against the calls of temporal duty, suggested throughout and explicit in one of Wolsey's speeches
(iii. ii. 144–50), reaches a unity in this at once religious and
royalistic splendour; while the King's fault itself is found to be
justified, as perhaps such a fault can only be justified, in its
creative purpose. That purpose is particularly concerned with
England, as a nation. National feeling is subtly present
throughout, as in the lords' talk of foreign fashions as a disgrace to British simplicity, or when even Katharine dislikes
Wolsey's Latin:

> O good my lord, no Latin . . .
> The willing'st sin I ever yet committed
> May be absolv'd in English . . .   (iii. i. 41, 48)

—through which a more than local importance shines, to be
compared with the King's remark later that the baby will thank
her godparents 'when she has so much English' (v. v. 15).
Even more important were our earlier suggestions that from

---

[1] The pealing of church bells will be found a natural and satisfying accompaniment.

Anne might be born a 'gem' to 'lighten all this isle' (II. iii. 79),
some great 'blessing to this land' (III. ii. 51). But even these
are details. Far more is to be involved here in Cranmer's
speech. All our long plot of intrigue and suffering, of religious
resignation and jovial mirth, the fall of Wolsey and advance of
Cranmer, Katharine's righteousness and Anne's sweetness, the
grand persons and raucous life-teeming crowds, all are subdued, offer homage to, this vision of Elizabethan England.
Especially is the eternity of religious insight at last integrated,
as earlier it was not, with the other excellence of seething life
(hence the broad fertility references in both our main crowd
descriptions); not in the King but, through him, in the child.
In laying his final prophetic emphasis on a child Shakespeare
follows a long tradition, Vergilian and Christian ; and the
works of Aeschylus and Sophocles show similar completions in
national statement. So our ritualistic drama, opening with
transcendental description and direct reference to prophetic
utterance (I. i. 92), flowers to its conclusion in prophecy.

Cranmer is the centre of a vast stage, composed of nobles,
ecclesiastics, crowds, the King himself, a glittering and packed
assembly. He is, as a man, nothing, a simple, artless soul; but
through him as its chosen instrument the great spirit blows,
as a clean wind, sweeping over a wide field of corn. His speech
moves with a massive, swaying movement, accumulating
greater and yet greater mass and, when seeming exhausted,
rising to a new self-begotten life, new energy and expansive
grasp.[1] No words in Shakespeare are more potently placed,
none so deeply loaded with a life's wisdom rolled within the
volumes of a single, yet for ever unfurling, speech. Nor does
anything in our literature demand a subtler understanding in
tone, emphasis, pause, and variation of speed and vocal colour:

> *Cranmer.*   Let me speak sir,
> For heaven now bids me ; and the words I utter
> Let none think flattery, for they'll find 'em truth.
> This royal infant—heaven still move about her—
> Though in her cradle, yet now promises
> Upon this land a thousand thousand blessings,
> Which time shall bring to ripeness : she shall be—

[1] This is a normal Shakespearian characteristic, though one more likely to be discovered in
the actual experience of stage speaking than by a purely literary analysis.

But few now living can behold that goodness—
A pattern to all princes living with her,
And all that shall succeed. Saba was never
More covetous of wisdom and fair virtue
Than this pure soul shall be : all princely graces,
That mould up such a mighty piece as this is,
With all the virtues that attend the good,
Shall still be doubled on her ; truth shall nurse her ;
Holy and heavenly thoughts still counsel her ;
She shall be lov'd and fear'd ; her own shall bless her ;
Her foes shake like a field of beaten corn,
And hang their heads with sorrow. Good grows with
                                                                her;
In her days every man shall eat in safety
Under his own vine what he plants ; and sing
The merry songs of peace to all his neighbours.
God shall be truly known ; and those about her
From her shall read the perfect ways of honour,
And by those claim their greatness, not by blood.
Nor shall this peace sleep with her ; but as when
The bird of wonder dies, the maiden phoenix,
Her ashes new-create another heir
As great in admiration as herself,
So shall she leave her blessedness to one—
When heaven shall call her from this cloud of
                                                                darkness—
Who from the sacred ashes of her honour,
Shall star-like rise, as great in fame as she was,
And so stand fix'd. Peace, plenty, love, truth, terror,
That were the servants to this chosen infant,
Shall then be his, and like a vine grow to him :
Wherever the bright sun of heaven shall shine,
His honour and the greatness of his name
Shall be and make new nations ; he shall flourish,
And, like a mountain cedar, reach his branches
To all the plains about him ; our children's children
Shall see this and bless heaven.   (v. v. 15)

The prophecy is followed by the King's, 'Thou speakest
wonders' (v. v. 56; cp. the use of 'wonder' in *The Winter's Tale*)
and Cranmer's reply, in which the pressure relaxes, in a manner thoroughly Shakespearian, for Shakespeare never concludes on a climax. But for the speech itself, something more

must be said: it would be pleasant to leave it, but the precision of meaning is such that a note is necessary.

'Flattery' (as though with an eye to future commentators) is explicitly ruled out. Heaven is imagined to 'move about' the child, as in Wordsworth's Ode where its 'immortality' broods over the child 'like the day'; both poets following a Gospel emphasis. The 'mighty piece' is the King standing by; but the reign of Elizabeth is to be characterized by yet greater splendours of virtue, truth and religion under a sovereign both loved and, with a shift of tone, feared. It is as though the simple purity of Cranmer were to be blended with the princely virtues and wisdom of Timon, Cerimon and Prospero: 'princely graces' vividly recalls Timon. Under Elizabeth the grace of Renaissance culture is to flower without dissociation from the traditional virtues of Christendom. But national action is also accordingly involved and the Queen will be no philosopher-prince merely, but terrible to her country's foes. Through her, however, good steadily, deep-rootedly grows. A rich fertility lies in 'which time shall bring to ripeness', 'corn' and 'vine', the last, with 'Saba' earlier, preserving a close Biblical reference. The sovereignty defined is no tyranny. Rather Elizabeth is to be the safeguard of each subject and his own, personal property, each man enjoying, in peace and safety, the fruits of his labours. Nor shall any inhuman state-monster usurp power over the ordinary man. All of Elizabethan lyric is in those 'merry songs', and in 'neighbour' reminders of Shakespeare's village life, of Dogberry and 'neighbour' Verges in *Much Ado about Nothing* (III. v. 19, 39) and Henry V's old man feasting his 'neighbours' on the eve of Crispin (*Henry V*, IV. iii. 45).[1] A more solemn thought enters with 'God shall be truly known', religion cleansed of hampering and distorting subtleties. Men shall no longer take pride in their own blood-descent, but rather, looking *up* to their sovereign, draw from her as exemplar of honour the finer aristocracy of the soul defined in the valorous comradeship of Henry V's Crispin speech and Cerimon's careful preference of 'virtue' and 'cunning' to 'nobleness' and 'riches' (*Pericles*, III. ii. 27). Such is our vision of Elizabethan strength, peace, happiness, and religion.

[1] The word has now lost the emotional overtones so clear in the authorized version of the Bible: 'Which now of these three, thinkest thou, was neighbour unto him that fell among the thieves?' (*St. Luke*, x. 36.)

But this is not all. Cranmer's words define not merely a single monarch's reign, but rather the Phoenix excellence, reminiscent of other Phoenix passages in Shakespeare, of an undying purity and blessedness settling here, on England. Though in contrast to our tragic mysticism this may seem a view of merely temporal felicity, yet the temporality is shot through with eternal meaning, and immortal. So, though heaven be yet remembered, and this earthly world considered a vale of 'darkness', yet the glories in time are to grow from those 'sacred ashes' of 'honour' and rise, as a star, as the 'eastern star' of Cleopatra's immortal end (*Antony and Cleopatra*, v. ii. 310), 'and so stand fixed', as that other imperial and Caesarean star in *Julius Caesar* (III. i. 60), or the star of love's unwavering perfection in Sonnet cxvi. Under the new sovereign, the age of our authorized version of the Bible, there will again be peace, plenty, love and, with uncanny remembrance, and a slight deepening of the voice, 'terror'; which shall all grow round him as a vine round a great tree; and this tree, Shakespeare's habitual image for honour of descent, is itself to grow, to expand, to make across the world new nations, great as itself, in every climate, east and west, north and south, wherever the sun visits earth; not by force, but by 'honour' and reputation. This is the great cedar already mentioned in the cryptic prophecy of *Cymbeline*, Shakespeare's proudest, most high-set, tree. Here, as in Shakespeare's wider universe, so throughout *Henry VIII*, pride and power-lust have been painfully expelled; but this new, royal, pride is itself born on the crest of a deep humility, whose recurring, bell-like, note is 'peace'.

The two dominating strains in *Henry VIII*, of temporal splendour and of tragic mysticism, are confluent in Cranmer's lines; for the sun-powers of temporal greatness are here expressed, not through Shakespeare's more resurgent rhythms, but rather through the falling cadences, and yet not quite those either, of Buckingham's farewell. There is a subtle countering, as of the temporal strength which is, unless chastened, weakness, by the spiritual humility that is, but only when put to temporal faith and service, greatest strength; and both are here; both power and peace.

All Shakespeare is here too: that little prophecy of Henry VI over the boy Richmond (3 *Henry VI*, IV. vi. 68), now grown to full stature;[1] the Bastard's 'This England never did nor never shall . . .' (*King John*, V. vii. 112) without its rant; old John of Gaunt's faith in 'this sceptred isle' (*Richard II*, II. i. 40), without his bitterness and fears; the long story of ill-fated kings and civil, and other, wars; of a prince's wildness, a Rabelaisian wit repudiating military ambition, and a Chief Justice; culminating in a warrior-hero and a play ending the first half of a life-work, as this the second, with a studied eulogy of peace (*Henry V*, V. ii. 23–67); the line of British kings stretching to 'the crack of doom' (*Macbeth*, IV. i. 117) that rises from the lowest murk of tyranny and evil; *both* Ulysses' order-speech *and* that tragic mysticism which it sets itself to answer and refute; all the satiric and nihilistic enquiries of the great tragedies and their advance to *Antony and Cleopatra*, whose Phoenix glamour is lustrous within Cranmer's words; the deep admiration, culminating in *Cymbeline*, of ancient Rome as prototype of empire; the profound Christianity of so many explicit passages[2] and, even more revealing, so many half-obscured side-lights of charity; the religious wisdom born of bitterness and tragedy reaching to the wonder of Marina's restoration and Hermione's resurrection, where tears—you can hear them in Cranmer's voice—contribute to an impossible joy, a tragic, chastened, eternal recognition; the wonder of childhood throughout those last plays, all miracles of 'great creating nature', felt here in the royal infant[3] and the seething, promiscuous, Caliban, crowds; the union of the commoner Posthumus with royal Imogen;

---

[1] The passage is :
> Come hither, England's hope. If secret powers
> Suggest but truth to my divining thoughts,
> This pretty lad will prove our country's bliss.
> His looks are full of peaceful majesty,
> His head by nature fram'd to wear a crown,
> His hand to wield a sceptre, and himself
> Likely in time to bless a regal throne.
> > (3 *Henry VI*, IV. vi. 68.)

Somerset remarks afterwards how
> Henry's late presaging prophecy
> Did glad my heart with hope of this young Richmond.
> > (3 *Henry VI*, IV. vi. 92.)

[2] Cranmer's lines are deeply soaked in Biblical reference : see the Arden notes.

[3] Remember the central importance of the crowned and tree-bearing child in *Macbeth* ; and compare with Shakespeare's progress through the Final Plays that of Racine from the tragic sequence culminating in *Phèdre* through *Esther* to *Athalie*, where, as in *Henry VIII*, a prophetic and national emphasis falls on (i) religion and (ii) a royal child.

the sheep-shearing festival of *The Winter's Tale*, indeed all
rustic comedy and lyric fun, all humour, music and 'merry'
song, all that is Autolycus; yes, and all that is strong government, all greater compulsions, on Hal to reject Falstaff, on
Hamlet to give place to Fortinbras, on Prospero to return to
Milan; all are softly, quietly offered, yet with few rejections, for
Falstaff and his scum of London are here too, if not in Cranmer's words, in the powerfully, almost brutally, realized mob
for which his prophetic spirit, the spirit of England, labours;
all are here in this soft-toned, yet enormous, music, as of a
voice greater than man's.

This, then, is the crowning act for which the Ariel of
Shakespeare's art has been steadily, from play to play, dis-
ciplined and matured. Therefore the prophecy cannot be
confined to the two sovereigns to whom it is directly offered.
Shakespeare thinks poet-wise, drama-wise, through persons or,
failing that, ritual and symbol, and has little truck with the
abstractions normally current as powers of thought; so here he
says nothing of England as a 'nation', still less of a national
'destiny', nothing of the 'community'; and yet, in working
his story, with all its tragic, historic and theological undertones, all its humanity and humour, and all its ritual and
crowds, to the culminating ceremonial from which the prophecy
flowers—as prophecy should flower from poetry, the next
newness from the old synthesis—so, in making his Cranmer
voice for the reigns of two contemporary sovereigns, he has not
only defined the indwelling spirit of his nation, but also outlined that greater peace, those 'olives of endless age', whose
cause that nation was, and is, to serve; has thus pushed his art
up to a proclamation and a heralding, lifting his whole life-
work to this point, with cumulative force and authority.

So the wheel comes full circle: 'and where I did begin,
there shall I end'. *Henry VIII* binds and clasps this massive
life-work into a single whole expanding the habitual design of
Shakespearian tragedy: from normality and order, through
violent conflict to a spiritualized music, and thence to the concluding ritual. Such is the organic unity of Shakespeare's world.